The Great Parade

Exhibition organized by
Pierre Théberge

The Great Parade

Portrait of the Artist as Clown

Edited by **Jean Clair**

Yale University Press, New Haven and London
in association with the
National Gallery of Canada, Ottawa
2004

Itinerary

Galeries Nationales du Grand Palais, Paris
12 March – 31 May 2004

National Gallery of Canada, Ottawa
25 June – 19 September 2004

The exhibition *The Great Parade: Portrait of the Artist as Clown* was organized by the National Gallery of Canada. It was co-produced by the Réunion des Musées Nationaux for its presentation in Paris.

Paris

The project was coordinated in the Exhibitions Department by Hélène Flon, and the transportation of works was managed by Jean Naudin. The exhibition was designed and installed by Didier Blin in collaboration with the staff of the Galeries Nationales du Grand Palais.

Ottawa

The project was coordinated in Exhibitions Management by Christine Sadler, and the transportation of works was managed by Diane Watier. The exhibition was designed by Ellen Treciokas.

Published by Yale University Press, New Haven and London, in association with the National Gallery of Canada, Ottawa

National Gallery of Canada
Chief of Publications: Serge Thériault
Editors: Usher Caplan, Marie-Josée Arcand
Picture editor: Colleen Evans
Translators: Marcia Couelle, Donald McGrath, Donald Pistolesi, Judith Terry

Yale University Press
Managing Director: John Nicoll
Éditions Gallimard
Art Books: Jean-Loup Champion

Design and typesetting: Fugazi, Montreal
Printing: Conti Tipocolor Arti Graphiche spa, Florence

Copyright © National Gallery of Canada, Ottawa, 2004

PRINTED IN ITALY

Front cover: George Luks, *A Clown* (cat. no. 55)
Back cover: Cindy Sherman, *Untitled #411* (cat. no. 89)

ISBN 0-88884-779-3 (NGC edition)
ISBN 0-300-10375-1 (Yale edition)

The Great Parade: Portrait of the Artist as Clown was organized by

Pierre Théberge, O.C., C.Q.
Director, National Gallery of Canada

Curatorial Committee

Jean Clair
Director, Musée Picasso, Paris

Mayo Graham
Director, National Outreach and International Relations, National
Gallery of Canada

Constance Naubert-Riser
Professor, Department of Art History, Université de Montréal

Didier Ottinger
Senior Curator, Musée National d'Art Moderne, Centre Pompidou

Ann Thomas
Curator, Photographs Collection, National Gallery of Canada

The presentation of the exhibition in Paris was overseen by Sophie
Aurand, Director of the Réunion des Musées Nationaux, in collabora-
tion with Marie-Claude Vitoux, Director of the Galeries Nationales du
Grand Palais.

Contents

Abbreviations

J.C. : Jean Clair
C.N.-R. : Constance Naubert-Riser
D.O. : Didier Ottinger
M.R. : Mélanie Racette
A.T. : Ann Thomas

Lenders to the Exhibition

The National Gallery of Canada is grateful to the following institutions and individuals whose generous loans made this exhibition possible.

Austria

Galerie Heinze, Salzburg 134

Österreichische Galerie Belvedere, Vienna 11, 12, 13

Belgium

Koninklijke Musea voor Schone Kunsten van België, Brussels 41

Ministère de la Culture de la Communauté Française Wallonie-Bruxelles, on loan to the Musée Félicien Rops, Namur 93, 94

Musée d'Ixelles, Brussels 128

Museum voor Schone Kunsten, Ostend 65

Canada

Landau Fine Art, Montreal 47

National Gallery of Canada, Ottawa 7, 8, 9, 39, 52, 64, 72, 78, 79, 83, 111, 114, 120, 139, 145, 146, 147, 193, 194, 195, 196, 197

Félix Quinet 81

Robert Walker 105

Denmark

Ordrupgaard, Copenhagen 90

France

Bibliothèque Nationale de France, Paris 150, 151, 152, 153, 154, 155

École Nationale Supérieure des Beaux-Arts, Paris 5

Fondation Cartier pour l'Art Contemporain, Paris 63, 88

Fondation Marguerite et Aimé Maeght, Saint-Paul-de-Vence 190

Galerie Loevenbruck, Paris 86

Bernard Houri 20

Madame Izis, Paris 58, 59, 60, 132

Herbert and Barbara Molderings Archive, Paris and Cologne 187

Musée Carnavalet, Paris 34, 35

Musée d'Art Moderne de la Ville de Paris 22, 23

Musée d'Art Moderne et Contemporain, Strasbourg 42

Musée d'Art Roger-Quilliot, Clermont-Ferrand 92

Musée d'Orsay, Paris 17, 32, 33, 40, 76, 106, 149

Musée des Arts Décoratifs, Paris 6

Musée des Beaux-Arts, Tourcoing 16

Musée du Louvre, Paris 3, 15

Musée du Petit Palais, Paris 19

Foreword

In the spring of 1998, early in my first year as Director, Jean Clair gave a lecture at the National Gallery of Canada during a Picasso exhibition. He spoke about the artist's "Italian period," beginning in 1917, when Picasso was working with the *Ballets Russes* on the gigantic stage curtain for Satie's *Parade*. The curtain depicts the classic clowns Harlequin (the netherworld rogue) and Pierrot (the mute poet) seated backstage among other circus figures, watching an angelic equestrian reaching heavenward, guided by a monkey.

While Picasso found meaning in the characters of the *commedia dell'arte* as allegorical representations of social figures of the past, they also seemed present in his contemporary world. So, too, did they stand for the many roles of the artist himself: critic, dissenter, outcast, wanderer, enchanter, acrobat, clown.

The cosmic symbolism of *Parade* rekindled a subject of mutual interest – that of nineteenth- and twentieth-century artists' continuing fascination with the circus and its denizens. An exhibition idea was born.

Jean Clair graciously accepted to head a curatorial team to organize with me, for the National Gallery of Canada, *The Great Parade: Portrait of the Artist as Clown*. In this exhibition we explore the circus as the locale for artists' imaginative expression, and the clown as a metaphor for the condition of the modern artist.

Singular credit must also be given to Jean Starobinski for his 1970 publication *Portrait de l'artiste en saltimbanque*, which was germinal to the development of the present exhibition.

I would like to express my gratitude to the members of the curatorial team who have worked so enthusiastically with me to orchestrate this exhibition, under the guidance of Jean Clair, Director of the Musée Picasso: Didier Ottinger, Senior Curator at the Musée National d'Art Moderne, Centre Pompidou; Constance Naubert-Riser, Professor of Art History at the Université de Montréal; and Ann Thomas, Curator of Photographs at the National Gallery of Canada. Each has also contributed in a valuable way to the catalogue. We thank Mayo Graham, Director of National Outreach and International Relations at the National Gallery of Canada, for her diligent coordination of all aspects of the exhibition. We would like to acknowledge as well the important contributions to the catalogue made by Sophie Basch, Professor of French Literature at the Université de Poitiers and member of the Institut Universitaire de France, with her essay, and Mélanie Racette, with her research. I am very pleased that the National Gallery of Canada is co-publishing the catalogue with two distinguished partners, Éditions Gallimard, Paris, and Yale University Press, London.

It is an honour for the National Gallery of Canada to have been joined by the Réunion des Musées Nationaux in presenting *The Great Parade: Portrait of the Artist as Clown* at the Galeries Nationales du Grand Palais. As a result, the exhibition is being showcased on both sides of the Atlantic – in Paris and in Ottawa. The Department of Canadian Heritage has provided assistance for the Ottawa venue through the Canada Travelling Exhibitions Indemnification Program.

Let me also express my sincere appreciation to the dedicated staff of the National Gallery of Canada, all of whom contributed to this exhibition's organization, and to the members of the Board of Trustees, whose support of this project demonstrates their firm commitment to originality and excellence.

As always, we are thankful for the goodwill and collaboration of lenders. Our gratitude is extended to colleagues in museums and to private collectors in Europe and North America who have been extremely generous in their support of this exhibition.

The Great Parade: Portrait of the Artist as Clown sets out to explore the magical world of the circus and its appeal to artists. It is a fascination we share with them.

Pierre Théberge, O.C., C.Q.
Director, National Gallery of Canada

13

Acknowledgements

The members of the Curatorial Committee wish to express their gratitude to all those who assisted them in their work, especially the following.

Evelyne-Dorothée Allemand
Daniel Amadei
Maxwell Anderson
Irina Antonova
Marie-Josée Arcand
Sylvie Aubenas
Juliette Armand
Sophie Aurand
Monique Baker
Anthony Bannon
Miles Barth
Philippe Bata
Chris Baxter
Frances Beatty
Herbert Beck
Christoph Becker
Jean-Claude Bellier
Neal Benezra
Hendrik Berinson
Trish Berube
Manuel Bidermanas
Didier Blin
Bénédicte Boissonnas
Pierre Bonhomme
Christian Bouqueret
Bernadette Bonnier
Jonathan Borofsky
Louise Bourgeois
Stéphanie de Brabander
Edward R. Broida
Stevens L. Brezzo
Bernhard Mendes Bürgi
Katia Busch
Helena Bussers
Usher Caplan
Sean Cavanaugh
Jean-Loup Champion
Hervé Chandès
Joanne Charette
Marie P. Charles
Gilles Chazal
Rebecca Cleman
Karen Colby-Stothart
James Conlin
Mark Cosdon
Barbara Balkin Cottle and
    Robert Cottle
Marcia Couelle
Henry-Claude Cousseau
Roger Cuckey
Sylviane Dailleau
Keith Davis

Jeanie Deans
Lisa Dennison
Alain Deplagne
Anne d'Harnoncourt
Nicole d'Huart
Jean Edmonson
Northild Eger
Colleen Evans
Andrea Fajrajsl
Richard L. Feigen
Louise Filiatrault
Marvin and Janet Fishman
Claude Fleury
Valerie Fletcher
Hélène Flon
Anne-Birgitte Fonsmark
Jean-Michel Foray
Merry Forresta
Lucian Freud
Gerbert Frodl
Jay Gates
Gilles Gheerbrant
Elizabeth Glassman
Stephen Glassman
Didier Gorce
Howard Greenberg
Martine Guichard
Anne Guilheux
Rolf Günther
Peter Hahn
Sabine Hartmann
Willis E. Hartshorn
Barbara Haskell
Françoise Heilbrun
Friedrich Heinze
Tom Heman
W.S. van Heusden
Erica E. Hirshler
Norbert Hostyn
Bernard Houri
Bill Hunt
Annie Jacques
Jane Jackel
David Jaffé
Carroll Janis
Jean-Noël Jeanneney
Jane Kallir
Steven Kern
Rudolf and Annette Kicken
Angela Koch
Michael Krapf
Thomas Krens

Suzanne Lacasse
Robert Landau
Aleksandr Lavrentiev
Baudoin Lebon
Serge Lemoine
Florence Le Moing
Madeleine Lequeux
Jean-Marc Léri
Hervé Loevenbruck
Glenn D. Lowry
Henri Loyrette
Bruce Lundberg
Ghislaine Mahé
Laure Beaumont-Maillé
Steve MacNeill
David McKee
Wataru Okada
Alain Madeleine-Perdrillat
François Martin
Donald McGrath
Glen McMillan
John Murdoch
Réjean Myette
Steven A. Nash
Jean Naudin
Jon Newsom
John Nicoll
Maria Tereasa Ocaña
Suzanne Pagé
Alfred Pacquement
Harry S. Parker
Lori Pauli
Yevgenia Petrova
Rainer Pfefferkorn
John B. Pierce, Jr.
Bianca Alessandra Pinto
Donald Pistolesi
Michel Poivert
Vincent Pomarède
Earl A. Powell III
Jean-Louis Prat
Grazia Quaroni
Françoise Reynaud
Andrea Rich
Ned Rifkin
Vavara Rodtchenko
Malcolm Rogers
Alexander S.C. Rower
Almine and
    Bernard Ruiz-Picasso
Christine Sadler
Philippe Salaün

Albane Salleron
Béatrice Salmon
Gerd and Christine Sander
Sabine Schulze
Sir Nicholas Serota
Innis Howe Shoemaker
Charles Saumarez Smith
Jean-Paul Springael
Michael and Judy Steinhardt
David Strettell
Elizabeth Stevens
Jeremy Strick
Bob Taylor
Marie-Dominique de Teneuille
Judith Terry
Yves Théoret
Serge Thériault
Ellen Treciokas
Pierre Vallaud
Marie-Claude Vitoux
Lauren Walker
Robert Walker
Diane Watier
Wendy Williams
Cynthia Young
Donald Young
Miguel Zugaza

Jean Starobinski

The Grimacing Double

There exist many studies on the origins of the clown and on the earliest appearances of Harlequin and his fellow *commedia* characters; the grandeur and decadence of Hanswurst have been explored in detail; historians have focused their attention on the fair, the circus, the music-hall; and there has also been some research (although not as much) into the images artists have made of the costumes, grimaces, and acrobatics observed in the world of popular entertainment. But what is the significance of the fascination exerted over artists for the past century or so by images of sideshows and circuses? The aim here is to try and define a little more clearly than hitherto the precise nature of the interest that prompted writers and painters of the nineteenth century to create so many pictures – to the point that they became commonplace – of clowns, *saltimbanques*, and fairground life.

The main reason for this interest was undoubtedly external: in the sooty atmosphere of an increasingly industrialized society, the world of circuses and fairs represented a glittering oasis of magic, an unspoiled piece of childhood, a realm where lively spontaneity, illusion, and simple feats of skill (or lack of it) combined to delight spectators weary of the monotonous burdens of serious life. More than almost any others, it seemed, these aspects of reality were begging to be captured in pictorial or poetic trans-cription. But this explanation, with its obvious socio-historical component, is not the only one. The choice of such a theme cannot be explained entirely by the powerful visual charm exercised by the gaudy colours of the fairground sideshow, their splash of brilliance in the general gloom of an ash-grey era. As well as pleasure for the eye there was another kind of attraction, a psychological link that caused the modern artist to feel a kind of nostalgic complicity with the microcosm of the parade, with uncom-plicated enchantment. In most cases, we can actually speak of an odd form of *identification*. For we soon realize that the use of the clown image is more than simply the choosing of a pictorial or poetic motif – it is an indirect and parodic way of questioning art itself. Since the Romantic era (although there were a few precursors), the buffoon, the *saltimbanque*, and the clown have served as the hyperbolic and deliberately *deforming* images that artists have taken pleasure in presenting of themselves and of the state of art. What they have offered is a distorted self-portrait that is far more than just a sarcastic or mournful caricature. Musset picturing himself as Fantasio; Flaubert declaring "My basic character, whatever people say, is that of a *saltimbanque* (letter dated 8 August 1846); Jarry, on his deathbed, identifying himself with his parodic creature, "Father Ubu will try to sleep"; Joyce claiming "I am only an Irish clown, a great joker at the universe"; Rouault painting his self-portrait again and again in the guise of Pierrot or a sad clown; Picasso surrounded by his inexhaustible collection of costumes and masks; Henry Miller meditating on the clown he was and had always been. An attitude so ceaselessly repeated, so obstinately reinvented over three or four generations, compels our attention. The ironic approach is an interpretation of self by self: it is a derisory vision of both art and artist. The criticism of bourgeois respectability is also an auto-criticism that targets the aesthetic vocation itself. Irony, in fact, has been a characteristic component of "modernity" for a little over a hundred years.

From the introduction to Jean Starobinski's *Portrait de l'artiste en saltimbanque* (Geneva: Skira, 1970). The French term *saltimbanque* is difficult to render in a single English word. Its etymology is similar to that of the English "mountebank" (both are from the Italian – *saltimbanco*, "leap-on-bench," and *montimbanco*, "mount-on-bench"), but "mountebank" is generally used to refer to a charlatan or itinerant quack. *Saltimbanque* in French denotes a tumbler or street entertainer, but also, by extension, simply someone who performs in public.

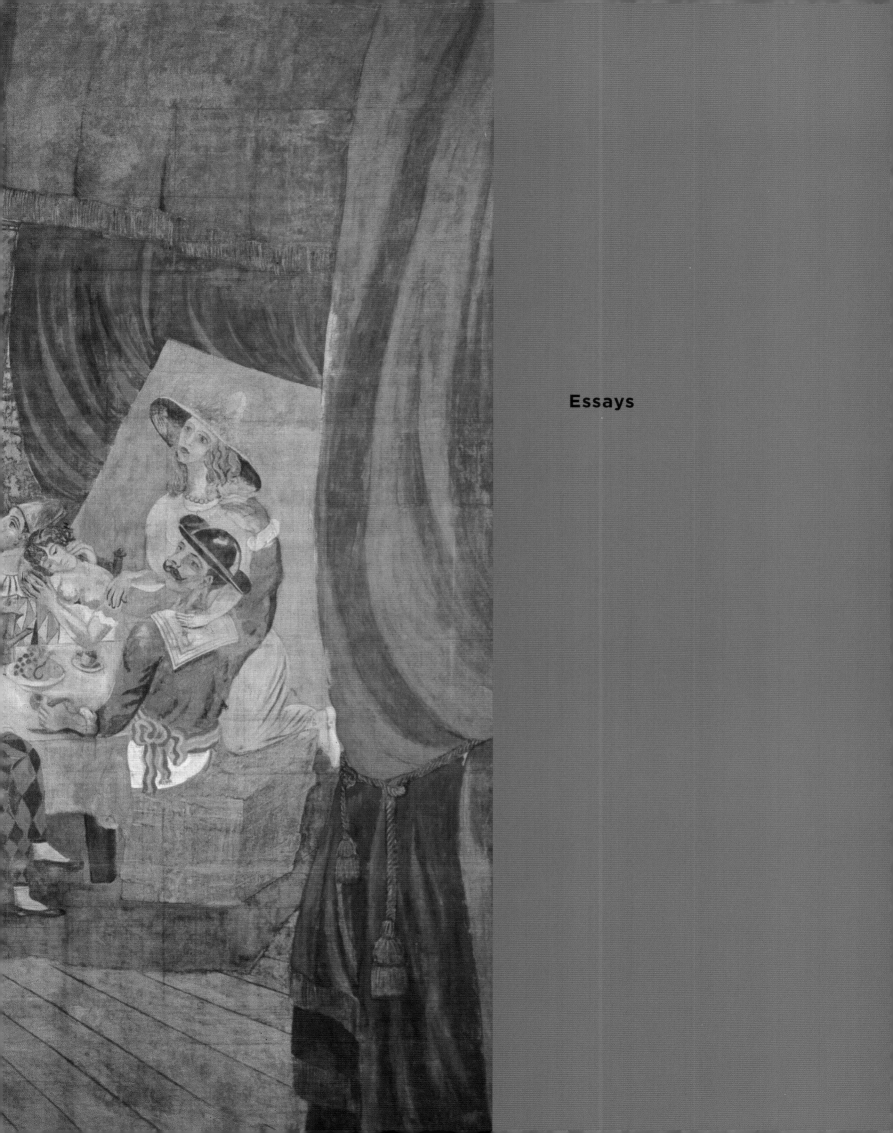

Essays

Jean Clair

Parade and Palingenesis
Of the Circus in the Work of Picasso and Others

... for it was the *graeculus histrio*, and not Greek culture,
as the naive are accustomed to say, that conquered Rome.

Friedrich Nietzsche, *The Gay Science*

Man, the first of the primates to walk upright, was also the first acrobat. Daring to stand up, hesitant, then making his way forward and, without falling over, finding his way on two feet, he was, among mammals, the first tightrope walker to follow the invisible thread of his own existence. While other creatures remained earthbound – crawling, hopping, limping – he alone took off. But more than that, this celestial clown, this Uranian acrobat unfazed by vertigo, who would henceforth position his head above his body and cast his gaze a little further afield, was the first to suspect that he bore within himself the mystery of his existence. Other animals concealed their sexual organs within the hollows of their flanks or at the base of their underbellies, whereas man exhibited his frontally, in plain view – a blinding presence, located at the centre of the circle described by the radii of his extended arms and legs. And he was not only a tightrope walker; he was also the acrobat who inscribed his body within that invisible wheel whose course would conquer the world. Knowing sex and inventing progress, he discovered death.

It is this supple and naked man of the first dawn who emerges, resurrected, in the circus.

To go to the circus is to go back to our origins. For there reigns the silence of a world in which man did not yet speak. The theatre, that aristocratic diversion, was the place of speech; it was there that language was refined over the course of centuries. But the circus, a more populist venue, would remain the place of the *infans*. For a long time, the performers were not permitted to speak there. And so expression took the form of mimicry, gesticulation, grimaces, pantomime, babbling, shrieks, and rumblings. These barbarous displays made the circus more akin to the world of animals and newborns, whose language it shared since the civilized tongue of stage actors was prohibited.[1]

The circus is also the locus of a world in labour. It is full of the strong odour of dung, the burnt smell of wheelwrights and forges, the aroma of perfumes and liniments, and the pungent fetor of animal secretions. You go back to your tent at a set time, like the nomad to his canvas tabernacle.

With the Spanish, said Picasso, it is church in the morning, bullfights in the afternoon, and the brothel in the evening. He neglected to mention the circus, though he himself, in those early years of the century, went almost every night to see the Cirque Medrano on Boulevard Rochechouart. On his way, at the bottom of Rue des Martyrs, he would pass by the itinerant circuses with their poorer cousins reminiscent of Gelsomina and Zampano in Fellini's film, those poor Columbines and bony athletes who plied their trade on rafts covered in patches of lung-red consumptive carpet, before being swept away by the tide of passers-by.

Church, bullfight, brothel ... the circus shares qualities with each. In its love of mirrors, crimson, and gilt, and in its penchant for bare and often equivocal bodies, it is so similar to the brothel that we often end up mistaking them for one another. Toulouse-Lautrec loved the circus with its equestrian acrobats and its Cha-U-Kao for the same reasons he loved the heat of the bordello.

From another perspective, the arena of the bullring and the arena of the fairground circus, simply in the way they look, both have commerce with the sphere of the gods. The circus, the *circulus* that designated the planetary orbits, is that magic space in which bodies escape gravity. Under the sky of the big top, bodies describe precise arcs, sketch out figures that, being akin to those of the zodiac, hint at fate. But the *circulus* was also that circle of charlatans and rhetors around whom crowds of gawkers congregated in Roman times. The circus is composed of the plebeian and the elect, the low and the divine, the soiled and the sublime, the resplendent and the sordid. The circus is a figure of the ancient *sacer*.[2] And the circus entertainer is also a criminal out of reach of human justice.

Together with their bags of tricks, the poor creatures who flesh out these genealogies and physiologies are, in all their banality, the visible signs of a hidden knowledge as well as the agents – priests and victims – of a sacrifice. "If we knew," wrote Apollinaire, "all the gods would waken." With regard to Picasso's *saltimbanques*, he wrote:

> The expectant mothers were no longer expecting the child, perhaps because of certain chattering crows and evil omens.

> Noël! They gave birth to future acrobats amid the familiar monkeys, the white horses, and the bearlike dogs.

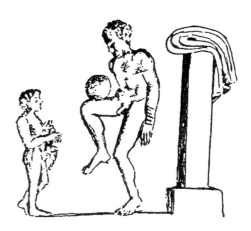

Figure 1
Attic funerary stele. *Bulletin de Correspondance Hellénique* 7 (1883), plate 19

Figure 2
Kottabos figure, Perugia. *Romisches Mitteilungen*, 1986, plate 12B

22

The adolescent sisters, treading and balancing themselves on the great balls of the *saltimbanques*, impart to those spheres the radiant movement of the planets. These girlish adolescents, children still, have the anxieties of innocence; animals teach them the religious mysteries. Some harlequins accompany the aura of the women and resemble them, neither male nor female ...

Hybrid beasts have the consciousness of the demigods of Egypt ... One cannot confuse these *saltimbanques* with mere actors on a stage. The spectator who watches them must be pious, for they celebrate wordless rites with painstaking agility.[3]

In these striking lines, the stage is transformed into a place of worship.[4] It evokes a distant Orient in the Alexandrian tradition, one in which the features of remote religions come together in a curious syncretism of miraculous fecundities, immaculate nativities, hermaphrodism, and the worship, finally, of sacred animals, among which one distinguishes horses, dogs, and apes.

◆

The acrobats of antiquity were, in fact, often associated with funeral ceremonies.[5] The game as rite, as "wordless rite," is possessed, said Apollinaire, of a "painstaking agility." The leap of the acrobat, the agility of the contortionist, the flexibility of the "human jellyfish," the apparent absence of a skeleton in the "India rubber man," the unstable equilibrium of the gravity-defying clown, the double somersault of the trapeze artist – all of these acts avert death while miming the irrepressible *élan* of life.

Going even further, we can say that regardless of the cultural context, the era, or the country, we find almost everywhere this same image of the hermaphrodite divinity (Apollinaire was right on the mark), sometimes male and sometimes female, balancing on one foot atop an unstable support, one arm slightly extended, dancing the world into creation. In the Hindu pantheon it is Shiva, with his many arms, like a juggler throwing and catching his various props. It is present in the ancient European world, and it can be seen in contemporary cultures as well. Myths, stories, and visual works portray this figure in a similar manner: unsymmetrical with respect to both pose and gender, this bisexual man or mythological character stands, arm extended and knee bent, poised to act. Attic funerary steles present precariously balanced figures performing gymnastic exercises; knee bent, one hand behind their back, they balance on their hips a ball like the worlds that revolve in space (fig. 1).

In the game of *Kottabos*, played in Greece, Magna Graecia, and Etruria up until the third century B.C., the player had to knock a precariously balanced disk – the *manes* – out of the hand of a statue poised in the form of an X atop a tall metal rod (fig. 2). In the game of *Askoliasmos*, played during the grape picking, players had to stand on one foot upon an inflated goatskin taken from the animal sacrificed to the gods by the ancient Dionysians. The same situation obtained with the game of *Empusa*, named after the one-legged demon, in Tarento. Farther away, in Siam during the sowing period, King Bancal was supposed to stand on his left foot all day long; if his right foot touched the ground, the throne would be shaken and the seeds would not sprout.

Many agrarian rituals feature a participant who is barefoot or who is required to stand on one foot. All of these games – ritualistic attitudes of prayer directed toward the gods, "wordless rites" of "painstaking agility" – were related to the growth of plants, but even more so to human fertility.

Why would this rite of balancing on one foot (distantly reincarnated in Picasso's child acrobats) serve to prolong the creation of the world and ensure the fecundity of its inhabitants? "Most likely," replies the ethnologist, "because an increased and intensified reproductive power is concentrated in a single member unshaken by the earth."[6]

Wouldn't Picasso have loved a magic capable of enhancing virility to such a point? The light child balanced on one foot atop an un-stable ball would continue to haunt the painter's imagery (fig. 3). Running through all his work, this figure describes the sacred game of the acrobats, in which the ball is the equivalent of the *sedes rotunda* of Fortune that spins haphazardly amid infinite worlds. Near the young acrobat, an older figure sits slumped upon a cube that could pass for the *sedes quadrata* of the Ancients. This is the aged athlete, tired of too much living and too much wrestling.

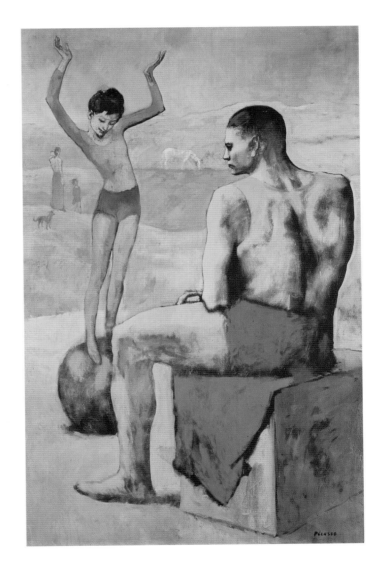

Figure 3
Pablo Picasso, *Acrobat on a Ball*, 1905, oil on canvas. State Pushkin Museum of Fine Arts, Moscow

24

We will find these images again in *Parade*, where they are
accompanied not only by a winged Pegasus but also by a baboon,
the sacred Sun animal (figs. 4 and 5). The circus belongs to a time
in which animals conversed with the gods, while within its own
enchanted circle men are deprived of speech. From 1905 to *Parade*,
apes and baboons in particular would reappear in Picasso's work,
companions of his actors and harlequins.

The image of the ape, seen originally as a *figura diaboli*, came into
the Western tradition from Eastern Christianity. But before the
Crusades, in the eleventh and twelfth centuries, the animal would be
brought back from the Orient with increasing frequency. It could be
seen henceforth in cities, where it appeared in marketplaces and
squares, often in the company of a bear, becoming the *animal familier*
of jugglers and acrobats. However, it soon lost its frightening aspect,
since perceiving it as the image of the devil grew more and more
difficult. On the contrary, it became a quasi-domestic animal whose
singular features would inspire comparisons with those of human
beings.[7] Thus did it find its way into the Romanesque bestiaries and
onto the narrative capitals of churches as *hominum deforma imago*.
The image of the ape became the symbol of the Fall – not of the
angels down the ladder of perfection, but of man. It became the
turpissima bestia simillima nobis.

To explain this hierarchical reversal, might we not consider the other
traditional figure that the ape would come to embody during the
Renaissance, when it served as the prototype of the painter and
sculptor?[8] Picasso cannot have failed to know – popularized as it
was by means of prints, and appearing even in Cesare Ripa's
Iconographia under the article on "Imitation" – the image of the ape
as *artifex*, originally portrayed in the *Genealogia Deorum* of
Boccaccio. *Ars simia naturae*: the artist, in copying nature, is akin
to the animal; the painter apes nature (cat. no. 3). Indeed, on New
Year's Day 1903, Picasso sketched a hasty caricature of himself
as a grimacing ape-man. Throughout his life he would emphasize
the resemblance between his facial features and those of the animal,
and he delighted in recalling it even in the final tragic self-portraits
made just before his death.

The physical proximity of the baboon and the human beings in *The
Acrobat's Family with a Monkey* (cat. 95) and the strong affection
that appears to unite them hark back to man's very ancient complicity with the animal conceived of as *simia naturae* – the juggler,
tightrope walker, harlequin, and painter.

And if, among all the species of ape that itinerant entertainers brought along with them, this baboon is the one in which Picasso appears to have taken a particular interest (so much so, in fact, that he never stopped drawing it),[9] is this not due to the sacred nature of the animal, *simia dei*? In ancient glyptics, the cynocephalus is often represented as an ithyphallic figure in the position of a sun worshipper and endowed with magic powers.[10] An animal sacred to the god Thoth-Hermes, the baboon also enjoyed a particular status among theriomorphic representations of the gods: it is a hermetic figure and, as such, is a direct relation within the divine family to its earthly counterpart, the Roman Mercury or the Greek Hermes, in other words the medieval harlequin, the guide of souls and the divinity of the two kingdoms.

At first a figure of the devil, the image of a fallen angel, the ape then became an image of fallen man, before being raised finally to the image of the artist. It has, therefore, known all the successive degrees of Nature and, at its highest reach, has gone so far as to serve as the emblem of the *artifex universalis*. Yet it has accomplished its ascension without ever renouncing its primitive infernal nature. It represents what Picasso himself always sought to embody in the extolling of his creative power and well into his old age: an animal nature so close to the world of the animals that he never ceased living among them.[11]

Menageries and Carnivals

Between the late nineteenth century and the early twentieth, between 1880 and the First World War, reveries centred around animals ran like a thread through literary and artistic works. One had Rilke's "Panther" as well as Franz Marc's herd of stags, bucks, and does. There was the Arcadia of Bonnard and Kerr-Xavier Roussel, populated by Edenic animals. In music there was *The Carnival of the Animals* (1885), *The Golden Cockerel* (1907), *Mother Goose* (1908), *The Nightingale* (1909), and *The Fox* (1916). Saint-Saëns, Rimsky-Korsakov, Ravel, Stravinsky … a whole menagerie marches by, perhaps for the last time. This recourse to fables in which animals talked and lived among us (so unexpected at the moment of modernity's triumph) was like a Noah's Ark, a gathering in of every species before the onset of the catastrophe in which humans would perish.

The sail of their salvation is most often just the shabby canvas of a rustic circus, or acrobats' platforms, or on occasion the threadbare carpet on a sidewalk where Rilke, once again, in the "Fifth Duino Elegy," has the acrobats and their *animaux familiers* – baboons, roosters, trained dogs and cats – execute, even unto the double somersault that concludes their act, the various figures of grace, cunning, and agility.[12]

Rilke may have been the first to suspect that the circus is the entryway to a higher world, and to a purgatory as well, where humans get ready to hurl themselves into the skies. Echoing, as it were, Apollinaire's "If we knew, all the gods would come to waken," Rilke imagines that if lovers could ever meet one another on the circus carpet they would see the unimaginable lives of the angels open up before them:

> Engel: es wäre ein Platz, den wir nicht wissen, und dorten,
> auf unsäglichem Teppich, zeigten die Liebenden, die's hier
> bis zum Können nie bringen, ihre kühnen
> hohen Figuren des Herzschwungs,
> ihre Türme aus Lust, ihre
> längst … [13]

Parade is the culmination, perhaps, of this long dialogue begun in the Middle Ages with the fabliaux, a dialogue that would blossom into the *Cabinet des fées* in the French classical period, when we still lived close to the animals, with their disguises and their seductive and deceitful speeches. At first, in the Paris of 1900, Picasso's acrobats still partook of the sadness and melancholy of the *fin-de-siècle*. In 1917, when he painted the curtain for *Parade*, they became the celebrants of a form of solar worship, the officiants of that Orphic hymn to the new world that had arrived with modernity.

It was in *Parade*, after all, that one would first hear the preposterous clattering and sputtering machine noises, the revolver shots, and the wailing of sirens that accompanied the appearance of new kinds of grotesques. These were the new world masters, giants decked out in the bright rags of modernity: skyscraper facades, loudspeakers, lamps and beacons, distress signals and alarms. In their din and appearance – we actually hear them before we can see them – something is irrevocably torn asunder. The robot takes the place of the marionette. A young American girl takes the place of Columbine. And the Managers take the place of the menagerie.

These processions of animals out of Eden, puppets, and melancholy clowns that advance toward us, driven forward by the oom-pah-pah of fairground music and the clamour of tumblers, disperse, come apart, scatter. They will be followed by unheard-of sonorities, new fanfares, deafening drums, until the cry of the first dawn, of a world in the aftermath of battle, intended at that point to be primordial, absolutely primordial, of a time before these civilized times, when animals and human beings spoke with one voice. The circus, this enclosure protected by its magic ring, would make the spell last a little longer.

♦

When humans lend their voices to animals, and puppets take on the appearance of men, and Pierrots at last seem – like women and wolves – subject to the phases of the moon, then we are no longer in the assured and glorious era of the Academy's centuries. For this is the replacement, the parody, the derisory funeral procession of that era. Parade becomes parody. And it is thus, as Jean Starobinski nicely put it, that the gods give way to clowns.[14]

All parades are parodies, and every parade is a paradise lost. Parades that stage – if only in an attempt to stop (which is the meaning of *parar* in Spanish) – the decay of the societies they display are sarcastic, boisterous self-representations of a world that they claim to celebrate but that no longer exists. They are the rumpus and hubbub of a relapse into chaos, as suggested by the name of the clowness Cha-U-Kao painted by Toulouse-Lautrec.[15] So it was that around 1880, at the height of capitalism and in a Vienna at the start of its decline, people hailed *The Triumphal Entry of Charles V into Antwerp*, as painted by Makart, and the *Joyous Entry* of the same monarch as commemorated by Henry Leys in Antwerp, in his murals for the city hall. These huge mechanisms are the final flourishes of processions honouring past glories, at a time when the shimmering raiment of the nobility had become nothing more than the garish cast-offs of clowns and strong men. Historicism buries history. The parade is its funeral procession.

What is the meaning of this moment when the fairground parade replaces the historical pageant?

When, in a studio a stone's throw from where Picasso would in the coming months revolutionize painting, the Montmartre artist Willette (whom Apollinaire happened to quite like) painted a seemingly light yet equally serious rendition of Pierrot's funeral procession (fig. 6), it was the pre-1914 world that he was burying. Above the rooftops of Paris, accompanied by the rumbling of a double-decker bus, in a nightmarish atmosphere, Pierrot reviews his life of pleasure. The story unfolds right to left, starting with his birth and ending in his suicide with a revolver.

The shot of that revolver sounds its echo in *Parade*. The period when the Great War was as much as thirty years away, a time marked by intense class struggle, the overthrow of authority, and the collapse of the old empires, was also the period in which those buffoons and puppets that had, a century earlier, taken over from the gods of Olympus gave way to the victors of the day. False emperors in period dress would be followed by true proletarians, the pariahs of whom Théophile Gautier had spoken,[16] and the athletes and record men of the modern world in their sporting attire. Picasso's *Parade* inaugurates this reversal. In it, between laughter and tears, the end of the old ways is played out.

This was also a return to the medieval farce that stood the world on its head. A reversal, a transmutation of values. It was Carnival time, a confounding of the quick and the dead. Harlequin led the dance, followed by his retinue. And it was a return to a certain mathematical perfection, to the skill and precision of the tightrope walker and juggler, but backed up this time by the science of mechanics. It marked the attainment, finally, of the precise form of beauty that Kleist had envisioned for the puppets of his theatre a century earlier. The automaton would take the place of Pierrot, and the robot that of Coppelia. The figures of Oskar Schlemmer's *Triadic Ballet* are also the heirs of the circus ring.

Figure 6
Adolphe Willette, *Parce Domine*, 1885, oil
on canvas. Musée du Petit Palais, Paris, on
loan to the Musée de Montmartre

Scala Paradisi

Two groups share the curtain that Picasso painted for *Parade*. The group to the right, comprised of seven characters including Harlequin, Pierrot, the Sailor, a Negro, and three young women, all seated around a table feasting (as in *The Wedding of Pierrette*), has been thoroughly studied and its sources in popular culture have been clearly identified.[17]

On the other hand, the group at the left, which includes the winged figure of a female circus rider and four animals – a white horse and its foal, a monkey, and a dog – has been less studied. No one seems to have thought about uncovering the meaning of this outwardly simple fairground parade in relation to the rest of the composition, to which it in fact provides the key.

Picasso contrasts the group of circus performers – highly individualized characters – with a group of figures who, unlike them, are not humans but mythological beings and animals out of fable. The winged horsewoman belongs to the realm of angels, just as the winged horse escapes its animal nature and becomes Pegasus, who is also an *angelos*, a messenger of the gods, a creature somewhere between earth and heaven, or between earth and hell – like so many other circus characters, but especially Harlequin, as we have seen.

Descended from the *commedia dell'arte*, not to mention his more remote sources in medieval folklore, Harlequin is the ancient Hellequin of the Wild Hunt, dwelling betwixt the two realms, ferry-

man of the dead, an unsettling creature who is by turns tender and cruel, clever and treacherous, a comic valet as well as a *magister ludi*. His bright, variegated attire links him to the jester and the buffoon, who are likewise distinguished from the rest of humanity by their ill-assorted livery. His clothes, just like the striped clothes of fairground entertainers, belong in fact to the category of clothing worn by "checkered" individuals. Arrayed in the *vestis scatata*, his checkered outfit, he displays the worrisome nature of those who wear striped livery, the *vestis virgata* – in other words, those who ply ignominious trades, prostitutes, executioners, blacksmiths (who work close to the fires of Hell), but also jugglers and buffoons. "Stripes do not exist on their own. In order for them to 'function' and take on their full meaning, they must be associated with or contrasted with other surface structures, mainly solid or semy, but also party, checkerboard, speckled, lozengy."[18] The diabolical figure of Harlequin partakes of this visual *varietas*, this *varius* of chromatic confusion, this "vair" that alludes to trickery, to lies, to threats, to the impure, to the antechamber of death and Hell.

Jean Cocteau became the interpreter of this variegated, nocturnal, and troubling nature of the harlequin when he wrote that, while he admired the harlequins of Cézanne and Picasso, he did not like Harlequin: "He wears a black mask and a costume of all the colours. After denying the cock's crow, he goes away to hide. He is a cock of the night."[19]

Figure 7
School of Mantegna, *Festina lente*. Palazzo Ducale, Mantua

28   It is the singular nature of these non-human creatures, animal or divine, that accords the circus props near them their particular meanings. On the ground, a spangled globe recalls the sphere of Fortune, the *sedes Fortunae*, upon which *Occasio*, with his bare nape and curly hair (the forelocks by which Opportunity must be skilfully seized), was said to balance (figs. 7–9).[20] There is also a drum to punctuate the succession of figures.

And, most important, there is a raised ladder. This balancing instrument is the one to which the circus rider, like Venice's *Fortuna alata* – a supernatural being, a denizen of the heavens perched on the winged horse – imparts meaning. The ladder, as well as the balancing apparatuses and the trapezes, are the successive rungs of a ladder, a great ladder of creatures that the circus embodies and that, under the big top representing the Firmament, transports us from the animal to the human, from the beasts of the menagerie to their tamers, from the *infans* stage to the adult and, finally, from man to the higher creatures that vault through the heavens.

But this ladder is, even more so, a representation of the *Scala Paradisi*, the great ladder of souls illustrating the spiritual progress of all animate creatures, from the animals to the angels – in other words, one of the great themes of ascension whose universality is attested to by the history of myths and religions.[21] Indeed, it is noteworthy that the term "paradise" is also part of the vocabulary of the theatre, where it designates the upper galleries.

This long and narrow ladder, the traditional peasant's ladder one sees all over Spain, would carry over unchanged into Picasso's *Crucifixion* of 1930. It is the same ladder that, laid against the Redeemer's cross, enabled the executioners first to raise him up and then to take him down from it. The acrobats' ladder, the one laid slantwise next to the spangled ball in *Parade* (emblematic of the celestial globe, the *axis mundi*) and flanked by an angel, like the ladder leaning against the sacrificial cross, is a transposition of the age-old iconography of the Ladder of Saint John Climacus,[22] which during the Byzantine era represented the soul's ascension into Heaven (fig. 10). Human beings go up and down its length. Some, supported by angels, climb up its rungs, while others are cast down into Hell by devils.

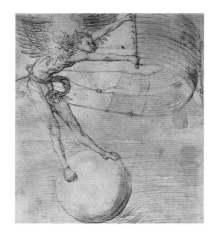

Figure 8
Peter Vischer the Younger (?), *Fortuna*, pen and ink heightened with white. Universitätsbibliothek, Erlangen

Figure 9
Mercury and Fortuna, from Andrea Alciato, *Emblemata* (Lyons, 1562)

In like manner, the figures that populate the circus have their different levels, from the monsters and demons, the bizarre characters and amazing animals down in the ring, to the superb creatures, the dazzling divas with their winged profiles, the ballerinas and trapeze artists flittering under the sky of the big top.

The Sad Clown

If the ladder in *Parade* recurs in *Crucifixion*, it serves above all to remind us that we have sometimes sought to see in Pierrot, the sad figure of the whiteface clown who is spared no humiliation, the very figure of Christ on the cross.

The white clown, the *Pierrot de la mort* – to borrow the title of a Charles Deburau pantomime (admired by Nerval, Gautier, and Baudelaire) based on the marvellous Jules Janin – the Pierrot who gets slapped, is always the one who dies unto himself, the propitiatory victim of human stupidity. The myth of the sad clown has been fuelling our imagination uninterruptedly since about 1860.[23]

We have already seen Willette, behind Montmartre's uproarious frivolity and amidst the sad gaiety of farandoles and balls, depicting the suicide of a "pessimistic and macabre" Pierrot. At the same time in Flanders, Ensor, who parodied Watteau's Gilles surrounded by masks of the *commedia dell'arte*, gave us a sinister Pierrot surrounded by disturbing mugs, just as he represented the scourged Christ encircled by the pack of ruffians and roughnecks who put him to death after torturing him. His countryman, Henry de Groux, also painted the publicly insulted Zola as half Pierrot and half deity (p. 61, fig. 4).

The image of the whiteface clown, humiliated to the point of death, reappeared in *He Who Gets Slapped* (cat. no. 61), Victor Sjöström's fine film of 1924, based on a story by Leonid Andreiev. A similar Christlike image of the clown appears yet again in Ingmar Bergman's film *Sawdust and Tinsel*, where the hero, his whitened face grimacing, carries home in his arms the body of his wife, who has been raped and beaten by a mob of circus performers. As in the song of Gianni Esposito, it is always

> sur un petit violon et pour quelques spectateurs
> S'accompagnant d'un doigt ou quelque doigt
> le clown [qui] se meurt.

Figure 10
Ladder to Heaven, late 12th century, tempera on wood. Monastery of Saint Catherine, Constantinople

For the clown, the circus ring is like the ancient Roman arena: "Morituri te salutant," he seems to cry as he makes his entry. This is the clown that Georges Rouault painted, and whose death Picasso depicted. On the other side of the Atlantic, it is the lurid clown painted by Walt Kuhn, and the tragic clown painted by Edward Hopper.

Two characters play a major role in the psychomachy of the circus. If the first is Pierrot, the second, as we have seen, is Harlequin. Their roles are sometimes reversed and even blend into one another. As Pierrot's character evolves over time, he becomes increasingly cruel, cynical, and murderous – in the 1842 play *Le Marchand d'habits*, for example, and a century later in Marcel Carné's film *Les Enfants du paradis*. Sometimes, as in the painting by Gérôme, they face off in a duel.

The Artist as Clown

The fairground entertainer is the original foreigner. He comes from outside, *foris*, and he lives outside the community. In Normandy he is the *horsain*, the one who comes from outside the country. He is the forester, the wild man, the man in the wood, as was Harlequin at the outset. He is *fors*, like the faubourg that extends beyond the city walls. The fairground entertainer is the opposite of the bourgeois. He is as disturbing as he is fascinating by virtue of the fact that he is without a permanent abode. He is the vagabond, the nomad, the wanderer, the social misfit, the outlaw, the *Sonderlinge*, footloose, marginal, unstable. And it is because of some sort of curse that he is constantly on the move.

If Pierrot can be seen to embody the myth of the crucified Christ, the nineteenth-century travelling circus performer is more generally compared with and often assimilated to the myth of the wandering Jew. He is indeed the most frequent embodiment of this figure, whose features Champfleury aptly observed in Courbet's portrait of the vagabond.[24] His prototype could very well be the "Vieux Saltimbanque" described by Baudelaire in 1861: "absolute wretchedness, wretchedness rigged out, most horrible, rigged out in comic rags, where necessity, much more than art, had introduced the contrast ... the wretched man! ... whose booth the forgetful world no longer wants to enter!"[25] But what Baudelaire especially sees

in him is the "the image of the writer who has survived the generation whose brilliant entertainer he was; of the old poet ..."[26] In fact, it is his own self that he recognizes, with terror, in the apparition of this fairground Ahasuerus.

The old gods who were appeased by fertility games and dances have given way to the buffoonish wandering players of the fairgrounds. The historical parade has been replaced by the circus parade. But it was the artist and the poet who found in the figure of the clown the final paradigm of their existence.

They had been pleased, up to that point, to compare themselves to the powerful. Painters claimed to be the equals of lords, and to deal with them on an equal footing. The lives of painters, from the Renaissance to the end of the eighteenth century, are full of anecdotes and legends recounting real or imagined episodes in which the artist seems to acquire the social status of the mighty of this world.

Many factors contributed to the toppling of the artist from his acquired status of nobleman down to that of vagabond. Many are the historical causes and sociological shifts that would account for how such an eminent member of the intellectual elite could fall so low as to become the abandoned old acrobat in which Baudelaire feared he recognized himself. The debasement of the image of the artist is, in fact, the history of modern painting. It transpired in two stages: from the Revolution until 1863 (if dates are required), and from 1863 until our own era. It was a slow decline – a decay of the profession, to quote Baudelaire once again, that at the same time signalled a forfeiture of social status.

And perhaps the very first symptom of this gradual decline was to be found in the approach to the spoken word.

First of all, when a painter – let us say Michelangelo, or Poussin, or La Tour – spoke with someone great and powerful, it was face to face, at the court, not in the solitude of the studio. Here it is the lord who is the master of speech, who owns it, who dictates its rules. Painting, for its part, does not speak. To express himself, the painter has only a mute art at his disposal – the voices of silence, as Malraux would say. Like Deburau of the Théâtre des Funambules, whom Balzac, Gautier, Nerval, and Nodier all recognized as a master, the painter does not speak. The failing of an art reduced to silence – or, if you will, of an ineffable art, an art that must make do only with sight and not with hearing – makes painting akin to the art of pantomime, the moment it claims to leave the mode of classical representation and enter that of Romantic or modern expression. The painter's modes of expression, those means he uses to express his deepest self, to share his emotions, passions, and inner states are, as in the case of Gilles or Pierrot, mimicry, gesticulation, grimaces. How can one express oneself when one is mute? But this is also to abandon moderation and enter a state of hubris.

That the painter, observing himself in a mirror, should begin to grimace in order to make himself heard already tells us that caricature would now take over from the art of the classical portrait, and that the harmonious composition of facial features seen in earlier portraiture would be replaced by a kind of de-composition. This means, too, that the painter would henceforth seek his model in the mime or the clown.

This is the beginning of a long and as yet largely unwritten history – from Romanticism to Expressionism, and from Expressionism to the present – of the links that around 1780 to 1830 united the art of mimicry and the art of painting, the science of expression and the practice of artists, physiognomy and the genre of the self-portrait.[27]

The gesture of the aged Liotard, with his toothless smile and his finger pointing in our direction, inaugurates a long list of confessional portraits in which the artist openly confides in us, through grimaces and sometimes parody, revealing what has become of him, whereas his predecessors, in a haughty silence and striking an immutable pose, affirmed what they had succeeded in being.

Here again, Baudelaire was the first to dwell at some length, intrigued and fascinated as he was by them, on the art of those who went by the names of *grimaciers* and *physionomanes*. Many such performers played at the Funambules, along with the acrobats and rope dancers. "In those already distant days, there lived in Paris a kind of physiognomanic clown, by name Léclaire, who often performed in suburban bars, wine-dives, and little theatres. His turn consisted in making faces; by the light of two candles, his face would depict all the human passions. It was like the notebook for the *Caractères des passions de M. Lebrun, peintre du roi*."[28]

To say this is to establish a very precise lineage connecting the "character heads" of Messerschmidt in Austria and the first essays in physiognomy of Lavater in Switzerland with the French tradition of "expressive heads" inaugurated by Charles Lebrun in France and continued by Traviès ("an outstanding artist," according to Baudelaire, "who did not in his day receive the delicate appreciation he deserved"[29]) and above all, of course, by Daumier.

In 1830, at a time when the mode of the *physiologies* (from those of marriage to those of crime) was making incursions into the theatre as well as into novels, the study of physical features that supposedly betrayed their owners' most intimate feelings and ideas, the assumed correspondence between the external body and inner tumult, was pushed to such a point that the grimace became the new rule of comedians, as well as of painters. One might say that the photograph, an instrument of scientific investigation supplying a cold and objective record of the data of the human body and its various affections, existed to supply an abundant harvest of expressive heads, like those that Adrien Tournachon and Nadar made with Charles Deburau, the son of the great Jean-Baptiste Gaspard Deburau, who had died in 1846.

The intrusion of photography into art would have its greatest success at this time. The legacy of the treatises on the passions and expressive heads can be found in the scientific, or supposedly scientific, photographs collected in the *Iconographie de la Salpêtrière* in 1895. In this monument to convulsive beauty that Albert Londe executed for Jean-Martin Charcot, the theatre of hysteria became the logical continuation of the Théâtre des Funambules, and the convulsions of *Hysteria Major* copied the poses of the contortionists then performing in the circuses. The clonic spasms of the brand new field of neurology became a close relative of fairground clownism.[30] Didn't the same Albert Londe, driven by the same scientific curiosity, execute a whole series of photographs of fairground acrobats' poses, becoming the first of a long line of photographers to be fascinated by the circus?

Harlequin, Pulcinella, and the Minotaur

The figure of Harlequin did not disappear from Picasso's painting, although during the 1930s and after it underwent a long eclipse. In fact, Harlequin was replaced by another denizen of the underworld, the Minotaur, characterized by Euripides as "a mingled and hybrid birth of monstrous shape," in which "two different natures, man and bull, were joined together." Born out of the loves of Pasiphae, the Minotaur inhabits the dark realms of the labyrinth of King Minos of Crete, for he too is an infernal divinity, like Harlequin. Thus Virgil relates that one of the doors of the Temple of Cumae bore an engraving of the Labyrinth at a point where a cave led to the underworld.[31]

And it was two curtains that marked the phases of the metamorphosis of the acrobat tumbler into a monstrous animal. On the *Mercure* curtain, the colour of Harlequin's suit, like that of his companion Pulcinella, stands apart from the form. The diamonds lose their outline. The "varied" regularity of the *vestis scatata* is dissolved. We are entering into those troubled times in which form would be the prey of an increasingly cruel graphic exasperation, when colour would become arbitrary and violent, and form and colour would part company. What we are in fact witnessing is the dismemberment of Harlequin's coat in the years leading to *Guernica* and the war.

Twelve years later, in May 1936, a second stage curtain for the Théâtre du Peuple, for Romain Rolland's *Le Quatorze Juillet*, gave the hermetic myth its whole strength. We see a dead Minotaur dressed in a costume that is none other than that of Harlequin; he is being carried by an eagle-headed monster in a desolate landscape with ruins in the background.

The Minotaur and the Hellequin, the figure of myth and the figure of fable, who are here merged into one, and wrapped in the same cloak, in their common annihilation seem to be saying that the omnipotence of those who inhabit the two kingdoms could not prevail against the barbarism of human beings.

At the end of Picasso's life, Harlequin reappears in the final self-portraits as a frightened old clown, a hallucinatory face poking out from the beyond and sweating with the fear of being plunged back into it for all eternity.

Caught between heaven and earth, between life and death, but also between the infinitely close world of the animals and the infinitely distant world of the angels, the acrobats' carpet that Picasso unfolds before our eyes ends once again on an image that evokes the fairground entertainers of Venice who, the day after Ash Wednesday, would execute the *svolo del angelo* or build human pyramids before the stupefied gazes of the gawkers.

It was Nietzsche who developed a parable of this arrogant and pathetic primate, man, who from his first appearance on the planet became an acrobat, who was so near and yet so far from the apes, and so self-assured that he already prefigured the modern Superman:

> When Zarathustra arrived at the nearest of the towns lying against the forest, he found in that very place many people assembled in the market square: for it had been announced that a tightrope walker would be appearing. And Zarathustra spoke thus to the people:
>
> *I teach you the Superman.* Man is something that should be overcome. What have you done to overcome him?
>
> All creatures hitherto have created something beyond themselves, and do you want to be the ebb of this great tribe, and return to the animals rather than overcome man?
>
> What is the ape to men? A laughing-stock or a painful embarrassment. And just so shall man be to the Superman: a laughing-stock or a painful embarrassment.
>
> . . .
>
> Man is a rope, fastened between animal and Superman – a rope over an abyss.[32]

1 In *Les Enfants du paradis* the overseer of the Théâtre des Funambules imposes a fine every time someone speaks or simply breaks the silence.

2 According to the definition given in Rudolf Otto's famous study entitled *The Idea of the Holy* (1917), the ambivalence of holiness that belongs to the sometimes beneficent and sometimes infernal world of the divine is a *sacer* consecrated to the gods and imbued with an indelible stain, august and accursed, worthy of veneration and provoking horror, partaking simultaneously of the terrifying and the fascinating, of the *mysterium tremendum* and the *mysterium fascinans*. Rudolf Otto, *The Idea of the Holy: An Inquiry into the Non-Rational Factor in the Idea of the Divine and its Relation to the Rational*, trans. John W. Harvey (London: Oxford University Press, 1958).

3 Guillaume Apollinaire, "Young Artists: Picasso the Painter," in *Apollinaire on Art: Essays and Reviews 1902–1918*, trans. Susan Suleiman (New York: Viking, 1972), p. 16.

4 See Jean Starobinski, *Portrait de l'artiste en saltimbanque* (Geneva: Skira, 1970), p. 117ff.

5 See Waldemar Deonna, "Le Symbolisme de l'acrobatie antique," *Latomus: Revue d'Études Latines* 9 (1953).

6 Françoise Héritier, "Moitié d'hommes, pieds déchaussés et sauteurs à cloche-pied," *Terrains: Carnets du Patrimoine Ethnologique*, no. 18 (March 1992), pp. 5–14, also in *Masculin-Féminin*, vol. 1, *La Pensée de la différence* (Paris: Odile Jacob, 1996), pp. 165–189.

7 H.W. Janson, *Apes and Ape Lore in the Middle Ages and the Renaissance* (London: Warburg Institute, 1952), p. 30.

8 Ibid., p. 291.

9 See Kirk Varnedoe, *Picasso and Portraiture* (New York: Museum of Modern Art, 1996), pp. 173–174.

10 Janson, *Apes and Ape Lore*, p. 306.

11 Brassaï describes him as follows: "Picasso might like or hate men, but he adored all animals, which were as indispensable to him as female company. At the Bateau-Lavoir he had three Siamese cats, a dog, a monkey, and a turtle; a tame white mouse lived in one of his table drawers. He loved Frédé donkey [Frédéric Gérard] … and the tame crow housed at the Lapin Agile … In Vallauris he had a goat, and at Cannes a monkey, etc." *Conversations avec Picasso* (Paris: Gallimard, 1964), pp. 239–240. It is generally known that the idea for the *Bestiary of Orpheus* came to Apollinaire after viewing wood engravings of animals in the studio on Rue Ravignan.

12 It was in Munich in 1915, in the apartment of his friend Herta Koenig, that Rilke admired *The Acrobat's Family*. He had met Picasso in Paris in 1906. The encounter with the painter and subsequently with the painting gave rise, in 1922, to the "Fifth Duino Elegy," which Rilke completed in the Tower of Muzot: "Wer aber *sind* sie, sag mir, die Fahrenden, diese ein wenig / Flüchtigern noch als wir selbst …" ("But tell me, who *are* they, these acrobats, even a little / more fleeting than we ourselves …"). Rainer Maria Rilke, *Duino Elegies*, rev. ed., trans. J.B. Leishmann and Stephen Spender (London: Hogarth Press, 1952), p. 55.

13 "Angel: suppose there's a place we know nothing about, and there, / on some indescribable carpet, lovers showed all that here / they're forever unable to manage – their daring / lofty figures of heart-flight, / their towers of pleasure, their ladders …" Ibid., p. 61.

14 Starobinski, *Portrait de l'artiste en saltimbanque*, p. 14.

15 The first two syllables of the clown's name are pronounced in the same way as *chahut* or "uproar," while the final syllable is pronounced in the same way as the French *chaos*.

16 Théophile Gautier, *Histoire de l'art dramatique en France depuis vingt-cinq ans* (Paris: Blanchard et Cie, 1858), vol. 5, p. 23.

17 Werner Spies, "*Parade*: La Démonstration antinomique – Picasso aux prises avec les *Scene popolari di Napoli* d'Achille Vianelli," in "*Il se rendit en Italie*": *Études offertes à André Chastel* (Rome: Edizioni dell'elefante; Paris: Flammarion, 1987), p. 679ff.

18 Michel Pastoureau, *L'Étoffe du diable: Une Histoire des rayures et des tissus rayés* (Paris: Le Seuil, 1991), pp. 33–34.

19 Jean Cocteau, "Dedication to Georges Auric" (preface to *Cock and Harlequin*), in *Cocteau's World: An Anthology of Writings by Jean Cocteau*, ed. Margaret Crosland (New York: Dodd, Mead and Company, 1972).

20 See Edgar Wind, "'Ripeness is All,'" in *Pagan Mysteries in the Renaissance* (London: Faber and Faber, 1958), pp. 89–99.

21 See, for example, Mircea Eliade, *Mythes, rêves et mystères* (Paris: Gallimard, 1957), pp. 133–164.

22 See Christian Heck, *L'Échelle céleste dans l'art du Moyen Age: Une Image de la quête du ciel* (Paris: Flammarion, 1997), p. 39ff.

23 See Francis Haskell, "The Sad Clown: Some Notes on a 19th Century Myth," in *French 19th Century Painting and Literature*, ed. Ulrich Finke (Manchester: Manchester University Press, 1972), pp. 2–16.

24 See Linda Nochlin, "Gustave Courbet's Meeting: A Portrait of the Artist as a Wandering Jew," *The Art Bulletin* 44 (1967), p. 209ff.

25 Charles Baudelaire, *The Parisian Prowler*, trans. Edward K. Kaplan (Athens: University of Georgia Press, 1997), 2nd ed., pp. 29–30.

26 Ibid., p. 30.

27 See in particular Judith Wechsler, *A Human Comedy: Physiognomy and Caricature in 19th-Century Paris* (London: Thames & Hudson, 1982).

28 Charles Baudelaire, "Some French Caricaturists," in *Selected Writings on Art and Literature*, trans. P.E. Charvet (Harmondsworth: Penguin Books, 1972), p. 230. Judith Wechsler (in *A Human Comedy*) writes "Léclaire" as "Leclerq" and "physionomane" as "physiomane."

29 Ibid.

30 See the essay by Sophie Basch below, pp. 57–63.

31 Virgil, *The Aeneid*, Book 6.

32 Friedrich Nietzsche, *Thus Spoke Zarathustra*, trans. R.J. Hollingdale (Harmondsworth: Penguin Books, 1969), pp. 41–43.

Didier Ottinger

The Circus of Cruelty
A Portrait of the Contemporary Clown as Sisyphus

Clowns are sad, right? It's a commonplace as unsubtle and cloying as the cream pies so vital to any sketch that aims to transform comedy into violent aggression, buffoonery into martyrdom. But while there emerged from the nineteenth century and a large part of the twentieth a long procession of gloomy Gilles, melancholy Pierrots, and other sad fools, more recent art offers a less maudlin and stereotypical image of the clown. Modern clowns have abandoned the sentimental realm to move toward the moral or the aesthetic. And they have intensified the traditionally carnivalesque inversion of values to the point where their extravagances give rise to an apparently meaningless chaos. The characters of popular entertainment may have seemed during the nineteenth century like a series of allegories of the artist (according to an equation where image = meaning). But the modern clown, as Francis Haskell has suggested, is the stuff of myth.[1] And as with myth, its significance is open, complex, contradictory.

The clowns of Bruce Nauman, Ugo Rondinone, Paul McCarthy, Jonathan Borofsky, Arnaud Labelle-Rojoux, and Olivier Blanckart share common ancestors: the Hanlon-Lees, a troupe of six Irish-born brothers who revolutionized clowning with their resounding slaps and wild somersaults, rendering almost instantaneously obsolete the silent art of mime. A saraband of baboons after a minuet of felines! It was undoubtedly not by chance that the Hanlon-Lees began performing in Paris in 1872 and were received there with such acclaim. The Parisian public loved them because they were the embodiment of a new collective sensibility. Deburau and the sad Pierrots had been the incarnation of a resigned melancholy. The "children of paradise," society's rejects trapped behind the scenes of the Théâtre des Funambules, observed onstage the spectacle of their own condition. "Gilles is the people. He is sad; he beats and is beaten, musician, poet, clown, simpleton, always poor like the people ..." wrote Jules Janin.[2] Pierrot, on the other hand, was the awkward butt of good-natured jokes, victim of a social destiny he endured with resignation. His tribulations offered a foretaste of the populist miserabilism that pervaded the songs sung later by Berthe Sylvia and Edith Piaf. Théophile Gautier saw him as "the proletarian of modern times, a pariah, passive, the crafty, saturnine outsider who watches the orgies of his masters. He is ashen-faced, delicate, his clothes are pale. One might feel compassion for him as a victim; but he has another side, he is an ominous figure, shifty, pallid, weak."[3]

The Commune marked a radical break with this more or less acknowledged identification of the people with figures of submission. The revolutionary impulse, not only frustrated but cruelly repressed, had transformed the melancholy smile into a bitter grimace, sentimentalism into sarcasm. The Hanlon-Lees' show offered an image of unfettered violence, of the chaos generated by a shattered dream. They introduced "epilepsy into pantomime," as Hugounet put it, "wild fantasy compounded by a macabre naturalism that changed laughter into rictus."[4] The Hanlon-Lees presented "the most stupefying concert full of slaps, kicks in the behind, disintegrating scenery, exploding cannons, railway trains rushing through the air, submerging the outlandish musicians in flames and smoke ... a nightmare come true!"[5]

Modern clowns are actors in a disorderly show, and they are often vulgar, violent, immoral – all excesses displayed by the Hanlon-Lees. Bruce Nauman's clowns have a sardonic air. Sometimes they are shown seated on a public toilet (fig. 1). Their violence, shamelessness, and crudeness reflect the approach of an artist who in a 1967 work proclaimed: "The true artist helps the world by revealing mystic truths." In the dialectic between the triviality of his clowns and the grandiloquence of his declaration, Nauman proves himself a worthy winner of a Max Beckmann Fellowship, which he was awarded in 1990.

The German artist for whom the fellowship was named never ceased to defend the metaphysical dimension of his art: "The artist in the contemporary sense is the conscious shaper of the transcendent idea."[6] A spiritual heir of Romanticism, Beckmann always imbued his idealist declarations with the same irony that prompted the many self-portraits showing him as a clown or acrobat – as Gilles in *Double-portrait Carnival* from 1925, for example, and as an acrobat in *Acrobat on the Trapeze* (fig. 2) from 1940. But this same sense of irony can also be detected in self-portraits that have nothing of the overtly clownish. *Self-portrait in Tuxedo* (fig. 3), from 1927, which presents Beckmann as an imperious member of the bourgeoisie, should be approached on a level that the artist's haughty pose tends to obscure. As in all his self-portraits, Beckmann is here questioning the artist's status, the role that society allows him to play. The meaning of *Self-portrait in Tuxedo* becomes clearer after a reading of "Der Künstler im Stadt" ("The Artist in the State"), a text written by the painter when asked to define his art's social role: "Workers ...

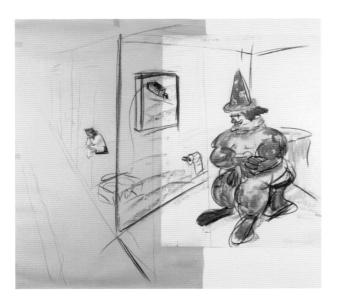

Figure 1
Bruce Nauman, *Clown with Video Surveillance*, 1986, watercolour, pencil, and collage on paper. Courtesy Mr. and Mrs. Jay Bernstein, Shoshana Wayne Gallery, Santa Monica

Figure 3
Max Beckmann, *Self-portrait in Tuxedo*, 1927, oil on canvas. Busch-Reisinger Museum, Harvard University Art Museums, Cambridge, Massachusetts, Association Fund

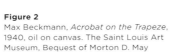

Figure 2
Max Beckmann, *Acrobat on the Trapeze*, 1940, oil on canvas. The Saint Louis Art Museum, Bequest of Morton D. May

Figure 4
Still from Bruce Nauman's *Manipulating a Fluorescent Tube*, 1969, video. Courtesy Electronic Arts Intermix, New York

should likewise appear in tuxedo or tails. Which is to say: We seek a kind of aristocratic Bolshevism."[7] A latent "clownism," composed of paradox and irony, characterizes this most famous of Beckmann's self-portraits.

On the one hand, he writes: "What we're missing is a new cultural centre, a new centre of faith. We need new buildings where we can practice this new faith and this new cult of man's balance, buildings in which to collect and present all that has become whole as a consequence of our newly acquired balance."[8] On the other, he portrays himself backstage, in circus trailers (*Birth*, 1938; *The Circus Wagon*, 1940, cat. no. 101), and declares that the artist must "take cognizance of the fact that he is a subservient member of society, nothing more in essence than a slightly better employee. His demands can, of course, be taken under consideration only when society's more essential needs for a family car and a vacation trip to the Pyramids have been satisfied."[9]

His paintings, his self-representations, both actual and metaphorical, play on the ambiguity surrounding the German words *Künstler* (artist) and *Artist* (circus performer). This "clownish" lineage throws light on the fundamental significance of Bruce Nauman's work, which consists to a large extent in the ironical debunking of modernist idealism (its teleology, its obsession with "purity"). Almost as soon as they appeared on New York's avant-garde stage, Nauman began re-presenting the objects of minimalist art as a series of practical jokes and tricks. He appropriated one of the fluorescent tubes that Dan Flavin had made the signature of his art and placed it in his own crotch, where it simulated a particularly radiant phallus (*Manipulating a Fluorescent Tube*, 1969, fig. 4). In his studio, the simple shapes of modernist formalism are overcome by a grotesque languor. The rigidity of hard-edged sculpture dissolves into limpness (*Untitled*, 1965), and his forays into body art and performance resemble music-hall skits. *Bouncing Two Balls between the Floor and Ceiling with Changing Rhythms* (1968) gleefully recasts the Wittgensteinian gloss of a certain branch of conceptual art, turning its exercises in applied tautology into a kids' game. *Art Make-Up* (1967–1968) and *Studies for Holograms* (1970) link body art to the circus dressing-room.

Figure 5
Stills from Pierrick Sorin's *La Bataille des tartes* (cat. no. 63)

Figure 6
Still from Victor Sjöström's *He Who Gets Slapped* (cat. no. 61)

Against the "Darwinism" of the avant-garde discourse (its idea of historical transcendence, the irreversibility of its model of artistic "evolution") Nauman offers the absurd litany, repeated in an endless loop, of his clowns (*Dirty Stories*, from 1987, shows two clowns facing one another, one of whom reels off the same absurd narrative, over and over). Nauman, who insidiously undermines the idealism integral to the modernist vision, takes on the clown's mission – that of reminding utopians of ordinary, existential reality, of countering their futurist projections with the orbits circumscribed by a circus ring, which he sees as the only possible framework for the human condition.

One of the standard devices of the art of clowning is endless and unbearable repetition. It serves as an excruciating illustration of the fate that condemns humanity to repeat itself – the same mistakes, the same recurring illusions born of the same impossible dreams. Like Camus's Sisyphus, clowns express a condition of absurdity from which only awareness and feigned submission can offer any hope of emancipation. And like the clown in Nauman's *Dirty Stories*, endlessly telling a story whose final word is also its first, Ugo Rondinone has a penchant for the absurdity of repetition. His installations are accompanied by short, throbbing musical pieces, only one or two minutes long, that are repeated over and over again.

Invited to participate in the États Généraux de la Poésie in Marseilles in 1992, Arnaud Labelle-Rojoux (Olivier Blanckart's clownish stooge) presented a performance in which he was regularly slapped every time he uttered a poet's name. In Pierrick Sorin's *La Bataille des tartes* (fig. 5) the endless repetition of its pie-in-the-face stunt causes the laughter it initially triggers among viewers to turn sour. The reiterated humiliations of this piece recall the unbearable slapping scene in Victor Sjöström's 1924 film *He Who Gets Slapped* (fig. 6).

The tragicomic litanies of clowns are the "Sisyphian" alternative, the realist antidote to the appeals and adulation directed at the "new man," who was so ubiquitous in the twentieth century. Albert Camus's remarks on Sisyphus apply also to the clown trapped within the circus ring: "His scorn of the gods, his hatred of death, and his passion for life won him that unspeakable penalty in which the whole being is exerted toward accomplishing nothing. This is the price that must be paid for the passions of this earth."[10]

Ugo Rondinone's clowns lie inside the white cube that symbolizes the "purity" toward which art long aspired. Embodying the same nightmarish chaos that the Hanlon-Lees conjured for their audiences, these clowns are all flabby, all struck down by some terrible intoxication. In their odd, scruffy clothes they look more like homeless people than music-hall stars (the grey blankets on which they rest their heads resemble those handed out to the destitute). In several installations they gaze into a broken mirror that confuses, fragments, and destroys both their own image and ours.

They epitomize the denial of any endeavour capable of generating meaning, order, or beauty; they are a "living" manifesto of anti-affirmation. The image of their apathy projected by Rondinone's installations is for Eric Troncy the exemplification of one of the clichés of contemporary art, "the absolute futility of the use of overhead projections in exhibitions, of the cinematographic device implying a duration that in reality is of benefit to no one."[11] Similarly, Rondinone's target paintings "smugly and cynically take up all the known artistic strategies: use of the repeated motif designed to produce the hallmark of 'the author,' the signature, the tight control of production in order to ensure rarity, recuperation, and adaptation of a historically resonant form (Jasper Johns, Kenneth Noland) …"[12] Rondinone's target is the same as Nauman's – the messianic, apodictic art of the avant-garde, whose self-imposed mission is to change the world. And like Nauman he sets the obscure pathways of the labyrinth against the triumphant avenue leading to a glorious future. The exhaustion of Rondinone's clowns has an "after-the-deed-is-done" feel about it. The nausea they inspire is tinged with the tension generated by a sense of imminent danger. What will they do, these great oafs, once their stupor wears off? Explaining the uneasiness inspired by these strange, sleeping forms, John Richardson recalls that for most Americans the image of the clown is now forever associated with that of the serial killer.[13] In 1978, after a lengthy manhunt, the ghastly crimes of John Wayne Gacy, Jr., were finally brought to a halt. The Chicago police had been trailing the man for months: dressed as Pogo the Clown, he had enticed some thirty children into his basement, whence they never emerged. Like the inhabitants of the town of Hamelin, forever wary of pipe players, American children have learned to be suspicious of clowns.

European adults have known for a long time that clowns have their dark side. Picasso, who during his Blue Period made Harlequin his alter ego, learned from Apollinaire that this *commedia dell'arte* character had a history and etymology linking him to the diabolical realm. The poet had added "Trismegistus" to Harlequin's name, thus recalling his relations with Hermes, guardian god of occult knowledge who also guided the shades of dead mortals to the underworld. The modern "Harlequin" can be traced back, through Old French, to Hellequin, an evil flying demon with an animal's face. According to the mysteries of medieval times, the role of Hellequin was to transgress social taboos. Harlequin's variegated costume reflects the shallowness of his character, his unpredictability, his lack of ideas and principles. It can even be seen as a symbol of his fundamentally immoral desire to relativize roles and human certitudes, his aim of demolishing ideas and images that are too simple, too unified. With his "chaotic" costume prefiguring Ugo Rondinone's broken mirrors, Harlequin accomplished on the moral and social levels the "kaleidoscopization" of values that Picasso, through Cubism, achieved in the visual realm. Like the Minotaur (the Spanish artist's other identifying emblem), whose bull's head bespeaks links to the bestial netherworld, Harlequin was for Picasso the perfect image of the artist-ferryman, a creature of the world in between.

Witnesses of the Hanlon-Lees' show remarked upon the "bestiality" of their performance, and Théodore de Banville described them as creatures that were "half man, half god."[14] Archetypes of the modern clown, they were dual figures, agents of the passage from one world, or one state, to another. Even now, when a clown tumbles into the circus ring his role is often to keep the audience amused in the gap between the acrobats and the bareback rider.

The dualism that is so much a part of the clown's nature is evident in the crude transvestite figure (half clown, half ballerina) created by Jonathan Borofsky. It is a sexual fantasy made possible by the semantic instability of the clown, its sponge-like capacity to absorb meaning, its determination to avoid synthesis and over-simplification. The inversion of the clown's sexual identity was described by Félicien Champsaur in 1901 in his novel *Lulu*, which features a clowness portrayed as a "barely feminized ephebe."[15] This androgyne rapidly gained fame. Toulouse-Lautrec represented it in the guise of the clowness Cha-U-Kao, and the couple formed by the Goncourt brothers in Edmond's novel *Les Frères Zemganno* reveals the clown's

Figure 7
Still from Paul McCarthy's *Painter*
(cat. no. 64)

latent androgyny: Gianni possesses "the beauty of a man's body,"[16] while his brother Nello, soon required to play the role of an "American lady circus rider," boasts "a svelte and femininely well-covered figure."[17] Apollinaire, for his part, pointed out the sexual ambiguity of Picasso's acrobats: "Some harlequins accompany the aura of the women and resemble them, neither male nor female."[18]

The androgyny of the clown figure is just one aspect of its polysemy. In attempting to capture its identity, André Suarès makes liberal use of the oxymoron. "It is the comic mirror of tragedy, the tragic mirror of comedy ... Silence is its loudest cry, stupor its eloquence."[19] "The expressive moment that separates laughter and tears is the quintessence of the clown's style ... It has to have a face that is not that of a child, nor of a death's head, but resembles both."[20] "The art of the clown is calculated improvisation."[21] "The clown is a moving skin covering a death's head. The skin, with its shivers of water and wavelike movements, expresses all the variety of life, of characters, and of passions. But the death's head is the immutable core."[22]

The clowns of contemporary art have inherited this dualism. Bruce Nauman describes them as incarnations of contradictory values: "I became interested in the idea of the clown in the first place because there is a mask, and it becomes an abstract idea of a person. And that's the reason, because clowns are in a sense abstract, that they become disconcerting ... It's hard to make contact with an idea or an abstraction. And also, when you think of vaudeville or circus clowns, there's a certain degree of cruelty and meanness."[23] The role Nauman makes them play emphasizes their dual nature. "The scene of the clown going to the toilet should be interpreted, in one sense, as a symbolic vision of the artist torn between private necessity and public obligation."[24]

The art of Paul McCarthy is essentially clownish, for it turns on its head the sublimation integral to art and inverts hierarchies, reducing to their most crudely human reality the abstractions produced by culture – both "high culture" and "mass culture." In this sense, his work is the perfect antithesis of Jeff Koons's. In the late 1960s McCarthy, like Nauman, ridiculed the formalist purism of the East Coast avant-garde, adding a "tail" to one of the cubes so loved by minimalists (*Skull with a Tail*). His performances from the 1970s

show him wearing clown and carnival masks, parodying B horror films.[25] On occasion he has made use of some of the most popular figures of children's culture (*Popeye*, 1983; *Pinocchio*, 1994), recycling them as the heroes of ketchup-splattered gore movies. His aim is to inject a massive dose of human reality (in the form of its organs and excretions) into the overblown symbols of gassy idealist entertainment. His target is the stereotyped, asepticized, "abstract" life of the theme park, and he employs the most expeditious methods in creating his brand of "realism." In order to illustrate his carnivalesque "inversion of values" he sometimes makes two photographs of the same space, which he then assembles with one image upside down (*Inverted Hallway*, 1970). His most explicitly clownish film, *Painter* (1995, fig. 7), features an artist. The work is a grotesque and parodic commentary on Abstract Expressionism, its legendary interiority (the artist, alone, acting out his life in the arena of the canvas) and expressive pathos. In another film (*Penis Brush Painting*, 1974), McCarthy, with more than a touch of Freudianism, overturns the sublimation of the creative process by using his own genitalia as a paintbrush – a "technique" also used by Labelle-Rojoux in his jokey *Painted with the Dick*, a work on canvas that portrays a pig.

Clowns (cat. no. 86), the performance created jointly by Arnaud Labelle-Rojoux and Olivier Blanckart, is in entirely the same spirit as their individual practices. Scoffing at both sentimental myths and artistic clichés, it is a response to Cézanne's transmutation into a hit-parade hero. The singer France Gall, already notorious for her love of aniseed-flavoured lollipops, turned the painter from Aix-en-Provence into a character in a pop song. Her hit "Cézanne peint" (Cézanne paints) is changed by Labelle-Rojoux and Blanckart into a cacophonic "cet âne peint" (this donkey paints). In the same performance, the Hollywoodian tragedy of Francis Bacon is transformed into butchery: Labelle-Rojoux brandishes a pig's leg in front of a blank canvas; Blanckart (the whiteface clown), confident of his grasp of things, asks "Is it ham?" and the other replies, "No, it's bacon"!

Figure 8
Jean Hélion, *Yellow Trickery*, 1970, acrylic
on canvas. Private collection

The irony of these clowns is thus directed at art itself. After a century of so-called "avant-garde" art, whose very name reflects its affinities with revolutionary militantism, today's "clownish" artists throw doubt upon its meaning and its ultimate goals. They are the clear-sighted witnesses of an art devoid of the Promethean ethos inherited from political ideologies and the religion of progress.

Two historical "clowneries" shed some light on the relationship between art and ideology.

Jean Hélion, who in the early 1930s had been a promoter of the first abstract avant-garde, believed for a time that the objectives of a certain form of avant-garde art and his dream of social and political reform could be combined. But the undermining of his revolutionary faith destroyed his abstract art: "It was in 1936, during the famous trials that saw the disappearance of at least ten of my friends, the very ones who had guided me toward Communism (Isaac Babel, Afinogenov, Kirchon, General Xermanius, and others, like Mandelstam, whom I knew only by reputation), that my Communist faith disintegrated ... It was when I stopped being Communist that I stopped being abstract."[26]

After 1936 Hélion made no further attempt to link changes in art with the development of a political reform movement. But his disillusionment was not sufficient to push him into the conservative camp. Even in the late 1960s a number of young "revolutionary" painters (such as Eduardo Arroyo and Gilles Aillaud) were stressing the topicality of his ideas and work. Like his, their militant commitment was

expressed in an art whose ironic (Arroyo) or metaphorical (Aillaud) dimension saved it from becoming a propagandist manifesto – a trap some of their painter contemporaries failed to avoid.

Returning to the figurative mode in the late 1930s, Hélion did not begin exploring clowns in his painting until three decades later. And they appeared at a significant moment. In 1967 the painter began attending the Cirque Medrano regularly. When the events of May '68 exploded beneath his windows, he turned almost naturally to the image of the clown as an antidote to the spontaneous lyricism of his support for the student revolt (fig. 8). "General strike today, 20 May. What a circus! And I mean it. I'm going to work on my circus today. Life is a circus!"[27] Clowns and their circular parades became, once again, a counterpoint to the "leaps forward" of unfolding History, "dialectical figures," a bulwark against the reduction of the world and its meaning to the schematism of over-simplified ideas. "Throughout my work," wrote Hélion in the spring of 1979, "I have sought the coincidence of the comic and the tragic; more precisely, the comic expression of the tragic."[28] The alternation between clowns and "revolutionaries" in his paintings from the late 1960s is a lesson in lucidity; its aim is to deflate those idealistic windbags who, claiming the best of intentions, invariably threaten to reduce art to a series of reassuring and simplistic notions. "Why did I go so far as to speak of 'the identity of contraries'? It had become routine, coming up with incisive expressions. The exact term was 'the kinship of contraries,' which leaves some room for difference and imposes on it an opposing stricture."[29]

Figure 9
Philip Guston, *The Studio*, 1969, oil on
canvas. Private collection, courtesy McKee
Gallery, New York

Philip Guston (fig. 9 and cat. no. 85) has also made use of a
"clownish" style and iconography to stay outside the modernist
mainstream. After having been one of the pioneers of Abstract
Expressionism, he created a scandal in 1969 by exhibiting paintings
linked both stylistically and iconographically to the cartoon and the
comic strip. Guston had come to realize that the ethical and political values that had historically justified and underpinned the modernist painting movement had had no impact whatever on reality and,
worse still, had degenerated into an authoritarian aesthetic dogma.
Taking a position diametrically opposed to the ill-considered dis-
courses that assimilated "modernist" form and "advanced" political
thinking, which had their roots in Clement Greenberg's 1939 essay
"Avant-garde and Kitsch,"[30] Guston explained that his adoption of
the kitschest of styles was actually the result of his political views.
"So when the 1960s came along I was feeling split, schizophrenic.
The war, what was happening to America, the brutality of the world.
What kind of man am I, sitting at home, reading magazines, going
into a frustrated fury about everything – and then going into my
studio *to adjust a red to a blue*. I thought there must be some way
I could do something about it. I knew ahead of me a road was lay-
ing. A very crude, inchoate road. I wanted to be complete again, as
I was when I was a kid … Wanted to be whole between what I
thought and what I felt."[31] Guston put on a clown's mask to follow
the "inchoate road" of the "impure" art to which he now aspired. In
the guise of comically hooded spooks, of truncheon-wielding puppets, he presented the critics and gurus of an art obsessed by the
ideal of purity. His self-portraits show a cartoon-like character lying
sprawled on his bed in a cloud of cigarette smoke. In denouncing
the Nixon administration (and sympathetically echoing Philip Roth's
parody *Our Gang*), he carefully distanced himself from the inevitable
ingenuousness of grandiloquence by adopting a comic-strip style.
In this way he underscored the fundamental ambiguity – the simultaneous grandiosity and ridiculousness – of any art that strives to
be the vehicle of a social or political message.

Uncontested master of "clownish" art, Guston portrayed edifying or
tragic subjects (floods, torture scenes, genocide) using an approach
that fused humour and tragedy, farce and pathos. In the final years
of his life he discovered Albert Camus's version of Sisyphus, and it
became for him the perfect allegory for a humanity condemned to
wrestle with contradictions, to transcend the meaning of its own

existence, to acknowledge the simultaneous fragility and irony of its effort. Camus writes: "Sisyphus teaches the higher fidelity that negates the gods and raises rocks. He too concludes that all is well. This universe henceforth without a master seems to him neither sterile nor futile. Each atom of that stone, each mineral flake of that night-filled mountain, in itself forms a world. The struggle itself toward the heights is enough to fill a man's heart."[32]

The history of the clown, whose myth, as Jean Starobinski has pointed out, "was formed during the Romantic age,"[33] is closely linked to that of irony. Romanticism employed irony as its favourite weapon against the edifice of neoclassical certitudes. To combat "neoclassical systematism," Friedrich Schlegel and the Romantics advocated complexity and its corollary, relativism: "Versatility consists not just in a comprehensive system but also in a feeling for the chaos outside that system."[34] This feeling for "chaos" was the heart of an aesthetic position that became a model for Romantic art. According to Charles Rosen and Henri Zerner, *Kunstchaos* has a favoured form – the oxymoron. It makes possible the alliance of contradictory qualities in a single object. Pierre Wat has defined Romanticism as "a split painting, an oxymoronic painting that reminds the viewer of his painful position as a modern man, in other words that renders the rational subject chaotic."[35]

The creation of chaos – the very antithesis of the dogma of perfection and purity – is a method used by clowns since time immemorial. The clowns of Nauman, Guston, and Hélion are the historical symptoms of a questioning of modernism's omnipotence. Like the clowns of the Romantic era, their goal is to loosen the stranglehold of neoclassicism, of an aesthetic that imposes on art a teleological model of perfection and "purification" (the progress of art, from Cubism to Abstract Expressionism, that has been the modernist bible). The unashamed vulgarity, the "impurity" so integral to a clownish approach, is the alternative to the process of self-purification defended by Greenbergian modernism.

In the direct lineage (as the literary tradition attests) of Gilles and Pierrot, our contemporary clowns are heirs to a Romanticism that aims to offer a more complex image of the world than the one fashioned exclusively by the tools of rationalism. The clowns in a shamanic trance shown by Paul McCarthy, like those of Ugo Rondinone, who

imagine a world composed of the shards of a shattered mirror, are the descendants of the Pierrot so loved by late nineteenth-century authors. Like their forerunner, they express a thought "that becomes integral to the peril of the Logos, that has its raison d'être in the peril it brings to bear on the Logos, that throws into discredit both the Body and the Word, that picks up along the way the doubtful prestige of the Grotesque and the Baroque, that unites the irreconcilable, that – far from being, like classical poetry, 'revoltingly healthy and virtuous' – is a 'seething swamp,' not a 'glass of clear water.'"[36]

Clowns are the messengers of a paradoxical lyricism, of an idealism tormented by doubt, of an absolute that must surely forever strike down materialism and scepticism, of the sublime modernity that in Thomas Mann's view can only be expressed through the grotesque.

A final hypothesis protects our clowns from all historicism. Their duplicity, the "challenge to the seriousness of our certitudes"[37] that they embody, makes them allegories of artistic creation itself.

Plato's theory of mimesis reduces all we call art to mere reproduction, making it nothing but a misleading reflection of the world. Artists thus become creators of simulacra, individuals who threaten the order of the city-state. In *The Republic*, the philosopher recommended the outright banishment of these troublemakers. Since, art has been forever trying to escape this harsh fate. Liberating it from the visible by making it "abstract" was one option. Making it subject to a teleology, affirming its "essence" and its "truth," also gave it a certain authority – almost as much authority as the ancient philosophy that had condemned it. The other avenue open to art (the realist option) is the acknowledgement of its "impurity." This results in an approach that applies to itself the wisdom acquired long ago by Sisyphus, an art that allows itself to dream while recognizing the illusory nature of its dreams, that never forgets the weight of the reality it pushes up the slope, like clowns ever conscious of the huge shoes they drag around the circus ring.

Clown wisdom: only he who admits to lying is telling the truth.

1   Francis Haskell, "The Sad Clown: Some Notes on a 19th Century Myth," in *French 19th Century Painting and Literature*, ed. Ulrich Finke (Manchester: Manchester University Press, 1972), pp. 2–16.

2   Jules Janin, *Deburau: Histoire du théâtre à quatre sous* (Paris: Éditions d'Aujourd'hui, 1981), pp. 75–76.

3   Théophile Gautier, *Histoire de l'art dramatique en France depuis vingt-cinq ans* (Paris: Blanchard et Cie, 1858), p. 317.

4   Paul Hugounet, *Mimes et Pierrots* (Paris: Fishbacher, 1889), p. 195, quoted by Jean de Palacio in *Pierrot fin de siècle* (Paris: Séguier, 1990), p. 40, note 13.

5   Monsieur du Paradis, in *La Lune rousse*, 23 June 1878, quoted by Sophie Basch in "Le cirque en 1879: Les Hanlon-Lees dans la littérature," in *La Vie romantique* (Colloques de la Sorbonne), ed. André Guyaux and Sophie Marchal (Paris: Presses de l'Université de Paris-Sorbonne, 2002), p. 23.

6   Max Beckmann, "The Artist in the State," July 1927, article for the *Europäische Revue*, in *Max Beckmann: Self-Portrait in Words*, ed. Barbara Copeland Buenger (Chicago: University of Chicago Press, 1997), p. 287.

7   Ibid., p. 288.

8   Ibid.

9   Max Beckmann, "The Social Stance of the Artist by the Black Tightrope Walker," in *Max Beckmann: Self-Portrait in Words*, p. 282.

10 Albert Camus, *The Myth of Sisyphus and Other Essays*, trans. Justin O'Brien (New York: Random House, 1955), p. 89.

11 Eric Troncy, "Ugo Rondinone: Where Do We Go, Ugo? – Clown and Out with Ugo Rondinone," *Art Press*, no. 227 (September 1997), p. 33, trans. p. 36.

12 Ibid., p. 35, trans. p. 37.

13 John Richardson, *Ugo Rondinone* (Paris: Galerie Almine Rech, 2001), n.p.

14 Théodore de Banville, *Critiques* (Paris: Charpentier, 1917), p. 422.

15 Quoted by Jean de Palacio in *Pierrot fin de siècle*, p. 49.

16 Edmond de Goncourt, *Les Frères Zemganno* (Paris: Charpentier, 1879), p. 35, quoted by Jean de Palacio in *Pierrot fin de siècle*, p. 47.

17 Ibid., pp. 47–48.

18 Guillaume Apollinaire, *Apollinaire on Art: Essays and Reviews 1902-1918*, ed. Leroy C. Breunig (New York: Viking, 1972), p. 16.

19 André Suarès, "Essai sur le clown," in *Remarques* (Paris: Gallimard, 2000), p. 25.

20 Ibid., p. 26.

21 Ibid., p. 31.

22 Ibid., p. 130.

23 *Bruce Nauman: Sculptures et installations, 1985–1990* (Lausanne: Musée Cantonal des Beaux-Arts, 1991), p. 34.

24 Ibid., p. 36.

25 "In one of the early pieces I wore a clown mask." Paul McCarthy and Ralph Rugoff, *Paul McCarthy* (New York: Phaidon, 1996), p. 136.

26 Jean Hélion, *Mémoire de la chambre jaune* (Paris: École Nationale Supérieure des Beaux-Arts, 1994), pp. 175–176, 181.

27 Jean Hélion, *Journal d'un peintre: Carnets 1929–1984*, ed. Anne Moeglin-Delcroix (Paris: Maeght, 1992), p. 60.

28 Ibid., p. 325.

29 Ibid., p. 373.

30 Greenberg writes: "Where there is an avant-garde, generally we also find a rear-guard. True enough – simultaneously with the entrance of the avant-garde, a second new cultural phenomenon appeared … that thing to which the Germans give the wonderful name *Kitsch*: popular, commercial art and literature with their chromeotypes, magazine covers, illustrations, ads, slick and pulp fiction, comics …"; and further on: "The encouragement of kitsch is merely another of the inexpensive ways in which totalitarian regimes seek to ingratiate themselves with their subjects." See "Avant-garde and Kitsch," in *Clement Greenberg: The Collected Essays and Criticism*, ed. John O'Brian, vol. 1, *Perceptions and Judgments* (Chicago: University of Chicago Press, 1986), pp. 11, 20.

31 Quoted by Robert Storr in *Philip Guston* (New York: Abbeville, 1986), p. 53.

32 Camus, *The Myth of Sisyphus*, p. 9.

33 Jean Starobinski, *Portrait de l'artiste en saltimbanque* (Geneva: Skira, 1970), p. 15.

34 Friedrich Schlegel, "Ideas," no. 55, in *Friedrich Schlegel's "Lucinde" and the Fragments*, trans. Peter Firchow (Minneapolis: University of Minnesota Press, 1971), p. 246.

35 Pierre Wat, *Naissance de l'art romantique: Peinture et théorie de l'imitation en Allemagne et en Angleterre* (Paris: Flammarion, 1998), p. 118.

36 Jean de Palacio in *Pierrot fin de siècle*, p. 234.

37 Starobinski, *Portrait de l'artiste en saltimbanque*, p. 15.

Ann Thomas

The Waking Dream
Photography and the Circus

The wide appeal of the circus is that it offers us a brief glimpse of triumph over the mundane. In an environment of glittering costumes, dramatic lighting, and rousing music, we experience for a short spell of time the achievement of what we have believed to be impossible. Death is defied, deviations from the norm are celebrated, and the solemnity of life is mocked. As Jean Starobinski has aptly described it, the circus is like a "waking dream."[1]

From the breathtaking moves of high-flying trapeze artists, to the steel-nerved acts of suavely attired lion tamers, to the daredevilry of human cannonballs, to the antics of clowns and midgets, the circus has traditionally offered its audiences a full range of intense thrills. At the same time, it has also been an unadulterated feast for the eyes. The play of multicoloured spotlights, the sequin-studded costumes, and the stylized, theatrical make-up all have a part in holding the attention of the circus audience and transporting them into a fantasy world far from the everyday. It is not surprising that the extreme and seemingly spontaneous nature of the circus, with its pageantry, romance, and excitement, as well as its social marginality, has always made it appealing to visual artists. It has inspired them to record and interpret its every aspect, in every medium.

At the point when photography was being established as a viable image-making technique, beginning in 1839, the theme of the circus was already quite popular in painting. It was a subject, however, that did not immediately lend itself to the new medium. Because of the low sensitivity of the first generation of plates and papers and the long exposure times that were required, overall views of circus interiors or of the action of parades and performers could not be obtained. Even much later in the century the results continued to be less than satisfactory. Furthermore, the technical limitations of the medium in its early decades were such that it was impossible to record colour. Being unable to render either of these two compelling aspects of the circus experience, nineteenth-century photographers confined themselves to the one area where successful results could be assured: portraiture.[2] Interestingly, even when the technical obstacles were finally overcome, photographers continued to enjoy making portraits of clowns, acrobats, and sideshow characters. The fidelity with which photography captured the human likeness made it especially popular as a portrait medium, and the circus was such a rich reservoir of human types that it proved irresistible to photographers.

The earliest circus portraits, dating from 1839 to the mid-1850s, were created by the daguerreotype process, the first effective method of making permanent, legible photographic images. Daguerreotypes were more commonly used to portray individuals or families of means, or people who occupied elevated stations in society, such as politicians, scientists, high-ranking military officers, and members of the nobility. Daguerreotypes of socially marginal figures like clowns, acrobats, or midgets thus constitute a rather rare subcategory, although in a sense they also can be regarded as belonging to the established genre of "occupational" daguerreotypes. The subjects of these pictures were not photographed in the context of the circus but rather posed in the daguerreotypist's portrait studio.

Three such images, by unidentified American daguerreotypists, are included in this exhibition: *William G. Worrell of Welch's National Circus and Theater* (cat. no. 37), *Portrait of an Acrobat, Valentine Denzer* (cat. no. 38), and *Tom Thumb* (cat. no. 120). The portrait of the midget celebrity Charles S. Stratton, who was commonly known as Tom Thumb, is endearing for its depiction of him as a person rather than as a human aberration. Presenting him full-length in a frontal, seated pose, the daguerreotypist has deliberately rejected the usual practice (as in fig. 1, for example) of posing a midget beside a normally or even abnormally large person as a means of calling attention to his size. Curiously, and no doubt unintentionally, the actual length of Stratton's body is further obscured by the disappearance of his feet into the darkness under his chair. In contrast to this representation of a childlike and rather defenceless figure, the daguerreotype portraits of the acrobats William G. Worrell and Valentine Denzer exude the grace and elegance of performers whose very livelihood depended upon projecting the most polished level of stage presence. The full-length standing portrait of Denzer, which shows evidence of the rough hanging of backdrop drapery, is clearly the work of a more primitive practitioner of the daguerreotype, while that of the seated William G. Worrell, whose costume has been enhanced by selectively applied colour, represents the height of sophistication in the Daguerreian art. The subtle hand-colouring – a technique adopted by daguerreotypists to compensate for their inability to actually record colour – adds a liveliness and festive mood to the image.

Given the fragility of the silvered surface of the daguerreotype plate, the addition of colour required a skilled hand. The plate was heated from its underside as pigmented resin was carefully dusted onto the areas of the image selected for coloration. Dissolved pigment was then applied to the surface of the image with a very fine-haired brush, enhancing pertinent features of the face, costume,

Figure 1
Charles Eisenmann, *General Willis Carver, Midget*, 1882, albumen silver print. Courtesy Michael Mitchell and ECW Press, Toronto

Figure 2
Kölnische Illustrierte Zeitung, April 1929. Archives of the City of Cologne

48

and props. Studio assistants with training or talent in painting were often given the job of applying the colour to the plate.

Even if the poses adopted by Worrell and Denzer are graceful, they are still those of the portrait studio; they are not in the least suggestive of the agility and beauty of the acrobats' movements in the circus ring. A quicker process than the daguerreotype was the negative-positive photographic process, employed to great effect by the Tournachon brothers in their sequenced portrait of the renowned French mime Charles Deburau as Pierrot (cat. nos. 32–35). The negative-positive process allowed photographers to capture one image after another in a matter of seconds, rather than minutes, while also enabling them to print a given photograph in large numbers. Félix Tournachon (known as Nadar) and his brother Adrien Tournachon[3] produced the fifteen sequentially numbered salted paper prints around the end of 1854, when they invited Deburau to pose for them as a means of publicizing their newly established studio. The photographs are, among other things, a telling indicator of the respected status that popular forms of entertainment such as pantomime, the circus, and variety shows had achieved within literary circles in France in the mid-nineteenth century.[4]

Striking in composition and scale, the images that comprise the sequence illustrate a delightfully playful narrative in which Pierrot assumes a variety of emotion-laden poses. Departing somewhat from this scenario is the initial image in the sequence, *Pierrot the Photographer* (cat. no. 34), which is probably the first iconic representation of "the artist as clown" in the history of photography. Standing beside a large-format camera mounted on a tripod, Pierrot is seen removing a plate-holder from the apparatus while directing the viewer's attention to the camera lens. The expression on his face, whitened by the application of flour,[5] is neutral and impassive. At least two writers have noted the layered meanings behind this image: on one level it is the photographer's self-portrait as clown, with Deburau as his stand-in,[6] and on another level it is a statement about the art of photography as a mimetic art, in the sense that both pantomime and photography base their representation of the world on a mute replication of reality.[7]

The genre of the circus-performer portrait represented by these daguerreotypes and the Tournachon brothers' Pierrot sequence has persisted well into our own time, as illustrated by Rhona Bitner's masterful life-size portraits of clowns and harlequins, a series she began in 2001 (cat. no. 117).

With their white-painted faces, which shifted at will from joy to sadness, clowns like the Swiss-born Grock in Europe and Jimmy Armstrong and Emmett Kelly in the United States were magnets for photographers working during the period 1920–1950. Umbo, a German photographer and Bauhaus graduate, was among the many artists fascinated by Grock. In 1929 he made a series of photographs of the popular entertainer applying make-up to transform his rather regular features into those of the much beloved clown figure and then acting out a range of expressions, from a rubber-faced smile of joy to a menacing grin (cat. nos. 53 and 54). Several images from the series were published that year in the *Kölnische Illustrierte Zeitung* (fig. 2). In contrast to Umbo's highly animated Grock, Jimmy Armstrong faces Weegee's camera with a soulful sadness, in an exaggeratedly foreshortened view (cat. no. 57). The picture is a masterpiece of its kind. Weegee, who exhibited a marked taste for the sensational and was known for his aggressive and outrageous conduct as a photographer, made clowns one of his specialties. While many of his negatives of clowns were subjected to distorting devices that allow the prints to be classified under the rubric of "trick photography," an exception is the haunting clown self-portrait he created by setting up his camera in the circus ring and capturing himself with a large-format Speed Graflex clutched to his breast as he chased after a clown (cat. no. 112). In identifying with the clown, the artist reveals himself as a creator and performer, but also as an outsider, a maverick, a butt of humour and ridicule, and a figure of self-deprecation.

In the entire history of photography, the subject of the artist as clown was never more joyously and impertinently represented than in the photographs documenting the dances and theatrical presentations performed at the Bauhaus in Germany in the 1920s. Teachers and students of this school – which offered a multidisciplinary program of design, architecture, theatre, dance, music, painting, sculpture, and photography at its various locations in Dessau, Weimar,

and Berlin – collaborated on all aspects of dance and theatrical performance, from writing scripts and composing scores to choreographing dances and designing sets and costumes, and then photographing the entire process. Through all this, the circus played an important role, both as subject matter and as source of inspiration, invigorating the performing arts with a fresh spontaneity.

"Show me how you celebrate, and I'll tell you who you are" was just one of the challenges issued by the artists of the Bauhaus, who emphasized self-revelation through music, dance, and masks. For many of them, the appropriate response to this maxim was to don a creatively designed clown costume, take up a musical instrument, and act out a scene created along the lines of a pantomime, circus, or variety show.

Foremost among the Bauhaus teachers who promoted the circus as an art form was Oskar Schlemmer, a German painter, choreographer, and designer who was in charge of the Bauhaus theatre department in Dessau from 1923 to 1929.[8] In 1923 he developed a curriculum for "The Stage Workshop of the Bauhaus in Weimar," in which he referred explicitly to the educational importance of the circus and variety theatre as well as the opera and ballet.[9] Schlemmer's stage work borrowed from popular art forms ranging from the circus and mime to music-hall entertainment and vaudeville. As Brenda Richardson has written, he believed that "incisive artistic structure could be etched in what was essentially comic, extemporaneous form, without sacrificing the integral properties of either."[10]

Among the Bauhaus photographs that show artists playing the role of clowns are those by T. Lux Feininger and Irene Bayer-Hecht. The artists depicted were, respectively, Oskar Schlemmer and Andor Weininger, the latter a designer of stages, sets, and costumes (including clown costumes), a founder of the Bauhaus jazz band, and a member of the Bauhaus theatrical group. Feininger's extended portrait of Oskar Schlemmer (cat. nos. 73 and 74) shows several different views of the artist playing the role of the "musical clown" in a piece by that name presented at the Bauhaus in 1927–1928 (performed, according to Adelheid Rasche, as an act of defiance against increasing political repression in Germany at the time[11]). One of the views is a full-face portrait of a bald-headed Schlemmer in white make-up wearing a clownish dress and white gloves. The intensely dramatic lighting adds a heightened sense of the strange and alien.

Figure 3
Harold Edgerton, *Russian Circus No. 2*, 1963, dye coupler print. National Gallery of Canada, Ottawa, Gift of the Harold and Esther Edgerton Family Foundation, Santa Fe, New Mexico, 1997

The other images show him playing the "mechanical cello." All of the photographs are set against a stark black background and vividly demonstrate the clean-edged, unromantic aesthetic of the Bauhaus, which privileged strong graphic appeal over emotional interpretation. Bayer-Hecht's tightly composed black-and-white portrait *Andor Weininger at the Eye-Ear-Nose-Throat Festival at the Bauhaus, Dessau* (cat. no. 72) similarly transforms the subject's face into a grotesque mask. Due to the skilful lighting and extremely foreshortened perspective, Weininger's nose and chin and the spectacles propped on his forehead emerge as the dominant elements in the composition.

Schlemmer and Weininger were kindred spirits whose clowning interests intersected. Schlemmer designed the clown costume that Weininger wore for his presentation in a "clownerie" performance on the occasion of the opening of the new Bauhaus school in Dessau in 1926. A year later Weininger appeared in yet another clown performance in the Bauhaus Eye-Ear-Nose-Throat Festival. He was also a dancer in the "Bauhaus dance," which was created from a traditional clown dance.[12] Schlemmer's love of the clown as a self-parodying figure, a social commentator, and a source of laughter grew out of his pleasure in watching some of Europe's most renowned clowns, including Grock and the Fratellini brothers, as well as Charlie Chaplin's film *The Circus*, which he saw in Berlin in February 1928.[13]

The idea of presenting oneself as a clown, or indeed of masquerading in any form, appealed to many painters and photographers in the twentieth century. Pablo Picasso enjoyed making himself up in clown faces and putting on silly hats as well as masks of his own creation, as is evident from the many photographs taken of him by Douglas David Duncan and other photographers. The mask that he wears in a 1949 portrait by Robert Capa (cat. no. 80) appears to be an Oceanic mask, probably one in his own collection of primitive art.

Although their works are not, strictly speaking, portraits of artists as clowns but rather self-portraits of artists clowning around, both Marcel Duchamp and Claude Cahun submitted themselves to similar acts of self-transformation before the camera. Marcel Duchamp's lithographed *Monte Carlo Bond* (cat. no. 79) is a playful, layered commentary on art, economics, and identity. Each print in the edition was made from a complex collage incorporating a photograph taken from a series that Man Ray had made of Duchamp in 1923

or 1924.[14] Man Ray's series illustrates the various stages of Duchamp lathering his face and hair with shaving cream and creating coifs, goatee beards, and horns out of the foam. It is a slightly demonic image of Duchamp, with his hair shaped into ram's horns, that appears on the bond in a circle of roulette squares. Other signature elements on the bond reflect Duchamp's interest in random numbers, chance, transformation, and word play.[15] The bond also bears the signature of "Rrose Sélavy," the elegant female alter ego invented by Duchamp and impersonated by him in another series of photographs made by Man Ray around the same period. It was this latter group of images that set the stage for Claude Cahun's major body of self-portraits addressing issues of identity, gender, and self-presentation. Particularly relevant to the theme of this exhibition is her series of clown-face self-portraits, one of which shows her holding a set of barbells and wearing a tee-shirt printed with the words "I AM IN TRAINING DON'T KISS ME" (cat. no. 136).

In Aleksandr Rodchenko's Russia of the 1920s and 1930s, the circus was seen as a performing art that would revolutionize the world of the theatre. The stage director Vsevolod Meyerhold, who was named head of the Petrograd division of the Theatrical Department of the People's Commissariat of Education in 1918, called upon workers in all the various branches of the theatre and the circus to join forces in the common cause of bringing their art to the people. In this spirit, the writer Vladimir Mayakovsky and the director (before becoming filmmaker) Sergey Eisenstein incorporated circus scenes into their stage productions. The circus element was sometimes used as a vehicle for celebrating and commenting upon political events, with the program notes jauntily presenting the cast under the heading "Working in the ring are …" Since it always appealed to a broad audience, the circus was well suited to serving the ideology of the newly formed socialist state. Among its early stars were the clown Vitaly Lasarenko and the animal trainer A.N. Aleksandr Fedotov, both of whom were photographed by Rodchenko in the 1930s, when they were with the Leningrad Circus (cat. no. 78).[16]

Rodchenko photographed the circus from the 1920s through the early 1940s. He had been fascinated by its special magic since early childhood. In a poignant passage in his autobiography, published in 1939, Rodchenko wondered whether a socialist country might not also need "ventriloquists, magicians, jugglers, magic carpets, fire

works, planetariums, flowers, kaleidoscopes?"[17] It was around this very time, while he was concentrating on the circus theme more intensely than ever, that Rodchenko was being persecuted by the government's cultural watchdogs. An assignment to supply photographs for a special "circus" issue of *SSSR na Stroike* ("USSR in Construction") in 1940 proved stimulating, but in the wake of the German invasion the following year the publication was cancelled.[18]

When Rodchenko resumed painting in the late 1930s, one of the subjects he returned to was the theme of the artist as clown. In his paintings of the period he depicts himself as a melancholy figure, often playing a musical instrument, and sometimes accompanied by a small dog. The wistfulness of these scenes is a reminder of the difficulties that plagued him after 1933, when he was accused by the authorities of falling under the foreign spell of modernism and was consequently restricted in his movements and his work. He was thus confined to fulfilling assignments for *SSSR na Stroike* and photographing official parades, athletic events, the theatre, and the Moscow Circus.[19]

Two distinctly different approaches are evident in Rodchenko's circus photographs. There are those that possess a romantic, dreamy mood, such as the slightly soft-focused images of *In the Interval* (cat. no. 102) and *The Rhine Wheel* (cat. no. 196), in which the photographer's attention seems to have been attracted by the dramatic light, the sparkle of the costumes, and the fresh beauty of a young female acrobat. Others, however, like *The Pyramid*

(cat. no. 197), encapsulate the dynamic, disciplined energy of the circus as well as its abstract beauty – aspects well matched to the hard-edged, geometric, Constructivist aesthetic that had always appealed to Rodchenko.

These works by Rodchenko belong to a genre of circus photographs made by a number of other photographers as well, including Umbo and Lisette Model. In Umbo's *Trapeze Artists* (cat. no. 187) and in Model's images titled *Circus, New York* (cat. nos. 193 and 194), clusters of human figures suspended in space and highlighted by dramatic shafts of light form static abstract geometries. Due to the pioneering efforts of Eadweard Muybridge, Jules-Étienne Marey, and Albert Londe, who dedicated their careers to the study of motion through the medium of photography, it gradually became possible to capture complex activities taking place in the circus ring. Albert Londe, in particular, was fascinated by the movements of circus performers and was probably the first person to photographically record acrobats and tightrope walkers in action (cat. nos. 162 and 163). Advances in photographic technology, such as faster film and paper emulsions and the invention of high-speed flash, would render obsolete Londe's technique of photographing a moving figure by means of a sequence of frames. Fifty years after the making of his studies of acrobats and tightrope walkers it became possible to capture both the gross and detailed aspects of the dynamic movements made by circus performers in a single frame.

While Londe was the first photographer to exploit the circus as a laboratory for recording motion, it was Harold Edgerton, the "magician of light," who brought to this field an entirely new level of descriptiveness through the use of stop-motion photography, as seen for example in his *Russian Circus, No. 2* (fig. 3) and *Moscow Circus* (cat. no. 195). In each of these images the simple actions of acrobats – one jumping and the other performing a tumble-turn – are captured as a sequence of movements shot at rapid intervals. Photographing the circus was a challenge to Edgerton in more ways than one, for he was accustomed to working in the highly controllable environment of a laboratory. In photographing live performances he was forced to adapt to the spotlighting of his subjects and to the unalterable series of events that made up the circus program.

It could be argued that the greatest contribution photography has made to the representation of the circus has been in the recording of events outside the ring, in the backstage areas. By showing circus people preparing for their performances, photographers have revealed to us how the ordinary is transformed into the spectacular and exotic. The metamorphosis of a person into the tragicomic figure of a clown is a subject especially well suited to the medium of photography, which through a rapid sequence of images is able to capture the essence of a process as it quickly unfolds.

In his poignant 1954 sequence of three images showing the celebrated clown Grock, suitcase in hand, leaving his trailer and entering the circus ring, Izis illustrates the solitary journey of the performer moving into the spotlight (cat. nos. 58–60). Black-and-white photography in particular is able to suffuse scenes like these with a strong sense of melancholy. One sees it in Leon Levinstein's portrayal of a man applying make-up in a handheld mirror in preparation for his clown performance (cat. no. 62), or in the image of an exhausted clown collapsed over his dressing-room table, his dog at his feet (cat. no. 103). In contrast, the contemporary photographer Robert Walker's large, vibrant giclée print (cat. no. 105) showing a rehearsal by Cirque du Soleil performers celebrates the colours and textures of the backstage, as well as the tensions experienced by performers preparing to step into the spotlight. Walker draws our attention as well to an unguarded moment of interaction between the photographer and one of the acrobats, who looks over his shoulder at the camera.

Behind the glamour of the ring and the exoticism of the sideshow booths, even the most colourful members of the circus – midget clowns, two-headed "monsters," fat ladies, tattooed and lizard-skinned men, all of the so-called human freaks – would cease to be "characters" and become ordinary people, leading ordinary albeit nomadic lives. If joining the circus was initially an avenue of escape for these individuals, it soon became a business – one with all the trappings of corporate affiliation, such as the "congress of clowns"

Figure 4
Bruce Davidson, *Circus Dwarf*, 1958, printed
c. 2000, gelatin silver print. Courtesy Bruce
Davidson / Magnum Photos

and the "congress of freaks." Nowhere is the self-contained "work world" of the circus better illustrated than in Edward J. Kelty's twelve-by-twenty-inch group portraits of the 1920s and 1930s in which acrobats, clowns, freaks, and musicians gathered in their respective groups for an annual photograph. Dressed in the costumes of their trade, the performers would be ranged from small to large (the order typically imposed by a group portrait), except for the "freaks," who naturally defied such conventional grouping methods and were placed in startling juxtapositions for maximum effect (cat. no. 119). Kelty was, in fact, a corporate photographer who specialized in the circus and built up a lucrative business in the sale of his panoramic group portraits of circus and sideshow performers.

Ironically, the traditional circus, which was based on the notion that people's deviations from a perceived norm (be it racial or physical) could provide a kind of entertainment, also created a society of its own that encompassed many racial groups and presented an enviable model of social integration. This is illustrated in August Sander's group portraits from the late 1920s or early 1930s of performers and circus workers enjoying each other's company in their off-hours (cat. nos. 98–100). One of these portraits (cat. no. 98) makes for an interesting comparison with Max Beckmann's 1940 painting *The Circus Wagon* (cat. no. 101).

Just as Sander's interest in portraying circus people in their daily lives can be traced back to paintings by Honoré Daumier and the young Pablo Picasso, so the theme of dwarfs has a long tradition in the history of art. John Gutmann and Bruce Davidson both created moving portraits of these popular circus figures, who were often referred to as "midget clowns."[20] In Gutmann's photograph (cat. no. 122) two standing midget clowns, one attired and made up for a performance and the other in undershirt and shorts, share an off-stage moment of friendship. The dressed clown places his arm around the shoulders of his colleague, who appears to be averting his gaze from the camera. As in many of the photographs that show circus performers going about their daily lives, the reality that Gutmann's picture conveys is of a self-contained society. From 1957 to 1959 Bruce Davidson entered into and observed closely the life of a midget clown named Jimmy (cat. nos. 104 and 141). An image from the series showing Jimmy eating in a restaurant (fig. 4) poignantly illustrates the feeling of vulnerability he experiences when he leaves the accepting world of his circus colleagues and ventures beyond. By

depicting the clown as the object of mocking curiosity on the part of fellow diners, Davidson has taken a thoroughly banal scene and turned it into a piercing comment on social behaviour.

The grandness and sense of presence with which Diane Arbus endowed her circus performers (cat. nos. 114, 137, 138) was partly a result of the way she successfully combined the clean-edged precision of August Sander's photographs with the boldly described and generous volumes of the images of her teacher, Lisette Model. But what is even more important is that Arbus brought to her work a genuine admiration for her subjects. She respected the toughness and courage of people who are forced to live on the margins. "Most people," she observed, "go through life dreading they'll have a traumatic experience. Freaks were born with their trauma. They've already passed their test in life. They're aristocrats."[21]

The wealth of photographic material devoted to the circus bears ample evidence of its enduring attraction to photographers. As we have observed, it is a subject that has been approached with widely differing intentions. From early on, there were those who aspired to record its drama and excitement, culminating in our own time in the most spectacular images of acrobats and trapeze artists frozen at shutter speeds on the order of hundred-thousandths of a second. Other photographers deliberately stripped away the glamour of the moment of performance, focusing instead on the banal routines of daily life behind the scenes. For some, the circus and its performers served mainly as a point of departure in exploring questions of identity, social differentiation, and marginalization. Most interestingly, modern photographers have also depicted, and even impersonated, circus figures as a means of presenting a metaphoric portrait of the artist. From the very outset, the circus proved to be a photographic subject that transcended itself, and we can safely assume that its mysterious appeal to the human imagination will be with us always.

1 Jean Starobinski, *Portrait de l'artiste en saltimbanque* (Geneva: Skira, 1970), p. 120.

2 One exception was the French photographer Albert Londe, who photographed trapeze artists and acrobats. These images, however, were captured outside the circus ring, under strictly controlled conditions.

3 Shortly after the making of this series of portraits of Deburau, the brothers had a falling-out and went their separate ways. Adrien eventually adopted his brother's pseudonym and called himself "Nadar jeune."

4 Among those who championed the circus were Gautier, Champfleury, and the Goncourt brothers. The latter claimed in 1859 that the only theatre they attended was the circus. See Sophie Basch, "Barbey D'Aurevilly et la critique de cirque," in *Le Cirque au risque de l'art* (Arles: Actes Sud, 2002).

5 At the beginning of the nineteenth century, mimes and clowns adopted the white face of Pierrot from the *commedia dell'arte*. It became the basic traditional make-up.

6 Maria Morris Hambourg in *Nadar* (New York: Metropolitan Museum of Art / Harry N. Abrams, 1995), p. 225.

7 See Philippe Hamon, "L'Image fabriquée," in *Imageries: Littérature et image au XIXe siècle* (Paris: José Corti, 2001), p. 60.

8 Andreas Bossmann, "Theaterreform-Lebensreform," in *Oskar Schlemmer: Tanz, Theater, Bühne* (Ostfildern-Ruit: G. Hatje, 1994), p. 25.

9 Hans M. Wingler, *The Bauhaus: Weimar, Dessau, Berlin, Chicago* (Cambridge, Mass.: MIT Press, 1978), p. 59.

10 Brenda Richardson, "The Nimbus of Magic: An Album of Schlemmer's Stage Work," in *Oskar Schlemmer: The Baltimore Museum of Art* (Baltimore: Baltimore Museum of Art, 1986), p. 162.

11 Adelheid Rasche, "Oskar Schlemmer als Festgestalter" in *Oskar Schlemmer: Tanz, Theater, Bühne*, p. 38.

12 Richardson, "The Nimbus of Magic," p. 117.

13 Rasche, "Oskar Schlemmer als Festgestalter," p. 38.

14 Although Man Ray was the author of the two series of photographs of Duchamp – Duchamp shaving and Duchamp as Rrose Sélavy – the concept was Duchamp's, and it was under his direction that these photographs were taken.

15 *Monte Carlo Bond* was originally made as a collage to be printed as a bond in an issue of thirty copies. Duchamp offered the bonds for sale at 500 francs each, yielding interest at a rate of twenty percent per annum. Robert Lebel describes the issue as follows: "As [Duchamp] spent more and more of his time on chess he perfected a system, half seriously and half in fun, designed to assure him a regular income from the roulette tables at Monte Carlo. For this purpose he floated a loan of 15,000 francs, divided into thirty bonds of 500 francs each redeemable by 'artificial drawings' and bearing the somewhat exorbitant interest of twenty per cent. The bonds resembled the standard article except for Duchamp's face, covered with shaving cream and topped by the horns of a faun or devil, on a ground of roulette squares. The play on words: 'Moustiques domestiques demistock,' printed over and over again in small green italics, formed the background of the bond. The issue was dated 1 November 1924 and endorsed by the Chairman of the Board of Directors, Rrose Sélavy. On the reverse an extract from the by-laws indicated that the company had as its purpose the exploitation of 'Trente et Quarante' and other mines on the Côte d'Azur as the Board of Directors might decide. Duchamp actually tried out his system at Monte Carlo and he insists, not without pride, that he succeeded in neither winning nor losing, which is, for him, the peak of financial success. He considers his martingale infallible in this respect but he also admits that if one perseveres long enough one can hope to win an amount equal to the wages of a clerk who works in his office as many hours as the gambler does in the casino." Robert Lebel, *Marcel Duchamp*, trans. George Heard Hamilton (New York: Paragraphic Books, 1959), p. 50.

16 A. Fevralsky, "Meyerhold and the Circus," in *The Soviet Circus: A Collection of Articles*, ed. Alexander Lipovsky (Moscow: Progress Publishers, 1967), pp. 225–230.

17 Alexander Lavrentiev, *Alexander Rodchenko: Photography 1924–1954* (Edison, N.J.: Knickerbocker, 1995), p. 34.

18 Rodchenko photographed acrobats, clowns, and trainers at the Moscow Circus, together with the photojournalist Georgy Petrusov. Rodchenko and Varvara Stepanova laid out all the pages.

19 Magdalena Dabrowski, Leah Dickerman, and Peter Galassi, *Aleksandr Rodchenko: Painting, Drawing, Collage, Design, Photography* (New York: Museum of Modern Art, 1998), p. 128.

20 This is a genetically caused condition known as achondroplasia that results in disproportionately small arms and legs.

21 Diane Arbus, *Diane Arbus* (New York: Aperture, 1972), p. 3.

Sophie Basch

Hysterical Clowns, Ridiculous Martyrs
The Writer's View

Like ape or clown, in monstrous garb
... we went round and round.

Oscar Wilde, *The Ballad of Reading Gaol*, 1898

The modernity in which Baudelaire perceived the meeting of the eternal and the transitory remains obscure.[1] The famous admonition "It is necessary to be absolutely modern," always misconstrued by those who quote it, heightens the paradox: Rimbaud gibes at the cult of the modern as Baudelaire does at the religion of progress. The ironic lover of "maudlin pictures, the painted panels over doors, stage sets, the back-drops of mountebanks, old inn signs, popular prints"[2] encounters the haughty melancholy of the "Vieux Saltimbanque" from *Le Spleen de Paris*.

The impossibility of assigning a historical sense to time came with the post-Revolutionary interest in manifestations of the unusual. In literature as in painting and music, attention was focused on the outcasts, the fringe, the fools, propelled centre stage by the aesthetic of the grotesque, the new principle governing "the genius of melancholy and meditation, the demon of analysis and controversy"[3] proper to modern times. Theoretician of Romanticism and the only truly epic poet of the nineteenth century, Hugo did not neglect to create the monstrous figures of Quasimodo and Gwynplaine, "The Man Who Laughs," the clown disfigured since childhood. Shakespeare supplants Racine. From Musset's Fantasio and Zemlinksy's Dwarf to Verdi's Rigoletto, Leoncavallo's Pagliaccio, and Schoenberg's Pierrot, grimacing, deformed, and fantastic silhouettes parade before the footlights.

The Circus as the New Temple

The triumph of the bizarre populated the Romantic universe with strange, macabre, and trivial creatures. Charles Nodier invented the "frenetic school" and Baudelaire the "satanic school" in the years when the circus, harbouring freaks and wonders, took hold as the new temple. By 1831, in *Barnave*, Jules Janin was asserting that the circus, with its "real blood" and "real tears," was superior to the theatre. In 1859 the circus is where the Goncourt brothers found "the only talents in the world that are incontestable, absolute like mathematics, or rather like a double somersault."[4] The circus spectacle renewed a connection with the sacred birth of tragedy and revived the medieval mystery play. Under the big top, modern man sought anew the transcendence that had disappeared from secularized naves and domes. Joris-Karl Huysmans saw the circus as "the masterpiece of the new architecture," where "at a prodigious height

worthy of a cathedral, cast-iron columns soar with matchless daring. The upward thrust of the slender stone pillars so admired in certain old basilicas seems timid and cumbersome beside these lightweight poles rising toward the gigantic arcs of the turning ceiling, linked together by extraordinary webs of iron, starting from all sides, lining, crossing, entangling their formidable beams."[5] Octave Mirbeau compared the decoration of the Cirque d'Été, with its "champlevé enamels set with gemstones, mosaic reliquaries, silver- and gold-work, thick lamé fabric" to "all the lavish finery of a defunct abbey."[6] By an effect of contagion, the consecration also influenced the historicizing architecture of the department stores, filling them with diabolical apparitions inspired by Willette and Chéret:

> C'est un bazar, avec des murs géants
> Et des balcons et des sous-sols béants
> Et des tympans montés sur des corniches
> Et des drapeaux et des affiches
> Où deux clowns noirs plument un ange.[7]

New Priests, New Madmen

New temples needed new celebrants. The clown, as the type was set in Paris around 1860, was a hybrid of the French Pierrot, the English jester, and the *commedia dell'arte* Arlecchino. It gained so great a following in the Anglo-Saxon world that Max Beerbohm noted, "If our English mimes want to improve themselves, let them be born again, of French parents."[8] By describing the "English Pierrot" in his 1855 essay "De l'essence du rire," with his wan complexion and red spots of phthisis, Baudelaire defined the French model of clown that had taken hold among his fellow citizens and with the rest of the world. Shortly after, granting this figure a metaphorical value, he imagined Poe as a juggler whose work reveals "hysteria usurping the throne of the will, conflict reigning nerves and mind, and man so out of tune with himself as to express grief with laughter."[9] The clown's shadow lengthened to loom over literature. Should a poet neglect to take up the subject of clowns, the clowns he might have invented were conjured up in his behalf: "Charles Cros may not have created any Pierrots, but if he had, his Pierrot would have drawn the greater part of its lyricism and whimsy from the marvels of the macabre and the wonders of science."[10] Jules Laforgue imagined a clownish Hamlet. Mallarmé praised the "Dorst brothers,

Figure 1
Two of the Hanlon-Lees in *Le Voyage en Suisse*, photograph possibly by Nadar, c. 1878–1879

those clowns, nay, those convulsionists, nay, those dancers of a strange quadrille, known by a calm and exasperated name: the Frétillants [Wrigglers]."[11] The deranged Pierrots represented by Henri Rivière and Jean Richepin, in their novels *Pierrot* (1860) and *Braves Gens* (1886) respectively, confirm the amiable moonstruck dreamer's transformation into a disturbing lunatic. This evolution had been foretold in 1833 by Théophile Gautier: before going completely mad, the painter Onophrius sees "the moon as the wan reclining figure of his intimate friend Jean-Gaspard Deburau, the great Paillasse of the Funambules."[12] The darlings of writers and artists, the sinister Irish clowns the Hanlon-Lees, Pierrots in black suits (fig. 1), accentuate the anxiety exuded by White Man.[13] Their success at the Folies Bergère in the 1870s coincided with the debut of a doctor, a prestidigitator performing in another kind of amphitheatre. Perceiving the carnival atmosphere of these public sessions, Joséphin Péladan wrote, "Theatre people are Charcots,"[14] prefacing a polemical pamphlet on the contemporary literary scene – a "Salpêtrière of literature" that provided "something to astonish the Charcots of criticism every morning, those nitwit charlatans." The polemicist concludes, "The clowns of hysteria make me smile."[15]

It could hardly be put better. The connection between the mechanical antics of clowns and hysterical epilepsy is blatant. Between 1852 and 1856 the neurologist Duchenne de Boulogne turned to Nadar's brother, Adrien Tournachon, to fix the "true smile" (true like the circus, true like the absolutely comical that was so dear to Baudelaire) induced by an electrical discharge to the face of a paralyzed patient.[16] In 1872 Darwin illustrated his book *The Expression of the Emotions in Man and Animals* with "mimodramatic" photographs by Oscar Rylander. Twenty years later, Albert Londe, in charge of the photography department at the Salpêtrière, alternated portraits of clowns with photographs of patients. Meanwhile, a semantic muddle transformed "clonic spasm" (from the Greek *klonos*, violent motion) into *clownisme*, as if acrobats' contortions had swayed medical terminology. And so, Bergson remarked on "the attitudes, capers, and movements that are what is properly 'clownic' in the art of the clown."[17] The hysteric's influence on circus and vaudeville delivery, which Rae Beth Gordon has described accurately without examining the historical causes[18] – is it not rather a coincidence, a sign of the will to reintroduce the irrational into a theatre that had become deconsecrated?

Figures 2 and 3
Illustrations by Enrico Mazzanti from the original 1883 edition and by Carlo Chiostri from the 1901 edition of Carlo Collodi's *Le avventure de Pinocchio, storia di un burattino*

There have always been buffoons, but never did they acquire the autonomy of the clown who blossomed along with industrialization like a burlesque double of the dandy, defying the world of the progressive upper middle class. When he had his picture taken in Foottit's cap, a few years before the attack of delirium tremens that made him execute the circus drawings that convinced Dr. Semelaigne of his lucidity, Toulouse-Lautrec was this clown; Nijinski too, the mystic acrobat Cocteau described as a "little monkey with sparse hair, wearing a skirted overcoat and a hat balanced on the top of his head":[19] the jester of the comic tradition found refuge among the deranged. In these modern temples that are the circus, the clown, possessed like a primitive actor, portrays a derisory, sarcastic intermediary. Like a tragedian of antiquity, the clown wears a grotesque mask that clings to his skin. He knows instinctively that *persona* designates a theatrical mask and that *personage* originally referred to an ecclesiastical dignitary. Like an archaic priest, he relies on make-up and ointments when he officiates. The clown's make-up, from the plaster white of the Hanlon-Lees to the motley of Albert Fratellini, jolts plausibility: the clown opts for the absolutely illusory, just as Villiers de Lisle-Adam, in *L'Ève future*, prefers the automaton to the actress, because the illusion is total and actualizes absence more radically.[20] Likewise, with Olympia, Hoffmann created the most deceptive of dolls, and Collodi, with his marionette Pinocchio (whom the story's first illustrators, Enrico Mazzanti and Carlo Chiostri, dressed as a clown),[21] the most ambiguous of the artificial children, whose strangeness is no less disturbing than the doll's (figs. 2 and 3). From the priest, the clown inherited ritual; from the automaton, with its expected repertoire of crystallized entrées, he took his stereotyped gestures, mechanical attitudes, and malice: he claimed the inept victory of the predictable. Like his make-up, his acting is based on excess: exasperating, useless, superfluous, the clown exceeds in every sense of the term. For fear of emptiness, this senseless being becomes clutter incarnate. Heralding Beckett's characters who babble on indefatigably, he gesticulates in order not to think.

The portrait of the artist as a clown appears to be the strange resolution of the old conflict between idolatry and iconoclasm. How could the degraded, ridiculed, offensive representation of the human figure supplant the holy image? The clownesque icon, a figurative blasphemy, could not be transformed into an idol: at once all too human and dehumanized, it founders into disfigurement. The circus world of artifice admits neither faces nor genders: the baggy costume that gradually replaced the suit worn by clown acrobats effaces the singularity of the man. Alfred Jarry exploited this abstraction by inflating the potbelly of Père Ubu, universal spineless character. If clownery disfigures, it also denatures. And it disturbs. It is striking to see those writers who are the most devoted to the circus – but from a milieu more familiar with legitimate theatre than with the popular stage – succumb to the temptation to make the clown a more respectable character. This zany of the sacred, who seems to ignore the paradox of the actor and no longer distinguishes being

Figure 4
Henry de Groux, *Zola Leaving the Court*
(*The Mocking of Zola*), c. 1898, oil on
canvas. Musée Émile Zola, Médan

60   and seeming, makes us profoundly uneasy. So then, we are anxious to effect the split. Many texts evoke the clown in mufti, unrecognizable on the street. A well-known short story by Jules Claretie (written soon after his novel on hysteria, *Les Amours d'un interne*) exploits this reassuring dichotomy. A dying child asks for the illustrious Medrano to be brought to his bedside. His father, a humble workman, hastens to the clown's residence, where he is received by an intimidating gentleman. The child does not recognize this Monsieur as his idol. The clown dashes off and returns in his make-up and loud costume. The child laughs and miraculously recovers. When the father anxiously asks how much he owes, the clown requests "permission to put on his calling card: Boum-Boum, acrobat doctor, general practitioner to little François."[22] Alongside the hysterical clown, laughter, the best medicine, stands vigil in the thaumaturgical clown.

Portrait of the Clown as Christ

If the frenetic clown is a product of noir Romanticism, the Christlike clown's heritage derives from another branch of the movement and revives the image of the Romantic Christ.[23] A grotesque Christology comes into play when Jesus, the Word made flesh, takes on the clown's absurd character and dons his cast-off suit, flanked by mortifying accessories, the instruments of the Passion held up to ridicule. The infiltration of the sacred into the circus finalized the separation of Ideal Beauty and divine transcendence: the Almighty Saviour abandons the creature, committing him, in a parodic sacrifice, to his irredeemable downfall. Dimly aware of the impossibility of its redemption, the audience degenerates along with him and crucifies the idiot (the Innocent par excellence) with its stupid laughter. "Forgive them," Paillasse seems to say, "for they know not what they do." Onstage meanwhile, word-juggler and comico-heroic martyr Cyrano de Bergerac takes quodlibets on his nose the way others take kicks on the behind, substituting a tirade for the cartwheels his circus-ring brothers answer their attackers with. For this sacrificial figure bounds over the ring fence to invade the world of letters. Attending an execution, Jules Vallès describes the condemned man, "pale as if he were already dead – the white face of a clown."[24]

Barbey d'Aurevilly compares the journalist Rochefort's face to the "frozen and fixed" chalk face of an English clown.[25] Léon Cladel describes the mystical hysteria gripping actors and audience at a fairground show:

> And the lanky circus performer convulsed in the cart, wriggling about as he gasped; while his ravaged skull, polished like old ivory, bobbed his variegated cap – the clown's omnicolour cap – in every direction, his fantastical bugle sent a shrill, triumphal fanfare into the air … The trusty companion, distraught, raised arms and legs, and throwing his voice, barked merrily, dancing like an epileptic, laughing like a maniac … The circle shrank. Everyone was equally dazzled, attracted, magnetized, fascinated, haunted, conquered by this rude charmer … They surrounded him, they felt his huge biceps, listened to his broad chest, rumpled the silk of his purple- and gold-striped shorts, kissed him, hugged him, entered him …"[26]

Images of Christlike clowns parade by fast and thick: in the same collection in which Claretie's "Boum-Boum" first appeared, Louis Mullem tells the curious tale of the Reverend Father Trimmel, who, anxious to "Americanize Catholicism," after having exhausted "all known means of liturgical enticement to procure a clientele of believers," came up with a "fantastic program" to excite general curiosity: hanging garlands and trapezes in the brightly lit church, the priest transformed a young acrobat into a "little Clown-Jesus" who flew vertiginously between the columns above the heads of the wonderstruck crowd.[27] Soon, Cocteau – a faithful member of the Nouveau Cirque's flock, for whom the trapeze artist's safety net represented "a no man's land between heaven and earth" – would write that "within even the most vulgar and aggressive spectacle is an angel that bursts forth."[28] More serious, André Suarès makes use of the clown to distinguish derision from caricature, which is directed at mediocre objects and lowly beings: "In Jesus on the Cross, the clown, if he dare, also sees the string puppet of divinity who is going to rot, crumble in the wind, and dance the jig … One may parody the divine: one does not caricature it without dissipating its divine quality, the way one dissolves a speck of amber in a tubful of laundry."[29] In the same way, for Henry Miller, friend of Rouault, Max Jacob, Chagall, and Léger, "a clown is a poet in action. He *is* the

story which he enacts. It is the same story over and over – adoration, devotion, crucifixion."[30] More recently, Angela Carter, evoking the "tumultuous resurrection of the clown" leaping from his circus coffin, saw in this mercenary of laughter "the very image of Christ."[31] A votive figure in a consecrated environment, the clown, with his codified and banal way of acting, is indistinguishable from the automaton, itself closely linked with the wax effigy. The latter takes us not to the circus but to its poor cousin, the fair, which also fascinated painters and poets.

Wax and Castoffs: The End of a Literal Identification

By closing the churches, the French Revolution reinforced the ban on wax statues, already shunned by classical aesthetics. Schlosser has magnificently recorded the *via dolorosa* of wax portraits, from the earliest funerary effigies to Madame Tussaud's and the Musée Grévin. "Today," the historian wrote in 1911, "proletarization has been accomplished: the wax sculpture has become art for fairground stalls, novelty stands, puppets, of scant social esteem and held in aesthetic contempt."[32] However, some artists attempted to restore the aristocratic dignity of this court art that had returned to the state of a primitive craft (Mario Praz collected some remnants of them in his Roman apartment). Whatever the sculptor's talent, though, the subject became inseparable from the exhibits of anatom-

ical freaks that democratized the *Panoptikum* and the photographs of the mentally ill that took up where the eerie naturalism of wax portraits left off. Visiting a workshop, Jean Lorrain, a devotee of fairs moreover, could not separate this sculpture from the modern context, which he projected on its creator: "It is Ringel, and now that I am seated in his studio peopled with monumental chalk-white statues and, scattered about on shelves, painted wax figures with disturbing frozen smiles, I watch the long, lithe boy with a ruddy blond complexion, thoroughly tanned, busying himself about a wetted head with the agility of a clown and the attentive suppleness of a prowling cat, and I cannot help reviewing in my mind all the more or less absurd and crazy stories I had been told about this Ringel."[33] The confusion of identities is total; we do not know which is the Golem – the sculptor or his creations.

From wax to freak, from freak to clown, the line is unbroken. The clown appeared both on the boards at the fair, beside Dr. Spitzner's waxes, and at the circus. Hence the necessity, greater than at the circus – for this is an even more marginal place – of sanctifying the field of fair exhibits, where the most disinherited mountebanks perform: those favoured by the gaze of writers and painters. The poets of Montmartre cabarets – where Maurice Rollinat, accompanying himself at the piano, enumerated in verse the macabre charms of an anatomical Venus[34] – attended the fair as if attending mass: "This Fair, this deformed church, this grand temple of ugliness, so necessary to man in his aspiration to beauty, we who had new hearts loved it. Its chapels, its flimsy stalls, were filled with children … A Virgin with a gargoyle head offered her legs to the hesitant touch of her adorers. Christ went by on the plaza, in a stable vest. Saint Peter ran a shooting gallery. The angel Gabriel threw himself among the lions as of yore but made you pay at the cash register."[35]

In the nineteenth century, artistic perception of the clown merged into the current reality of the circus, and incidentally of medicine. Only Italian has an expression for such a phenomenon of intimate junction: *immedesimazione*. In the twentieth century – which witnessed the decline of this spectacle that can no longer be viewed as a subject of modern life the same as before, weakened by popularization, undermined by competition from vaudeville and then the movies – travesty was treated as a neoclassical motif, necessarily by means of allusion and parody.[36] If the theme continues to fascinate, the acrobats' approach is no longer immediate but *beside* reality, historically and sociologically out of synch: in 1926 Siegfried Kracauer already considered the circus an anachronism and the clown a prehistoric exhibit, "ein paläontologisches Schaustück."[37]

The merger of artist and acrobat did not last a hundred years. Émile Zola (fig. 4) laid these Siamese twins to rest in a memorable scene in *L'Oeuvre*, a partly autobiographical novel where the author appears in the guise of the writer Sandoz, opposite the painter Claude Lantier, in whom the reader discerns a great deal of Cézanne, a little of Manet and something of Zola himself. It is doubtlessly not insignificant that Lantier's funeral cortege rolls past deserted booths and circuses and merry-go-rounds. But, before evoking this last journey suffused with all the squalor of the fairground, Zola describes another burial, at the Clignancourt fair, where Sandoz and Lantier again meet up with an old acquaintance, Chaîne, an unsuccessful painter and copyist who has become the owner of a booth, "a very ornate sort of chapel" at the back of which, "in a kind of holy of holies," hang the artist's three masterpieces: "It was the sight of them in all their splendour that made Claude exclaim, 'Good God, but they're wonderful … and perfect for that job.' The Mantegna especially, with its gaunt simplicity, was rather like a faded print nailed up for the enjoyment of simple folks, while the meticulous, lopsided rendering of the stove, balanced by the gingerbread Christ, looked unexpectedly funny."[38] The Romantic irony that permeated the century comes out here with unprecedented ferocity. Zola's solicitude toward Chaîne's dismal paintings coincides with the taste of Rimbaud, tired of "celebrities of modern painting and poetry," for "maudlin paintings." On the eve of Symbolism, artist meets acrobat in a fairground booth, the ultimate Salon des Refusés, between a crucified copy and a depiction of an edible Christ.

1   See Antoine Compagnon, "Baudelaire devant l'éternel," in *Dix Études sur Baudelaire*, ed. André Guyaux (Paris: Honoré Champion, 1993), pp. 71–111.

2   Arthur Rimbaud, "Alchemy of the Word" (1873), in *A Season in Hell & The Drunken Boat*, trans. Louise Varèse (Norfolk, Conn.: New Directions, 1961), p. 49.

3   Victor Hugo in "Préface de *Cromwell*" (1827).

4   Jules and Edmond Goncourt, *Journal: Mémoires de la vie littéraire* (Paris: Robert Laffont, 1989), vol. 2, p. 491.

5   Joris-Karl Huysmans, "Le Salon officiel de 1881," in *L'Art moderne* (Paris: UGE, 1975), pp. 198–199.

6   Octave Mirbeau, *L'Écuyère* (1882), in *Oeuvre romanesque* (Paris: Buchet-Chastel, 2000), vol. 1, p. 787.

7   Émile Verhaeren, "Le Bazar," from *Les Villes tentaculaires* (1895), in *Poésie complète* (Brussels: Labor, 1997), vol. 2, p. 285. "'Tis a bazaar, with walls gigantic / Gaping basement, balcony, attic, / And cornice topped with tympanum / Posters, banners, flags outstrung / Where two black clowns an angel pluck."

8   Max Beerbohm, "Latin and Anglo-Saxon Mimes," *The Saturday Review*, 13 April 1901, p. 467.

9   Charles Baudelaire, "Edgar Allan Poe, His Life and Works" (1857), in *Baudelaire: Selected Writings on Art and Literature*, trans. P.E. Charvet (Harmondsworth: Penguin Books, 1992), p. 185.

10   Gustave Kahn, *Montmartre et ses artistes* (Paris: Librairie Artistique et Littéraire, 1910), p. 29.

11   Stéphane Mallarmé, in *La Dernière Mode*, no. 4 (18 October 1874), p. 8.

12   Théophile Gautier, *Les Jeunes-France* (1833), in *Oeuvres* (Paris: Robert Laffont, 1995), p. 57.

13   On these clowns who captivated Europe and the United States, see Mark Cosdon, "Prepping for Pantomime: The Hanlon Brothers' Fame and Tragedy, 1833–1870," *Theatre History Studies* 20 (June 2000), pp. 67–104.

14   Joséphin Péladan, *La Décadence latine, éthopée, VI: La Victoire du mari* (Paris: Dentu, 1889), p. 27.

15   Han Ryner, *Le Massacre des Amazones: Étude critique sur deux cents bas-bleus contemporains* (Paris: Chamuel, 1899), pp. 13–14.

16   André Jammes reproduces some of these photographs in "Duchenne de Boulogne, la grimace provoquée et Nadar," *Gazette des Beaux-Arts*, December 1978, pp. 215–220.

17   Henri Bergson, *Le Rire: Essai sur la signification du comique* (1899), in *Oeuvres* (Paris: PUF, 1959), p. 414.

18   Rae Beth Gordon, *Why the French Love Jerry Lewis: From Cabaret to Early Cinema* (Berkeley: Stanford University Press, 2001).

19   Jean Cocteau, *The Difficulty of Being* (1947), trans. Elizabeth Sprigge (New York: Coward-McCann, 1967), p. 44.

20   Ross Chambers has developed the subject in *L'Ange et l'automate: Variations sur le mythe de l'actrice, de Nerval à Proust* (Paris: Lettres modernes, 1971).

21   On the iconographic career of the famous *burattino*, whose adventures were first published in book form in 1883, see Valentino Baldacci and Andrea Rauch, *Pinocchio e la sua immagine* (Florence: Giunti-Marzocco, 1981).

22   Jules Claretie, "Boum-Boum," in *Le Livre de Pochi, écrit pour Judith Cladel et ses petites amies* (Paris: Monnier, de Brunhoff et Cie, 1886), p. 25.

23   On the metamorphoses of Christ in the nineteenth century, see Frank Paul Bowman, *Le Christ romantique* (Geneva: Droz, 1973) and *Le Christ des barricades, 1789–1848* (Paris: Le Cerf, 1987).

24   Jules Vallès, "La Guillotine," *Le Cri du Peuple*, 30 April 1884, in *Oeuvres* (Paris: Bibliothèque de la Pléiade, 1990), vol. 2, p. 1354.

25   Jules-Amédée Barbey d'Aurevilly, quoted in Henri Rochefort, *La Lanterne* (Paris: Jean-Jacques Pauvert, 1966), p. 10.

26   Léon Cladel, "L'Hercule" (1864), in *Les Va-nu-pieds* (Paris: Charpentier, 1881), pp. 275–277.

27   Louis Mullem, "La Nuit de Noël: Fantaisie américaine," in *Le Livre de Pochi*, pp. 79–83.

28   Jean Cocteau, *Souvenir Portraits: Paris in the Belle Epoque* (1935), trans. Jesse Browner (New York: Paragon House, 1990), p. 41.

29   André Suarès, "Remarques sur le clown, suite" (November 1917), in *Remarques* (Paris: Gallimard, 2000), p. 126.

30   Henry Miller, *The Smile at the Foot of the Ladder* (New York: New Directions, 1958), p. 46.

31   Angela Carter, *Nights at the Circus* (London: Chatto and Windus / Hogarth Press, 1984), pp. 118–119.

32   Julius von Schlosser, *Histoire du portrait en cire* (1911), afterword by Thomas Medicus (Paris: Macula, 1997), p. 144. On puppets and wax effigies in literature, see Bernhild Boie's fine study, *L'Homme et ses simulacres: Essai sur le romantisme allemand* (Paris: Librairie José Corti, 1979).

33   Jean Lorrain, *Buveurs d'âmes* (1893), in *Masques et fantômes* (Paris: UGE, 1974), pp. 212–213.

34   See Maurice Rollinat, "Le Monstre" and "La Dame en cire," in *Les Névroses* (Paris: Charpentier, 1883).

35   Georges d'Esparbès, "Les forains," in *Les Demi-Cabots* (Paris: Charpentier et Fasquelle, 1896), pp. 203–205.

36   For example, Louis-Ferdinand Céline's *Guignol's Band*, Vladimir Nabokov's *Look at the Harlequins!* and Romain Gary's *Les Clowns lyriques*.

37   Siegfried Kracauer, *Drei Pierrots schlendern: Die Söhne von François Fratellini im Pariser Cirque d'Hiver*, in *Aufsätze 1915–26*, quoted in Alessandro Fambrini, *La vita è un ottovolante: Il circo nella letteratura tedesca tra 800 e 900* (Pasian di Prato: Campanotto, 1998), p. 25.

38   Émile Zola, *The Masterpiece* (1886), trans. Thomas Walton and Roger Pearson (Oxford: Oxford University Press, 1999), pp. 416 and 361.

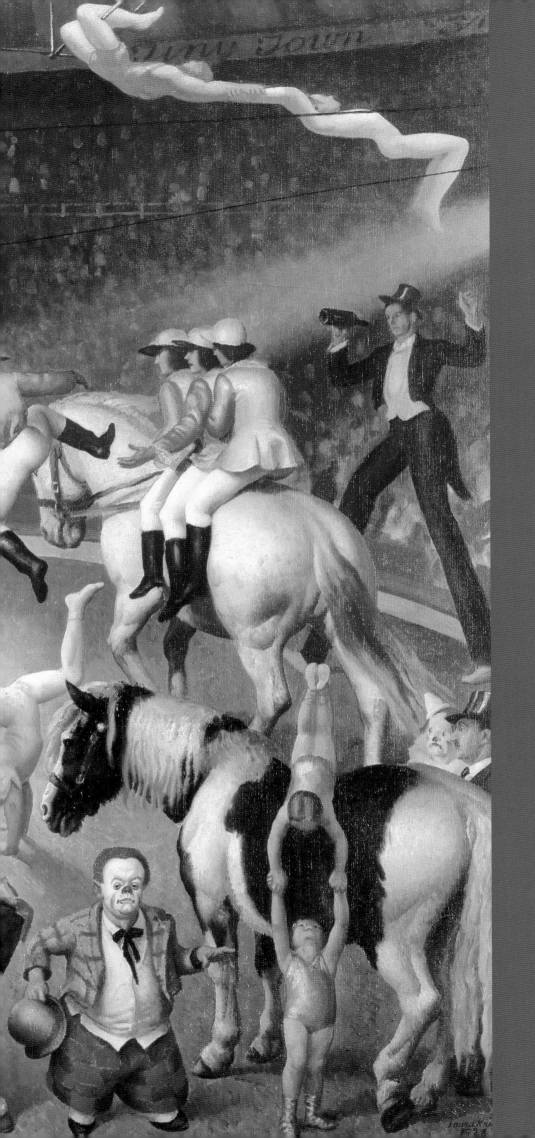

Catalogue

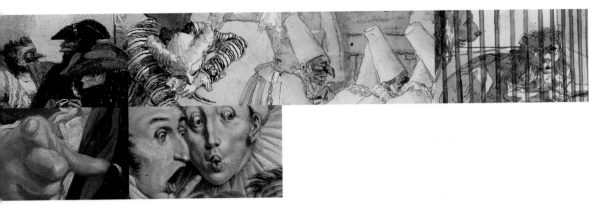

Il Mondo Novo

When the circus and its illusions are presented as the site of truth,
what remains of the tradition of the Great and the Beautiful?
The antics of Pulcinella as depicted by Giandomenico Tiepolo, in
a Venice in decline, sounded the first warning that the gods were
about to be supplanted by the clowns.

Jean Starobinski

Il Mondo Novo, the new world, was the world of those Northern Italian fairground shows that, during the late eighteenth century, went from town to town exhibiting various optical devices offering phantasmagorias of distant landscapes. These enchanted visions, which heralded the cinema, were accompanied by *saltimbanques*, travelling entertainers of all descriptions. Such spectacles announced a shift in European sensibility, signalling the appearance of a taste for the odd and the foreign, for unknown animal species like the rhinoceros, and for the "savages" of exotic lands; and, too, for the mixing of genres, from heroic to comic, and of social classes, from noble to common.

An interest among painters in physiognomy (Lavater) and in the expressions and poses that would be described by psychiatry and neurology (Charcot and the study of hysteria) breathed new life into the art of portraiture. Artists no longer hesitated to depict grimaces, bizarre gestures and facial expressions, the most grotesque disguises – even injuries and sickness. A new portrait gallery emerged, independent of the old canons, one that sometimes aped the singular features of the circus world.

J.C.

1
Antoine Watteau
Italian Comedians probably 1720

Antoine Watteau
Valenciennes, France, 1684 – Nogent-sur-Marne, France, 1721

On the death of his teacher in 1702,[1] the young Jean-Antoine Watteau left his native Valenciennes for Paris, where he worked briefly for a painter who had his premises on the Pont Notre-Dame. Around 1705 he joined the studio of Claude Gillot, a painter and draftsman whose repertoire included many subjects taken from the *commedia dell'arte*. Gillot had a decisive influence on Watteau, who henceforth drew frequent inspiration from the actions and costumes of the most popular Italian characters featured in the sideshows of Paris's two biggest fairs, Saint-Laurent and Saint-Germain: Harlequin, Mezzetin, Scaramouche, the Doctor, and the naive Pierrot. Watteau left Gillot around 1708 to work with the fashionable decorative painter Claude III Audran, who punctuated his arabesque-filled panels with figures taken directly from fairground shows. Although Watteau was made an *agréé* of the Académie Royale in 1712, when he presented a theatrical fiction entitled *Les Jaloux* that had Pierrot as the central figure, he did not submit his diploma work until 1717. This painting, *The Pilgrimage to Cythera*, also highly theatrical, established him as a painter of *fêtes galantes* and the creator of this new genre. A few years later he executed the monumental *Pierrot* (also called *Gilles*), whose model may have been the Italian fairground actor Belloni. Stricken with tuberculosis, Watteau travelled in 1719–1720 to London, where he consulted the physician and collector Richard Mead, for whom he painted *Italian Comedians* (cat. no. 1).[2]

In this meticulously composed work, Pierrot stands at the centre of a group of *commedia dell'arte* characters like those seen often at Parisian fairs, where they presented their comical intrigues as pantomimes. Dressed in the traditional white satin suit with a ruff at the neck, Pierrot is accompanied by an elegant and fashionably gowned *prima donna*. To the left of the painting, behind a jester and two children, one of the actors tinkers with Mezzetin's guitar,

while he, in his striped costume, pays court to a young ingénue. Gesticulating beside him is his rival Harlequin, wearing the customary diamond-pattern outfit and black leather half-mask. On the right we recognize the elderly bearded figure of Pantaloon, without his mask. Brighella, standing in front, introduces us to the hero of the fairground troupe, Pierrot, who adopts his usual stiff pose, arms held rigidly by his sides. The small smile playing on his lips is a hint that he may have triumphed in the farce that has just ended. As in a number of Watteau's other paintings, including *Pierrot Contented* (c. 1712) and *The Foursome* (c. 1714), the precise meaning of the image is today something of a mystery. It is generally agreed, however, that the actors have gathered to receive their final round of applause.

In 1825 the mime Jean-Baptiste Gaspard Deburau (1796–1846) began performing the role of the innocent, well-meaning Pierrot at the Théâtre des Funambules, on Paris's Boulevard du Temple, where he met with huge acclaim. Between 1830 and 1860, through the popular art form of pantomime, a whole generation of writers discovered in this *commedia dell'arte* character a new hero. During the nineteenth century, literary and theatre critics soon reinvented him as the alter ego of the alienated artist, radically reshaping the type and giving birth to a mythology based on the Romantic vision of a Pierrot vacillating between gaiety and melancholy. This transformation can be closely linked to the new interest shown in Watteau's work during the same period, and to the readings of it offered by such famous authors as Gautier, Baudelaire, and the Goncourt brothers.

C.N.-R.

---

1   Scholars agree on this date of 1702, but there is still some uncertainty about the identity of his teacher. Watteau may have been apprenticed to the painter Jacques Albert Gérin (c. 1640–1702) or to the sculptor Antoine Joseph Pater (1670–1747).

2   See Margaret Morgan Grasselli and Pierre Rosenberg, *Watteau 1684–1721* (Washington, D.C.: National Gallery of Art, 1984), pp. 440–444.

James Ensor

Ostend, Belgium, 1860 – Ostend, 1949

James Ensor was born to an English father and a Flemish mother. His mother ran a souvenir shop where Ostend carnival masks and accessories were sold, and as a youth he never missed a family outing to the famous Bal du Rat Mort (Dead Rat's Ball) during Mardi Gras. As a student at the Académie Royale des Beaux-Arts in Brussels from 1877 to 1880, he became friends with Théo Hannon, the author of an 1886 pantomime entitled *Pierrot macabre*, and with Ernest Rousseau, his companion in youthful diversions like the circus, the theatre, and masquerades. The charades and playlets that he and Rousseau performed provided inspiration for later paintings, such as *Masquerade* (1891) and *Duel of the Masks* (1892). Returning to Ostend in 1880, he set up a studio in his parents' attic and perfected his training by copying drawings by Rembrandt, Callot, Watteau,* Goya,* Daumier,* and other masters. It was there, in 1883, that he produced one of his best-known self-portraits, a homage to Rubens, his favourite painter; in 1888 he reworked it, adding a flowered hat (cat. no. 65).

The carnival bric-a-brac of the family shop made its first appearance in the 1883 painting *Scandalized Masks*, where Ensor's cynical vision of the human comedy is already evident. Masks, skeletons, and Pierrot figures recurred frequently in his work from then on, expressing both his obsession with death and a growing loathing for his detractors. The masks often "hid" famous and patently recognizable political, scientific, and artistic personalities of the day, sparking the outrage with which his works were greeted at the annual exhibitions of Les XX, the avant-garde group that he joined in 1883. Public rejection of his art led him to liken his misery to that of the persecuted subject of *Christ's Entry into Brussels in 1889* (1888–1889), a grand socialist parade with the haloed Saviour barely visible in a throng of soldiers, gentlefolk, workers, and politicians of all stripes in raucously laughing masks. The banner proclaiming "Vive la Sociale" attests to the anarchistic convictions of the artist, who categorically condemned all "doctrinaire hoopla" and government and religious institutions, charging them with restricting individual and artistic freedoms. In *The Strange Masks* (cat. no. 41) he is the masked violinist slumped limp on the floor, overwhelmed by the scorn of the grotesque figures representing the other members of Les XX in their dispute with him. In 1899, replicating his earlier image of himself in a flowered hat, he pictured himself in a sea of masks denoting human turpitude, recalling the Flemish tradition of Bruegel the Elder.

As his prodigious creativity began to wane in 1900, his paintings became mere variations on his earlier work. In 1906 his friends Albin and Emma Lambotte gave him a harmonium, and he devoted more and more time to music. Between 1906 and 1911 his lifelong fancy for the colourful world of the carnival inspired him to compose a pantomime ballet, *La Gamme d'amour* (*Flirt de marionnettes*), first performed at Galerie Giroux in Brussels on 17 January 1920.

M.R.

2
James Ensor
The Puzzled Masks 1930

3
Jean-Baptiste-Siméon Chardin
The Monkey as Painter c. 1739–1740

Jean-Baptiste-Siméon Chardin

Paris, 1699 – Paris, 1779

Between 1733 and 1748 Jean-Baptiste-Siméon Chardin devoted himself almost exclusively to genre painting.[1] One of the works from this period, *The Monkey as Painter* (cat. no. 3), exhibited at the Salon of 1740, capitalizes on a theme seen widely through engravings from the late sixteenth century on and very fashionable in Chardin's time.[2] The source of this painting subject was a precept formulated by Italian theorists in the early Renaissance – *ars simia naturae* ("art apes nature") – with the aim of reinstating the imitation of reality as art's primary function. It was the Northern Flemish school of the seventeenth century[3] that first translated this dictum into an image. As H.W. Janson has explained:

> Flemish seventeenth-century painters … seized upon *ars simia naturae* for purposes of their own. Disregarding the philosophical or aesthetic implications of the simile, they visualized it, in the most literal fashion, as an ape actually performing the artist's task, an image replete with humorous and satirical possibilities … Apes had been utilized to parody human actions in Northern European art ever since the thirteenth century … In the beginning, it had been mostly the nobility and the clergy whose characteristic doings were thus re-enacted; but in the sixteenth century, when they were no longer confined to the margins of manuscripts, these *drôleries* came to embrace an ever wider variety of classes and occupations.[4]

This iconographic tradition was based on the monkey's ability to imitate human activities, which over the centuries had earned it a unique place in the established bestiary of Western art.[5] Pierre Rosenberg has this to say:

> Eschewing vulgarity, even betraying a certain affection for the macaques he portrays, Chardin shows us a "successful" painter, seated on a stool, wearing a cocked hat with a feather and a brown frock coat trimmed with gold. Before him are a sketching board, a rag, a jug, a pan for washing brushes, a stone for grinding pigments, a small flask of oil, a roll of blue paper, a knife … Why should we not see this painting, which possesses a touch of humour rare in Chardin's work, as simply the French response to the Flemish *singeries* that were so hugely popular in Paris at the time?[6]

The success of the painting is definitely rooted in the human urge to laugh and to mock our fellows. The comic effect is created by the perfect resemblance between the animal and the practice it parodies – hence the importance of reproducing every detail of the usual studio paraphernalia. The astute art lover may even have spotted an allusion to acts seen often in the great Parisian fairs of Saint-Germain and Saint-Laurent, where animal trainers would exhibit monkeys who could dance a minuet, operate a cup-and-ball game, play the violin, and even perform on a tightrope. Dressing the animals in the appropriate costume was an essential part of the joke, for it made them seem even more familiar.

But what precisely is being mocked in this image of a painter? The artifice of painting itself? The vanity of clients seeking flattery? The impish power of the portraitist to improve his subjects' looks? The answer lies perhaps in the monkey-painter's gaze, which is directed beyond the confines of the canvas, as if he were examining his own reflection in a mirror. More than a simple amusement, this portrait of the artist as a monkey executing a self-portrait not only ridicules the self-portrait genre but also prefigures a paradigm shift in the way artists perceived themselves. The following centuries would yield portraits of the artist as a grimacing Pierrot (Doré,* cat. no. 42), as a tragic clown (Rouault,* cat. no. 45), and, more recently, as an aging and nearly naked body (Freud,* cat. no. 84). Once called "noble painter," artists had gradually lost their bearings, and their own self-images reflect their new status after having watched, helplessly, as the "gods were … supplanted by the clowns."[7]

C.N.-R.

1   For the full biographical context, see Florence Bruyant in *Chardin* (New Haven and London: Yale University Press, 2000), pp. 19–25. After 1748 Chardin turned increasingly to still life.

2   This picture and its pendant, *The Monkey as Antiquarian*, were both included in the Salon of 1740. Both were also engraved in 1743 by Pierre-Louis Surugue *fils*. See Pierre Rosenberg, *Chardin, 1699–1779* (Cleveland: Cleveland Museum of Art, 1979), p. 222. Watteau had explored the theme around 1712: two engravings by L. Desplaces, *Painting* and *Sculpture*, executed after paintings on the same subjects (now lost), are allegories in which the role of the artist is played by a monkey.

3   In the sixteenth century, celebrated engravings by Pieter van der Borcht (1540–1608) showed monkeys practicing a variety of professions (barber, soldier, schoolmaster) or enjoying leisure activities such as dancing and skating. In the seventeenth century, David Teniers the Younger continued this Flemish tradition, depicting a number of more elaborate scenes showing dressed-up monkeys: *A Festival of Monkeys* (1633), *School for Monkeys*, and, most notably, *The Monkey as Painter*, all now at the Prado.

4   H.W. Janson, *Apes and Ape Lore in the Middle Ages and the Renaissance* (London: Warburg Institute, 1952), p. 308.

5   See the essay by Jean Clair in this catalogue (pp. 24–25) for a discussion of the metaphorical meanings – positive and negative – associated with the monkey over the centuries.

6   Rosenberg, *Chardin*, p. 224.

7   Jean Starobinski, *Portrait de l'artiste en saltimbanque* (Geneva: Skira, 1970), p. 12.

73

Henry Fuseli

Zürich, 1741 – Putney Hill (near London), 1825

Born Johann Heinrich Füssli, into a well-known family of artists, writers, and collectors, Henry Fuseli taught himself drawing by copying old prints from the collection of his father, Johann Caspar Füssli (1706–1782). He was forced by his father to become a clergyman, and studied theology from 1759 to 1761 at the Hochschule Carolina in Zürich, where he came under the influence of the Swiss scholars J.J. Bodmer (1698–1783), and J.J. Breitinger (1701–1776). Much impressed by their critique of the classical ideal published in the journal *Discourse der Mahlern* in 1723 and by their emphasis on genius and imagination, Fuseli studied Shakespeare, Milton, Dante, Homer, and the *Nibelungenlied*; these would remain his principal iconographical sources throughout his subsequent artistic career. During his years as a student he also met and became friendly with Johann Kaspar Lavater (1741–1801). Obliged to leave Zürich in 1763 as the result of political difficulties, he went to Germany and then settled in London, where he gave up theology and developed an interest in the theatre. In 1768 he was encouraged by Sir Joshua Reynolds to become a painter, and two years later he went to Rome to learn his craft. On his return to London in 1778 he began moving in intellectual circles, and by 1781 had become famous as the creator of the strange painting entitled *The Nightmare*, which set the tone for the remainder of his oeuvre. He generally drew his themes from literature, but the real subjects of his pictures were dreams, secret passions, and unconscious desires, which he translated into the most extraordinary images. In the years that followed, he illustrated the French edition of Lavater's *Physiognomische Fragmente*,[1] a book defending the thesis that human character can be deduced through the study of facial features. Fuseli was elected to the Royal Academy in 1790, and began teaching there in 1801. While fulfilling this public role, he also produced a private series of watercolours illustrating human perversion.

Among Fuseli's very earliest drawings is a series of twenty-nine sketches representing a jester, dated 1757–1759. According to the artist, the images were copied from a book by Rudolf and Conrad Meyer and Gottfried Stadlern, published around 1640, entitled *Das Narrenbuch*.[2] However, Gert Schiff believes this jester image was more likely based on sixteenth-century tales about the peasant clown Till Eulenspiegel, whose irreverent pranks were aimed at the aristocracy, the bourgeoisie, and the clergy.[3]

The best known of these drawings, *Fool in a Fool's Cap Having His Portrait Painted* (cat. no. 4), which is indeed entirely in the Till Eulenspiegel spirit, reveals Fuseli's taste for caricature and role playing. A jester, wearing the traditional belled cap, poses for a painter whose quite unusual approach and fool's costume seem to reflect more than a touch of madness. Shown with one knee resting on a low chair, his thick-lensed pince-nez giving him a rather short-sighted look, and his hand-rest (normally held in the left hand) on the floor propped up against the canvas, the painter is beginning his portrait by painting the bells on the model's hat! The jester, moreover, is casting a decidedly sceptical look at the artist's technique. Fuseli has obviously taken delight in inverting his characters' traditional roles. Executed long before he decided to become an artist, the work seems to be thumbing its nose at painting in the Grand Manner.

Over the nineteenth century, the elitism that characterized the painting profession during its classical period was gradually supplanted by a new standard of excellence grounded in the Romantic notions of "inspiration" and "genius." At the dawn of the Second Empire, the life of the artist, made more precarious by a considerable swelling of the ranks, was often compared by writers to that of a jester or a *saltimbanque*. As Jean Starobinski so clearly saw, this was far more than a simple comparison: it was "an odd form of *identification*. For we soon realize that the use of the clown image is more than simply the choosing of a pictorial or poetic motif – it is an indirect and parodic way of questioning art itself."[4]

C.N.-R.

---

1   The German edition, *Physiognomische Fragmente zur Beförderung der Menschenkenntniss und Menschenliebe*, was published by Heinrich Steiner in four volumes, with illustrations and plates, in Leipzig and Winterthur between 1775 and 1778. A French edition, *Essai sur la physiognomonie, destiné à faire connoître l'homme & à le faire aimer*, was published in four volumes, with illustrations and portraits, in The Hague between 1781 and 1803 (the publisher is unidentified). The first English edition, *Essays on Physiognomy: Designed to Promote the Knowledge and the Love of Mankind*, was published by John Murray et al. in London between 1789 and 1792.

2   No copy of this book has ever been found, and it is now believed to be fictitious. See Gert Schiff, *Johann Heinrich Füssli, 1741–1825* (Zürich: Verlag Berichthaus, 1973), vol. 1, p. 39.

3   Ibid., p. 42. According to the catalogue raisonné established by Schiff, Fuseli became interested in the character of Till Eulenspiegel and created a cycle of images between 1758 and 1760 in which he is represented, as was the tradition, in all sorts of grotesque situations.

See Schiff, vol. 1, p. 44, and vol. 2, plates 274-277; *Fool in a Fool's Cap Having His Portrait Painted* is apparently the first image in the Till Eulenspiegel series.

4   Jean Starobinski, *Portrait de l'artiste en saltimbanque* (Geneva: Skira, 1970), p. 7.

4
Henry Fuseli
*Fool in a Fool's Cap Having His
Portrait Painted* 1757–1759

5
Giambattista Tiepolo
Punchinellos Cooking c. 1735

Giambattista Tiepolo
Venice, 1696 – Madrid, 1770

Father of Giandomenico* and Lorenzo, who served for many years as his assistants, Giambattista (Giovanni Battista) Tiepolo was one of the greatest Venetian painters of the eighteenth century. His frescoes adorn churches and royal palaces in Italy (Udine, Bergamo, Milan, Venice), Germany (Würzburg), and Spain (Madrid, Aranjuez). He was a practitioner of painting in the Grand Manner, famous for interpretations of historical, mythological, and religious subjects in which he deployed an extraordinary, almost theatrical sense of composition and a vivid, light-filled palette. But Giambattista also left a vast graphic oeuvre (over fifteen hundred drawings and prints), and it is in these works – less flamboyant than the frescoes, more freely inspired, more caricatural – that we encounter the character of Punchinello.

Punchinello (Pulcinella in Italian), who originated in the region of Naples, was a member of the commedia dell'arte cast. He was a popular figure in theatres and carnivals – a greedy buffoon with neither morals nor brains, dressed all in white like a Neapolitan peasant, wearing a high conical hat and a mask with an eagle's beak, humpbacked and potbellied ("because he had two different fathers," as the Neapolitan legend went), and contrasting sharply with society gentlemen of the time, with their black capes and tricorne hats. Giambattista Tiepolo devoted himself to illustrating Punchinello's antics, and Domenico followed suit, giving the character his own unique twist. The Tiepolos' Punchinellos became caricatural figures symbolic of the decadence of their era, when what counted above all was appearance. Often presented in groups, these identical Punchinellos formed a kind of new, egalitarian society, where no trick, not even the cruellest of jokes, was too dirty to play.

The drawing entitled Punchinellos Cooking (cat. no. 5)[1] illustrates a custom once observed in Verona.[2] On the last Friday of Carnival, known as "gnocchi Friday," young people from one of the city's poor neighbourhoods, dressed as Punchinello, would gather in the Piazza San Zeno and prepare gnocchi in a huge earthenware pot. They would then invite the chief magistrate to join them for the feast, washed down with a glass of wine. These drawings by Giambattista Tiepolo, which illustrate the rather dissolute habits of his hero – Punchinello drunk, Punchinello sick, Punchinello peeing – can likely be seen as a reprise by the artist of the comic and ridiculous situations performed for over two centuries by the members of commedia troupes (Harlequin, Punchinello, Columbine), first in fairground sideshows and ultimately before aristocratic and royal audiences in private mansions and palaces.

C.N.-R.

---

1   This drawing is part of a series that offers a comic account of the various stages involved in making gnocchi. The group has been dated by George Knox to c. 1735; see "The Punchinello Drawings of Giambattista Tiepolo," in *Inter-* *pretazioni Veneziane: Studi di storia dell'arte in onore di Michelangelo Muraro*, ed. David Rosand (Venice: Arsenale, 1984), pp. 439–446.

2   Emmanuelle Brugerolles and David Guillet, *Les Dessins vénitiens des collections de l'École des Beaux-Arts* (Paris: École Nationale Supérieure des Beaux-Arts, 1990), p. 106.

Giandomenico Tiepolo

Venice, 1727 – Venice, 1804

Oldest son of the great painter and decorator Giambattista* Tiepolo, Giandomenico (Giovanni Domenico) worked closely with his father from 1750 until the latter's death in Madrid, in 1770. After an eight-year stay in the Spanish capital Domenico returned to Venice and resumed his painting career. Admitted to the Accademia dei Pittori as a *maestro*, he served as its director from 1780 to 1783. Until 1797 he devoted himself to completing the frescoes adorning the Tiepolo family villa at Zianigo, near Mirano, which have since been transported to Venice and remounted at the Museo del Settecento Veneziano di Ca' Rezzonico. His own artistic personality emerged clearly in 1757 when he began creating genre scenes that were quite different from the historical and religious subjects painted by his father at the Villa Valmarana in Vicenza, built by Palladio in 1566; Domenico had been entrusted with the decoration of the *foresteria*, or guest lodgings, adjoining the villa, and there he gave free rein to his abundant talent.

Among these genre scenes was the first version of *Il Mondo Novo* ("The New World"), the image of a village carnival to which the artist would return twice more during his career, ending with the great fresco painted in 1791 for the villa at Zianigo. The exhibited work (cat. no. 6) is a small version on canvas dating from about 1765. The painting depicts a regular attraction at country fairs of the time: a crowd is gathered around a small building to observe, in amazement, coloured prints being displayed by means of an optical device.[1] A mountebank, perched on a stool, is commenting on these *vues d'optique*, or "perspective views," with the aid of a pointer. This kind of entertainment generally presented pictures of another world, distant and unreal, calculated to excite the villagers' curiosity and stimulate their imaginations. Here, as scholars have pointed out, the painter also offers us a strange kind of "reverse theatre," where almost all the characters are seen from behind, ordinary folk and society types alike. Some are masked, some not, but we cannot make out a single face, and class distinctions seem blurred. All are experiencing the same curiosity, the same illusion, the same mystification. The artist thus casts an ironic eye on the way Venetian society generally liked to see itself. A wind of social change already stirring in the rural areas around Venice had yet to be felt in the city itself.[2] The work points to this shift toward a "new world."

During his summer stays in Zianigo between 1770 and 1791, Domenico allowed his imagination to roam free in his redecoration of the family house, peopling the walls of several of the rooms with multiple Punchinellos, who jump, dance, swing, and substitute in all sorts of ludicrous situations for the classical heroes of ancient legend. The resulting images testify to the artist's incomparable skill in rendering movement and theatrical effects.

In the final decade of the eighteenth century, when the power of the doges and the great trading families was being threatened by an economic and political crisis (the French army was on Venice's doorstep), Domenico, now in his seventies, produced an extraordinary series of 104 drawings in graphite and ink called *Diversions for Children* (c. 1797–1804, cat. no. 8). In a tone of considerable sarcasm, the series represents all sorts of tribulations encountered by a community of Punchinellos in their everyday lives – birth, love affairs, the circus, arguments over gnocchi, death. It is a moving and dramatic evocation of Venice's festive and independent spirit, created as the city's political power was declining after its occupation by Napoleon's troops. In the great Carnival of life, even the impossible may one day become possible.

C.N.-R.

---

1 Although the painting shows neither the optical device nor the pictures, experts have identified this fairground attraction as its subject. See Harry Mathews, *Giandomenico Tiepolo*, trans. Martin Winckler (Paris: Flohic, 1993); Stéphane Loire, *Settecento: Le Siècle de Tiepolo* (Lille: Palais des Beaux-Arts, 2000), p. 166; and especially Frances Terpak in *Devices of Wonder: From the World in a Box to Images on a Screen* (Los Angeles: Getty Research Institute, 2001), pp. 344–353.

2 In the final decades of the eighteenth century, two things were happening: on the one hand many Venetian families were building country homes and thus transforming relations between city dwellers and the rural population, while on the other the urban bourgeoisie and aristocracy were maintaining their traditional lives of pleasure and opulence at a time when the city was facing serious economic, social, and political problems. Scholars believe that toward the end of his life Tiepolo was well aware of the major changes ahead.

6
Giandomenico Tiepolo
Il Mondo Novo c. 1765

7
Giandomenico Tiepolo
*An Encounter during a Country
Walk* c. 1791

8
Giandomenico Tiepolo
Punchinello Visits a Circus
c. 1797–1804

9
Giandomenico Tiepolo
The Lion's Cage c. 1791

82 10
Francisco Goya
The Straw Mannikin 1791–1792

Francisco Goya

Fuendetodos, Spain, 1746 – Bordeaux, 1828

Born into a family of modest means, the young Francisco José de Goya y Lucientes trained as a painter with José Luzán in Saragossa from 1760 to 1763. In 1763 he joined the Madrid studio of the brothers Francisco and Ramón Bayeu, whose sister Josefa he married in 1773. Under the auspices of Francisco, a court painter, he was hired by the Royal Tapestry Factory of Santa Bárbara in the winter of 1774 to produce weaving designs for the royal residences of El Pardo and San Lorenzo del Escorial. Between 1774 and 1792 he painted more than sixty tapestry cartoons in the manner of French and Flemish genre scenes. He took his subjects from the life of ordinary people, depicting various types and characters engaged in their leisure pursuits. One of his last cartoons, *The Straw Mannikin* (cat. no. 10), portrays a familiar feature of Spanish Carnival, in which a group of women toss a straw dummy up and down on a blanket, symbolizing the reversal of male and female roles. These populist subjects reflect the tastes of the liberal court of Charles III, where it was popular to show a "common touch" by imitating lower-class attire and amusements. Elected to the Real Academia de Bellas Artes de San Fernando in 1780, Goya was appointed painter to the king in 1786 and court painter in 1789.

Following a serious illness in the winter of 1792 that left him nearly deaf, he became withdrawn and, while convalescing in Cádiz in 1793, focused his work on a universe of violence and madness. Back in Madrid, he turned to social satire. *Los caprichos*, a first series of eighty prints published in 1799, reveals black humour that scathingly condemns the shortcomings of his contemporaries. The turbulent political context of the early nineteenth century deepened his pessimism.[1] Appalled by the massacres committed by the French in Spain until their retreat in 1814, the enlightened and Francophile painter became the bitter denunciator of *Los desastres de la guerra* (*The Disasters of War*). Between 1815 and 1824 he brought the same inexorable lucidity to bear on the political and social reality of the new regime in a final, uncompleted print suite that continues to defy interpretation, *Los disparates*.[2]

The Spanish word *disparate* – which literally means nonsense or absurdity, something beyond reason or outside the norm – is the only clue that Goya left behind, in the titles of thirteen plates. In spite of the surreal atmosphere and incongruous aspect of these images, Nigel Glendinning maintains that the subjects, while unconventional, relate to Spanish Carnival customs practiced in Goya's day, such as the dance of the giants, the wearing of two-headed masks, and the display of monstrous figures in public places.[3] All of them, he believes, serve to question authority, Carnival being the one period during which the reversal of social hierarchies and traditional values was permitted.

Only one etching in this series explicitly refers to a carnival performance: *Punctual Folly* (cat. no. 145). In it, a young woman balances on the back of a horse, which in turn appears to be balancing on a flexible cord, like a tightrope walker – an impossible feat, and one that is apparently unnoticed by the crowd in the background. Goya skilfully plays with illusion here, for the horse's hooves and the cord are, in fact, firmly on the ground. This becomes clear when one focuses on the crowd: the spectators are not positioned below the horse, looking upwards, but behind it, on the same level, looking down. Thus the horse is not a real tightrope walker after all, and this image may be a bitter comment on the general credulity of ordinary Spaniards.[4]

Fearing the reign of terror resulting from the absolute power re-established by Ferdinand VII in 1823, Goya obtained the king's permission to seek medical treatment in France for six months. His real intention was to flee, and in May 1824 he sought refuge with friends in Bordeaux before going to Paris, where he lived on Rue Marivaux. Returning to Bordeaux later that year, he took pleasure in the circus acts at the annual carnival, many images of which appear in Album H, his final sketchbook.

C.N.-R.

1   In 1808 the invasion of Napoleon's forces toppled the Spanish monarchy, and Joseph Bonaparte replaced the Bourbons on the throne. The popular uprising against the invaders sparked a long period of guerrilla warfare that ended in 1814 with the retreat of the French troops and the ascension to the throne of Ferdinand VII, acclaimed by his supporters as "the desired one." But the hopes thus raised were quickly dashed when the new king immediately abolished the liberal constitution promulgated by the Cortes in 1812, restored an absolute monarchy, revived the Inquisition

tribunal, and shut down universities, theatres, and newspapers. Ceding to widespread pressure in 1820, Ferdinand VII reinstated the Cortes constitution and civil liberties, which remained in effect until 1823.

2   This suite of etchings, which went unpublished during Goya's lifetime, came to have two titles. In 1864, after acquiring eighteen of the copper plates, the Real Academia de San Fernando issued the prints under the title *Los proverbios*. The title *Los disparates* comes from

Goya's notations on a number of artist's proofs, and is often used today to designate the entire series. The exact number of plates and their sequence is not known, nor are Goya's titles for some of them.

3   Nigel Glendinning, "Goya's Disparates" in *Goya: Neue Forschungen – Das international Symposium 1991 in Osnabrück*, ed. Jutta Held (Berlin: Mann-Verlag, 1994), p. 158. Glendinning cites two sources of primary importance concerning Spanish Carnival festivities: Caro Baroja, *El carnaval* (Madrid: Taurus, 1965) and Luis Antonio González Marín and Ignacio

María Martínez Ramirez, *Historia de la comparsa de Gigantes y Cabezudos de Zaragoza* (Saragossa: Ayuntamiento de Zaragoza, 1985).

4   Clifford S. Ackley, "The Disparates," in *The Changing Image: Prints by Francisco Goya*, ed. Eleanor A. Sayre (Boston: Museum of Fine Arts, 1974), p. 251.

Franz Xaver Messerschmidt

Wiesensteig (south of Stuttgart), 1736 –
Pressburg (now Bratislava, Slovak Republic), 1783

After early training under his uncles, the well-known sculptors J.-B. Staub (Munich) and P.-J. Staub (Graz), Franz Xaver Messerschmidt began studying at Vienna's Akademie der Bildenden Künste in 1755. By 1760 he was already receiving commissions for official portraits (busts, statues, and bas-reliefs) of the aristocracy and members of the court of Maria Theresa, Empress of Austria, which he executed in a traditional Austro-Bavarian Baroque style. In 1765 he spent several months studying in Rome; on his return, according to an early source, he moved to the magnificent residence of one of his friends, the celebrated Viennese doctor Franz Anton Mesmer (1734–1815), who had recently completed a thesis on the influence of the planets on the human body (*De planetarum influxu in corpus humanum*, 1766).[1] Appointed to the position of assistant professor at the Academy in 1769, Messerschmidt purchased a property not far from Mesmer's. The following year he began showing the first symptoms of the "psychosis" that was apparently the source of the eccentric behaviour responsible for his deteriorating relations with his colleagues. When the Academy's sculpture chair came free in 1774 he was refused the position because for three years he had "shown signs of some confusion."[2] Deeply hurt, he left Vienna for good in May 1775, retiring first to his native village of Wiesensteig until 1777 and then settling near Pressburg, where he died in 1783.

From 1770 until the end of his life Messerschmidt devoted himself almost exclusively to making "character heads" (cat. nos. 11–13).[3] The sixty-nine busts he produced were divided into two groups by Friedrich Nicolai,[4] the first consisting of those reminiscent of Roman statuary circa A.D. 69–96 and the other consisting of the heads expressing passions or emotions, many of which were based on Messerschmidt's own image reflected in a mirror. Despite the artist's isolation, his notorious eccentricities and nonconformism attracted eminent visitors. Nicolai travelled to see him in Pressburg in 1781. In a detailed account of the visit, the author wrote that while working Messerschmidt "looked into the mirror every half minute and made, with the greatest exactitude, precisely that grimace which he just needed."[5] Whatever the motives behind this obsessive compulsion, there is an element of self-mockery to the bizarre enterprise that had clearly not escaped the people who in the early nineteenth century exhibited the busts as a curiosity, in a stall at the Prater.[6] And although these essentially private works (the titles were added after the artist's death) have given rise to a number of controversial interpretations, their enigmatic quality still has the power to fascinate. As Michael Krapf has observed: "The thoroughly 'modern' feature of Messerschmidt's aim in producing the 'character heads' is that his preoccupation with serial self-inquiry can be rediscovered, by way of the 'Sturm und Drang' period and Romanticism and Secessionism around 1900, in the aggressive self-questioning of artists and art scholars in our own day."[7]

Because he himself, standing in front of a mirror, adopted the expressions he portrayed, Messerschmidt's highly personal explorations were in a sense akin to the work of the clown, for he used the "character head" as his means of communicating emotion. This man of the Enlightenment has emerged as the source of a new self-exploration in contemporary art: in the work of Bruce Nauman,* which is by no means devoid of self-mockery, Messerschmidt's concept is reformulated in a series of holograms entitled *Making Faces* (1968), where the artist twists his face into expressions that verge on the grimace.

C.N.-R.

1   Albert Ilg, *Franz Xaver Messerschmidt's Leben und Werke* (Vienna and Leipzig, 1885), quoted by Michael Krapf in *Franz Xaver Messerschmidt, 1736–1783* (Vienna: Barockmuseum Österreichische Galerie Belvedere; Ostfildern-Ruit: Hatje Cantz, 2003), p. 24.

2   Extract from a note written by Count von Kaunitz, charged with conveying the Academy's objections to the appointment to Maria Theresa, quoted by Ernst Kris in *Psychoanalytic Explorations in Art* (New York: International Universities Press, 1952), p. 130.

3   Krapf, *Franz Xaver Messerschmidt*, pp. 45–47. Invoking the friendship between Messerschmidt and Mesmer (both men were born in Swabia), the author proposes the interesting theory that the "character heads" were inspired by expressions the artist had observed on the faces of patients undergoing one of the "magnetic cures" developed by Mesmer in 1773–1774.

4   Friedrich Nicolai (1733–1814), publisher and editor of numerous journals, was considered one of Berlin's foremost "enlightened thinkers." See Krapf, *Franz Xaver Messerschmidt*, p. 39.

5   Friedrich Nicolai, *Beschreibung einer Reise durch Deutschland und die Schweiz im Jahre 1781*, vol. 6 (Berlin and Stettin, 1785), quoted by Kris in *Psychoanalytic Explorations in Art*, p. 136.

6   Krapf, *Franz Xaver Messerschmidt*, p. 10. The Prater is Vienna's most popular fun fair.

7   Ibid., p. 11.

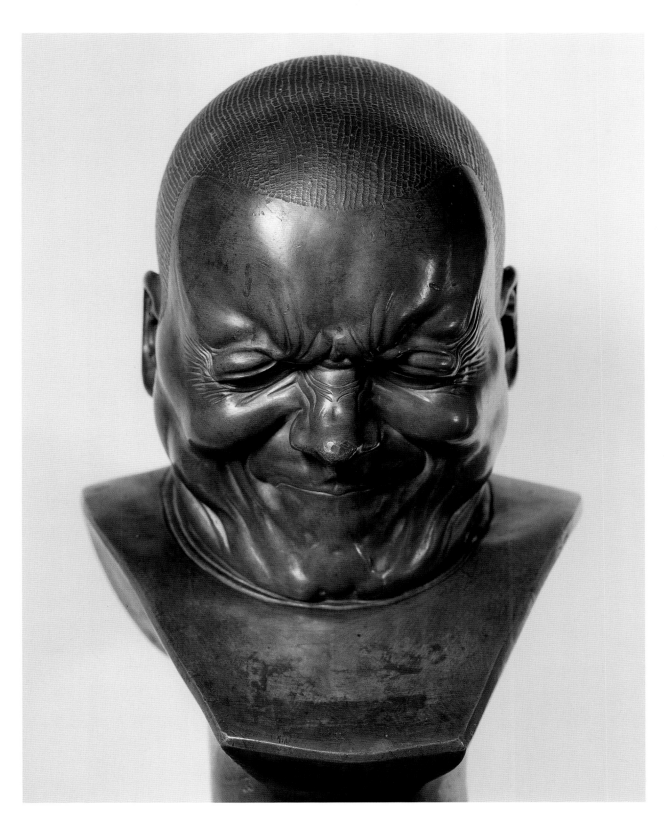

11
Franz Xaver Messerschmidt
An Arch Rascal after 1770

12
Franz Xaver Messerschmidt
A Dismal and Sinister Man
after 1770

13
Franz Xaver Messerschmidt
An Old Cheerful Smiler after 1770

Jean-Étienne Liotard
Geneva, 1702 – Geneva, 1789

Jean-Étienne Liotard's father was a Huguenot from Montélimar who had settled in Geneva following the 1685 revocation of the Edict of Nantes. Liotard was initiated into the art of the miniature by Daniel Gardelle (1679–1753). In 1723 he went to seek his fortune in Paris, where he was apprenticed for three years to Jean-Baptiste Massé (1687–1767), a portraitist, miniaturist, and engraver. He developed a particular affinity for the medium of pastel and executed a number of portraits of family and friends. However, despite his remarkable ability to capture a likeness, his status as a miniaturist meant there was little future for him in Paris.[1] He therefore set off in 1735 for Naples, and spent the next two years travelling in Italy. In 1738 he sailed for Constantinople in the company of two English noblemen,[2] remaining there until 1742 and making his living executing portraits of diplomats. It was at this point that he began wearing Turkish dress – the first stage in the construction of his "persona." Late in 1742 he was invited to the court at Jassy, capital of Moldavia (now Romania), where he spent ten months painting members of the aristocracy. He also adopted the large fur hat worn by his models and, most strikingly, a huge Moldavian-style beard. By September 1743 he was at the court of Vienna. Well received by Empress Maria Theresa, he soon became part of her entourage. In a self-portrait dating from 1744 he fully assumes his role as "the Turkish painter,"[3] the nickname earned by the unusual costumes and beard that reflected his independent and nonconformist nature. His "Oriental" appearance eventually became a trademark to which he owed at least part of his fame. In 1745 he resumed his career as an itinerant portraitist, travelling across Europe and painting some of the great figures of his time. Between 1746 and 1753 he remained in Paris, where he considerably enhanced both his reputation at court and his fortune. In 1755 he spent some time in London and later went to Amsterdam; after marrying the young Marie Fargues there in 1756, he returned permanently to Geneva.[4]

Liotard the portraitist did not generally flatter his models. Favouring the fragile and subtle medium of pastel, he represented their faces realistically and accurately. And he made no exception for his self-portraits.[5] The unusual painting entitled *Liotard Laughing* (cat. no. 14) is one of a series of self-portraits executed between 1765 and 1770. It had been some

years since the artist had portrayed his own face, for his preceding exercises in the genre date from the second Parisian sojourn, which extended from 1746 to 1753. Anne de Herdt describes the work as "sensitive, human, and prosaic … with a modesty not evident hitherto."[6] The costume is simple: a blue jacket with a white ruff, and a red cap. In this half-length portrait the artist has represented himself without the usual attributes of the painter. It is thus not so much the act of painting that is his subject as his own identity, and indeed the image possesses the same psychological intensity as the other self-portraits from this period. Focusing on the face and the hand, the painting shows a white-haired, beardless man, serene but with a mischievous look in his eye, wearing a broad, mocking smile that (with a verisimilitude that breaches the bounds of decorum) reveals a number of missing teeth. He gazes directly at the viewer, who actually takes the place of a mirror, and with his right forefinger points tantalizingly to someone or something invisible to us outside the frame.

Mysterious and highly original, *Liotard Laughing* is open to multiple readings. Is it simply a reflection on the fleetingness of youth, with a moralistic undertone reminiscent of the Flemish painting of which Liotard was so fond? Or is it a playful exploration of the relationship between self-representation and the mirror image? Or can we see it, as Anne de Herdt suggests, as "Liotard playing the role of Liotard, a comic actor standing on an empty stage conjured simply by the heavy green curtain hanging at the right of the composition"?[7] Claude Reichler's penetrating analysis of the self-portraits as a group adopts a fresh perspective and throws a revealing new light on this particular painting: "Each of his portraits is a variation on the theme of the relationship to self … in Liotard's work, this relationship reflects an inner theatricality … The 'staging' of the self emerges through a mix of mystery and irony that both divulges and cloaks the complacency of the self-image … the representational mechanism anticipates in a quite remarkable way the clown figure and its invariable mockery."[8]

C.N.-R.

1 Anne de Herdt, *Dessins de Liotard* (Geneva: Musée d'art et d'histoire; Paris: Réunion des Musées Nationaux, 1992), p. 11ff.

2 Sir William Ponsonby, future Earl of Bessborough, and the Earl of Sandwich, later First Lord of the Admiralty.

3 Now in the Uffizi in Florence, this painting is signed and inscribed in French in the upper-left corner: "J.E. Liotard of Geneva nicknamed The Turkish Painter painted by himself in Vienna in 1744."

4 The young woman of twenty-seven, from a Dutch Calvinist family, had agreed to the marriage on one condition: that her fiancé sacrifice his famous beard, which by that time reached down to his belt.

5 The artist made self-portraits regularly from the start of his career (1727), and if we count all the oils, pastels, drawings, engravings, and enamels, there are between twenty and thirty extant. I am grateful to Madame Renée Loche, joint author of the catalogue raisonné currently under preparation, for having provided me with this information.

6 Herdt, *Dessins*, p. 240.

7 Ibid., p. 242.

8 Claude Reichler, "Liotard avec variations: Les Autoportraits de Jean-Étienne Liotard," in *Genava* 26 (1978), pp. 221–228.

89

Joseph Ducreux
Nancy, 1735 – Paris, 1802

Born in the Duchy of Lorraine, Joseph Ducreux set off in 1760 to try his luck in Paris, where he became a student of the famous portraitist Maurice Quentin de La Tour (1704–1788). He began receiving commissions in 1762, and was soon specializing in pastel bust portraits; he also started working in oils, taking instruction from Jean-Baptiste Greuze (1725–1805). His most prestigious commission came in 1769, when the Duc de Choiseul, first minister to Louis XV, asked him to execute the portrait of the young Dauphin's new fiancée, Marie-Antoinette, Archduchess of Austria. In order to complete his task, Ducreux spent the months from February to November in Vienna. As soon as Louis XVI ascended to the throne in 1774, his consort showed her gratitude to the artist by making him "first painter to the queen." Even with this honour Ducreux never succeeded in gaining entry to the Académie Royale, largely because of his irascible nature.[1] Denied access to the annual Salon du Louvre, he exhibited at the 1783 Salon de la Correspondance[2] "two images of his own person, one showing him laughing, and the other a large half-length portrait, picturing him dressed in a red frock coat, yawning and stretching like someone who has just woken up. These extravagant depictions of himself must have amused onlookers and guaranteed a certain popular success."[3]

After the fall of the Ancien Régime, Ducreux miraculously escaped imprisonment, although in 1791 the former favourite of the queen was obliged to take refuge in London. During his stay there he exhibited five portraits at the Royal Academy and published three humorous engravings, self-portraits in the "expressive heads" mode that reveal his interest in facial expression and role playing: *The Tearful Gambler, Discretion, The Laugher*.[4] In executing these works he may have been trying to impress London society, renowned for its love of caricature. Whatever the case, on 15 August 1791 Ducreux returned under somewhat obscure circumstances to Paris,[5] where he at last took part in the official Salon, now open to all. Critical reaction to some of his previously exhibited works was fairly negative – there was talk of the "yawner who would make a lackey laugh," and, worse still, of a "yawn-inspiring Ducreux."[6] He nevertheless continued to make pictures of his own grimacing

face, presenting another version at the Salon of 1793, *Portrait of the Artist with the Features of a Mocker* (cat. no. 15). Here, mouth open and teeth revealed, the artist points with his right index finger directly at the spectator, whom he seems to be addressing. A social offence (showing one's teeth) has undoubtedly been committed: "Citizen" Ducreux, now no longer a servant of the court, appeals directly and somewhat arrogantly to the people, either in an effort to reinstate honest humour or in mockery of a public that refuses to offer him their approval or understanding.

But the "clownish" nature of his contributions did not go unnoticed by his contemporaries. Beside number 160 in the brochure for the Salon of 1795, *Citizen Ducreux by Himself*, we read: "He has given himself a forced laugh that does not reflect his true character." The following year the *Mercure de France* published comments about his painting *The Laugher* that provide an interpretative key: "What bad taste to exhibit oneself over and over at the Salon, and to exhibit oneself invariably in some crude or silly pose! ... He's like a boulevard face-puller."[7] The author of these words, and no doubt the public too, associated facial contortion with the small-time theatres on Boulevard du Temple. And Ducreux was indeed making a "spectacle" of himself. His very stance in the 1793 self-portrait is that of a fairground barker. The distinctly unorthodox approach to self-portraiture that he had adopted in the early 1780s may have been inspired by Lavater's work on physiognomy, and it can certainly be compared to the explorations conducted in isolation by Messerschmidt* between 1770 and 1783. Like the enigmatic Viennese sculptor, he made his own physiognomy an object of study and undertook the extraordinarily difficult task of capturing its alterations in the mirror – a feat that required a total understanding of the working of the facial muscles.

Despite its marginality, Ducreux's project of translating emotion into facial expression was revived in the following century by Boilly* (cat. no. 16), Daumier,* and finally Doré,* whose marvellous, proto-Expressionist *Pierrot Grimacing* (cat. no. 42) can be seen as its culmination.

C.N.-R.

1 Georgette Lyon, *Joseph Ducreux (1735-1802), premier peintre de Marie-Antoinette: Sa Vie, son oeuvre* (Paris: La Nef de Paris, 1958), p. 67.

2 Ibid., pp. 67-73. The artists who exhibited at this Salon certainly formed an eclectic group; nevertheless, for a decade or so it constituted an alternative to the Salon du Louvre, which it aimed to rival.

3 Prosper Dorbec, "Joseph Ducreux (1735-1802)," *Gazette des Beaux-Arts*, 3rd ser., 26 (1906), p. 206.

4 Lyon, *Joseph Ducreux*, p. 78.

5 Ducreux was "linked to David," who had apparently made a portrait of one of his daughters (Dorbec, "Joseph Ducreux," p. 209). David was an active revolutionary, and served as a Deputy to the Convention. On 21 June 1791, the fleeing Louis XVI was arrested in Varennes, and the royal family's days were henceforth numbered.

From 1791 on, Ducreux was among the "Friends of the Constitution" (Lyon, *Joseph Ducreux*, p. 87).

6 Lyon, *Joseph Ducreux*, p. 80.

7 Ibid., p. 105. The author provides the source of this review: *Mercure de France*, "Deloynes" series, vol. 18, Salon of 1796, p. 978.

15
Joseph Ducreux
Portrait of the Artist with the Features of a Mocker c. 1793

16
Louis-Léopold Boilly
Thirty-Five Expressive Heads c. 1825

Louis-Léopold Boilly

La Bassée, France, 1761 – Paris, 1845

The son of a wood carver, Louis-Léopold Boilly learned the art of trompe l'oeil painting from Dominique Doncre in Arras (1779–1784). He settled in Paris in 1785 and soon earned acclaim for the romantic scenes that made him one of the most promising successors of Fragonard and Greuze. During the Revolution he espoused the themes of civic rectitude promoted by the school of David, but under the Consulate, Empire, and Restoration he turned to depicting popular bourgeois pastimes on the streets of Paris and in gaming houses, theatres, salons, and cafés (*Entrance of the Ambigu-Comique*, 1819). By 1800 the rising middle class had produced a clientele for his small bust portraits, which reveal a keen interest in the study of human character as theorized by the Swiss theologian Lavater in his *Essays on Physiognomy* (1775–1778). Between 1823 and 1828 he concentrated on facial expressions and gestures that reveal emotions, producing the famous lithographic suite *Grimaces* and a surprising painting, *Thirty-Five Expressive Heads* (cat. no. 16). This was the first time "expressive heads" – traditionally

engraved or drawn – had been rendered in painting. A threesome appears at the centre of the composition: an old man in tears (the artist's father) with his gesticulating son, at right, and his turbaned wife, at left. To accentuate the caricatural expressions of the variously grinning, furious, and stupefied faces, Boilly used fun-house mirrors. The Pierrot at the upper right suggests that he also may have been inspired by the art of grimacers, the popular performers who grossly contorted their faces to make audiences laugh. Around 1833 his attraction to the world of entertainment led him to paint *Carnival Scene, Boulevard du Crime*, which pictures Harlequin, Punchinello, and Pierrot on a fine winter afternoon in a crowd in front of the Porte Saint-Martin Theatre on Boulevard du Crime.

M.R.

II Parade

Weights they carry round or square
Drums and golden hoops
Those wise beasts the bear and monkey
Beg pennies along the road

Guillaume Apollinaire

All parades are parodies, and every parade is a paradise lost. The parade that stages – if only in an effort to arrest (which is the meaning of *parar* in Spanish) – the decay of the society it puts on display is actually a sarcastic and boisterous self-representation of the world that it purports to celebrate but which no longer exists. The "triumphal entries" that history painting so loved to depict during the 1870s were huge mechanisms designed to transmit the final thunder of processions honouring past glories, at a time when the shimmering raiment of the nobility had become nothing more than the garish cast-offs of clowns and strong men. Historicism buries history. The parade is its funeral procession.

J.C.

Honoré Daumier

Marseilles, 1808 – Valmondois, France, 1879

After studying drawing at the Athénée Royale des Arts and the Académie Suisse in Paris, Daumier was apprenticed in 1825 to the lithographer Zéphirin Belliard. An ardent Republican, he took part in 1830 in the three days of revolution known as the "Trois Glorieuses." From then on, he focused his efforts on political satire, contributing first to *La Caricature* and later to *Le Charivari* (1832), anti-monarchist papers founded by Charles Philipon. That same year a caricature of King Louis-Philippe entitled *Gargantua* led to Daumier's incarceration in Sainte-Pélagie prison. His political convictions remained firm, however, and in 1834 he produced an irreverent print, *Lower the Curtain, the Farce Is Ended*, portraying Louis-Philippe as the clown Paillasse – the first appearance of the clown image in his work – and likening the debates of the parliamentary *hémicycle* to a fairground show. The government's prohibition of political caricature in 1835 forced the artist to turn to social satire, which occupied him for some years. In a famous 1839 lithograph titled *The Parade* he depicted the *Charivari* journalists as public entertainers openly derisive of society's ills. Shortly after the proclamation of the Second Republic in 1848, Daumier the lithographer became, somewhat belatedly, Daumier the painter. As a result of the new government's innovative art policy, he began receiving commissions.

The authoritarian regime established after Napoleon III's accession to power on 2 December 1852 resulted in his dismissal from *Le Charivari* in March 1860. Philipon had finally succumbed to the fear of censorship, and until the publisher's death in 1863 Daumier was obliged to devote his energies increasingly to watercolour and oil painting. The precariousness of his career is perhaps the deep-rooted explanation for the appearance in his work of the "poor *saltimbanque*," a metaphor for the misunderstood artist. It was a theme that had already been explored by a number of his literary acquaintances, including Théophile Gautier, Théodore de Banville (whose *Odes funambulesques* of 1857 he came close to illustrating) and Charles Baudelaire ("Le Vieux Saltimbanque," 1861). The literary figure of the "sad clown," which echoed the everyday reality of Paris's fairgrounds in a number of ways, no doubt fuelled this identification.

Daumier was not interested in the grandiose spectacles put on by the permanent circuses of his time. Specialists generally agree that the figures represented in his works come from the poorer social milieu of travelling entertainers, individuals who were not attached to any official circus and were thus, of necessity, condemned to itinerancy.[1] Daumier's choice can be explained by the political situation: under the Second Empire, the police were constantly harassing fairground folk, seen by many as undesirable marginals. Increasingly strict regulations had forced them into the suburbs of Paris, and when Baron Haussmann, charged by the emperor to clean up the capital, demolished Boulevard du Temple between 1860 and 1862, street entertainers had already deserted the neighbourhood.

Performers Resting (*Strong Man and Pierrot in the Wings*) (cat. no. 91), an exemplary image of the sad clown, illustrates both Daumier's interest in this iconic figure and his unique way of exploiting its metaphorical potential. The strong man's serious and attentive expression leaves no doubt as to the ill fortune that has befallen Pierrot (the proletarian hero), shown seated on his drum, exhausted, impoverished, crushed by despair. The theatrical lighting reinforces the pathos of the scene. By keeping bodily and facial expression to a minimum, Daumier here offers a powerfully understated picture of the bleak life of the fairground entertainer. Executed during the 1860s, when the "caricaturist" was enduring the effects of censorship and the "artist" was earning negative reviews for his contributions to the Salon ("Caricature ruins a painter's hand," wrote Philippe de Chennevières), this scene seems to summarize Daumier's own career: like these fairground players, he was an artist "for the people."

C.N.-R.

1   See Paula Hays Harper, *Daumier's Clowns: Les Saltimbanques et les Parades, New Biographical and Political Functions for a Nineteenth-Century Myth* (New York: Garland, 1981); Bruce Laughton, *Honoré Daumier* (New Haven and London: Yale University Press, 1996); Colta Ives, Margret Stuffmann, and Martin Sonnabend, *Daumier Drawings* (New York: Metropolitan Museum of Art / Harry N. Abrams, 1992).

17
Honoré Daumier
The Sideshow c. 1865

James Tissot

Nantes, 1836 – Buillon, France, 1902

In 1856 Jacques Joseph Tissot (who only later took the name of James) went to Paris to study painting with Louis Lamothe and Hippolyte Flandrin. Between 1859 and 1870 he devoted himself successively to painting Romantically inspired medieval subjects, portraits, and contemporary genre scenes, all in an academic style. He was involved in the Paris Commune, and after its fall in 1871 he took refuge in England, where he became an observant chronicler of Victorian high society and women's fashions. Throughout his London period, women were the main focus of his work. Returning to Paris in 1882 following the death of his mistress, Mrs. Kathleen Newton, he undertook a major series of fifteen large paintings featuring Parisian women of diverse social backgrounds, from upper-class ladies to shop girls. Each one, shown engaged in an activity characteristic of modern womanhood, is captured from life in a kind of "freeze-frame" image. The plan was to reproduce each painting in an etching and accompany it with a poem or short text by a famous author. Tissot exhibited this ensemble at Galerie Sedelmeyer in Paris in 1885 and then again the following year at Arthur Tooth & Sons in London.

Three paintings from this suite are circus images. *The Circus Lover* highlights several elegant ladies in the audience at the Cirque Molier, an amateur circus that was all the rage in Paris; the central figure of *The Tightrope Walker* is a performer with whom Tissot had a brief affair on his return from London;[1] and *Ladies of the Chariots* (cat. no. 18) pictures "real Batignolles girls" parading in Roman chariots beneath the electric lamps of the Hippodrome de l'Alma. The painting faithfully reproduces the splendour of this iron and stone edifice, with its glass roof and its rows of comfortable seats capable of accommodating up to eight thousand spectators.

Among the new occupations of modern Parisian women, those linked to the world of entertainment attracted the attention of numerous painters during the 1880s. Here Tissot introduces us to the girls of humble background who worked in the large circuses. Their glittering costumes and the solemn atmosphere of the parade preceding the race have prompted the Tissot scholar Willard Misfeldt to draw an interesting parallel between this painting and Alphonse Daudet's novel *Sapho*, published in 1884. Daudet describes the costume of one of his heroines, Rosa, a former "lady of the chariots" at the Hippodrome. Rosa's lover recalls their first meeting: "It is twenty years since I went to live with Rosa, – twenty years since, on my return from Italy after my three years' incumbency of the Prix de Rome, I went into the Hippodrome one evening and saw her standing in her little chariot, coming down on me round the turn in the ring, whip in air, with her helmet with eight lanceheads, and her coat covered with gold scales fitting tight to her figure to the middle of her leg. Ah! if any one had told me …"[2] Tissot's image seems to be an almost exact visual rendering of this passage. Or perhaps it was the reverse – perhaps it was Daudet who drew inspiration from his friend's painting. Both certainly convey the audience's fascination with these industrial-era goddesses and the erotic atmosphere that enveloped them. As Jean Starobinski has aptly pointed out, these divinities represented "the exotic fringe at the edges of the bourgeois world … enigmatic strangers who possessed the suppleness, the vigour that made them the perfect tormentors."[3] Tissot was conscious of the latent eroticism of these vast, elaborate shows. Like the female bareback rider or Huysmans' Miss Urania,[4] the "lady of the chariots" "simultaneously offers and withholds herself in the shamelessness of a commercial exhibition."[5] Impervious to the roar of the crowd, she even adopts the rather stiff pose of an elegant society lady, thus rendering respectable the top-hatted gentlemen's secret desires.

C.N.-R.

1   David Brooke, "James Tissot's Amateur Circus," *Boston Museum Bulletin* 67, no. 347 (1969), pp. 4–17.

2   Quoted in Willard E. Misfeldt, "James Tissot and Alphonse Daudet: Friends and Collaborators," *Apollo* 123 (February 1986), p. 114. This translation from Alphonse Daudet, *Sapho* (Greenwich, Conn.: Appleby & Company, 1939), p. 95.

3   Jean Starobinski, *Portrait de l'artiste en saltimbanque* (Geneva: Skira, 1970), pp. 42–47.

4   J.K. Huysmans, *À Rebours* (Paris: Gallimard, 1989), p. 206. In this novel, which dates from 1883, Miss Urania appears thus to the hero, Des Esseintes: "… long, white teeth … a short nose … short-clipped hair … an American girl with a supple figure, sinewy legs, muscles of steel, arms of iron. She had been one of the most famous acrobats at the *Cirque*." This translation from J.K. Huysmans, *Against the Grain* (New York: Dover, 1969), pp. 97–98.

5   Starobinski, *Portrait de l'artiste*, p. 46.

18
James Tissot
Ladies of the Chariots 1883–1885

Fernand Pelez

Paris, 1843 – Paris, 1913

The little-known artist Fernand Pelez learned the funda-mentals of painting from his father, the Parisian painter Fernand Pelez de Cordova (1820–1899). Pelez *fils* continued his academic training in the studios of Félix-Joseph Barrias and Alexandre Cabanel, first exhibiting paintings at the Salon in 1866. Abandoning history painting in 1880, he began making genre scenes portraying the poverty of the working-class people who inhabited Paris's most depressed neigh-bourhoods. Pelez approached the theme (already explored by Daumier,* Courbet,* and Degas*) with an almost photo-graphic exactitude. At the Salon of 1885 he showed *Poverty – At the Opéra*, a melancholy work that reveals the humble background of the young dancers it depicts. Two years later, he presented the Salon with a harsh view of the plight

of homeless children in his work *A Nest of Poverty*. The world of popular entertainment is the subject of the huge five-panel work from 1888, *Grimaces and Misery*, also known as *Circus Performers* (cat. no. 19). Exhibited at the official Salon the same year that Seurat* presented his *Circus Sideshow* at the Salon des Indépendants, Pelez's vast work meticulously – and in a spirit of powerful social censure – depicts the miserable fate of travelling entertainers. As the clown delivers his patter, we see nothing but weariness on the faces of the young trapeze artists and the musicians.

Fairs, prohibited for reasons of public health and safety by Napoleon III in 1860 (when Paris's suburbs were annexed), had been authorized again in 1881 by the chief of police.[1] Their reinstatement was a victory for itinerant entertainers: troupes streamed into the capital, vying for the attention of an increasingly discerning public that did not hesitate to go as far afield as Saint-Cloud or the fair at Neuilly. As early as 1853, at the start of the Second Empire, the poet

19
Fernand Pelez
Grimaces and Misery (Circus Performers) 1888

Théodore de Banville had described the fate of these travelling show people: a life of woe dedicated to making others
laugh. In an essay entitled "Les Pauvres Saltimbanques"
he pointed out the similarity between the travelling entertainer and the poet, both "artists": "*Saltimbanques*, and poor
saltimbanques indeed, these inspired poets, these actors
intoxicated with passion, these eloquent voices, these violin
and lyre players, these brilliant marionettes, whose condition is first to weep, and after to make the crowd weep and
laugh! For what is a *saltimbanque*, pray tell, if not an independent, free artist who performs marvels to earn his daily
bread, who sings in the sun and dances under the stars,
with no hope of becoming part of any academy?"[2] Placed
alongside the poet's words – which constitute one of the
founding texts of the "sad clown" myth – Pelez's painting
illuminates their metaphorical meaning, for symbolically the
clown and the artist are two facets of the same reality.
During the 1880s increasing industrialization was threaten-
ing the existence of both.

C.N.-R.

1   Christiane Py and Cécile
Ferenczi, *La Fête foraine
d'autrefois: Les Années 1900*
(Lyons: La Manufacture, 1987).

2   Théodore de Banville, quoted
in Philippe Andrès, *Théodore de
Banville (1823–1891): Parcours littéraire et biographique* (Paris:
L'Harmattan, 1997), p. 79.

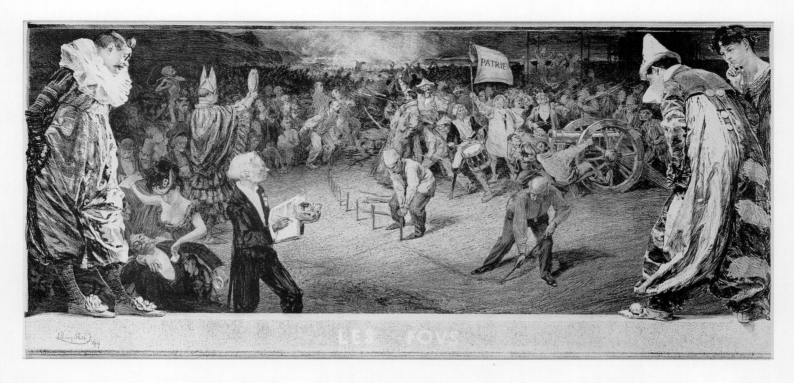

20
František Kupka
The Fools 1899

František Kupka

Opočno, Eastern Bohemia (now Czech Republic),
1871 – Puteaux, France, 1957

After formal training in Prague, from 1888 to 1891, and in Vienna, from 1891 to 1893, František (or Frank) Kupka made Paris his permanent home, returning to Austria and Germany only for short visits. Following the death of his companion Maria Bruhn in 1898 he moved to Montmartre to live with a former Moulin Rouge cancan dancer known as La Goulue ("The Glutton"). Like Toulouse-Lautrec before him, Kupka decorated her booth at the Foire du Trône (the Foire au Pain d'Épice) on Place de la Nation. In 1899 he rented a studio above Aristide Bruant's cabaret on Boulevard Roche-chouart and frequented Montmartre chansonniers, for whom he designed posters. He was a prolific illustrator, and that same year he produced an ambitious two-colour lithograph, *The Fools* (cat. no. 20), in which two clowns and a female

personification of free thought crowned with laurels appear as powerless spectators of the tragic human comedy. In a lithograph published in the fashionable art magazine *La Vie en Rose* in 1900 he represents himself enthroned on a podium in the middle of a Montmartre fair behind two monuments honouring Steinlen and Willette: the former is flanked by a black cat and a white cat, and the latter by three tightrope walkers, two of them in Pierrot costume. After a short period of membership in the Section d'Or Cubist group in Puteaux in 1906, he turned to Fauvism before breaking with figuration in 1910 to become a pioneer of abstract art.

M.R.

21
Pierre Bonnard
The Parade (or *The Fair*)
1892

Pierre Bonnard

Fontenay-aux-Roses, France, 1867 – Le Cannet, France, 1947

Pierre Bonnard earned a law degree in 1888 and studied at the Académie Julian and the École des Beaux-Arts before joining the Nabis. He began attending the Cirque Medrano in the late 1880s, and in 1892 painted his first circus scene, *The Parade* (or *The Fair*) (cat. no. 21), using a pointillist technique similar to that of Seurat.* The following year he made twenty lithographs to illustrate Claude Terrasse's music album *Petites Scènes familières*, including one drawing entitled *At the Circus, Haute École*. Between 1894 and 1897 he produced circus scenes notable for their bold layout in the Japanese style, which strongly influenced his work

(*Circus*, 1894; *Equestrienne*, 1897). Although best known for his paintings of interiors, Bonnard produced illustrations for Louise Hervieu's *L'Âme du cirque* (1924) and a drawing, *Circus Vision* (1926), for Gustave Coquiot's *En suivant la Seine*. He moved to the south of France in 1925, and in 1936 undertook *The Circus Horse* (completed in 1946), a last nod to his fondness for equestrian circus acts.

M.R.

22
Georges Rouault
Circus (The Parade) 1905

Georges Rouault

Paris, 1871 – Paris, 1958

Georges Rouault's fascination with the circus extended back to his childhood. Around 1902 he abandoned the mytholog- ical subjects that he had been painting in the 1890s under the influence of his master, Gustave Moreau. A fervent Catholic, Rouault advocated a Christian "universal socialist republic," which he believed would counter both the pervasive mate- rialism of dehumanizing industrialization and the overly spiritualist philosophy of Bergson. He shared the enthusi- asms of two friends who had converted to Catholicism – Joris-Karl Huysmans, with whom he spent some time in 1901 at the abbey at Ligugé, in Poitou, with the aim of found- ing an artists' community, and the virulent polemicist Léon Bloy, whom he met in 1904. In a 1905 letter to another friend, the Symbolist writer Édouard Schuré, he explained the source of his interest in the circus: "For me, since the end of that happy day when the first star to shine in the fir- mament touched my heart – I know not why – I have uncon- sciously seen it as a source of considerable poetry. The travellers' cart drawn up beside the road, the scrawny old horse grazing in a meagre pasture, the old clown seated in the corner of his caravan mending his shiny, multicoloured costume, the *contrast* between the brilliant, glittering things made to amuse and a life that is so *infinitely sad* if we see it from a little way off ... Then I extrapolated it all. I saw clearly that the 'Clown' was me, was us, almost all of us ..."[1] Based on this realization, Rouault portrayed himself as a sombre-faced buffoon in *Head of a Tragic Clown* (cat. no. 45). In November 1904 he exhibited a series of forty- four paintings at the Salon d'Automne (which he helped found), and a third of the group consisted of works devoted to the circus. He repeatedly depicted circus artists, espe- cially clowns (cat. nos. 22, 24, 44, 45), seeking to illustrate the paradox at the heart of their nomadic existence: the obligation to perform as public entertainers in spite of their inner pain. In 1911 he became friendly with the writer André Suarès and began a correspondence with him that throws a good deal of light on his work. The following year Rouault moved to Versailles, settling on Rue de l'Orangerie not far from the home of the philosopher Jacques Maritain, to whom he had been introduced by Léon Bloy.

In 1913 the dealer Ambroise Vollard, much impressed by Rouault, began lengthy negotiations to purchase his studio stock.[2] After becoming the artist's official dealer in 1917, Vollard commissioned him to execute a number of illus- trated books, and for a while Rouault concentrated on mak- ing prints. Recollections of the circuses of his childhood provided the material for two new books, *Cirque de l'Étoile filante* (1938) and *Divertissement* (1943), for which he cre- ated both text and illustrations. While working on these artist's books, Rouault was also taking part in the tapestry revival that occurred in France between the wars.[3] In 1932 he produced two cartoons on circus themes for the Aubusson factory: *Pierrot* and *The Wounded Clown*. In these later works, Pierrot is essentially identified with the figure of Christ: he embodies the same love and self-sacri- fice, and like Christ he is the butt of the world's mockery and incomprehension. Rouault's religious beliefs and pen- chant for solitude led him to employ the sad clown and the circus as pretexts for a meditation on the meaning of life, somehow outside the course of history. His singular vision nonetheless challenges the spectator, ceaselessly posing the question that appears in the 1948 album *Miserere*: "Who does not wear a mask?"

C.N.-R.

1 Georges Rouault, "Lettre à Édouard Schuré," in *Sur l'art et sur la vie* (Paris: Gallimard, 1971), p. 150.

2 The negotiations took four years. In 1914 Vollard took posses- sion of 770 unfinished paintings, promising the artist that he would have the rest of his life to complete them. And Rouault did indeed re- work the same subjects until 1956.

See Fabrice Hergott and Sarah Whitfield, *Georges Rouault: The Early Years, 1903-1920* (London: Royal Academy of Arts, 1993), p. 68.

3 He owed his involvement to a meeting with Marie Cuttoli, wife of the vice-president of the Senate. A major patron of the arts, she helped revive the Aubusson factory by promoting the hiring of Jean Lurçat.

23
Georges Rouault
The Wrestler (Parade) 1905

24
Georges Rouault
The Parade 1907

Walter Sickert

Munich, 1860 – Bathampton, England, 1942

Walter Richard Sickert, whose family settled in England in 1868, gave up an acting career in 1881 to study painting with Whistler from 1882 to 1885. He visited Degas* at his Paris studio in 1883, and in 1885 went with him to Dieppe. There, under the master's influence, he executed his first painting on the circus theme, *The Circus*, representing the inside of the Pinder big top. From 1887 to 1889 London music-hall audiences provided subject matter for his finest Impressionist canvases. In the summer of 1889 a new Pinder Circus show in Dieppe inspired an engraving of a young girl on a pony. Between 1898 and 1905 he pursued his interest in popular theatre during extended stays in Venice (*Venetian Stage Scene*, 1901). On a trip to Paris in 1906–1907 he turned his attention to cafés-concerts in paintings like *Gaîté Rochechouart* (1906), where a trapeze artist figures inconspicuously in the background. In 1915, while summering at the Brighton home of his friend, the painter and collector Walter Taylor, he attended nightly variety shows staged at the local beach by the Highwaymen (directed by manager Jack Sheppard, this troupe became Jack Sheppard's Brighton Entertainers in 1920). Costumed as Pierrot during the first act and in blazers and straw boaters for the second, the performers put on three or four shows a day. Back in London, Sickert worked from his beachside sketches to produce a highly colourful canvas, *Brighton Pierrots* (cat. no. 25), which offers a glimpse of an evening performance for an audience made sparse by the war. In 1920 he paid a final tribute to Degas* in *The Trapeze*, a personal version of the famous *Miss Lala at the Cirque Fernando* (cat. no. 148). That same year he made one last portrayal of the music-hall world. After 1927 he focused on the actors at Sadler's Wells in London.

M.R.

25
Walter Sickert
Brighton Pierrots 1915

26
Fortunato Depero
My Plastic Ballets 1918

Fortunato Depero

Fondo, Austria-Hungary (now Italy), 1892 – Rovereto, Italy, 1960

Born in a region of Trentino that was then still part of the Austro-Hungarian Empire, Fortunato Depero studied at the Scuola Reale Elisabettina in Rovereto, an applied arts school with a strongly interdisciplinary approach. He soon began working in a range of fields: after serving as an apprentice decorator for the 1911 Turin Exposition he returned to Rovereto, where he produced drawings and plaster sculptures of a vaguely Symbolist or Social Realist flavour, illustrations inspired by the visions of Alfred Kubin, and poems. In 1913 he published at his own expense a collection of his recent work entitled *Spezzature*. At the same time, in Rome, he met Marinetti, Boccioni, and Balla, the founders of Futurism, a movement that meshed perfectly with both his early training and his creative imagination. Quickly displaying a mastery of the rules of plastic dynamism, Depero began experimenting with the movement of forms in space. It was from one of his recent texts, "Complessi plastici," that Balla drew inspiration in co-writing with him in 1914–1915 the famous manifesto "Ricostruzione futurista del'Universo." Around this time Depero began making his "plastic complexes," small sculptures in such humble materials as cardboard and wood. His constructions of pure abstract forms, called "plastic-motor-noise complexes," were a synthesis of states of mind, sounds, visual images, and movements. Exhibited in Rome in 1916, these various innovations attracted the attention of Diaghilev, director of the Ballets Russes. In 1917, commissioned by him, Depero executed the costumes designed by Picasso* for the ballet *Parade*.

The artist's meeting in Capri with the Swiss writer and Egyptologist Gilbert Clavel would prove decisive. Under Clavel's influence Depero refined his approach to set design and formed his style – a blend of Futurism, Cubism, metaphysics, Surrealism, and the fantastic. In April 1918 he produced *Balli plastici* ("Plastic Ballets"), a musical mime piece in five acts, presented at the Teatro dei Piccoli puppet theatre in Rome by the Gorni dell'Aqua puppet company. In a ballet of "grotesque humour," extraordinary marionettes of painted wood jumped, danced, and performed on stage like mechanical actors. After this success Depero moved to Viareggio, on the coast, where he reinterpreted in painting

the huge parade that constituted the final dance of Act 5 (cat. no. 26). The painting is constructed like a theatre stage, with the numerous superimposed planes characteristic of Depero's scenography, peopled by groups of colourful, stylized characters seemingly frozen in the movements of their march. The painting offers a fairly clear picture of what the puppet ballet must have been like – an excellent example of a "plastico-theatrical reconstruction of the world" and thus entirely in the spirit of the manifesto drawn up by Balla and Depero in 1914–1915.

From then on, Depero dedicated himself to an intense pursuit of Futurism in every realm, transforming his house into the "Casa d'Arte Futuristica" (1920), creating costumes and stage sets (for New York's Roxy Theater and for the ballet *American Sketches*, both in 1929), participating in major exhibitions (Paris, 1925, Venice Biennale, 1925 and 1936, Milan Triennial, 1925 and 1934), decorating interiors (Ristorante Zucca, New York, 1928), designing posters, making illustrations for newspapers (*La Sera*, Milan) and magazines (*Dinamo*, 1934), and writing manifestos. In 1941 he created a large mosaic to be installed at the Esposizione Universale in Rome, a world's fair originally scheduled for 1942 and then cancelled because of the war (though many of its pavilions were in fact completed). Depero seized every opportunity to proclaim his revolutionary approach to space-time, and his fevered imagination produced a distinctive Surrealist vision featuring a combination of mechanical movement, multiple perspectives, and the interplay of shade and bright colour.

C.N.-R.

111

Max Beckmann

Leipzig, 1884 – New York, 1950

Max Beckmann trained at the Grossherzogliche Sächsische Kunstschule in Weimar. In 1903 he made the first of many trips to Paris, where he haunted the nightspots of Montmartre and the Cirque Medrano. In 1918–1919 he denounced the horrors of war and revolution in the lithographic portfolio *Hell*, the cover of which bears his likeness in a Harlequin collar. He went on to make frequent use of carnival, cabaret, and circus masks and props to compose enigmatic stagings in his paintings.

Beckmann inherited the Romantic notion that the artist was God-like. In *Wilhelm Meister's Apprenticeship*, Goethe defines the purpose thus assigned to creators: "Ultimately they must raise themselves above the commonplace in such a manner that the entire community of man feels ennobled in and by their works."[1] Emerging from the horrifying slaughter of the trenches, which he witnessed as a medical orderly, Beckmann briefly tried to place his faith in a social and political utopianism of this kind. Friedrich Ebert, on becoming the first president of the Weimar Republic in 1919, gave echo to Goethe's affirmation: "Here, in Weimar, we must achieve the transition from imperialism to idealism, from world power to spiritual grandeur."[2] That year saw the founding of the Weimar Bauhaus, and in the new school's original manifesto Walter Gropius embraced the young Republic's utopian dream: "Together let us wish for, conceive, and create the new construction of the future, which will embrace architecture and sculpture and painting in a single form destined to rise one day toward heaven from the hands of millions of workers, like the crystalline symbol of a new faith."[3]

When asked by the poet Kasimir Edschmid to express his conception of the artist's role in society in the *Tribune der Kunst und Zeit* in 1918, Beckmann had responded with a similarly religious and edifying vision: "Someday I want to make buildings along with my pictures. To build a tower in which humanity can shriek out its rage and despair and all its poor hopes and joys and wild yearnings. A new church."[4]

However, it was not easy for Beckmann to maintain this optimism. His painfully fresh war memories and the reality of a German society torn by revolutionary unrest were hardly conducive to angelic pursuits. The clearest indications of his enormous doubts and of the actual irony with which he viewed his social role can be found in his *Self-portrait as Clown*, painted in 1921. Here the prophet is revealed

as buffoon, the guide as martyr. Beckmann's image of himself as a clown is presented in a pose borrowed from Gothic renderings of the mocking of Christ. Gropius and Ebert's cherished dream becomes a masquerade, for reality is impervious to utopianism; the artist is condemned to be the ephemeral dissipater of his own inexorable ennui, the inoffensive titillater of his dulled conscience. By now Beckmann's view of the world, of reality itself, had come to resemble the shows he saw at carnivals, circuses, and cabarets. Here was the "veil of *maya*": the dream world infiltrating the real world, and social conventions and power politics merging with the illusions of the theatre, circus, or cinema. Clowns, actors, and performers gradually became major figures of the "Beckmann Circus" announced by the artist on the frontispiece of the portfolio *Der Jahrmarkt* (cat. nos. 27, 129, 130, 179). In 1927, when asked about "the social position of the artist," Beckmann had two different responses. His public statement was that "the artist in the contemporary sense is the conscious shaper of the transcendent idea. He is at one and the same time the shaper and the vessel. His activity is of vital significance to the state, since it is he who establishes the boundaries of a new culture."[5] But his private message at the same time was quite different: "The artist can know nothing of religion, politics, and life. He must not forget that sylphlike presence that he is, his only purpose consisting in sprinkling the world with brightly coloured pollen. He must serve the amusement and the delight of the mighty."[6]

In 1944, exiled in Amsterdam (then under Allied bombardment), Beckmann went to the circus almost every day. His diary entry for 17 August reads: "Idled at length at the Busch Circus under a radiant sun. The weather was nice and I saw loads of 'my paintings'!"[7] For him, the beasts in their cages, the clowns, and the acrobats had more presence and humanity, were more imbued with an acute sense of life's fragility, than the bombing, the battles, the din of human madness echoing in the distance.

Beckmann moved to the United States in 1947. He taught at Washington University in Saint Louis and then at the Brooklyn Museum School of Art in New York. He revisited the circus theme one last time before his death, in the bronze sculpture *Back Bend* (*The Acrobat*) (cat. no. 191).

D.O.

1 Quoted in Thomas Gaehtgens, *L'Art sans frontières* (Paris: Le Livre de Poche, 1999), p. 397.

2 Friedrich Ebert, opening speech to the National Assembly, July 1919.

3 Walter Gropius, *Programm des Staatlichen Bauhauses Weimar*, April 1919, n.p.

4 Max Beckmann, "Creative Credo" (1918), in *Max Beckmann: Self-Portrait in Words*, ed. Barbara Copeland Buenger, p. 185 (Chicago: University of Chicago Press, 1997).

5 "The Artist in the State" (1927), ibid., p. 287.

6 Beckmann, "The Social Stance of the Artist by the Black Tightrope Walker" (1927), ibid., p. 282.

7 Max Beckmann, *Écrits*, ed. Barbara Stehlé-Akhtar, trans. Philippe Dagen (Paris: École Nationale Supérieure des Beaux-Arts, 2002), p. 281.

27
Max Beckmann
The Tall Man, plate 4 of the portfolio
Der Jahrmarkt ("The Annual Fair")
1921

28
Dame Laura Knight
Charivari (or *The Grand Parade*) 1928

Dame Laura Knight

Long Eaton, England, 1877 – London, 1970

After studying briefly in France in 1889, Laura Johnson moved with her family the following year to Nottingham, where she enrolled in the local art school. It was there that she visited Wombwell's Circus at the famous Goose Fair, originally a market event that has also had a fun park from the time the first merry-go-round was installed in 1855. She married the painter Harold Knight in 1903 and settled in London in 1919. Her first circus drawings, of the Bertram Mills Olympia Circus, date to the early 1920s. Around the same time, she drew the Fossett family – one of Great Britain's oldest circus dynasties – at Agricultural Hall in Islington. In 1923–1924 Bertram Mills gave her special permission to paint his star performers during rehearsals and backstage. This direct contact with the circus resulted in the remarkable 1928 painting *Charivari* (or *The Grand Parade*) (cat. no. 28), where all of the big top attractions appear together in the same flattened space. Between 1930 and 1932 she accompanied the Carmo Circus on summer tours around England, and her sketches and memories of the performers' difficult life continued to inspire paintings, prints, and drawings into the 1950s. After recounting her experiences with the Carmo troupe in a first autobiography, *Oil Paint and Grease Paint* (1936), she wrote and illustrated a biography of the acrobat clown Joe Bert, *A Proper Circus Omie* (1962), and produced a second autobiography, *The Magic of a Line* (1965).

M.R.

Reginald Marsh

Paris, 1898 – Dorset, Vermont, 1954

In 1920, straight out of Yale University, Reginald Marsh moved to New York and began drawing for *Vanity Fair*. At the suggestion of the editor-in-chief, Frank Crowninshield, Marsh visited the Coney Island beach, sideshows, and carnival rides that would later become his subjects of choice. He illustrated vaudeville reviews in the *Daily News* from 1922 until 1925, at which time he joined the staff of the newly founded *New Yorker*. In the 1920s he also painted caricature curtains for the Greenwich Village Follies and designed sets for the Provincetown Players. After seeing the works of Old Masters on a trip to Paris in 1925, he took classes with John Sloan* and Kenneth Hayes Miller at the Art Students League. During the Depression he rambled the streets of New York, photographing and sketching working-class leisure pursuits. He also captured the milling crowds at his favourite haunts – movie houses, dance marathons, burlesque shows, and the circus – in tempera paintings and etchings executed in a fluid, dynamic style.

In *Pip and Flip* (cat. no. 29), a tightly packed, colourful crowd elbows its way past the ballyhoo at Coney Island, where two Black dancing girls undulate seductively in an attempt to entice patrons in to see the sideshow freaks advertised on the banners behind them. One banner features Pip and Flip, twin "pinheads" supposedly from Peru (actually Elvira and Jenny Snow, born in Georgia). True to form, Marsh, who liked to garb his voluptuous female figures in scanty attire, has given this "exotic" duo a come-hither allure that has little to do with the modest appearance seen in their photographs.

C.N.-R. and M.R.

29
Reginald Marsh
Pip and Flip 1932

30
Fernand Léger
*The Great Parade on a Red
Background* 1953

Fernand Léger

Argentan, France, 1881 – Gif-sur-Yvette, France, 1955

Léger developed a passion for the circus as a child in Normandy, where the arrival of travelling troupes always caused great excitement in his quiet little village. He moved to Paris in 1900, and in 1908 settled at La Ruche, the artists' colony in Montparnasse. There he met Blaise Cendrars, Apollinaire, and Max Jacob, with whom he regularly attended the Cirque Medrano on Boulevard de Rochechouart. He was called up in August 1914, and his experiences at the front profoundly affected his creative focus, which shifted to the depersonalized world of mechanization. In 1918 he explored simultaneity in circus-theme paintings that associate the dynamic routines of acrobats with the rhythmic energy of machines. A close friend of the famous clowns Paul, François, and Albert Fratellini, he made an ink drawing of them in 1920, designed Cubist costumes for them, and often invited them to his Normandy farm in Lisores during the 1930s. Living in the United States during the Second World War, he was captivated by the agility of the Ringling Bros. and Barnum & Bailey Circus acrobats twirling forty metres above the ground in Madison Square Garden. In America his work evolved toward realist figuration, as seen in the supple bodies suspended in space in *The Divers*, a series begun in Marseilles prior to his departure from France, and in *Acrobats in Grey*, another series.

Léger returned to France in December 1945.[1] The following year he began elaborating on his favourite theme for an artist's book consisting of sixty-three lithographs and a handwritten text, published in 1950 by Les Éditions Tériade.[2] The text, titled "Le Cirque," marks a break with the machine aesthetic and proclaims not only his lifelong passion for circus routines but also his profound fascination with the form and dynamism of circles. "Go to the circus. Nothing is as round as the circus. It is an enormous bowl in which circular forms unroll. Nothing stops, everything is connected, the ring dominates, commands, absorbs."[3] During the final years of his life the circus became the main subject of a vast series of drawings, gouaches, and paintings that culminated in 1954 in the huge and masterful *Great Parade*.[4] The final composition for this definitive state of the work appears in quasi-monochrome in *The Great Parade on a Red Background* (cat. no. 30).

Among the works that lead up to this apotheosis, *The Acrobat and His Partner* (cat. no. 189) is especially notable for its originality. Spinning round himself, the acrobat stands out against a multicoloured background that recalls the circus ring. His partner holds a ladder used by aerialists in death-defying routines[5] such as the one in which two acrobats balance on either end as it spins full circle. Executed without a net, this act epitomizes the inherent danger of the popular entertainment Léger so loved.

The reintroduction of human figures in his painting underscores the artist's wish for the general public to enjoy direct contact with art, as at the circus. As Peter de Francia points out, "Léger's concept of 'the spectacle of modern life' formed the very essence of his art and always remained central to his concerns. He saw it as inseparable from his belief in a 'mass audience,' first mentioned by him in 1919. His social and political commitments were rooted in the notion that a visual language suited to the twentieth century had to be created. It had to be accessible, simple, and free from aesthetic trappings."[6] Contrary to Beckmann,* whose work he admired, Léger did not see the circus as a staged drama playing out the sad fate of humanity condemned to masquerade, but as a grand, joyful spectacle, ringing with sound, colour, and unpredictable magic that never fails to charm.

C.N.-R.

1   Before leaving New York, he joined the French Communist Party.

2   Léger had originally asked Henry Miller to write a text for the book. When Miller procrastinated, Tériade opted for a text by Léger modelled on those by Matisse and Rouault. Miller published his circus piece in 1948 as *The Smile at the Foot of the Ladder*.

3   The text published by Tériade appears in Fernand Léger, *Functions of Painting*, trans. Alexandra Anderson (New York: Viking, 1973), pp. 170–177. This passage is found on p. 172.

4   The painting, which measures 300 by 400 centimetres, is now in the collection of the Solomon R. Guggenheim Museum in New York.

5   Laid flat on a trapeze, the aerialists' ladder served in performing daredevil high-flying acrobatics and balancing acts. Known in French as *l'échelle du diable* or *échelle de la mort* (the devil's ladder, or ladder of death), these spectacular routines were popularized by the Marty brothers in nineteenth-century Europe.

6   Peter de Francia, "An Introduction to Fernand Léger's Circus," in *Fernand Léger: Recent Paintings & Le Cirque* (New York: Buchholz Gallery, 1950), p. 26.

119

31
Fernand Léger
The Parade, first state 1950

III Ecce Homo

A clown is a poet in action. He *is* the story which he enacts.
It is the same story over and over – adoration, devotion, crucifixion.
A rosy crucifixion, of course.

Henry Miller

His face was bloody; his hands also, and thorns were in his scalp …

Samuel Beckett

Between the late Middle Ages and the mid-eighteenth century many pictures were created of the mocking of Christ, jeeringly decked out with reed sceptre and purple robe as he is presented by Pilate to the people. With the advent of Romanticism, these images seem to have been replaced by that of the sad clown, a sorrowful and ridiculous figure displayed from the stage of a fairground stall to the laughing and shouting crowds.

From Victor Hugo's unforgettable portrait in *L'Homme qui rit* of a clown disfigured since childhood, to Professor Unrath dressed as a pathetic buffoon in the film *The Blue Angel*, the figure of the tragic clown fascinated the modern imagination. The whiteface Pierrot was a pariah, an annoyance, a secular version of the Man of Sorrows. With the Romantics the clown eventually became a grotesque jester flanked by the instruments of his own mortification, a modern Christ, a figure whose place in the circus world lay somewhere between the monsters and the angels, and whose extreme humanness inspired both laughter and tears.

J.C.

Nadar

Paris, 1820 – Paris, 1910

After quitting medical school Gaspard Félix Tournachon turned to writing, penning short stories and entertainment reviews in the 1840s under the pseudonym Nadar. He began drawing caricatures for *La Silhouette* and *Le Charivari* in 1846, but still continued to pursue his literary ambitions. In June 1848 he wrote *Pierrot ministre*, a topical political satire in the form of a pantomime, to be played by Charles Deburau in the lead role. After the commercial failure of *Panthéon Nadar* (1854), a large series of lithographs deriding the French intelligentsia, he took up photography and joined his brother Adrien in his studio at 11 Boulevard des Capucines, where he produced portraits of well-known artists and writers. During his brief collaboration with Adrien he asked Deburau to pose for fifteen "expressive heads" designed to promote the studio (cat. nos. 32–35).

Following in the footsteps of his famous father, Jean-Baptiste Gaspard Deburau, Charles Deburau played to packed houses at the Théâtre des Funambules on Boulevard du Temple. In the first of the Tournachon brothers' portraits, as assembled in the original album, he appears as Pierrot in the photographer's role. *Pierrot the Photographer* (cat. no. 34) is a delightfully playful and clever image. It not only addresses the contemporary interest in the picturing of human expres-

sion and gesture but also makes a whimsical commentary on another passion of the day: photography. Attired in his elegant baggy white costume, his face powdered with flour, Pierrot stands beside the camera, one hand directing the viewer's (or sitter's) attention to the apparatus while the other prepares to expose the plate. With subtle wit, the picture alludes to the professional muteness shared by mimes and photographers.

A bitter quarrel ended the brothers' association in 1855, and the rights to the Deburau photographs were disputed in two much-publicized lawsuits, in 1856 and 1857. Nadar – who was operating his own studio at 113 Rue Saint-Lazare and later at 25 Boulevard des Capucines – prevailed. Sometime between 1855 and 1859 he produced a portrait photograph of the mime Paul Legrand, a fixture at Théodore de Banville's Folies-Nouvelles since its opening in 1854. He also wrote a pantomime for this theatre, *Pierrot boursier* (1856). Around 1883 the famous tragedienne Sarah Bernhardt sat for him costumed as Pierrot, the role she was then playing in Jean Richepin's *Pierrot assassin*.

M.R. and A.T.

Adrien Tournachon

Paris, 1825 – Paris, 1903

At the urging of his older brother Félix Tournachon, known as Nadar, Adrien Tournachon gave up painting in 1853 to study photography with Gustave Le Gray. With the backing of a banker friend, Félix set him up in a studio at 11 Boulevard des Capucines, which Adrien, calling himself "Nadar jeune," began operating in the summer of 1854. Félix assisted in the management in September of that year and asked the mime Charles Deburau to pose as Pierrot for a series of "expressive heads" shot by Adrien. After the job was completed, the brothers quarrelled and went their separate ways. The Pierrot series won a gold medal at the 1855 Exposition Universelle, but only Adrien received the honours. This momentary success enabled him to open a new studio under the name of Tournachon, Nadar jeune et Cie, at

17 Boulevard des Italiens, and earned him a commission for a photographic portrait of Empress Eugénie. During the same period he produced an album of medical photographs for Duchenne de Boulogne, a neurologist at the Salpêtrière hospital. In 1856–1857 he was involved in two lawsuits with Félix, who was claiming rights to the portraits of Deburau. Ordered by the court to cease using the name "Nadar jeune," he continued to live off his brother until acute depression forced him into a mental hospital, where he spent the last ten years of his life.

M.R.

32
Nadar and Adrien Tournachon
Pierrot Imploring 1854–1855

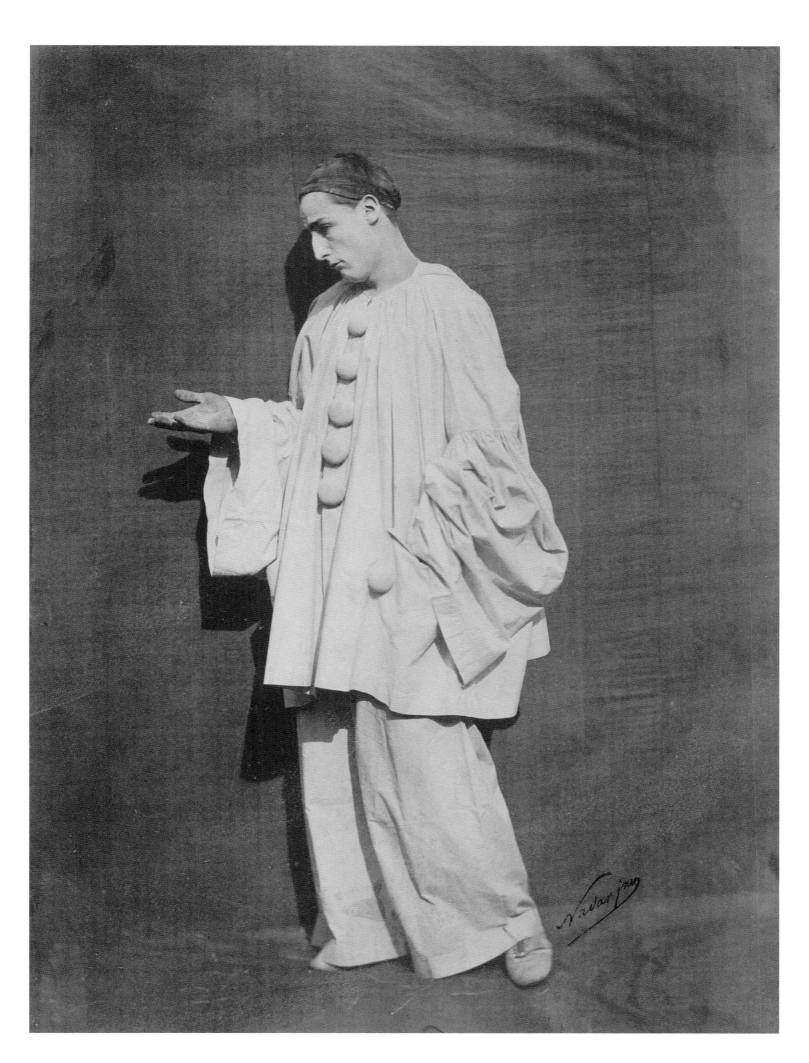

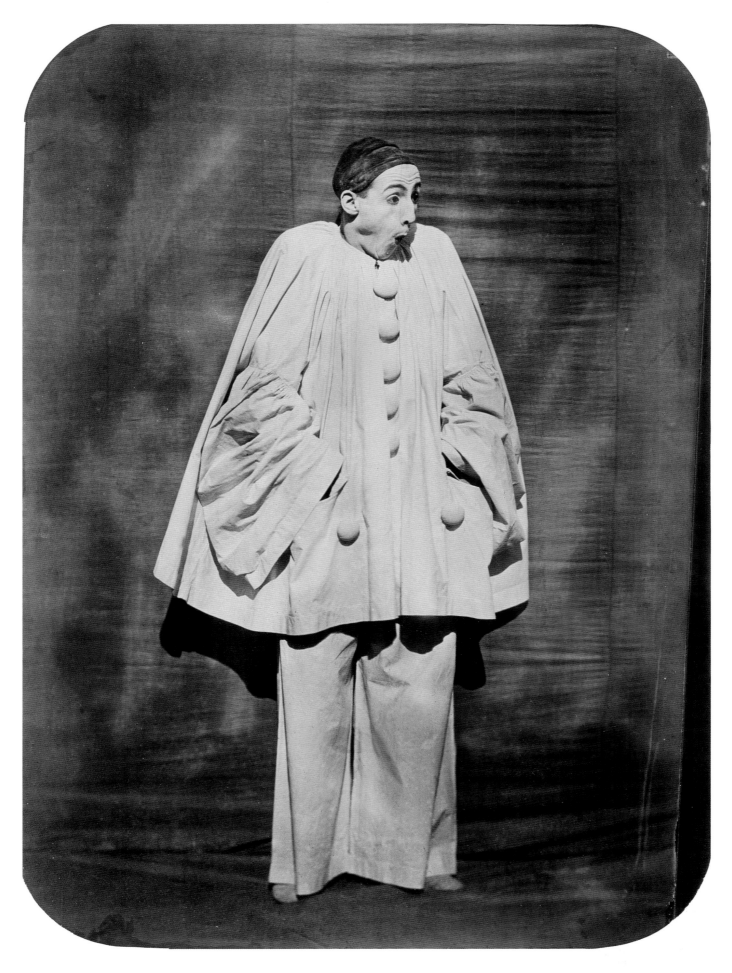

33
Nadar and Adrien Tournachon
Pierrot Surprised 1854–1855

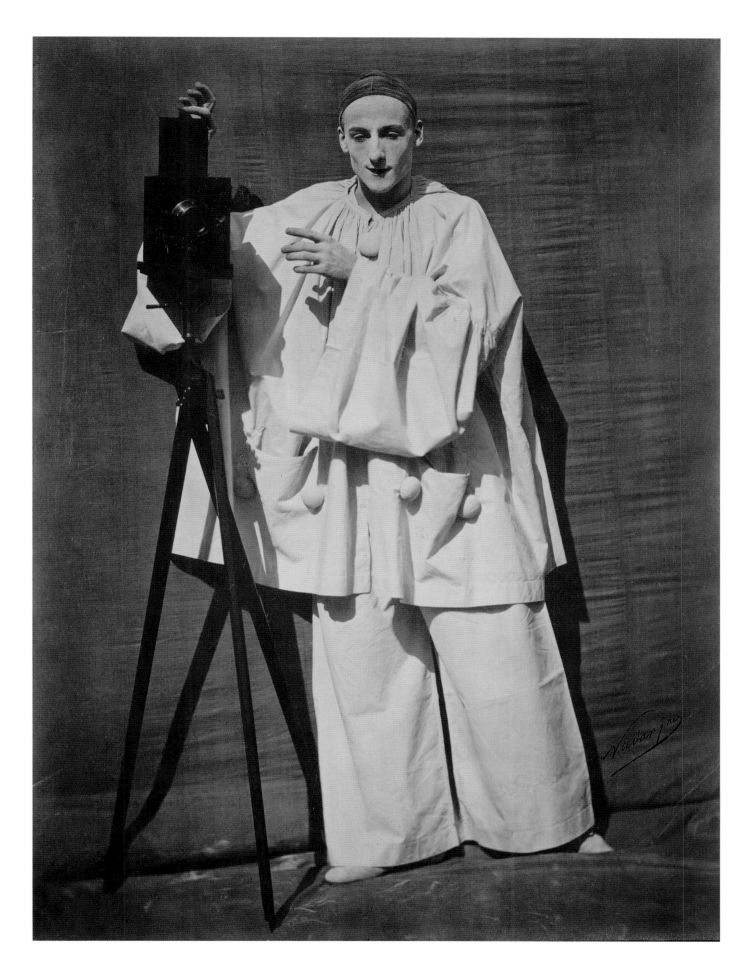

127

34
Nadar and Adrien Tournachon
Pierrot the Photographer 1854–1855

35
Nadar and Adrien Tournachon
Pierrot 1854–1855

36
Les Enfants du paradis, film directed
by **Marcel Carné**, France, 1945

37
Unidentified photographer
(American, mid-19th century)
William G. Worrell of Welch's
National Circus and Theater 1855

38
Unidentified photographer
(American, mid-19th century)
Portrait of an Acrobat, Valentine Denzer c. 1855

39
Gustave Courbet
The Black Arm 1856

Gustave Courbet

Ornans, France, 1819 – La Tour-de-Peilz (near Vevey), Switzerland, 1877

Gustave Courbet was the son of a prosperous landowning farmer from Doubs. After studying at the Collège Royal in Besançon, he arrived in Paris in 1839 with plans to enter the legal profession, but decided instead to become a painter. Although he took a few courses at the Académie Suisse, he claimed to be self-taught, preferring to copy the Old Masters at the Louvre. He submitted works to the Salon regularly, but with little success. After the fall of the July Monarchy and the establishment of the Second Republic in 1848, he attracted the attention of the critic Champfleury (1821–1889), an ardent defender of Realism, and began frequenting the Brasserie Andler with his friend Max Buchon. It was there that he was introduced to Daumier* and to the socialist philosopher Pierre-Joseph Proudhon (1809–1865), who was to become an important influence. Courbet created something of a scandal at the Salon of 1850 with his painting A Burial at Ornans, which portrays – with realism and a minimum of sentimentality – the rural population of his native region. Fiercely opposed to academicism and a declared enemy of the Second Empire, Courbet organized his own "Pavilion of Realism" at the 1855 Exposition Universelle in Paris, in order to show his huge painting-manifesto, The Painter's Studio, which had been rejected by the Salon jury. Among the figures in the left-hand part of the painting, who represent, in the artist's own words, "the people, misery, poverty … the exploited,"[1] we can spot a queue-rouge and a fairground strong man who would have been familiar participants in the parades commonly seen on Boulevard du Crime.[2]

Although Courbet was not as preoccupied with the world of fairground entertainers as his contemporary Daumier,* one of his drawings of 1856, The Black Arm (cat. no. 39), does feature another popular character, Pierrot. The work, actually a commission, signals the artist's interest in the théâtre à quatre sous,[3] as it was created for the poster of Fernand Desnoyers's pantomime in verse entitled Le Bras noir,[4] presented at the Théâtre des Folies-Nouvelles on 8 February 1856, in which the role of Pierrot was played by Paul Legrand.[5]

The plot of Le Bras noir, recounted by a narrator, unfolds as follows: Pierrot's father, the elderly Cassandre, wishes him to marry Chimène, daughter of the wealthy Polichinelle. But Pierrot loves Nini, a coquette somewhat past her prime, who arrives accompanied by the Negro Scapin, whom she intro-

duces as her brother but who is in fact her lover, as well as being an arrant rascal and a liar, and violent to boot. Scapin steals the bag in which Cassandre has hidden his fortune. Pierrot, witness to the theft, starts a fight with Scapin. Each pulls one of the other's arms off and proceeds to hit his opponent with it. When his detached arm disintegrates, Pierrot beats Scapin soundly with the latter's own arm and kills him. Pierrot, minus an arm, seeks help from the doctor Roïdamos, who uses his saliva to stick back the arm Pierrot is holding – Scapin's black arm. Now Pierrot has one white arm and one rude, violent, black one. The misdeeds Pierrot commits with his black arm land him in prison. He manages to escape, but the black arm comes off when the jailer makes a grab at it. Pierrot, again one-armed, takes to his heels, but

> … a mad black arm,
> Enormous, strong, like a terrible revenge,
> Rears up before its prey, in the middle of the road.
> Pierrot, seeing the hand, loses his feet,
> Terror turns him to stone … Thus the black arm
> Guards Pierrot – a terrible sentinel![6]

Courbet has chosen to illustrate the climax of the drama, the moment when the black arm rises up in the terrified Pierrot's path; the horror-stricken Nini has run off, abandoning at Pierrot's feet the bag that Scapin had stolen from Cassandre. In the end, Pierrot returns the money to Cassandre and marries Chimène.

The character of Pierrot had evolved in its passage from fairground sideshow to theatre. The servant of the commedia dell'arte – young, naive, honest, often victim of those craftier than he, vulnerable, quick to fall in love – had by the nineteenth century become a more substantial character who carried a certain symbolic weight. In the pantomime illustrated here, he is the embodiment of white honesty, victim and ultimately vanquisher of the forces of evil, which are invariably black. And Paul Legrand, even more than Deburau, would turn him into one of the most complex and sensitive of the traditional commedia dell'arte characters, making him actually weep on stage.[7] The character was to be taken a step further still in Pierrot lunaire by the Belgian author Albert Giraud, where he became a fusion of love, reverie, and cruelty.

C.N.-R.

1   Gustave Courbet, in a letter written to Champfleury in the fall of 1854, reproduced in Gustave Courbet, 1819–1877 (Paris: Réunion des Musées Nationaux, 1977), p. 246. (This excerpt taken from Letters of Gustave Courbet, trans. Petra ten-Doesschate Chu [Chicago: University of Chicago Press, 1992], p. 131.) See also Hélène Toussaint's excellent analysis of The Painter's Studio, in Gustave Courbet, 1819–1877, p. 247ff.

2   This was the nickname given to Boulevard du Temple. According to Toussaint (ibid., p. 248), the presence of a queue-rouge (the name of a type of clown who wore a red

wig with a tail of hair) and a fairground strong man is proof of the artist's sympathy for travelling entertainers.

3   In 1846 Champfleury had become the first author to compose and sign the scenario of a pantomime, Pierrot valet de la mort. This piece was followed in 1847 by Pierrot pendu, presented at the Théâtre des Funambules. See Louisa E. Jones, Sad Clowns and Pale Pierrots (Lexington: French Forum, 1984), pp. 63–64 and 100–118. It was Champfleury, moreover, who retained this drawing by Courbet in his collection.

4   A woodcut made after Courbet's drawing served as the frontispiece for the thirty-six-page brochure of Le Bras noir (Paris: Librairie Théâtrale, 1856). Desnoyers (1828–1869), a regular at the Brasserie Andler, was a member of Murger's circle and also knew Courbet and Champfleury. An admirer of Courbet's, he was the author of a study on Realism that appeared in the 9 December 1855 issue of L'Artiste. He also wrote a book on the Salon des Refusés (1863), in which he advocated the abolition of the jury system. See La Promenade du critique influent: Anthologie de la critique d'art en France, 1850–1900 (Paris: Hazan, 1990), p. 128.

5   Since 1825, the mime Jean-Baptiste Gaspard Deburau had put Pierrot in the spotlight with his brilliant interpretation of the role at the Théâtre des Funambules, on Boulevard du Temple. After his death in 1846, he was succeeded by his son Charles. But the younger Deburau had a rival, Paul Legrand, who began competing with him in 1854, playing the role at the Théâtre des Folies-Nouvelles, also on Boulevard du Temple.

6   Desnoyers, Le Bras noir, p. 34.

7   Tristan Rémy, Jean-Baptiste Deburau (Paris: L'Arche, 1954), pp. 176–177.

133

40
Honoré Daumier
Crispin and Scapin c. 1863–1865

41
James Ensor
The Strange Masks 1892

Gustave Doré
Strasbourg, 1832 – Paris, 1883

In 1847–1848 the precociously talented Gustave Doré, whose father had already signed a three-year contract on his behalf, published his first caricatures in Charles Philipon's *Journal pour Rire*. Ambitious, and fully aware of the hierarchy of genres, he aspired to be a painter. In 1848 he began attending the studio of the highly sought-after painter Ary Scheffer, and in 1850 presented his first landscapes at the Salon. He was both prolific and popular. During the 1850s and 1860s he illustrated the great masters of European literature – Rabelais, Dante, Shakespeare, Cervantes, La Fontaine – in a fluid, imaginative, and Romantically inspired style. Yet despite his success as an illustrator, his regular contributions to the Salon as a painter failed to impress. Around 1854–1855 he executed a series of twelve large canvases under the title *Paris tel qu'il est*, using a powerfully Social Realist approach. This monumental ensemble (now lost) included a painting known through a lithograph made at the time by E. Vernier, which appeared in 1859 in Philipon's monthly *Le Musée Français-Anglais*. Called *A Family of Acrobats*, it depicts four itinerant entertainers whose features betray their gypsy origins.

During his many travels Doré made sketches of human "types," which he later used as source material. Like certain writers, he was attracted to *saltimbanques*, and undoubtedly also to the acrobatic part of their show. His first biographer, the American journalist Blanche Roosevelt, reported that even as a child he was drawn to gymnastics, which he practiced all his life, and that he often socialized with street acrobats.[1] Indeed, it was in the guise of a gymnast that André Gill depicted him in a caricature portrait that appeared in *Le Charivari* in 1864 (fig. 1). When Doré explored the theme in his large 1874 painting entitled *The Performers* (cat. no. 92), also known as *The Injured Child*, he imbued it with a highly personal significance. Philippe Kaenel has commented

perceptively: "To better understand these two works, one would need to examine the iconography of childhood in Doré's work, his intense relationship with his mother, and his sense of destiny. During the 1870s, when his disappointments as a painter obliged him to turn to other media, such as etching, watercolour, and sculpture, the feeling of failure, the existential anxieties of advancing age, and the death impulse threatened to get the better of him ... In *The Performers* the child prodigy, the worldly acrobat feels somehow *injured*, with no real consolation other than his mother's profound conviction that he is a genius."[2]

The painting may seem anecdotal, the young acrobat full of pathos. But seeing it within the context of Doré's late career helps us grasp its hidden dimension. Known as an "Orleanist" sympathizer (a supporter of King Louis-Philippe, deposed in 1848), he had by 1859 become the official illustrator of the Second Empire and its foreign policy. His status in high society was crowned by an invitation to spend ten days at the Château de Compiègne in 1864. In 1870–1871, during the time of the Paris Commune, Doré and his mother were forced to take refuge at Versailles. Although he enjoyed a degree of success in London in the 1870s, the official art world under the Third Republic continued to denigrate his painting, leaving him with a profound sense of failure. The child acrobat of 1874 probably reflects his own perception of his career as painter. But the choice to represent a circus rehearsal (a thoroughly modern theme, given the huge popularity of the Cirque Fernando, open since August 1873 in Montmartre and attended regularly by Stevens, Manet, Gill, Bonnat, and Degas*[3]) may have been a deliberate strategy on Doré's part, designed to appeal to that year's critics.

C.N.-R.

---

1   Blanche Roosevelt, *Life and Reminiscences of Gustave Doré* (New York: Cassel & Co., 1885).

2   Philippe Kaenel, *Le Métier d'illustrateur, 1830–1880: Rodolphe Töpffer, J.J. Grandville, Gustave Doré* (Paris: Messene, 1996), p. 279.

Kaenel also mentions that "Doré's mother was in the habit of dressing in an exotic, bohemian style." It is worth noting that 1874 was the year in which she became gravely ill. See

the unpublished letter from Doré to Messieurs Fairless and Beeforth, quoted by Samuel Clapp in *Gustave Doré, 1832–1883* (Strasbourg: Musée d'Art Moderne, 1983), pp. 29–30.

3   J. Valter, "Le Cirque Fernando," *Paris-Journal*, 13 March 1874.

137

42
Gustave Doré
Pierrot Grimacing

Figure 1
André Gill, *Gustave Doré*, 1864,
from *Le Charivari*

43
Albert Londe
Portraits of Clowns 1887

Albert Londe

La Ciotat, France 1858 – Rueil, France, 1917

Admitted to the Société Française de Photographie in 1879, Albert Londe joined the clinical photography laboratory of La Salpêtrière hospital in Paris in 1882 as a chemical mixer and soon became the laboratory's director. Using a mechanical shutter of his own invention, he explored the possibilities of gelatin-silver bromide, a dry-plate process that requires exposure of just a fraction of a second. The high-speed shutter, designed to deconstruct bodily movement in successive photographs, allowed him to document Dr. Charcot's work with hysterical patients. In 1887 he founded the Société d'Excursions des Amateurs Photographes. As part of his research into capturing the body in motion, he photographed clowns and acrobats at the Hippodrome de l'Alma (cat. nos. 43, 162–163). In 1893 he demonstrated the capabilities of his new twelve-lens photochronograph at a public showing at La Salpêtrière. The discovery of X-rays in 1895 prompted him to open the first hospital radiology laboratory in Paris.

M.R.

44
Georges Rouault
Clown with a Drum c. 1906–1907

45
Georges Rouault
Head of a Tragic Clown 1904

46
Georges Rouault
Parade (detail), Acrobat c. 1907–1910

Kees Van Dongen

Delfshaven, Netherlands, 1877 – Monte Carlo, 1968

After having attended art school in Rotterdam from 1894 to 1896, Kees Cornelis Theodorus Maria Van Dongen went to Paris in 1897, where he survived by working as a wrestler and carnival roustabout. He settled permanently in Paris in 1899, around which time he produced a first carnival-themed drawing, *Raoul's Debut*, influenced by the circus illustrations of Henri-Gabriel Ibels then appearing in *L'Écho de Paris* and *Gil Blas Illustré*. But it was a stint as a straight man with the famous troupe Chez Marseille that brought the circus squarely into his work. He did ink drawings and watercolours of carnival parades in 1904, and in 1905 he painted the acrobats, clowns, and bareback riders of the Cirque Medrano, which he often attended with Picasso.* That same year he exhibited at the Salon des Indépendants, with two canvases of the steam-powered merry-go-rounds seen at the Montmartre and Neuilly fairs, and took part in the Salon d'Automne, which saw the coining of the term "Fauvism." Settling into a studio at the Bateau-Lavoir in 1906, he produced several circus-themed works, among them the famous *Old Clown*, posed as Watteau's* *Gilles*, and *The Clown Who Believes Himself to Be President of the Republic* (cat. no. 47). In 1908 he moved to rooms across from the Folies Bergère and produced new Fauvist paintings of circus and cabaret performers. His postwar popularity as a society painter came as a result of his liaisons with the Marquise Casati, in 1913, and Jasmy Jacob, in 1916.

M.R.

47
Kees Van Dongen
The Clown Who Believes Himself to Be President of the Republic
c. 1905–1907

Pablo Picasso

Málaga, Spain, 1881 – Mougins, France, 1973

After moving with his family to the Galician city of La Coruña in 1891, the young Pablo Ruiz Picasso took a keen interest in the theatre, as seen in his backstage drawing of the Teatro Principal done in 1894. During his studies from 1895 to 1897 in Barcelona at La Lonja, the school of fine arts, an affair with the stunt rider Rosita del Oro sparked his lifelong passion for the circus. This dual attraction to show business coincided with his penchant for masquerade, which first materialized in the 1897 *Self-portrait in a Wig* (cat. no. 66) and, much later, would see him get himself up as a clown to amuse visitors.

Returning to Barcelona in 1899 after just a few months at the Academy in Madrid, he became a familiar figure at the Els Quatre Gats café, a favourite haunt of bohemian artists and writers. Late that year, his *Pierrot Celebrating the New Year* won a prize in a carnival handbill competition organized by the avant-garde magazine *Pèl i Ploma*. In 1900 he began dividing his time between Barcelona and Paris. His work now would reveal the strong influence of Steinlen, Toulouse-Lautrec,* and Degas,* in the form of cabaret and circus motifs: *The Blue Dancer* and *Booth at the Fair* from 1900, and *La Nana* (cat. no. 124) and *Clown with a Monkey* from 1901.

After the suicide of his friend Casagemas in 1901, his work reflected a more pessimistic vision, evident in two canvases from that year that mark the beginning of his identification with the Harlequin figure: *Harlequin* and *The Two Saltimbanques*. These were followed by the artist's Blue Period, during which Harlequin and Pierrot gave way to images of the dispossessed and their wretched life in cabarets and bordellos. Living at the Bateau-Lavoir from 1904, Picasso hobnobbed with carnies on hand for the Montmartre fair and went to the Cirque Medrano several times a week to applaud clowns like Ilès, Antonet, Alex, Rico, and Grock and visit with them after the show.

This close contact with the circus profoundly affected his painting, which now focused on the performers' private lives, in a palette dominated by tones of rose (cat. nos. 164 and 210). Although he felt that the itinerant *saltimbanques* best reflected his condition as an artist, he chose Harlequin to represent him in a series of gouaches evoking family life (cat. no. 95), a discreet allusion to the child he never had with his mistress Madeleine. Around the same time, he cast himself as Harlequin in *At the Lapin Agile* (1905), seated at a bistro table with the bewitching Germaine Florentin (née Gargallo) and with Frédé, the owner, playing the guitar.

In 1907 Picasso and Braque set off the Cubist revolution, and Harlequin became a mere motif, good for deconstructing form into geometric facets. It was not until 1915, in the Cubist canvas *Harlequin*, that this figure again took on personal meaning, its cruel expression attesting to the painter's despair during the illness that took the life of his companion Eva that year. In 1917 Picasso returned to the circus with the ballet *Parade* (cat. nos. 204, 208, 209, 211). Working with Cocteau, Diaghilev, and Massine, he designed the sets and costumes in Rome from February to April, and then returned to Paris to complete the stage curtain. While he was in Italy he attended *commedia dell'arte* performances with Diaghilev, Stravinsky, and Massine in Naples, and this experience led to a new show for the Ballets Russes, *Pulcinella*, for which Picasso created the sets and costumes in 1919. His impressions of Italy prompted a return to an "Ingresque" realism in classical-style paintings (*Pierrot*, cat. no. 50) and portraits of children (*Paul as Harlequin*, cat. no. 201). Still, he retained some of his Cubist techniques for major works such as *Three Musicians* (1921), in which he again appears as Harlequin, this time with his friends Apollinaire and Max Jacob, as Pierrot and a monk.

In 1930 Picasso began taking his son Paulo to the Cirque Medrano, where the rubber man's contortions inspired a series of canvases on the Acrobat theme. By now more drawn by circus acts than by carnival folk, he celebrated the tightrope walker's high-wire daring in a series of oils entitled *Circus* (1933). Years later, in 1954, the circus resurfaced in lithographs portraying tumblers, dancers, and masked actors. After settling in Mougins in 1961, he revisited the characters of his early works one last time, between 1970 and 1972, in some of the etchings of *Suite 156*, where acrobats and naked stunt riders perform for actors and audience, and in paintings and drawings of Harlequin and Pierrot figures.

M.R.

48
Pablo Picasso
Head of a Jester 1905

49
Vasily Shukhayev and
Aleksandr Yakovlev
Self-portraits (Harlequin
and Pierrot) 1914

50
Pablo Picasso
Pierrot 1918

51
José Gutiérrez Solana
The Clowns 1920

José Gutiérrez Solana

Madrid, 1886 – Madrid, 1945

Born in the Salamanca district of Madrid on Carnival Sunday, José Gutiérrez Solana was obsessed from the outset with the grotesque, multicoloured masks that soon became a key subject of his painting. Born into a family of wealthy aristocrats, he drew carnivalesque characters and funerals even as a child. After being tutored by José Díez Palma, a teacher at the Escuela de Artes y Oficios Artísticos in Madrid, he studied at the Real Academia de Bellas Artes de San Fernando from 1900 to 1904. Until moving to Santander, in 1909, he spent time with the Generación del 98 group at the Café de Levante. This literary movement opened his eyes to the decadent, morally "black" Spain to which he refers in his first book, *Madrid, escenas y costumbres* (1913), and in depictions of life in the city's slums. Fiestas, fairs, merry-go-rounds, wax figures, and clowns appear in his paintings from the 1920s and 1930s (cat. no. 51), which meld the grotesque and the macabre in pure Spanish Baroque style.

M.R.

149

Paul Klee

Münchenbuchsee (near Bern), 1879 – Muralto-Locarno, 1940

Paul Klee's studies in Munich from 1898 to 1901 were followed by a six-month trip to Italy. Between 1903 and 1905 he produced his first truly personal works – a series of etchings entitled *Inventions*, whose satirical mood was inspired by the plays of Aristophanes. Three of these prints, which picture a *Comedian*, reveal Klee's interest in masks and grimaces, whose power to convey the tragicomic aspects of the "human comedy" he would exploit throughout his career. In May 1906 the artist was impressed by the tightrope act that was part of a show presented in Bern by the famous Knie family.[1] He had his first contact with Cubism in 1912, during a short stay in Paris, where he also spent an evening at the Cirque Medrano.[2] Small comical figures began making their appearance that year in his ink drawings. Inspired by the circus, but also by puppet theatre and the characters of the *commedia dell'arte*, he used them to caricature the "dramas" of everyday life. In 1913 he attended a performance in Munich of Schoenberg's* lyrical melodrama *Pierrot lunaire*, whose revolutionary originality thrilled him and confirmed his decision to align himself with the avant-garde.[3]

Klee made frequent reference to clowns, jugglers, and acrobats during the First World War years as a means of suggesting the modern artist's vulnerability and marginality in an unsettled art market. Given the precariousness of the times, the act put on for an audience by a circus performer symbolized perfectly the situation of the artist who was obliged to "take risks" in order to attract attention and carve out a niche for himself in a market that placed a premium on innovation. In March 1917, while he was on active duty in Gersthofen, near Augsburg, the Berlin magazine *Der Sturm* featured Klee's 1914 drawing *Acrobats* (cat. no. 167) on its cover. The aim of the publication's editor, Herwarth Walden, was to disseminate in a pacifist context an idea held widely in the Expressionist milieu during the war: the artist's existence, symbolized in this work by the free fall of the trapeze artists, is a precarious one.

Invited to teach at the Bauhaus in Weimar in 1920, Klee turned three years later to the metaphorical image of the tightrope walker balancing on his wire (cat. no. 168). It was a motif that had already been exploited before the war by Kirchner and Heckel, the founders of Die Brücke (1905), who used it as the transposition of a Nietszchean idea that appears in a text of crucial importance to the Expressionist generation – *Thus Spoke Zarathustra*.[4] As Janice McCullagh has noted: "The image was an especially potent one because it functioned directly as the model of an artist who physically exemplified the ideal of the artist's ultimate heroic commitment."[5]

Seen within the context of the extremely politicized debates taking place at the Weimar Bauhaus in 1923,[6] the metaphor of the tightrope walker takes on an added significance. A number of scholars have noted the presence of a highly schematicized face in the lower part of the image.[7] Above the head of this thinker, and very clearly joined to it, a trestle-like scaffold supports the wire on which the tightrope walker is balanced and which he has reached by means of the ladder to the left of the structure. Klee executed this lithograph in 1923 for a portfolio entitled *Kunst der Gegenwart* ("Contemporary Art"). He had already explained in his lectures the metaphor's potential: "The tightrope walker with his pole as a symbol of the 'balance of forces.' He holds the force of gravity in balance (weight and counterweight). He is a pair of scales."[8] Here Klee was employing two images to convey the delicate position in which Gropius found himself that year, obliged as he was to achieve a balance between the original vision and educational goals of the Bauhaus and the political pressures that were forcing him to integrate art with technology and industry so as to ensure the institution's financial viability.[9]

The figure of the clown recurred in Klee's work during his Dessau period (cat. no. 52) and up until his death in 1940. It can be seen in his large ink drawings, and there is a *Harlequin* among the large gouaches that he made at the very end of his career.

C.N.-R.

1 *The Diaries of Paul Klee, 1898-1918*, ed. Felix Klee (Berkeley: University of California Press, 1964), p. 205.

2 Ibid., p. 269.

3 Ibid., p. 276. After having noted his admiration for the work, Klee added these significant words: "Platze du Spiess, ich glaube Dein Stündlein schlägt!" ("Burst, you Philistine, methinks your hour has struck!").

4 See the excerpt quoted below, p. 281.

5 Janice McCullagh, "The Tightrope Walker: An Expressionist Image," *The Art Bulletin* 66, no. 4 (December 1984), p. 644.

6 See Chapter 10 in Élodie Vitale, *Le Bauhaus de Weimar, 1919-1925* (Brussels: Pierre Mardaga, 1989).

7 Comparisons have also been drawn between this work and images created in 1922 by Oskar Schlemmer for the second Bauhaus logo and by H. Bayer for the poster of the 1923 summer exhibition. See Georg Graf von Matuschka, *Annäherungen an Paul Klee, 20 Bildinterpretationen* (Nuremberg: Kunstpädagogisches Zentrum im Germanischen Nationalmuseum, 1987), pp. 35–45, and Wolfgang Kersten, *Paul Klee Übermut, Allegorie der künstlerischen Existenz* (Frankfurt am Main: Fischer, 1990), p. 24ff.

8 *Paul Klee: The Thinking Eye – The Notebooks of Paul Klee*, ed. Jürg Spiller (New York: George Wittenborn Inc., 1964), p. 197.

9 The Bauhaus gained international attention as a result of the exhibition held in Weimar in the summer of 1923. But the catastrophic post-war economy and a conservative return to power gave rise to new hostilities. After its closure on 1 April 1925, the Bauhaus was forced to move to Dessau, and Klee followed.

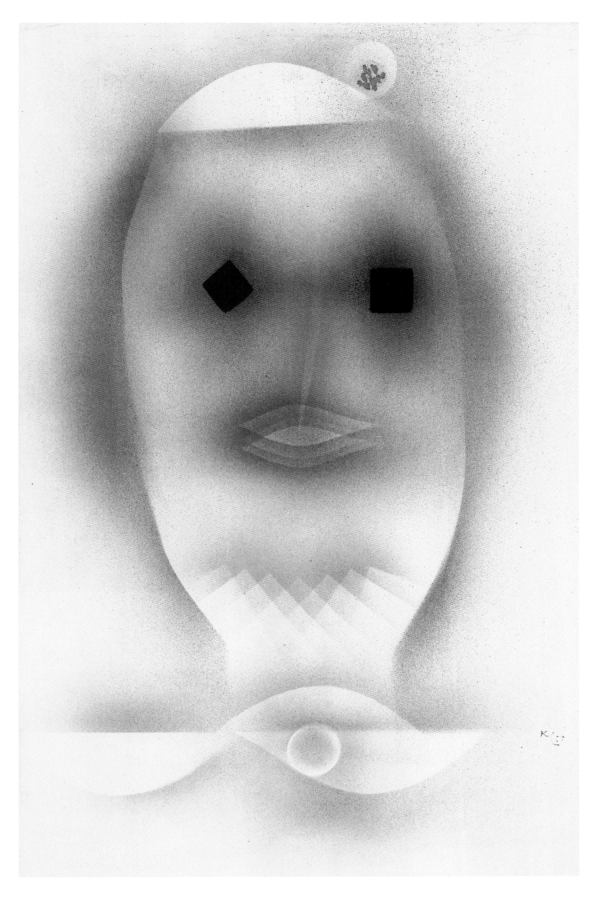

52
Paul Klee
Wintery Mask 1925

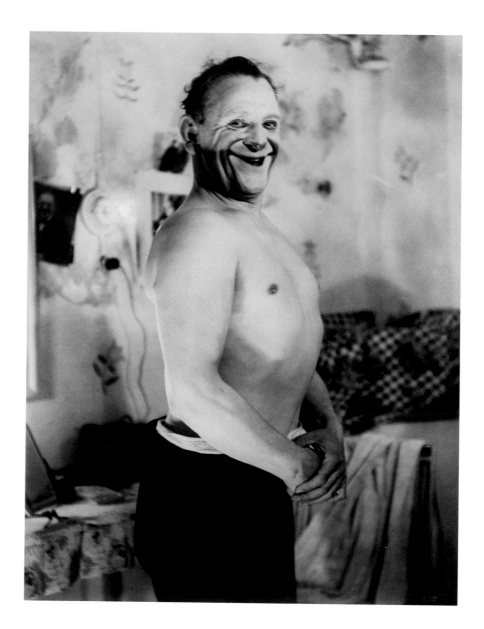

53
Umbo
Grock 18 1929

Umbo

Düsseldorf, 1902 – Hannover, 1980

Otto Umbehr studied at the Weimar Bauhaus from October 1921 to December 1922, after which he moved to Berlin and worked at assorted jobs, including movie poster painter, assistant cameraman, and clown. By 1926 he was making his first photo-collages, using found photographic images, as in *Street Scene*, which represents acrobats in the middle of a crowded street bordered on both sides by large buildings. He taught himself portrait photography that same year, and opened a studio with Paul Citroën, a former Bauhaus classmate. Two years later he founded the Dephot photo agency with Simon Guttmann, and in 1929, under the pseudonym Umbo, he sold a series of shots of Adrien Wettach metamorphosing himself into the famous clown Grock (cat. nos. 53 and 54). This was his first success as a photojournalist.

He was enchanted by trapeze and acrobat routines and captured them in several photo-essays that appeared in the *München Illustrierte Presse* in 1930 and the *Berliner Illustrirte Zeitung* in 1932 (cat. no. 187). After the Dephot agency was shut down by the Nazis in 1933, he worked freelance, mainly for the Ullstein publishing house, and continued to specialize in performing arts subjects until being called up for military service in 1943. In subsequent decades he worked as a freelance press photographer for various magazines and also taught photography at a number of institutions in Germany.

M.R.

54
Umbo
Grock 1929

152

154

55
George Luks
A Clown 1929

George Luks

Williamsport, Pennsylvania, 1867 – New York, 1933

After a short stint at the Pennsylvania Academy of the Fine Arts in Philadelphia, George Benjamin Luks pursued intermittent studies in Düsseldorf, Munich, Paris, and London between 1885 and 1894. Returning to the United States, he hired on as an artist-reporter for the *Philadelphia Press*, where he met Robert Henri, John Sloan,* and Everett Shinn.* In 1896 he moved to New York and obtained work as a cartoonist for the *New York World*, where "The Animals Start a Circus and Make the Men Perform" appeared that year. From 1897 on, he devoted himself almost exclusively to painting in the rough, realistic style of his mentor Robert Henri. Luks exhibited as a member of The Eight in 1908 and was represented in the 1913 Armory Show. He taught at the Art Students League from 1920 to 1924 and then opened his own school. A visit to a fair in Hadlyme, Connecticut, in the late 1920s rekindled his interest in the flamboyant world of the circus, which he expressed in two paintings, *The Circus Tent* and *A Clown* (cat. no. 55).

M.R.

56
Walt Kuhn
The Blue Clown 1931

Walt Kuhn

Brooklyn, 1877 – New York, 1949

In 1897, while working for a sports shop that also rented out theatrical costumes, Walt Kuhn began forming friendships with the actors he met backstage during deliveries. From 1901 to 1903 he attended the Colarossi Academy in Paris and the Königliche Akademie der Künste in Munich. He then returned to New York, where he produced variety acts at the Kit Kat Club and the Penguin Club. He was back in Europe as an organizer of the Armory Show between 1910 and 1913. Show business, including several musical revues, overshadowed his painting from 1920 until 1925, when he took up his brush again. In 1929 he began a series of portraits – clowns, acrobats, and showgirls – typical of the vigorous realism of his mature period (*The Blue Clown*, cat. no. 56). During the 1930s and 1940s he was a familiar figure at

Ringling Brothers performances in New York (cat. no. 135). He obtained a press pass in 1941 and would go backstage every night to hobnob with the clowns and acrobats, who provided material for new paintings. After designing clown entrées (never used) for the troupe, he spent three months with them in Florida in 1948, in their Sarasota winter quarters. Returning home in April, he sold a short article titled "Sketches in Sawdust," together with nine circus drawings, to *Collier's* magazine.

M.R.

Weegee
The Clown Jimmy Armstrong 1943

Weegee

Zloczow, Austria-Hungary (now Poland), 1899 – New York, 1968

Having immigrated to the United States with his family in 1910, Arthur (born Usher) H. Fellig, with no formal training in photography, found work as a darkroom assistant for the *New York Times* and the Wide World Photos syndicate in 1921, then joined Acme News Pictures in 1924. He began as a freelance press photographer in 1935 and soon made a name for himself with lurid, late-night shots of sensational events. Around 1938 he dubbed himself "Weegee," by some accounts a reference to his seemingly telepathic ability – as if using a Ouija board – to locate crimes and disasters and then be the first on the scene. Given carte blanche by the start-up paper *PM Daily* in 1940, he expanded his coverage of New York by night to include scenes of popular entertainment that he shot with an infrared flash in darkened

venues: circus acts at Madison Square Garden, vaudeville at Sammy's Bowery Follies, movie house audiences. Attracted to circus stars, he photographed the clown Jimmy Armstrong and the "human cannonball" Victoria Zacchini in 1943 (cat. nos. 57 and 113) and Emmett Kelly, the famous Auguste, in 1945. He worked in Hollywood as a technical consultant and bit actor from 1947 to 1952. During the 1960s he produced optically distorted photographs, some of circus subjects, using everything from mirrors to kaleidoscopes.

M.R.

Izis

Marijampole, Lithuania, 1911 – Paris, 1980

Israel Bidermanas began training as a photographer's apprentice in Marijampole in 1924. Arriving in Paris in 1931, he first did touch-up work at the Arnal studio, then operated a commercial studio. During the Nazi occupation he went into hiding near Limoges. On his return to Paris in 1945 he was introduced to Brassaï and Surrealist photography. Izis (as he began to sign his work) was attracted to even the most humble carnivals and circuses. He photographed a troupe of touring performers in the Old Port of Marseilles in 1949 and the August Holiday fair in London in 1952. But it was the tumbling clowns at the Foire du Trône on Place de la Nation in Paris and in public squares in Bordeaux and Lagny that most delighted him (cat. nos. 132 and 140). During the 1950s he captured them repeatedly in compassionate images that reveal the fatigue and weariness underlying the ostensible joy of the circus parade. A devotee of the Swiss clown Grock, he followed the big top to Cannes and Toulon. His photographs of fairs, and of the Fanni, Napoléon Rancy, Medrano, and Amar circuses,

as well as the Cirque d'Hiver in Paris, were published in 1965 in a book entitled *Le Cirque d'Izis*, with an introduction by the poet Jacques Prévert and four original drawings by Marc Chagall,* his friend since 1954.

Included in this survey of Izis's circus work done between 1949 and 1962 are two sequences of Grock behind the scenes. The poignant sequence entitled *Grock*, composed of three photographs shot in Toulon in 1954 (cat. nos. 58–60), dramatically captures the journey of the clown from the point at which he leaves his dressing-room trailer, suitcase in hand, to the moment before he enters the ring, his back now turned to the photographer, the curtain opened wide to reveal a spotlight shining on him. Dubbed "Monsieur Loyal" by Prévert, Grock was deeply committed to the circus and came out of retirement at the age of seventy-five to return to the life that he loved. These three images bear a hint of melancholy as they describe the passage from backstage to centre stage. While it was undoubtedly Izis's intention to strip away some of the magic and illusion of the circus, he was probably also responding to the personality of Grock himself, who was seen by Prévert as a rather philosophical figure, "a musician and also a metaphysician."

M.R. and A.T.

58
Izis
Grock, Toulon 1954

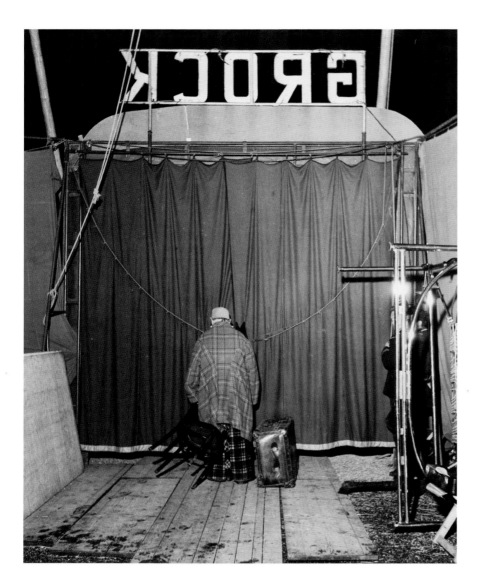

59
Izis
Grock, Toulon 1954

60
Izis
Grock, Toulon 1954

61
He Who Gets Slapped, film
directed by **Victor Seastrom**
(Victor Sjöström), United States
1924

62
Leon Levinstein
Circus c. 1965

Leon Levinstein

Buckhannon, Virginia, 1910 – New York, 1988

In 1946 Leon Levinstein moved to New York and found work as a graphic artist at the Colby Advertising Agency. He began taking photographs in his free time in 1948 and enrolled in classes with Alexey Brodovitch and Sid Grossman. In 1953 he left advertising to concentrate exclusively on photography. Until 1968 he spent much of his time scouring various neighbourhoods in and around New York – the Lower East Side, Times Square, Coney Island – in search of urban subjects that he depicted in a powerful, direct style. Around 1965 his attraction to the margins of society led him to examine the circus, and especially the solitude of its performers, which may have mirrored his own (cat. nos. 62 and 103). Although he was featured in a solo exhibition in 1956, he was largely unknown to critics and the public at the time of his death in 1988.

M.R.

Pierrick Sorin
Nantes, born 1960

After studies at the École des Beaux-Arts in Nantes from 1983 to 1988, Pierrick Sorin made his first "autofilmages," self-filmed moments from his real or invented private life. In 1989 he abandoned Super 8 in favour of video. An avowed Chaplin fan, he began producing short slapstick pieces in which he plays simpletons who are the hapless victims of either some ridiculous assault or their own bumbling: one is showered with an avalanche of books while speaking to the camera (*J'ai même gardé mes chaussons pour aller à la boulangerie*, 1993), another spills a bowl of cocoa on an important document (*L'Incident du bol renversé*, 1993), and yet another is set upon by pie-throwing attackers (*La Bataille des tartes*, cat. no. 63). Although the buffoonery of these clumsy characters at first draws laughter, it often leaves viewers with an uneasy feeling. In 1995 Sorin turned to "little virtual shows," video installations in which filmed images are projected onto actual settings. Acting for others, he played a lead role in Sophie Comtet's 1998 film *Les Bruits de la ville* and appeared on stage in Robert Lepage's "technological cabaret" *Zulu Time* in 1999. That same year he incarnated a magician in the video installation *Sorino le magicien* and created *Titre variable*, his less than kind interpretation of seven members of a family. Shrunk to Lilliputian size, these farcical characters appear as virtual images superposed on a backwards-spinning turntable. As they vainly attempt to move forwards, arms flailing, despair gradually paints their faces.

M.R.

163

63
Pierrick Sorin
La Bataille des tartes 1994

Paul McCarthy

Salt Lake City, Utah, born 1945

Schooled in painting, photography, and filmmaking (University of Utah, 1966–1968; B.F.A., San Francisco Art Institute, 1969; M.F.A., University of Southern California, 1973), Paul McCarthy has made a career of performance art. Early on, he played the clown in performance videos evoking a castration complex and other sexual disorders. In *Experimental Dancer – Rumpus Room* (1975) he dances, face hidden by a clown mask, penis clenched between his thighs. *Class Fool* (1976), also a video, shows him masked, writhing among audience chairs, a ketchup-smeared doll between his legs, chanting "penis as daddy's baby." In 1987 he began producing his performance/installations in television studios. *Bossy Burger* (1991) was shot on the discarded set of an old sitcom, *Family Affair*, with McCarthy, in full chef's regalia, clown shoes, and a *Mad* magazine Alfred E. Neuman mask, hosting a sordid cooking show. He went on to update the violent urges and unconscious conflicts veiled by the cloying narratives of television sitcoms and Disney cartoons in installations like *Heidi* (in collaboration with Mike Kelley, 1992) and *Pinocchio* (1994). He appeared again as a clown in the 1995 video installation *Painter* (cat. no. 64), where the viewer is invited into a messy artist's studio to observe the shooting of a video in it; McCarthy, sporting a rubber nose, plays a manic, third-rate painter absorbed in creating his Abstract Expressionist paintings and clashing with his dealer and collectors.

M.R.

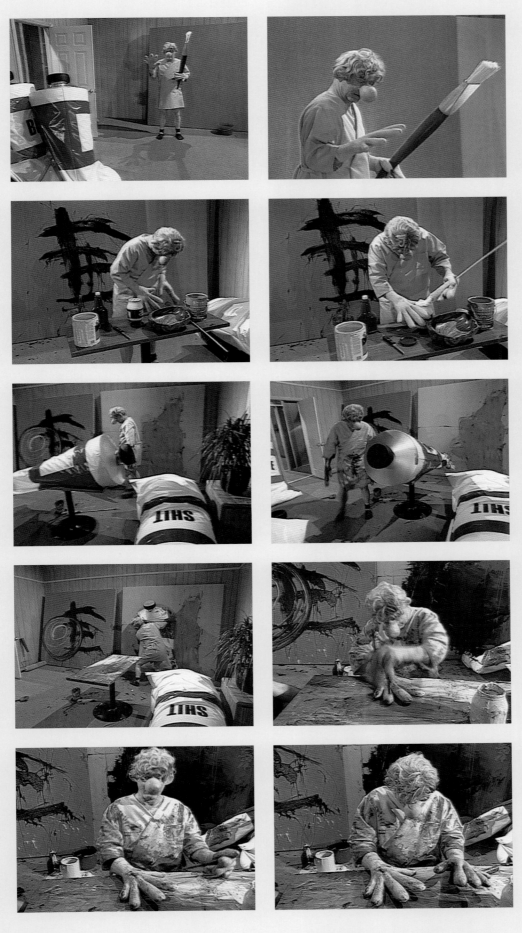

64
Paul McCarthy
Painter 1995

IV Portrait of the Artist

The problem of the actor has troubled me for a very long time. I was unsure … whether it is only from this angle that one can approach the dangerous notion of the "artist" – a concept that has heretofore been treated with unpardonable generosity … that art of perpetually playing at self-concealment which in animals we call mimicry – until finally this capacity, accumulated from generation to generation, becomes domineering, unreasonable, intractable, an instinct that learns to command other instincts and produces the actor, the "artist" (the buffoon, the teller of lies, the fool, the jester, the clown …)

Friedrich Nietzsche

The temptation for artists to depict themselves in a ridiculous or grotesque manner was not new to the eighteenth century. Evident even in certain Hellenistic and Roman portraits, the taste for self-parody found wide expression in the Middle Ages. But Romanticism galvanized the movement. Artists, who had once aspired to rank alongside the mighty of this world, now saw themselves as outcasts, *marginaux*, *Sonderlinge*, as asocial vagabonds and small-time performers, and they often looked to the circus for their models. That the development of the modern circus coincided with this paradigm shift is highly significant.

J.C.

65
James Ensor
Ensor with a Flowered Hat 1883–1888

66
Pablo Picasso
Self-portrait in a Wig 1897

Henri de Toulouse-Lautrec

Albi, France, 1864 – Château de Malromé, Langon, France, 1901

Having moved to Paris with his family in 1872, Henri de Toulouse-Lautrec displayed his very early interest in the circus in a group of drawings executed after a trip to an "American circus" in January 1874.[1] In 1878, bedridden for a lengthy period with a fractured thighbone, he occupied himself by drawing and experimenting with painting. He was encouraged in these pursuits by his father's friend René Princeteau, an animal painter. The young Henri began attending Princeteau's studio in 1881 and would sometimes accompany him to the Cirque Fernando, the smallest of Paris's circuses, which had been built in 1875 at the foot of the Butte Montmartre. After a period of academic art studies from 1882 to 1886, the nonconformist aristocrat began taking his subjects from the world of leisure. In 1886 he rented a studio on Rue Caulincourt – very near the Cirque Fernando[2] – in a neighbourhood that was full of nightclubs, dance halls, and open-air cafés dedicated to the amusement of the middle classes.[3] Until 1888 he was especially fascinated by a difficult act performed by the circus's female horseback riders and directed by Fernando himself, ringmaster's whip in hand. When the Moulin Rouge opened in October 1889 a large painting by Toulouse-Lautrec entitled *At the Cirque Fernando: Equestrienne* (1887–1888) was hung permanently over the bar, displaying to the locals what must have been a rather familiar scene. Toulouse-Lautrec was also a regular at the Cirque d'Hiver and the Cirque Molier, but his favourite circus was the Nouveau Cirque on Rue Saint-Honoré, opened in 1886 by Joseph Oller. With a ring that doubled as a swimming pool, it offered the most spectacular show in Paris. In 1892 he produced a series of studies based on an aquatic Japanese-style act presented at the Nouveau Cirque called *Papa Chrysanthème*.[4]

Toulouse-Lautrec also made several portraits of Cha-U-Kao,[5] a female dancer, clown, and acrobat who performed under this stage name at two of Oller's establishments, the Nouveau Cirque and the Moulin Rouge. One painting (cat. no. 106), in which her clown persona is signalled by the prominent ribbon adorning her tuft of white hair, reveals her in the privacy of her dressing-room, a setting that conveys the suggestion that she is both star and courtesan. In the mirror in the upper-left corner we can just make out the reflection of a man in evening dress. A year later Cha-U-Kao reappeared in the first plate of the album of lithographs entitled *Elles* (cat. no. 107), apparently confirming the middle-class belief that the circus was the gateway to prostitution.

Confined to the Folie Saint-James mental hospital in Neuilly for three months in 1899, Toulouse-Lautrec drew about forty circus scenes based on recollections of his twenty years as a devotee (see cat. nos. 150–161).[6] They featured, among other subjects, the famous Nouveau Cirque clowns Foottit and Chocolat (with whom he had become friendly), the Baronne de Rhaden, Cha-U-Kao, Monsieur Loyal, Molier, the tightrope walker from the Jardin de Paris, and the bear Caviar. The lively style, remarkable detail, and meticulous execution of the drawings – proof he had not lost his memory – resulted in his "liberation" from the hospital.

When he was commissioned in 1901 by his friend Paul Leclercq to make a lithograph for the cover of one of his short stories, *Jouets de Paris*, Toulouse-Lautrec pictured himself as a clown, alone against a white ground (cat. no. 67). And we see in this final self-portrait the same distinctive signs – the thick lips and pince-nez – that he employed habitually in his self-caricatures. He was perhaps revealing once more the challenge he had had to face all his life – his deformed body, the very image of the buffoon, targeted mercilessly by Paris's cartoonists. But who was he? The sadistic and cynical Foottit, whose costume and toupee he wears, or Chocolat, the object of so much contempt and violence? The darkly sketched figure leaves no doubt: he is both, for the two characters were fused in the tortured career of an artist who was at once cynic and victim.

C.N.-R.

---

1   "During my holidays I went to an American circus, where I saw eight elephants who walked on their heads." Letter to Madeleine Tapié de Céleyran, January 1874, in *The Letters of Henri de Toulouse-Lautrec*, ed. Herbert Schimmel (Oxford: Oxford University Press, 1991), p. 9.

2   Adrian, *Histoire illustrée des cirques parisiens d'hier et d'aujourd'hui* (Bourg-la-Reine: Paul Adrian, 1957), pp. 91–112. According to Adrian (p. 103) the Cirque Fernando contained two thousand seats, half of which were "third class," an indication of the "populist" character of this establishment.

3   Industrialization was giving rise to urban expansion, and the need to amuse the burgeoning work force stimulated the entertainment industry under the Third Republic.

4   One of these studies served as the cartoon for a stained-glass piece by Louis Comfort Tiffany, exhibited in 1895 at the opening of the first Salon de l'Art Nouveau in Paris.

5   This pseudonym was a play on the French words *chahut* (rumpus) and *chaos*. The *Chahut* was also the name given to a frenetic, almost acrobatic dance, a kind of outgrowth of the cancan, that swept through Paris's dance halls and open-air cafés during their heyday in the closing decade of the nineteenth century. This type of dance had developed prior to 1848, but it had been judged obscene and was prohibited. When it made its triumphant return under the Third Republic, it apparently became so wild and complicated that it was generally left to professionals. For more on this subject, see Jean-Claude Lebensztejn, *Chahut* (Paris: Hazan, 1989), pp. 48–65.

6   Toulouse-Lautrec had planned to publish these drawings in the form of an album on the circus. The album was published posthumously in 1905, by Manzi, Joyant et Cie.

171

67
Henri de Toulouse-Lautrec
Cover for "Jouets de Paris" 1901

68
Unidentified photographer
Henri de Toulouse-Lautrec with
Jane Avril's Fur Boa c. 1892

69
Unidentified photographer
Henri de Toulouse-Lautrec with
Foottit's Hat c. 1894

Arnold Schoenberg

Vienna, 1874 – Los Angeles, 1951

The son of Jewish Viennese shopkeepers, Schoenberg displayed unusual musical talent as a boy and began composing in earnest after taking lessons with Alexander von Zemlinsky in 1894. His early post-Romantic works, including *Verklärte Nacht* (1899) and *Pelleas und Melisande* (1903), were well received, but around 1907 he began moving toward a new style, replacing Western tonal structures with what would become known as "atonality." Outraged by this break with tradition, Viennese society turned its back. Nasty, even anti-Semitic caricatures, acerbic reviews, and a dwindling call for his music took their toll on the composer, who lost all self-confidence. It was then that he turned to painting.

In 1905 Schoenberg and his wife had sat for several portraits by the young painter Richard Gerstl. Schoenberg now sought instruction from Gerstl, convinced that painting would advance his pursuit of the *Gesamtkunstwerk* (the "total work of art") and simplicity. In November 1908 Gerstl, whose secret affair with Mrs. Schoenberg was discovered by her husband at Gmunden during the summer, committed suicide. This ordeal deeply distressed the composer for many years and compounded the pain of his being shunned by Viennese society. From December 1908 until 1912, uninhibited by formal training, he freely poured himself into a strange series of Expressionist self-portraits, or "gazes"[1] – in all, some sixty paintings and numerous drawings. Little by little, the facial features of these portraits receded to a blur, leaving the focus on the eyes; hence the title *Gaze*, or *Vision* (cat. no. 70). With these spare means and this fixed gaze, the painter sought to transcribe his various moods in works that reveal his inner tensions, in a manner similar to that of the "Expressionist" Viennese modernism of Schiele and Kokoschka, heavily infused with an indefinable angst. The quest for authenticity that lay at the heart of these preoccupations rested on the questioning of the individual. To achieve this, Schoenberg scrutinized his image in a mirror until the features dissolved, leaving an obsessive presence, like a strange mask, but without the empty eyeholes. The presence of the gaze is actually more suggestive of make-up, which, on stage, serves to intensify facial expressions. Thus, the resemblance with Schoenberg gradually disappears, giving way to the evocation of a sad, silent clown, such as the great Deburau.

Jean Clair describes the undated portrait *Hatred* (cat. no. 71) as "a frontal figure, Schoenberg himself, arms raised, eyes bulging, hair on end, with a blood-red sun in the place of his heart blazing like a malefic monstrance."[2] Apart from the title, the elements of this portrait can be found in a collection of poems by the Belgian Symbolist Albert Giraud, published in Paris in 1884 as *Pierrot lunaire: Rondels bergamasques* and freely translated into German by Otto Erich Hartleben (Berlin, 1893).[3] The latter was the source of the verses for the melodrama *Pierrot lunaire* that the Leipzig actress Albertine Zehme commissioned from Schoenberg in 1912. As a setting for her speech-song (*Sprechgesang*) recitation, he wrote an atonal composition for five players on eight instruments (piano, flute/piccolo, clarinet/bass, violin/viola, and cello).

In May 1933 Schoenberg, who had lived mainly in Berlin since 1911, fled Germany. In July, during a brief stay in Paris, he abandoned the Protestantism he had embraced in 1898 and converted back to Judaism, out of a sense of solidarity with the persecuted. In October he immigrated to the United States and settled in Los Angeles, where he remained active in theoretical research, teaching, and composing.

C.N.-R.

1 Kandinsky, whom Schoenberg met in 1911 and with whom he corresponded, was quick to grasp the affinities between painting and music in his new friend's quest, and he expressed it in his contribution to a collective tribute, *Arnold Schönberg, in höchster Verehrung*, published in Munich in 1912: "He paints them in order to bring to expression those stirrings of his soul that cannot find any musical form." It was Kandinsky who gave the title *Vision* to certain of the "gaze" paintings. See Arnold Schoenberg, "Notes (on the relationship with Kandinsky) 5.8.1934," *Journal of the Arnold Schoenberg Institute* 2, no. 3 (1978), p. 236. Quoted in *Arnold Schoenberg: Regards* (Paris: Musée d'Art Moderne de la Ville de Paris, 1995), p. 74.

2 Jean Clair, "Parades et Simulacres," in *Programme du 55ᵉ Festival d'Art Lyrique d'Aix-en-Provence*, Summer 2003.

3 Schoenberg arranged twenty-one of the poems in three groups of seven, forming an arrangement that has sometimes been interpreted as a narrative: in the first part, Pierrot the moonstruck poet and dandy muses on his unrequited love; in the second, Pierrot the thief celebrates "the gruesome Eucharist" and is threatened by the moon; in the third, a sentimental and cruel Pierrot assaults Cassander and sails home to Bergamo on a water lily with a moonbeam for a rudder. At the time, the Pierrot figure was omnipresent on stage and in literature, notably in Jules Laforgue's *Complaintes* (1885) and *L'Imitation de N.-D. La Lune* (1886). But Giraud's character is at once more buffoonish, more cruel, and more of a dreamer. The section subtitled "Red Mass," which Jean Clair relates to the painting *Hatred*, is the climactic moment of the melodrama: "With hand upraised in blessing / He holds aloft to trembling souls / The holy crimson-oozing Host: / His ripped-out heart – in bloody fingers – / At the gruesome Eucharist" (trans. Robert Erich Wolf, Nonesuch Records, 1971).

70
Arnold Schoenberg
Vision 1910

71
Arnold Schoenberg
Hatred c. 1912

72
Irene Bayer-Hecht
Andor Weininger at the
Eye-Ear-Nose-Throat Festival
at the Bauhaus, Dessau 1927

Irene Bayer-Hecht

Chicago, 1898 – Santa Monica, California, 1991

After studying at the Hochschule für Bildenden Künste in Berlin in the early 1920s, Irene Hecht lived in Paris in 1923–1924, where she met Fernand Léger* and Pablo Picasso.* Following her marriage to Herbert Bayer in 1925 she audited classes at the Dessau Bauhaus and took applied arts and photography courses at the Akademie für Graphische Künste und Buchgewerbe in Leipzig. It was during that time that she photographed the Bauhaus theatre workshop partici-pants (*Balancing Act*, 1927). One of these photographs is a close-up of Andor Weininger, painter, set designer, and member of the troupe, made up as a clown for the Eye-Ear-Nose-Throat Festival organized by Oskar Schlemmer at the Bauhaus in 1927 (cat. no. 72). Bayer-Hecht separated from her husband in 1928 and settled in Berlin. In 1938 she moved to the United States, where she gave up photog-raphy and became a translator.

M.R.

T. Lux Feininger

Berlin, born 1910

Son of the painter Lyonel Feininger, Theodore Lux Feininger began taking photographs in 1925. From 1926 to 1932 he studied at the Dessau Bauhaus, where he took introductory courses with Josef Albers, László Moholy-Nagy, and Joost Schmidt. He also attended theatre workshops given by the painter, choreographer, and designer Oskar Schlemmer, whose work he admired. With Schlemmer's help, he photographed the Bauhaus troupe in bold stage sets that reveal the experimental nature of the workshops, which were reviving early forms of popular entertainment – puppet shows, cabaret performances, and the circus (cat. nos. 73 and 74). In 1929 Feininger began devoting most of his time to painting. He moved to New York in 1936, and gave up photography altogether in 1952.

M.R.

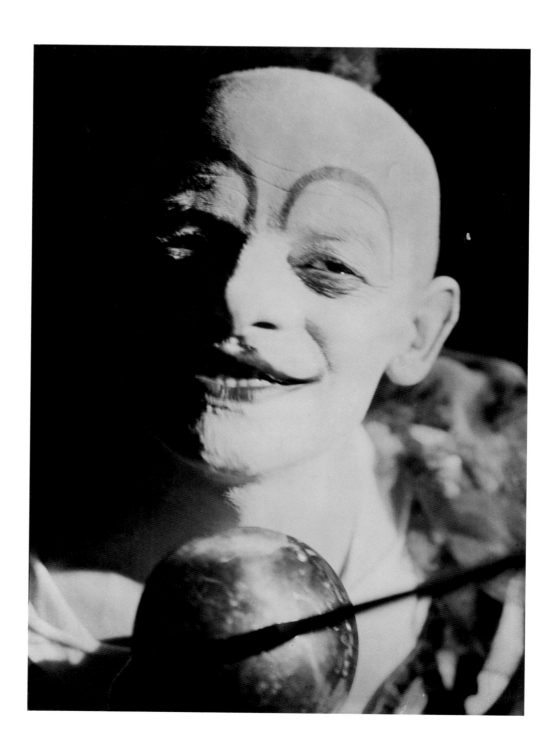

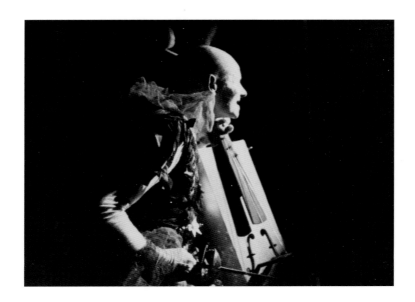

73
T. Lux Feininger
Oskar Schlemmer as Musical Clown
c. 1927

74
T. Lux Feininger
Oskar Schlemmer as Musical Clown
with Mechanical Cello c. 1927

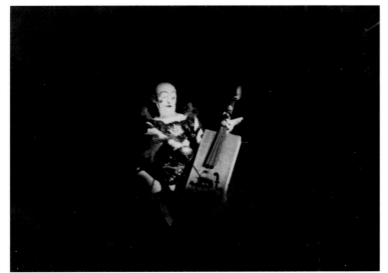

Herbert Ploberger

Wels, Austria, 1902 – Munich, 1977

After training at the Vienna Kunstgewerbeschule from 1921 to 1925, Herbert Ploberger spent several months in Paris in order to be present at the 1925 World's Fair, where some of his work was on display in the German Pavilion. He moved to Berlin in 1927 and showed in the first Neue Sachlichkeit exhibition at the Neumann-Nierendorf Gallery. One remarkable painting from 1925, *Scherben Bringen Glück* (cat. no. 75), features a clown in a closed space surrounded by fragments of various objects. His whitened countenance prefigures a 1927 self-portrait of the artist in the bathroom, masked in shaving soap. The similarity of the two paintings suggests that Ploberger saw himself as a clown, recognizing that artists and clowns – marginal members of society – play parallel roles. After the war he did stage design in Linz and Vienna, before settling in Munich in 1950, where he created sets and costumes for plays and movies.

C.N.-R.

75
Herbert Ploberger
*Scherben bringen Glück (Broken
Crockery Brings Good Luck)* c. 1925

76
Pierre Bonnard
The Boxer (Self-portrait) 1931

Francis Picabia

Paris, 1879 – 1953

Francis Picabia's early paintings, which reflected the shifting currents of late Impressionism and the influence of Pissarro and Sisley, brought him instant critical and commercial success. Around 1910 his art underwent a significant change, largely resulting from his encounter with the innovative and subversive ideas of Gabrielle Buffet and Marcel Duchamp.* Buffet, a musician whom he married in 1909, professed an art freed of all realism, while Duchamp, whom he first met in 1910, was merrily questioning the foundations of artistic practice and the very definition of art itself. Henceforth, Picabia's work became at once abstract and mechanistic. As the only European artist in New York for the Armory Show in 1913, he was the darling of the American press, which saw him as embodying the full audacity of modern art. During that trip to the United States he painted his first truly abstract pieces. In New York again in 1915, he drew "mechanomorphs" for Stieglitz's magazine *291*, depicting some of the leading figures of the New York avant-garde as mechanical objects: an electric lamp (Paul Haviland), a camera (Stieglitz), a spark-plug (*Portrait of a Young American Girl in a State of Nudity*). Like Duchamp in *The Large Glass* (1915–1923), he presented the sex act as a grotesquely cynical play of pistons and gears. Returning to Europe, Picabia became the commander-in-chief of Parisian Dadaism. At the official Salons, he exhibited works inspired by industrial design (*The Warm Eyes*, 1921), and strings stretched across an empty frame (*Dance of Saint Guy*, 1922) behind which he dreamt of installing white mice on a metal running wheel. When the Salon juries rejected his submissions, he flooded the opening events with rancorous tracts. Declaring Dadaism dead almost as quickly as he had embraced it, he turned to canvases incorporating macaroni and corn plasters (*Feathers*, c. 1925) and to vividly colourful "Monsters," swirling with streamers and confetti. The elegant, mythological "Transparencies" series, done in the late 1920s, saw him return to the fold of an art dear to the major dealers and collectors. But this return to grace was cut short by his shift to brutally austere realism in the early 1930s.

The mid-1930s brought a period of dark doubt, both artistic and existential – he separated from his second wife, Germaine Everling; financial problems forced him to sell the Château de Mai; and his 1936 exhibition at the Chicago Art Club was a flop. Stylistically, he played musical chairs, trying his hand for a few months at biomorphic abstraction, taking another stab at the "Transparencies," having a go at Photorealism, returning to "brutalism." It was during this period, from 1935 to 1937, that he painted a series of melancholy clowns. The earliest of these show up indistinctly in the background of one of the "Transparencies" – *Clowns* (1935)[1] – functioning as an ironic, disillusioned comment on the classical figure subject. By 1936 they turn into haggard, full-face portraits, evoking an interior life that contrasts sharply with their masks and make-up (*Fratellini the Clown*, cat. no. 77). It is hard not to see them as self-portraits, allegories of the artist and his condition. Picabia's interest in clowns was not new. *The Cacodylic Eye* (1921), a painting primarily composed of the signatures of Parisian art and show business luminaries, includes a photograph of the Fratellini brothers, signed by all three.

For the artist who, in Dadaist flight, called himself *Funny Guy*, *Pharamousse*, and *Le Loustic* ("The Rascal"), the mid-1930s were the beginning of a period of terrible uncertainty. In 1940–1941 he painted a *Pierrot Hanged*. Never before had he so frankly expressed the wrenching conflict between his naive, childlike veneration for art and his doubts as to its survival.

D.O.

77
Francis Picabia
Fratellini the Clown
1936

183

1   William A. Camfield, *Francis Picabia* (New York: Solomon R. Guggenheim Museum, 1970), no. 369.

Aleksandr Rodchenko

Saint Petersburg, 1891 – Moscow, 1956

A leading exponent of Soviet Constructivism and its subsequent radical form, Productivism, Aleksandr Mikhailovich Rodchenko took up photography in the winter of 1923–1924. The following April he produced a series of six portraits of his close friend Vladimir Mayakovsky. In the fall of 1925 he experimented with new formal approaches in photographs of his Moscow apartment building on Myasnitskaya Street, oblique-angle shots from above and below that testify to his originality. An unsigned letter published in *Sovetskoe Foto* in April 1928 accused him of copying the formalist aesthetic of Western photographers. He worked as a photojournalist during the 1930s but was unable to win back the esteem of the Communist authorities. In 1935 he returned to painting; the resulting series of portraits of himself as a clown, inspired by Picasso's *saltimbanques*, expresses his bitterness at the lack of official interest in his work. In 1940 a lifelong fascination with the circus led him to photograph the Moscow Circus with Georgy Petrusov for the magazine *SSSR na Stroike*, but the intended issue was never published.

Vitaly Lasarenko was famous in his day as a circus clown and a wit. He entertained his audiences with breathtaking feats on the trapeze and with satirical acts that attracted government officials and political party representatives. While most of Rodchenko's circus photographs taken between 1935 and 1940 fall into two stylistic categories – soft-focus romanticism and hard-edged Constructivism – his dynamic portrait of Vitaly Lasarenko (cat. no. 78) is unique in its bold, space-filling composition and expression of movement. The lunging form of the Harlequin figure in black-and-white costume exudes excitement, conveying the photographer's barely contained anticipation of an act of outrageous physical daring or political parody. Rodchenko was the victim of political repression during this period, and the circus and its performers, like Lasarenko, would have afforded him some emotional relief. In 1943 circus motifs emerged again in decorative paintings of acrobat and clown routines rendered in a fluid, synthetic style.

M.R. and A.T.

78
Aleksandr Rodchenko
The Clown Vitaly Lasarenko
1940, printed later

Marcel Duchamp

Blainville, France, 1887 – Neuilly-sur-Seine, France, 1968

Marcel Duchamp tried his hand at various styles, including Symbolism, Cubism, and implied motion, as in the famous 1912 *Nude Descending a Staircase, No. 2*. He then began painting and drawing the bridal-theme studies that would lead to the creation of *The Bride Stripped Bare by Her Bachelors, Even* (*The Large Glass*). These, he noted, were inspired by carnival skill-testing games, "where dummies, often in wedding garb, offered themselves up for decapitation by anyone with a good aim."[1] Tongue in cheek, he set out to make a work of art that would not be "of art," and in 1913 he produced his first readymade, *Bicycle Wheel*. Arriving in New York in 1915, he began assembling non-pictorial materials for *The Large Glass*, a monumental work that he pronounced "definitively unfinished" in 1923. In 1918, after one last canvas ironically titled *Tu m'*,[2] he turned his back on "conventional"

painting. By then he was exploring Dadaism and playing professional chess. While in Monte Carlo for a tournament in 1924, his preoccupation with chance led him to develop a system for breaking the bank at the casino. To raise money for testing it, he issued his lithographed edition of *Monte Carlo Bonds* (cat. no. 79), based on a collage that included elements of an actual bond as well as a comical photograph of Duchamp taken by his friend Man Ray, in which he appears with a shaving-soap beard and coiffure – the latter strikingly reminiscent of the horned wig worn by the famous clown Geronimo Medrano (fig. 1). This was not the first time Duchamp had represented himself in disguise (*Belle Haleine*, 1921; *Rrose Sélavy*, 1923–1924).

C.N.-R.

187

---

1   Marcel Duchamp, *Duchamp du signe: Écrits* (Paris: Flammarion, 1975), p. 247.

2   The title can be filled in with any verb that starts with a vowel. As Duchamp meant this to be his last painting, two possible readings are *tu m'ennuies* – "you bore me" – or *tu m'emmerdes* – a coarser phrase with the same meaning.

Figure 1
J.J. Faverot, *Geronimo Medrano, known as Boum-Boum*, 1888

Robert Capa

Budapest, 1913 – Thai-Binh, Vietnam, 1954

Accused of conspiring with the Communists, Endre Friedmann was expelled from Hungary in 1931. He sought refuge in Berlin before going to Paris in 1933, where he found work as a magazine photographer and assumed the name Robert Capa. In 1936 his powerfully troubling pictures of the Spanish Civil War established his reputation as a war photographer. In 1944, while covering the Second World War for *Life* magazine, he spent time with Picasso* and other artists in Paris. In August 1948 he photographed the painter and his family on the beach at Vallauris Golfe-Juan, near Antibes. A year later, after a brief stay at Matisse's home in Cimiez, he returned to Vallauris and produced a humorous portrait of Picasso, who liked to get himself up as a clown (cat. no. 80).

M.R.

80
Robert Capa
Pablo Picasso, Vallauris, France, 1949
1949, printed c. 1992

Marc Chagall

Vitebsk, Belorussia, 1887 – Saint-Paul-de-Vence, France, 1985

Marc Chagall's passion for the circus took root when, as a boy in Vitebsk, he saw a family of touring acrobats perform "on our poor road, for three or four spectators." After studying art in Vitebsk and Saint Petersburg from 1906 to 1910, he moved to Paris and found lodging at La Ruche, the artists' colony in Montparnasse, where Fernand Léger* was also living. A friend of Cendrars, Apollinaire, and Delaunay, he developed a personal blend of Cubism, Orphism, and Russian icon art in his early Paris paintings (cat. no. 183). He visited his homeland in 1914, intending to stay just three months, but the outbreak of war kept him from leaving. It was not until 1923 that he returned to Paris. Over the next four years the art dealer Ambroise Vollard commissioned him to produce four print suites, including one on the circus. During the winter of 1926–1927 he painted nineteen gouaches in preparation for this series, from sketches made in Vollard's private box at the Cirque d'Hiver. The fantastical characters of "Cirque Vollard" – a clown carrying a donkey, an acrobat on horseback in an Eiffel tower costume, an animal-headed acrobat, a rooster-man – are playfully transposed in weightless space that retains only the coloured light of the circus.

This poetic conception became a hallmark of all of Chagall's circus-related work (cat. no. 184). After a visit to the Cirque d'Hiver in 1955 to observe the shooting of scenes for a feature film, he depicted circus acts in a painting, *The Great Circus* (1956), and in a series of lithographs. Six of the lithographs, along with the nineteen gouaches done for Vollard, served as the basis for the set of twenty-three colour and fifteen black-and-white lithographs that he began putting together in 1962, to be published by Tériade in 1967 as an artist's book, *The Circus*, with poems by the painter (cat. no. 81).

M.R.

191

81
Marc Chagall
Untitled 1967

Giorgio De Chirico
Vólos, Greece, 1888 – Rome, 1978

Born to Italian parents, Giorgio De Chirico studied at the Polytekhnikon in Athens from 1900 to 1905 and at the Akademie der Bildenden Künste in Munich from 1906 to 1909. In Munich he attended major theatrical events with his brother, the painter, musician, and playwright Alberto Savinio (pseudonym of Andrea De Chirico). He took a keen interest in the work of Adolphe Appia, Gordon Craig, and Georg Fuchs, who were rewriting the scenic principles of modern theatre in Germany. On 14 July 1911, after a year in Italy, he joined Savinio in Paris. His enigmatic canvases, which often suggest a stage where the curtain has just risen and the actors are about to enter, attracted the attention of Picasso* and Apollinaire at the Salon des Indépendants in March 1913. Writing in *Les Soirées de Paris*, Apollinaire termed his paintings "metaphysical landscapes." In 1918, at the end of the First World War, De Chirico settled in Rome and joined the anti-Futurist Valori Plastici group. While hailed in Paris as a hero of Surrealism, he was making a startling return to neoclassicism. In the ensuing polemic with the avant-garde, he positioned himself as the heir of the Old Masters, a *pictor classicus*. By larding his paintings with literary references and allusions to ancient art and the Greco-Roman culture of his childhood, borrowing conventional poses and stances and copying famous paintings and sculptures, he managed to achieve, with some degree of irony, a "general theatricalization of the artistic practice."[1]

His aptitude for set design led him at the same time to theatre work. In November 1924 he returned to Paris to design sets for the ballet *La Giara* (which is based on a one-act play by Pirandello, whom De Chirico had met in Rome in the early 1920s), to be performed by Rolf de Maré's Ballets Suédois.

This first scenic creation marked the beginning of a long collaboration with the finest troupes of Europe. Between 1924 and 1971 he created the sets and costumes for twenty-six ballets, pantomimes, and operas performed in Paris, Berlin, London, Athens, Florence, Rome, and Milan. These included Stravinsky's *Pulcinella* (1919), produced in 1931 at the Lyceum Theatre in London in a new choreography by Boris Romanov, although as De Chirico himself admitted, his inspiration came largely from Picasso's design for the original 1920 production.[2]

Settling in Rome for good in 1944, as the Second World War drew to an end, he continued to vary historicist styles and references in his painting, running the gamut from neoclassicism to neo-Baroque. With a penchant for self-portraits dating to his school days in Munich, he began a new series in the late 1940s, adopting the Baroque style that he himself had condemned in the magazine *Valori Plastici* in 1921. Here he appears against backdrops of landscapes or turbulent skies (borrowed from his set designs), garbed in antiquated costumes that he considered picturesque and well suited to showcasing his painterly skills. For the *Self-portrait in Seicento Costume* (cat. no. 82) he went so far as to borrow an actual costume – a plumed hat and an embroidered velvet doublet with white lace – from the Teatro dell'Opera in Rome. One may detect in this work a parodic comment on De Chirico's own claim to greatness, but at the same time it is also a retort to his detractors, like André Breton, who felt that his genius was irretrievably lost.

M.R.

---

1   Giovanni Lista, *De Chirico* (Paris: Hazan, 1991), p. 103.

2   Letter from De Chirico to Jean Cocteau, 1 April 1931.

82
Giorgio De Chirico
Self-portrait in Seicento Costume
1947

83
Joseph Beuys
La rivoluzione siamo Noi (We Are the Revolution) 1972

Joseph Beuys

Krefeld, North Rhineland, 1921 – Düsseldorf, 1986

Born into a middle-class Catholic family from which he very soon felt the urge to escape, Beuys ran away with a travelling circus in 1938, working for a while as a roustabout, putting up posters and looking after the animals.[1] He was posted to the Russian front in 1942 as a combat pilot, and crashed in 1943 in the steppes of the Crimea, not far from Sebastopol. According to his own account, he was picked up and nursed by a Tatar tribe[2] – an episode considered apocryphal by some specialists,[3] though it constitutes one of the sources of the "Beuys myth." From 1947 to 1951 he studied at the Düsseldorf Kunstakademie producing drawings and sculptures that reveal an interest in a form of primitive symbolism. After undergoing a serious depression between 1955 and 1957, he began developing his personal theory on sculpture, which he saw as an energetic process in which each of the materials used (notably, in his own work, animal fat and felt) would be selected for its specific properties (solid or liquid, cold or hot, mineral or organic, insulative or conductive).

In 1961 Beuys was appointed professor of monumental sculpture at the Düsseldorf Kunstakademie. By the following year he found his ideas about art meshing with those of the neo-Dadaist Fluxus group, introduced to him by Nam June Paik, who taught at the same institution. At the Festum Fluxorum Fluxus concert in 1963, which he helped organize,

he performed two of his own musical works, *Siberian Symphony, First Movement* and *Composition for Two Musicians*, which marked the beginning of a long series of "actions," or performances, aimed at demolishing the boundaries between art and life. These early "actions" introduced Beuys's "artist-shaman" character, played by himself, gaunt-faced and wearing a large felt hat – described in 1966 by Troels Andersen as "a fantastic figure, halfway between clown and gangster."[4] As Heiner Stachelhaus has rightly pointed out, "humour, satire, seriousness, and profundity combine in various ways in Beuys's work, and it is not rare to hear a burst of 'dada'-type jokes."[5]

By 1967 Beuys had become deeply involved in politics. He was a founder of the German Student Party, and in 1972 he led a demonstration protesting the Düsseldorf Kunstakademie's enrolment policies.[6] An image entitled *We Are the Revolution* (cat. no. 83) shows him in Naples that year, dressed in his trademark outfit of jeans, fisherman's jacket, and felt hat, marching determinedly toward the spectator. In 1980 he ran as an official candidate for the Green Party. With his talent for undermining conventional ideas about art, he continued – as artist, performer, and politician – to shock and provoke, right up until his death in 1986.

M.R.

---

1   His parents tracked him down to the Upper Rhine valley, where the small circus was touring, and brought him back home.

2   His account is quoted in *Joseph Beuys* (Paris: Centre Pompidou, 1994), p. 249.

3   Benjamin H.D. Buchloh, "The Twilight of the Idol: Preliminary Notes for a Critique," *Artforum* 18, no. 5 (January 1980), pp. 35–43.

4   Troels Andersen, quoted by Heiner Stachelhaus in *Joseph Beuys*, trans. David Britt (New York: Abbeville, 1991), p. 136.

5   Heiner Stachelhaus, "Le rire de Joseph Beuys," in *Joseph Beuys* (see note 2), p. 358.

6   As a result of this demonstration, Beuys was dismissed from his job at the Kunstakademie by order of Johannes Rau, Minister of Science and Research for North

Rhine-Westphalia. He subsequently became embroiled in a lengthy legal battle and won reinstatement on 7 April 1978.

Lucian Freud

Berlin, born 1922

Lucian Freud, the grandson of Sigmund Freud, moved with his family to England in the summer of 1933, following Hitler's rise to power earlier that year. In 1939 he became a naturalized British subject. He studied sculpture at the Central School of Arts and Crafts in London, and painting at the East Anglian School of Painting and Drawing in Dedham, headed at the time by Cedric Morris. In the late 1940s he did portraits in the Neue Sachlichkeit style typified by the work of Otto Dix* and Georg Grosz in the 1920s. Since then his primary focus has been on male and female nudes in which every bodily imperfection is made evident. In the 1980s he painted several personal versions – homage, pastiche, parody – of works by Watteau,* Chardin,* Ingres, Cézanne, and other masters. In the background of one of two portraits of Baron H.H. Thyssen-Bornemisza done between 1981 and 1985 he reproduced a detail of Watteau's* famous *Pierrot Contented*, from Thyssen's collection. This Watteau also served as the basis for the enormous 1981–1983 composition *Large Interior, W11 (after Watteau)*, in which family and friends perch on a bed in the artist's studio in poses similar to those of Watteau's Italian actors, who are seated on a stone bench in a corner of a verdant garden.

After seeing the Australian performance artist Leigh Bowery strut his stuff at London's Anthony d'Offay Gallery in 1988, Freud asked him to pose and painted him frequently from 1990 until his death from AIDS in 1994. Bowery became his favourite model and inspired a new comic-grotesque vision of the human body (cat. no. 144). In 1993 Freud, who had done many self-portraits over the years, demonstrated an acute capacity for self-deprecation as well in a representation of his own body, aged and naked except for a pair of unlaced boots, his hands clutching the tools of his art (cat. no. 84). In the 1994 *Leigh under the Skylight* Bowery stands nude on a platform like a sideshow freak, displaying his gargantuan build, calling to mind the potbellied clown "El Tio Pepe Don José" portrayed by Picasso* in several paintings and drawings from his Rose Period, such as *Family of Saltimbanques* (1905). Since Bowery's death Freud has continued to rigorously record the unattractive and emaciated, or coarse and bloated, bodies of a number of different models, with their grotesque and even monstrous faces.

M.R.

84
Lucian Freud
Painter Working, Reflection 1993

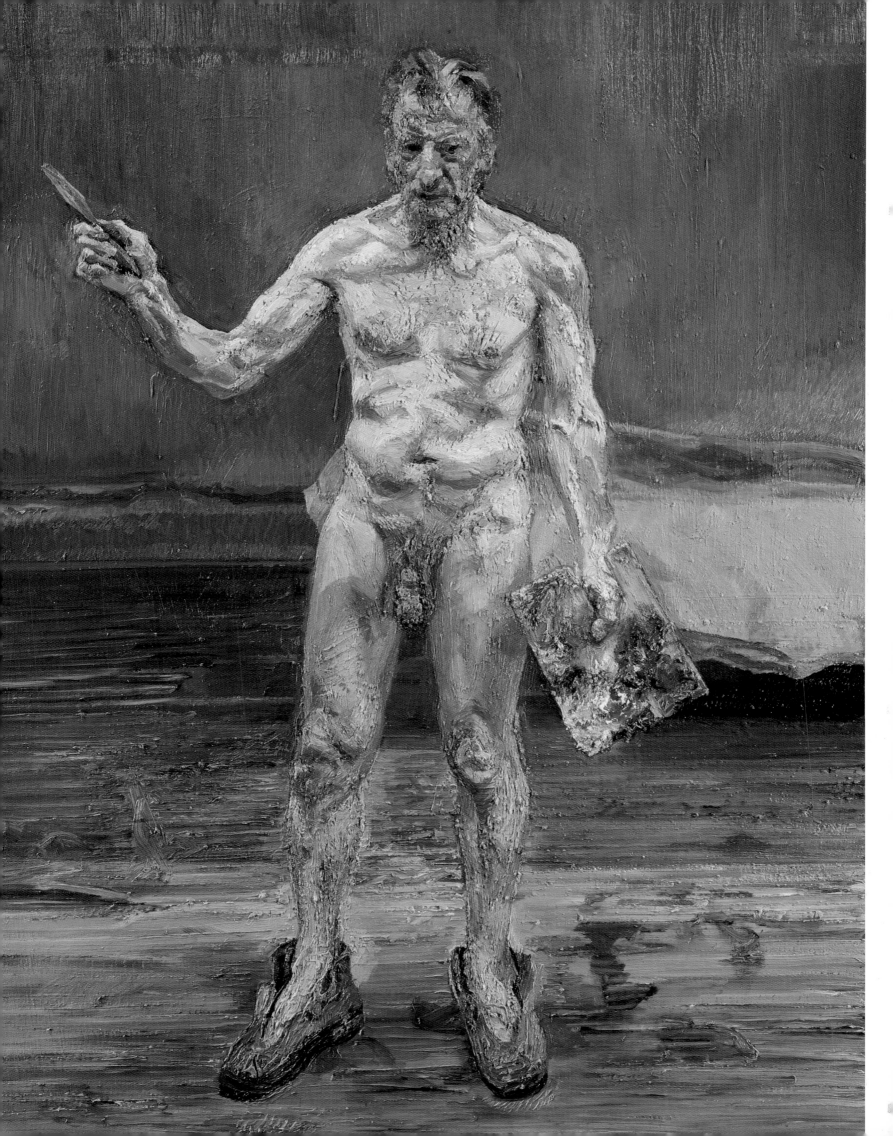

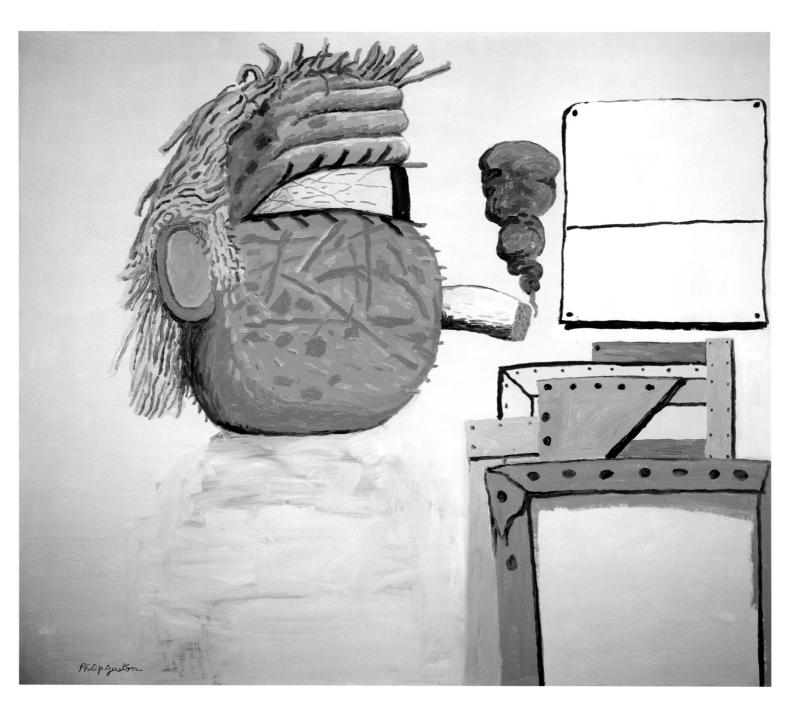

85
Philip Guston
Painter's Head 1975

Philip Guston

Montreal, 1913 – Woodstock, New York, 1980

Philip Goldstein (he later changed his name to Guston) moved with his family to Los Angeles in 1919. An avid comic book fan, he took a correspondence course from the Cleveland School of Cartooning in 1926. He attended the Manual Arts High School from 1927 to 1929 and studied briefly at the Otis Art Institute in 1930. He had no other formal training, but on his own he found lasting inspiration in Italian Renaissance painting and in the work of Léger,* Picasso,* and De Chirico.* A growing commitment to social and political activism revealed itself in the painting *Conspirators* (c. 1930), containing his first depiction of hooded Ku Klux Klansmen. His admiration for the Old Masters, especially Watteau* and Giandomenico Tiepolo,* is evident in the enigmatic canvas *If This Be Not I* (1945), where the masked and costumed children could be straight out of a Venetian carnival scene. In the late 1960s, after having been a hero of Abstract Expressionism for two decades, Guston did an abrupt about-face, returning to figuration in works that call on both caricature and cartooning. In addition to the leitmotifs of old hobnailed shoes, empty paint pots, and smouldering cigarette butts that litter these canvases (as in *Painter's Forms*, 1972), the hooded Klansmen of his early work reappear, Ubuesque symbols of the artist's condition. In his words: "They are self-portraits. I perceive myself as being behind a hood."[1] Pictured observing or discussing colour field paintings, or attending vernissages, these figures served to parody the art world. In 1973, after abandoning the hoods, Guston began making caricatural paintings of himself as a one-eyed, lima-bean-shaped head (cat. no. 85).

M.R.

---

1   Philip Guston quoted in Robert Storr, *Philip Guston* (New York: Abbeville, 1986), p. 56.

Olivier Blanckart

Brussels, born 1959

A self-taught artist, Olivier Blanckart worked at various temporary jobs before settling in Paris and taking up performance art in 1991. It was then that he made his first public appearance as "Jean-Michel," a former École des Beaux-Arts student turned vagrant who would disrupt gallery openings and other chic art events, loudly declaiming disconcerting texts and brandishing posters with quotations from the conceptual artist Joseph Kosuth. In Blanckart's view artists are always outcasts, like the "invisible man" in some of his 1996 performances. In 1992 he founded Galerie des Urgences, an AIDS prevention and information centre for which he created "works" in the form of petitions, tracts, and posters. Social protest and pastiches of the mass culture of consumerism are the two complementary poles of his art, which he renders in everything from kitsch sculptures of packaging materials (*Remixes*) to photographic self-portraits mimicking pictures of well-known personalities seen in the media (*I & Other Portraits*). In 1997 he targeted performance art itself in a caustic parody entitled *Clowns* (cat. no. 86), presented together with Arnaud Labelle-Rojoux at the Trafics festival in Nantes. In this send-up of a classic circus entrée, Nono and Lolo – a whiteface clown and an Auguste – quarrel over a blank canvas while spouting rude puns and impudent comments on the practice and history of art. Ravachol, a seductive and vulgar killjoy played by Annie-Laurie Le Ravallec, persistently interrupts them. This self-mocking exercise, which was also planned quite consciously as an act of bad taste, fared badly with audiences, who were incensed at the ridiculing of contemporary art. Blanckart continues to produce packaging sculptures and to stage controversial performances on social and political themes.

M.R.

Arnaud Labelle-Rojoux

Paris, born 1950

Arnaud Labelle-Rojoux first became intrigued by the Auguste character when he saw Albert Fratellini's clown act as a boy, and he long treasured an autographed picture postcard from him. He has always been an enthusiastic fan of slapstick and burlesque comedy films, especially those featuring Charlie Chaplin, W.C. Fields, and Benny Hill. From 1966 to 1968 his passion for movies was so great that he went almost daily to the Cinémathèque Française in Paris. He was admitted to the École des Beaux-Arts in 1969, and in 1970 he began (though never finished) writing a book on burlesque comedy. In 1973 he enrolled at the Sorbonne for a year of study toward a master's degree, but then went no further with it. In 1976 he began making his mark in performance art circles as an "actor" (*Gold Digger*, 1980) and theorist (*L'Acte pour l'art*, 1988), but public recognition came chiefly as a result of the 1996 publication of his book *L'Art parodic*. Over the years he gradually lost interest in performance, claiming that it had abandoned its subversive vocation. Before leaving it completely, he made an appearance at the 1997 Trafics festival in Nantes, together with Olivier Blanckart, in a scathing parody of performance itself. Here his grotesquely zany Auguste character embodied the general condition of contemporary artists, who have been reduced, in his opinion, to playing the clown. "The Auguste, and I'm sure of this, frightens kids more than he makes them laugh. He is a disfigured being in grotesque get-up, always shouting, making inappropriate gestures, playing the regressive fool ... He is a sort of burlesque Quasimodo, not just an ordinary kitsch figure, somewhere between a waif on black velveteen and a needlepoint of Elvis in a rhinestone-studded white suit, but a real monster harking back to medieval carnivals, to man's 'accursed share,' to everyone's repressed nature."[1] Since 1997, Labelle-Rojoux has produced drawings, photo-collages, and eclectic art events such as the Nonose Club, where he hosted performances and readings presented in the format of television "talk shows."

M.R.

1 Arnaud Labelle-Rojoux and Olivier Blanckart, "Un Rêve de fiasco," *Art Press*, no. 20 (special issue), 1999, p. 143.

86
Olivier Blanckart and
Arnaud Labelle-Rojoux
Clowns 1997

87
Christian Boltanski
The Joker 1974

88
Christian Boltanski
Comic Vignettes: The Reward 1974

Christian Boltanski

Paris, born 1944

A self-taught artist, Christian Boltanski gave up painting in 1968 in favour of short films, mail art, performance, installation, and photography. In 1974–1975, distancing himself from the austerity of his early works, which had dealt with childhood, memory, and death, he briefly assumed the fictional persona of a clown he called "Christian Boltanski," for whom he invented a life and memories. In *Comic Vignettes* (cat. no. 88) – sequential groups of hand-coloured, captioned photographs – this rather poor clown uses exaggerated gestures and expressions to revive stereotyped characters from his childhood: young Christian, the mother, the father, the doctor, the priest. In September 1974, inspired by a Munich museum dedicated to the German comedian Karl Valentin (1882–1948), Boltanski exhibited *Comic Vignettes* at the Westfälischer Kunstverein in Münster, complete with posters, records, films, costumes, and sets tracing the imaginary career of the now supposedly dead clown. During the exhibition he performed with a ventriloquist's dummy called "Little Christian." Also in 1974 he explored the ambiguity between reality and performance in an artist's book, *Quelques Interprétations par Christian Boltanski*, in which he comically plays various caricatural roles. Before shedding the clown's mantle in late 1975, he approached the subject of suicide in another artist's book, *Les Morts pour rire*, where black-and-white photographs juxtaposed in before-and-after pairs show him preparing to kill himself and then slyly revealing that it was all a hoax.

M.R.

Cindy Sherman

Glen Ridge, New Jersey, born 1954

While a student at the State University of New York at Buffalo, Cindy Sherman made a first set of photographs featuring herself in various disguises, including that of a female Auguste (*Untitled, A–E*, 1975; see cat. no. 142). In 1977, influenced by feminist and postmodernist theories of representation, she undertook a critique of mediated images of women as conveyed by B-movies of the 1950s (*Untitled Film Stills*, 1977–1980), television (*Rear Screen Projections*, 1980–1981), and the fashion world (*Fashion*, 1983–1984, 1993–1994). In the mid-1980s her work evolved toward carnivalesque imagery featuring grotesque beings (*Fairy Tales*, 1985), filth and trash (*Disasters*, 1986–1989), and hyper-sexed mannequins (*Sex Pictures*, 1992). This mixture of humour and revulsion culminated between 1994 and 1996 in the series *Horror Pictures*, tightly cropped images of the distorted figures of her earlier work.

Untitled #411 (cat. no. 89) belongs to a series of clown photographs made by Sherman in 2003 in which she explores the conventions of visual gags as they relate to clown make-up and the practice of clowning. This head-and-shoulders portrait of Sherman in the guise of a clown is set against a gradated background that shifts from a pale yellow at the bottom, to a saccharine shade of pink, to blood red at the top. The clown identity of the character is indicated by the traditional white face, the red on the nose and mouth, and the black around the eyes. The design painted on Sherman's lower lip gives the impression of buck teeth, while the vertical red streaks that bisect her eyes are like bleeding gashes. The immediate effect is simultaneously menacing and goofy. But it is only on closer examination that the image gives up its full meaning. For visible through the transparent layers of the blue chiffon scarf is an orthopaedic neck brace of the type worn by victims of whiplash, serving perhaps as a reminder that there is a human price to be paid, literally and figuratively, for the short-lived merriment that clown antics produce.

Rochelle Steiner has interestingly observed that Sherman's artistic method is analogous in some ways to that of the professional clown: "What is strikingly similar between Sherman's creative process and the way clowns create personas is the hermetic approach they take: like the artist in her work, 'a clown is their own writer, director, costumer, make-up artist, and prop man.'"[1]

M.R. and A.T.

---

1   Rochelle Steiner and Lorrie Moore, *Cindy Sherman* (London: Serpentine Gallery and Art Data, 2003), p. 20.

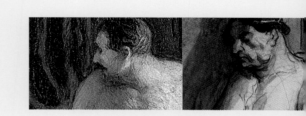

v Endgame

At the far end of the row of booths ... I saw a pitiful *saltimbanque*, stooped, worn out, a human ruin, leaning back against one of the posts of his shack ... But what an intense and unforgettable gaze he cast over the crowd and the lights ... I said to myself: I have just seen the very image of the old writer who has outlived his generation, which he brilliantly amused, or of the old, friendless poet ... whose booth the forgetful world no longer wants to enter!

Charles Baudelaire

A sense of abandonment, of no longer being understood by the public, was part of the new marginalization and "pathologization" of the artist, seen henceforth as "accursed," a nomad living on the fringes of society – like the circus that sets up its tent in outlying districts and vacant lots.

J.C.

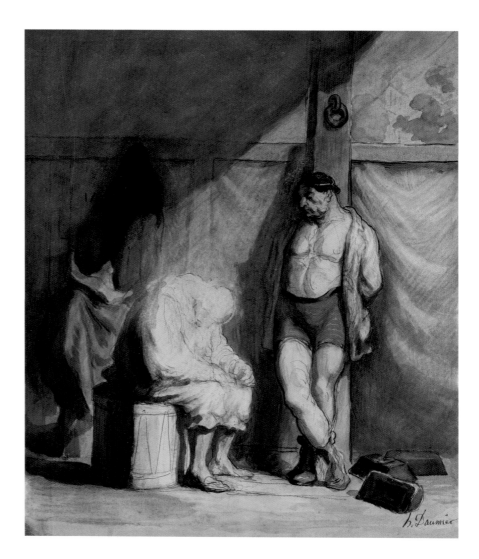

91
Honoré Daumier
Performers Resting (Strong Man and Pierrot in the Wings) c. 1865–1870

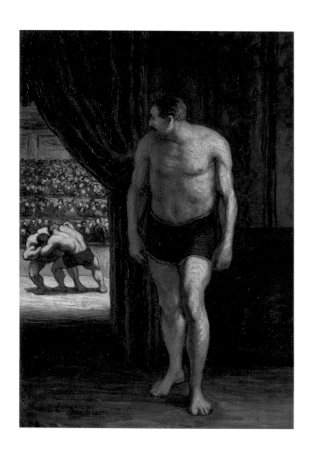

90
Honoré Daumier
The Wrestler c. 1852–1853

92
Gustave Doré
The Performers 1874

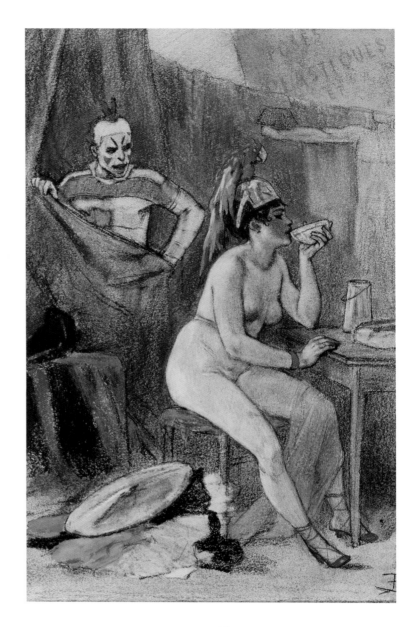

93
Félicien Rops
The Intermission of Minerve c. 1878

Félicien Rops

Namur, Belgium, 1833 – Paris, 1898

As a student at the Free University of Brussels, Félicien Rops joined forces with Charles De Coster in 1856 to found the magazine *Uylenspiegel*, in which his satirical lithographs appeared. Under the influence of Charles Baudelaire, whom he met in 1864, he went on to unmask the perversity and hypocrisy of modern ways in bitingly graphic erotic drawings. After settling in France in 1874, he soon became the illustrator of choice for the literary avant-garde. Between 1878 and 1881 he created his suite of *One Hundred Lighthearted Sketches for the Pleasure of Decent People* (cat. nos. 93 and 94), inspired by the Théâtre Érotique on Rue de la Santé in Paris. Among the licentious drawings in this series are several images of street performers that illustrate women's hold over men, males being reduced to foolish clowns at the sight of female nudity. Captivated by carnival folk and gypsies, Rops depicted a muscular aerialist in an 1882 etching that emphasizes the marginality of these itinerants, with whom he identified. During the 1880s he gradually replaced scenes of modern life with more decisively Symbolist works, deploying his erotic, morbid imagination in a satirical vein.

M.R.

94
Félicien Rops
*Venus and Cupid: Love Blowing
His Nose* c. 1878

John Sloan

Lock Haven, Pennsylvania, 1871 – Hanover, New Hampshire, 1951

From 1892 to 1894 John Sloan attended night classes at the Pennsylvania Academy of the Fine Arts in Philadelphia, studying with Thomas Anschutz. He worked as a sketch artist for the *Philadelphia Inquirer* from 1892 to 1895 and for the *Philadelphia Press* from 1895 to 1903, before becoming an advertising designer. In 1904 he moved to New York, where, under the influence of Robert Henri, he painted scenes of working class life that he presented in the 1908 group exhibition of The Eight. One of his rare circus-theme works, *Old Clown Making Up* (cat. no. 96), came about as a result of borrowing a clown suit for a costume ball; he later asked the owner, a professional model, to pose for the painting. In 1913 he showed seven pieces at the Armory Show. From 1920 on, he spent almost every summer in Santa Fe, New Mexico, where he became a keen observer of native Americans, and where he enjoyed drawing the parade floats at the local annual fair, whose special charm he captured in the 1924 painting *Travelling Carnival*.

M.R.

215

96
John Sloan
Old Clown Making Up 1910

Edward Hopper

Nyack, New York, 1882 – New York, 1967

After studying at the New York School of Art from 1900 to 1906, Hopper worked initially as a commercial artist. He spent three periods of time in Paris, travelling as well to other major European cities. During his first sojourn, from October 1906 to August 1907, he frequented the Louvre (not far from his hotel), went to the theatre, and observed the Mardi Gras festivities. He made numerous rapid sketches of people he encountered in daily life and a number of water-colours that reveal his fascination with certain "Parisian types." He also discovered the poetry of the Symbolists, which resonated strongly in him. In December 1913, after having sold a painting at the Armory Show, he settled in a studio on New York's Washington Square. It was there

that he executed from memory a large picture inspired by his recollections of Paris, giving it the French title *Soir Bleu* (cat. no. 97); the painting represents his first exploration of the theme of urban loneliness, a leitmotif of his later work.

One is immediately struck by the immobility of the charac-ters in this work and by their social diversity: at the table on the left is a pimp, in the centre a man wearing a Basque beret, a soldier, and a whiteface clown, and on the right a bourgeois couple in evening dress. Seated on a *terrasse* – possibly in the "old fortifications" neighbourhood, surrounded by the unconventional entertainment spots that attracted respectable society and demimonde alike – these "Parisian types" seem indifferent to the haughty presence of a heav-ily made-up prostitute, whose gaze travels far beyond the

97
Edward Hopper
Soir Bleu 1914

scene. The clown, as Gail Levin has pointed out,[1] is likely a self-portrait. Hopper, still virtually unknown in 1914, apparently identified with the melancholy Pierrot, a symbolic figure employed frequently by French novelists and poets since the latter half of the nineteenth century to convey the precariousness of the modern artist's existence.

After the critics' harsh reception of *Soir Bleu*, which they judged too "Parisian," Hopper turned once again to painting the monotony of the American city, in realist works that eventually made his reputation. Having seen Marcel Carné's 1945 film *Les Enfants du paradis* (cat. no. 36) in 1960, in

which the actor Jean-Louis Barrault movingly plays Pierrot, Hopper again identified with the white-faced naif in his final canvas, *Two Comedians* (1965), presenting himself and his wife Jo as *commedia dell'arte* characters, near life's end, taking their final bow at the front of a theatre stage.

C.N.-R. and M.R.

---

1   Gail Levin, *Edward Hopper: The Art and the Artist* (New York: W.W. Norton & Co., 1980), pp. 62 and 264.

August Sander

Herdorf, Germany, 1876 – Cologne, 1964

Having learned his trade as a photographer's apprentice in Berlin, Magdeburg, Halle, and Leipzig from 1899 to 1901, August Sander joined the Greif studio in Linz as senior operator in 1901, became a partner in 1902, and bought out the concern in 1904. In 1910 he opened a studio in Cologne and photographed the peasants of nearby Westerwald in an objective style at odds with the pictorial aesthetic then in fashion. During the 1920s he produced sixty portraits of Germans that were published in 1929 as *Antlitz der Zeit* ("Faces of Our Time"). This paved the way for his far more ambitious project, *Menschen des 20. Jahrhunderts* ("People of the Twentieth Century"), a vast visual "encyclopaedia" documenting the entire German people, classified by walk of life. The sixth of the book's seven chapters, "The Big City," includes images of misfits that people the urban landscape: workers and performers from the Barum Circus, carnies, gypsies, hoboes, and tramps (cat. nos. 98–100).

As a professional class, circus performers offered Sander an unparalleled opportunity for group shots of people from diverse cultural backgrounds. More interested in portraying the unmasked face of humankind than the glamour of costumed performers entertaining audiences under the big top, he captured life behind the scenes. Reminiscent of Beckmann's *Circus Wagon* (cat. no. 101), *Circus Artistes* (cat. no. 98) shows ushers, acrobats, and other performers grouped casually outside one of the wagons. Some are still in costume, while others, in robes, seem to have been hastily pulled from their dressing-rooms. But even those in costume have dropped their guise and pose as ordinary people. A cross-section of cultures and human and professional types, this work encapsulates in itself the "People of the Twentieth Century."

The rise of the Nazis to power in 1933 forced Sander to continue his work in relative secrecy. Despite the loss of some 30,000 negatives to a fire at his studio in 1946, he persevered steadily with his project, which remained unfinished at the time of his death in 1964.

M.R. and A.T.

98
August Sander
Circus Artistes 1926–1932,
printed 1975

100
August Sander
Circus Artiste 1926–1932,
printed 1980

99
August Sander
Circus Workers 1926–1932,
printed 1974

101
Max Beckmann
The Circus Wagon 1940

102
Aleksandr Rodchenko
In the Interval 1940, printed later

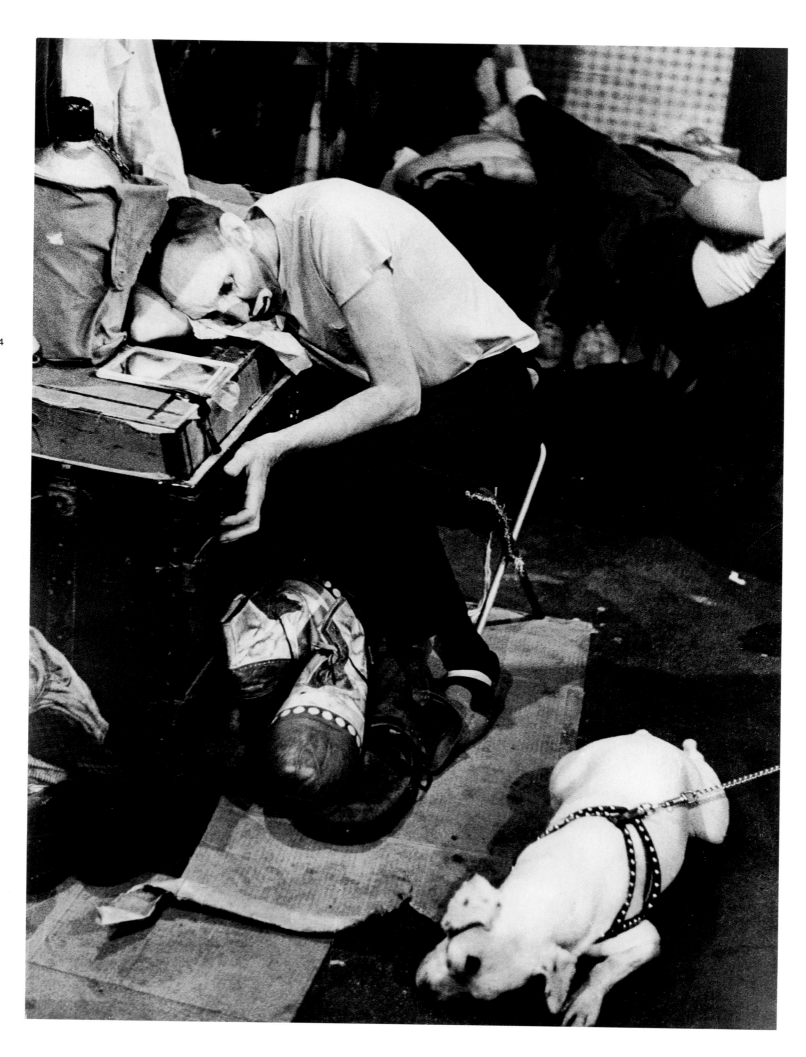

103
Leon Levinstein
Circus c. 1965

104
Bruce Davidson
Circus Dwarf, Palisades, N.J. 1958,
printed 2003

Bruce Davidson

Oak Park, Illinois, born 1933

After studying at the Rochester Institute of Technology in 1951, Bruce Davidson went to work for Eastman Kodak in Manhattan in 1952, and then briefly attended Yale University in 1954. Returning to New York in 1957 after two years of military service near Paris, he worked for a while as a photojournalist for *Life* magazine before joining Magnum Photos in the winter of 1958. At the suggestion of the Magnum archive director, he photographed a small travelling circus performing in Palisades, New Jersey: an acrobat rider leading an elephant, a lion tamer, a human cannonball, and clowns. Where the troupe went, he went, joining the cannonball and his family in the truck that hauled the cannon. His principal subject was a dwarf clown named Jimmy, whose everyday gestures he captured in photographs that demystify the life of the circus and reveal his compassion for society's misfits and downtrodden (cat. nos. 104 and 141). In 1959 he returned to independent photojournalism and shot a piece for *Esquire* on the Jokers, a Brooklyn street gang, before turning his camera on the lives of Blacks in the South (*Black Americans*, 1962–1965) and Harlem (*East 100th Street*, 1966).

M.R.

Robert Walker
Montreal, born 1945

Robert Walker studied painting at Sir George Williams University in Montreal from 1964 to 1969. After attending workshops given by Lee Friedlander at Montreal's Optica Gallery in 1975, he decided to turn to photography. He moved to New York in 1978 and made Manhattan the subject of a series of colour photographs in which the teeming juxtaposition of billboards, facades, and phone booths on Times Square jars the senses, exemplifying how our consumer society bombards us with a superfluity of images. At one point Walker photographed the famous Rockettes both on stage and behind the scenes at Radio City Music Hall. In 1988 he left New York and turned his camera on large European cities. In 1990, in Montreal, he captured the Cirque du Soleil troupe preparing for a European tour of *Saltimbanco* in intimate photographs inspired by Degas's* paintings of life backstage at the Opéra (cat. no. 105).

M.R.

105
Robert Walker
Backstage – Cirque du Soleil 1990,
printed 2002

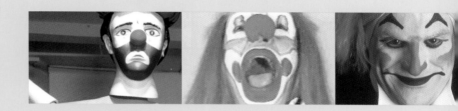

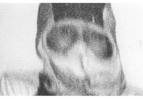

VI Rumpus and Chaos

The fairground was always the place of choice for poets and musicians seeking inspiration ... There we would see the mermaid in her boat, the lion tamer in his cage, wrestlers challenging their opponents, and the beautiful Zephyr in his sky-blue leotard ... But the real discovery of the show was Miss Aérogyne, the flying woman ...

With the month of May our evenings became more colourful. The Ballets Russes returned, and Pulcinella was back onstage. Picasso showed me a large portfolio of forty or fifty sketches he had done.

Jean Hugo

106
Henri de Toulouse-Lautrec
The Clowness Cha-U-Kao 1895

107
Henri de Toulouse-Lautrec
*Seated Clowness – Mademoiselle
Cha-U-Kao* (from *Elles*) 1896

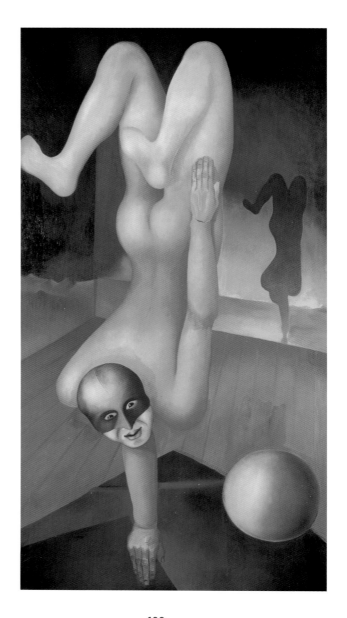

108
Heinrich Maria Davringhausen
The Acrobat c. 1920

Heinrich Maria Davringhausen

Aachen, Germany, 1894 – Nice, France, 1970

Heinrich Maria Davringhausen began teaching himself how to paint in 1911. In 1913 he enrolled at the Düsseldorf Kunstakademie. Exempted from military service during the First World War, he spent time in 1914 in Ascona, Switzerland, where he met Carlo Mense, Georg Schrimpf, and the dancer Mary Wigmann. After moving to Berlin in 1915, he spent time with the Left-leaning Expressionists at the Café des Westens, but by 1917 he had adopted a realistic style that presaged his adherence to the principles of the Neue Sachlichkeit movement. From 1918 to 1921 he lived in Munich, where he had his first solo exhibition, at the famous Hans Goltz Gallery. *The Dreamer* (1919), *The Acrobat* (cat. no. 108), and *The Black-Marketeer* (1920–1924) are among his characteristic portraits, done in a dry, spare manner.

C.N.-R.

233

109
Fernand Léger
Cubist Charlie 1924

234

110
Gaston Lachaise
Female Acrobat, also called
Abstract Figure c. 1935

Gaston Lachaise

Paris, 1882 – New York, 1935

Gaston Lachaise studied sculpture in Paris at the École Bernard Palissy from 1895 to 1898, and at the École des Beaux-Arts in 1898, where he was hailed as a prodigy. He began exhibiting his work at the Salon in 1899. In 1902 he met Isabel Dutaud Nagle, an American, who would become his muse. As a means of earning his passage to follow her home to Boston, he produced Art Nouveau jewellery for the designer René Lalique. Arriving in the United States in 1906, he found work assisting the sculptor Henry Hudson Kitson on large war memorials, which he gave up shortly after moving to New York in 1912. On his own, he produced statuettes of voluptuous and often explicitly erotic female nudes, one of which was exhibited at the 1913 Armory Show. Lachaise became an American citizen in 1916 and married Isabel Dutaud Nagle the following year. Several of his polished bronzes from the 1920s suggest the fluid movements of female acrobats, while their simplified, swelling contours recall Isabel's mature figure. In an autobiography written in the early 1930s Lachaise acknowledged his great admiration for circus performers who boldly push themselves to the absolute limit. As a child he had been struck by the death-defying acrobatics of a certain stunt rider, which later provided the motif for the sculpture *Equestrienne* (1918). Between 1931 and 1935 he worked primarily on public sculptures, including works that adorn the gardens of great American institutions like the Museum of Modern Art and the former Rockefeller Center in New York. At the same time he also produced smaller, more intimate works with titles such as *Abstract Figure* or *Female Acrobat* (cat. no. 110). These have been described by Jean Clair as "among the most striking examples of the art of their period": the acrobat's entire body is reduced to her sex, its "external morphology emphasized to excess."[1] That which was hinted at, but concealed, in Toulouse-Lautrec's portraits of female clowns – notably his *Seated Clowness* (cat. no. 107) – becomes plain as day here.

C.N.-R. and M.R.

---

1   Jean Clair, "Gaïa et Gorgô" in *Rétrospective Gaston Lachaise (1882–1935)* (Roubaix: Musée La Piscine; Paris: Gallimard, 2003), pp. 45–46.

Lisette Model

Vienna, 1901 – New York, 1981

In 1933 Elise Felice Amélie Seybert, called Lisette, gave up music and decided to teach herself photography. After her father's death in 1924 she moved to France, together with her mother and sister. Her earliest subjects included beggars and vagrants on the streets of Paris and the idle rich on the Promenade des Anglais in Nice. In 1937 she married the painter Evsa Model, and the following year they moved to New York, a city whose great energy inspired the many street scenes she was to photograph. She contributed to several magazines in the 1940s, including *Harper's Bazaar*, for which she produced the famous Coney Island bathers series in 1942. In the mid-1940s a particular interest in the marginal occupants of the city, whom she sought out on the streets and in bars, hotels, and card dens, led her to Hubert's Dime Museum and Flea Circus at 42nd Street and Broadway, home to oddities like the "Living Skeleton" and Albert-Alberta.

Model mined a rich reservoir of imagery provided by large circuses as well as modest sideshows (cat. nos. 111, 193, 194). But ultimately it was the outrageousness of sideshow performers like the "half man, half woman" Albert-Alberta that appealed to her most. Of the six frames she made of this character with her Rolleiflex, *Albert-Alberta, Hubert's 42nd Street Flea Circus* (cat. no. 139) is the most revealing and,

therefore, daring. The self-styled hermaphrodite has removed the satin cloth that veils his body in most of the other shots and draped it insouciantly over his shoulders, along with his boa, revealing a curious composite of male and female attributes. Below, a silky smooth leg adorned with an anklet and pom-pommed high heel shoe contrasts with a darkly hairy leg, Oxfords, and a conventional man's sock. Above, an artificial female breast is exposed alongside a male breast. Close examination shows that Model cropped the negative tightly, eliminating the extraneous details of the overhanging mirror to produce an image that resonates with vitality and audacity.

A photo-essay of Model's early circus work appeared in *Harper's Bazaar* in August 1945. From about then until the early 1950s she photographed Barnum & Bailey's Greatest Show on Earth at New York's Madison Square Garden, and around 1956 she captured the routines of tightrope walkers and acrobats high above the Ringling Brothers ring, before turning her camera to jazz musicians and actors.

M.R. and A.T.

111
Lisette Model
Circus, New York 1945

238

112
Weegee
Weegee as Clown 1943

113
Weegee
The Human Cannonball 1943

240

114
Diane Arbus
*Albino sword swallower at
a carnival, Md.* 1970, printed 1973

Diane Arbus

New York, 1923 – New York, 1971

Diane Arbus's fascination with the eccentric and grotesque was stimulated in part by visits to Hubert's Dime Museum and Flea Circus on New York's 42nd Street, which included among its attractions Professor Heckler's performing fleas, Lentini the "Three-legged Wonder," and the famous Albert-Alberta, "half man, half woman," who was photographed by Lisette Model* around 1945. After starting out in fashion photography in the 1940s, Arbus went on to study with Alexey Brodovitch in 1955 and took classes with Model in 1956 and 1957. In 1959 she began going to Coney Island, with its sideshows and its "World in Wax Musée." Circus and sideshow performers were among her earliest personal subjects. The first photo-essay that she sold to *Esquire* magazine, in 1960, was a series of portraits of eccentrics, shot in a simple, direct style. A keen admirer of August Sander's* circus photographs and of Tod Browning's* 1932 film *Freaks* (cat. no. 123), she turned her camera in 1970 to carnival performers in Maryland: an albino sword swallower, a girl in a circus costume, a tattooed man, a hermaphrodite in a trailer. Shortly before taking her own life in 1971 she produced some of her most expressive images in a series of photographs of the mentally handicapped.

Made in the year before she died, *Tattooed man at a carnival, Md.* (cat. no. 137) shows Arbus as a mature portraitist. Captured in a half-length frontal standing pose, the subject fills almost the entire picture frame. By shooting from close in, Arbus enables us to isolate and make out the snake, eagle, and star tattoos that adorn the man's torso and the cigarette-smoking human skull on his forehead. A few drooping flags that adorn the roof behind a sideshow marquee suggest the context of a fairground. This is a portrait made in the heroic style, in which Arbus clearly displays her admiration for life's most eccentric characters, whose presence causes us to "wonder all over again what is veritable and what it is to become whoever we may be."[1] Arbus understood that for a portrait to be effective it had to be more than just a faithful likeness of the sitter – above all it had to address the existential issues of personal and social identity. In Arbus's view, the tattooed man, like the other eccentrics she photographed, was "the author and the hero of a real dream."[2]

M.R. and A.T.

241

---

1   Diane Arbus, "The Full Circle," *Harper's Bazaar*, November 1961, quoted in *Diane Arbus: Magazine Work* (New York: Aperture, 1984), p. 14.

2   Ibid.

Jonathan Borofsky

Boston, born 1942

After settling in New York in 1966, Jonathan Borofsky developed a conceptual approach to art in *Counting from One to Infinity* (1969–), which consists of a stack of sheets of graph paper with handwritten numbers on both sides in a continuous sequence. In 1971, while continuing to count, he began sketching and noting his dreams on the pages, and the following year these jottings inspired several paintings. In one of them, *Man on a Tightrope at 2,354,128 and 2,531,117* (1978), the tightrope walker symbolizes the artist's desire to be free of mundane constraints. The same metaphor is found in the large wall painting *I Dreamed a Dog Was Walking a Tightrope* (1979). Various characters that Borofsky acknowledges as self-portraits have recurred in his drawings, paintings, and sculptures since the late 1970s, and have enabled him to form a critique of his own role as an artist. In the kinetic sculpture *The Dancing Clown at 2,845,325* (cat. no. 115), a three-dimensional version of a 1981 drawing entitled *Entertainer (Self-portrait as Clown)*, Borofsky appears as a cross between a ballerina and a hobo clown, posing before a closed curtain on a stage-like platform. The work incorporates a muffled recording of his rendition of Frank Sinatra's "My Way," while the clown kicks her/his leg up into the air like a French cancan dancer. Recognizing the self-mockery, critic Robert Mahoney described the piece as the artist's sad but funny comment on his own work and on the art world.[1] In 1989 a new version of this sculpture was affixed to the facade of a building near the beach in Venice, California, where street performers often entertain the crowds.

M.R.

1   Robert Mahoney, "Pygmalion à Disneyland: L'Histoire de l'art et l'histoire de la mécanique chez Jonathan Borofsky," *Artstudio*, no. 22 (Fall 1991), p. 116.

115
Jonathan Borofsky
The Dancing Clown at 2,845,325
1982–1983

244

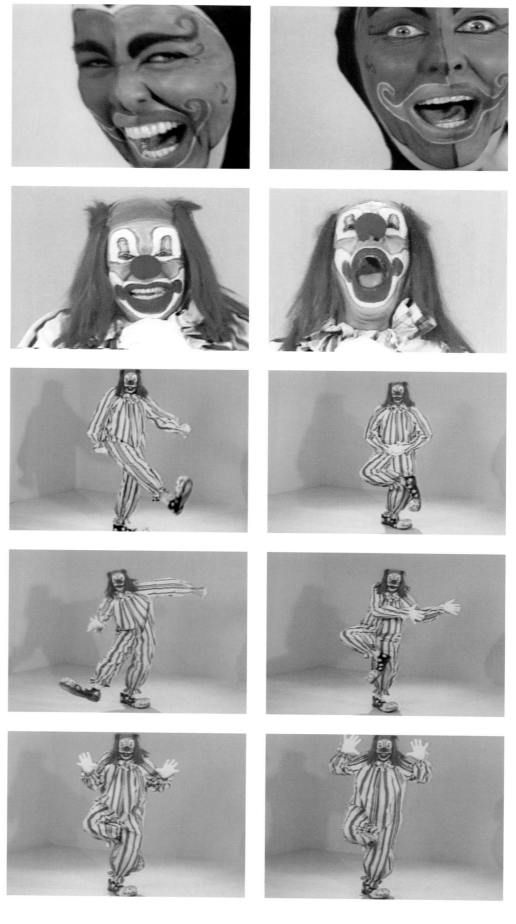

116
Bruce Nauman
*Clown Torture (Dark and Stormy
Night with Laughter)* 1987

Bruce Nauman

Fort Wayne, Indiana, born 1941

Bruce Nauman turned away from painting very early in order to pursue his interests in sculpture, photography, perform-ance, and video. For a long period, from 1967 to 1990, he worked with the clown figure, its mask of make-up creating an abstract, troubling, and utterly uncommunicative presence. In 1967 he filmed himself applying four successive layers of colour to his face, turning the act of putting on make-up into a subject of art. The following year he produced an initial series of holograms, *Making Faces (A–K)*, in which his three-dimensional face is distorted in eleven different grotesque grimaces. Nauman began making neon works in 1970. Two of these signs, from 1985, echo burlesque com-edy – *Mean Clown Welcome* and *Punch and Judy: Kick in the Groin, Slap in the Face* – the latter portraying an alterca-tion worthy of the legendary puppets so wildly popular at seventeenth-century English fairs. But Nauman's depictions of absurd situations, which always end in escalating violence,

are not meant for laughs. In the 1986 video installation *Violent Incident*, a bad slapstick joke turns an intimate din-ner into a brawl. The ambitious six-screen installation *Clown Torture* from 1987 features the misadventures of five clowns who endlessly repeat the same gestures and words, creat-ing an unbearable profusion of visual and audio stimuli that inflicts the clowns' "torture" on the viewer. The clown is subjected to still more explicit violence in the 1990 video installation *Shadow Puppets and Instructed Mime*, where an androgynous mime meekly obeys the commands barked by an anonymous voice, struggling into uncomfortable posi-tions similar to Nauman's postures in the 1969 holographic series *Full Figure Poses*.

M.R.

Rhona Bitner

New York, born 1960

Rhona Bitner owes her lifelong fascination with the circus to a children's book, Mischa Damjan's *The Clown Said No*. After graduating from New York University in 1981, she worked briefly as an assistant in John Coplans's photography studio, and then trained at the International Center of Photography while studying typography at the Parsons School of Design. Not content to focus on subjects at home, she toured the globe from 1990 to 1998 to attend performances by major circuses (Bouglione, Knie, Moscow, Shanghai, Beijing). Shooting inconspicuously from the audience, she captured the performers in the ring: acrobats, aerialists, and clowns in close-up, lit only by spotlight, isolated in a black void. To Bitner's surprise, viewers of the resulting series, entitled *Circus*, often found the heavily made-up clowns troubling. This led her to modify her perception of the clown as a figure who, far more than being an amusing entertainer, embodies the tragicomic condition of man. In 2001 she began a new series, *Clown* (cat. no. 117), consisting of life-size portraits done in her studio. Motionless and in sharp focus against a black ground, the performers stare directly into the camera, returning the viewer's gaze.

C.N.-R.

117
Rhona Bitner
from the series: Clown 2001

Ugo Rondinone

Brunnen, Switzerland, born 1963

Ugo Rondinone studied at the Hochschule für Angewandte Kunst in Vienna from 1986 to 1990 before moving to Zürich to develop a practice that includes drawing, painting, sculpture, photography, and video. The clown figure, epitomizing the artist's condition, has recurred frequently in his work since 1995. This tragicomic character appeared initially in a large graffiti piece, and then in *Please?* (1996), an assortment of self-shot Polaroids, artfully scattered on the floor, showing the artist in clown make-up with a fake nose and red wig. In *Dogdays Are Over*, a video installation first shown in a solo exhibition at Zürich's Museum für Gegenwartskunst in 1996, seven monitors placed on the floor present limply lounging silent clowns (all played by actors), their evident boredom a disconcerting subversion of the amuser's traditional role. Viewers of these passive, sullen-faced buffoons are further embarrassed by the uproarious laughter that is showered on them from ceiling speakers as they move through the room, making them not the recipients but the object of the mirth. Two more recent installations, *A Horse with No Name* (2000) and *If There Were Anywhere but Desert: Tuesday* (cat. no. 118), feature fibreglass clowns – cast from life, then painted and costumed – in various states of collapse. Rondinone has lived and worked in New York since 1996.

M.R.

118
Ugo Rondinone
*If There Were Anywhere but Desert:
Tuesday* 2002

VII Monsters and Marvels

The world is coming to an end. Humanity is on its last legs.
A Barnum of the future shows the decadent men of his era
a beautiful woman from ancient times, artificially preserved.
"What?" they might say, "can humanity have been that beautiful?"
But they wouldn't say that. A decadent man would admire
himself, and would see beauty as ugliness.

Charles Baudelaire

A hermetically circumscribed universe inhabited by
startling creatures, a world alternately beauteous and
grotesque, a gathering of ballerinas, athletes, and
freaks (like those who give Tod Browning's film its
name), the circus offers a graphic example of the *scala
naturae*, the great ladder of being that extends from
the lowest shelf of the curiosity cabinet heavenwards
all the way to the last row up in the gods. The animals
themselves are part of this progression of living forms,
by which the spectator is amazed, terrified, and repelled.

J.C.

CONGRESS of FREAKS with RINGLING BROTHERS and BARNUM & BAILEY (COMBINED) CIRCUS
SEASON — 1929

119
Edward J. Kelty
Congress of Freaks 1929

Edward J. Kelty

Denver, Colorado, 1888 – Chicago, 1967

After serving in the First World War, Edward Kelty settled in New York. Around 1920 he was working as a lab technician for several commercial photography studios. His first visit to Coney Island was in the summer of 1921, to take publicity shots of the Luna Park attractions and sideshow freaks. In February 1922 he opened Century Flashlight Photographers Inc., specializing in banquets and weddings. During summers, he would follow small touring circuses along the East Coast, assembling the performers and crews for spectacular group shots made with a large-format camera (cat. no. 119). In 1929 he became the first photographer to use a flash to capture the derring-do of the Ringling Brothers acts at New York's Madison Square Garden. After business fell off during the Depression, he gave up wedding photography to follow circuses around the Midwest and West. He covered his last circuses around 1942, before moving to Chicago and giving up photography.

M.R.

120
Unidentified photographer
(American, mid-19th century)
Tom Thumb c. 1847–1848

121
Irena Rabinowicz-Rüther
François (Dwarf from the Sarrasani Circus) 1925

Irena Rabinowicz-Rüther

Cologne, 1900 – Dresden, 1979

The first woman to be admitted to the Dresden Kunstakademie, in 1919, Irena Rabinowicz trained with Otto Gussmann (1899–1926). Her classmates included Otto Dix* and Hubert Rüther, whom she married in 1921. She is known chiefly for her portraits, including that of Richard Tauber (1920), one of the greatest tenors of the twentieth century. After her studies she travelled in France and Italy. In 1925 she painted *François* (cat. no. 121), the portrait of a famous dwarf from the Sarrasani Circus. Hans Stosch (1873–1934), who used the stage name Sarrasani, built a home for his exotic circus on Dresden's Carolaplatz in 1912.

C.N.-R.

John Gutmann

Breslau, Germany (now Wroclaw, Poland), 1905 –
San Francisco, 1998

From 1923 to 1927 John Gutmann trained at the Staatliche Akademie für Kunst und Kunstgewerbe in Breslau with the Expressionist painter Otto Mueller. He then moved to Berlin, where he took classes at the Akademie der Bildenden Künste in 1929 and 1930 and produced paintings on themes borrowed from the entertainment world – the circus, cabaret shows, and jazz groups. In 1933 the Nazis banned him from teaching or exhibiting his work. Forced to emigrate, he learned photography just a month before leaving for the United States and secured a contract with the Presse-Foto agency in Berlin, to which he sent his work after moving to San Francisco in late 1933. In 1936 he set off on a long cross-country tour that eventually took him to New Orleans to cover the Mardi Gras festivities for the Pix agency in New York. A series of photographs of touring circus performers taken in San Francisco in 1939 and 1940 demonstrates his passion for American pop culture (cat. no. 122). From 1938 on, he devoted an increasing amount of time to teaching at San Francisco State College, where he introduced a photography program in 1946.

M.R.

122
John Gutmann
Midget Clowns 1939

258

123
Freaks, film directed by **Tod Browning**, United States, 1932

124
Pablo Picasso
La Nana 1901

Otto Dix

Untermhaus, Germany, 1891 – Hemmenhofen, Germany, 1969

After apprenticing for several years as a decorative artist, Otto Dix studied at the Kunstgewerbeschule in Dresden from 1909 to 1914, and then served in the army until 1918. As a student at the Dresden Kunstakademie from 1919 to 1922 he produced Dadaist paintings denouncing the failings of postwar bourgeois society. In the 1920s his anti-military and anti-bourgeois views evolved into a deep sympathy for various types of social outcasts, including prostitutes, war invalids, and circus people. His earliest painting on a circus theme, *Suleika, the Tattooed Wonder* (1920), represents Maud Arizona, a famous carnival attraction who appeared mainly in German port cities.

Reprising the subjects of some of his earlier watercolours, Dix cast a critical eye on the Weimar Republic in his 1922 suite of etchings entitled *The Circus*. Among the inspirations for these prints were Dresden's famous Sarrasani Circus as well as the Ringling Brothers Circus, which had toured Germany in 1920. Some of the etchings, such as *International Riding Act* and *American Riding Act*, are manifestly allegorical commentaries on the political situation of the time. Others, often paralleled in a watercolour, depict typical circus figures in a harsh, caustic style, as in *Disdainers of Death – Two Artistes* (cat. no. 125) and *Female Animal Tamer* (cat. no. 126). While the former image embodies sadism and sexuality, the latter reflects Dix's fascination with the marginality of circus folk, who are not only exempt from the strictures of bourgeois morality but also risk their lives with every performance. In this respect, they illustrate the demands of the artistic life in general; like Nietzsche's tightrope walker, all artists must walk a fine and dangerous line. In a different spirit, the small 1923 watercolour and collage *Circus Scene* (cat. no. 180) renders the energy of the big top in robot-like figures.

In 1925 Dix became a leading exponent of the Neue Sachlichkeit movement. He obtained a teaching position at the Dresden Kunstakademie in 1927 but was dismissed by the Nazis in 1933. After his release as a prisoner of war in 1946, he retired to his home in Hemmenhofen, where carnival parades and village costume balls inspired three paintings in which he reflects on the meaning of life: *Masks in Ruins* (1946), *Masks in the Street* (1952), and *Alemannic Masks* (1954).

C.N.-R.

125
Otto Dix
Disdainers of Death – Two Artistes
1922

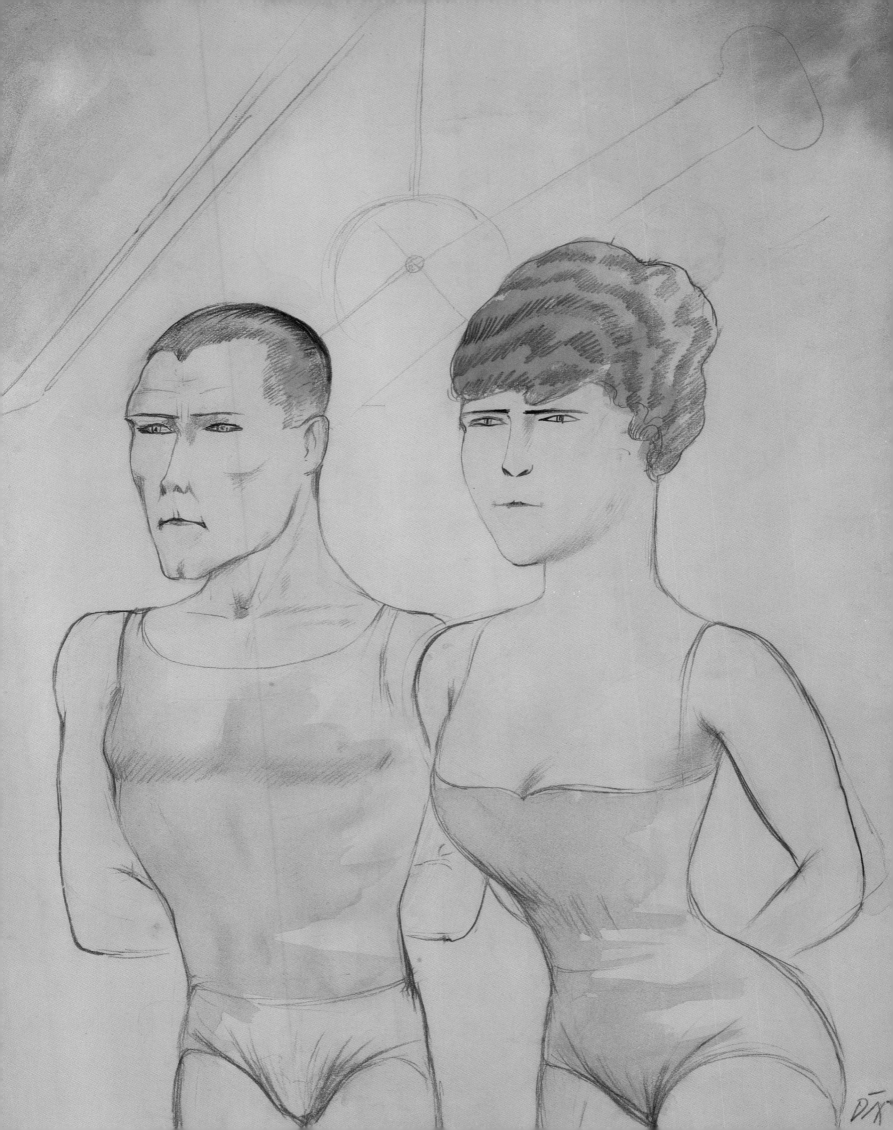

126
Otto Dix
Female Animal Tamer 1922

127
Otto Dix
Female Animal Tamer 1922

128
Félicien Rops
Saltimbanque

129
Max Beckmann
The Snake Woman, plate 10
of the portfolio *Der Jahrmarkt*
("The Annual Fair") 1921

130
Max Beckmann
The Negro, plate 6 of the portfolio
Der Jahrmarkt ("The Annual Fair")
1921

131
John Steuart Curry
Baby Ruth 1932

132
Izis
Foire du Trône 1960

John Steuart Curry

Near Dunavant, Kansas, 1897 – Madison, Wisconsin, 1946

John Steuart Curry trained at the Art Institute of Chicago from 1916 to 1918, joined Harvey Dunn's studio in Tenafly, New Jersey, in 1919, and went to Paris to study with Vasily Shukhayev in 1926. During his Paris stay he saw and admired circus scenes by Seurat* and Toulouse-Lautrec* from the 1890s. In 1927 he set up a studio in Westport, Connecticut, where he produced *State Fair* (1928), *Female Acrobat* (*High Diver*) (exhibited in 1929, reworked in 1937), and *The Medicine Man* (1931), all from memories of carnival shows seen during his childhood in Kansas. In 1932 he accompanied the Ringling Brothers Circus on a three-month tour through New England, painting the troupe's star performers, among them Baby

Ruth (cat. no. 131). His hundred or so sketches of the show's high points served as the basis for another series of canvases that he completed back in Westport, including *The Flying Codonas* (1932). In 1934, under the auspices of a New Deal program, he created two wall paintings for a Westport school: *Tragedy*, portraying an aerialist's fall, and *Comedy*, depicting the buffoonery of clowns.

M.R.

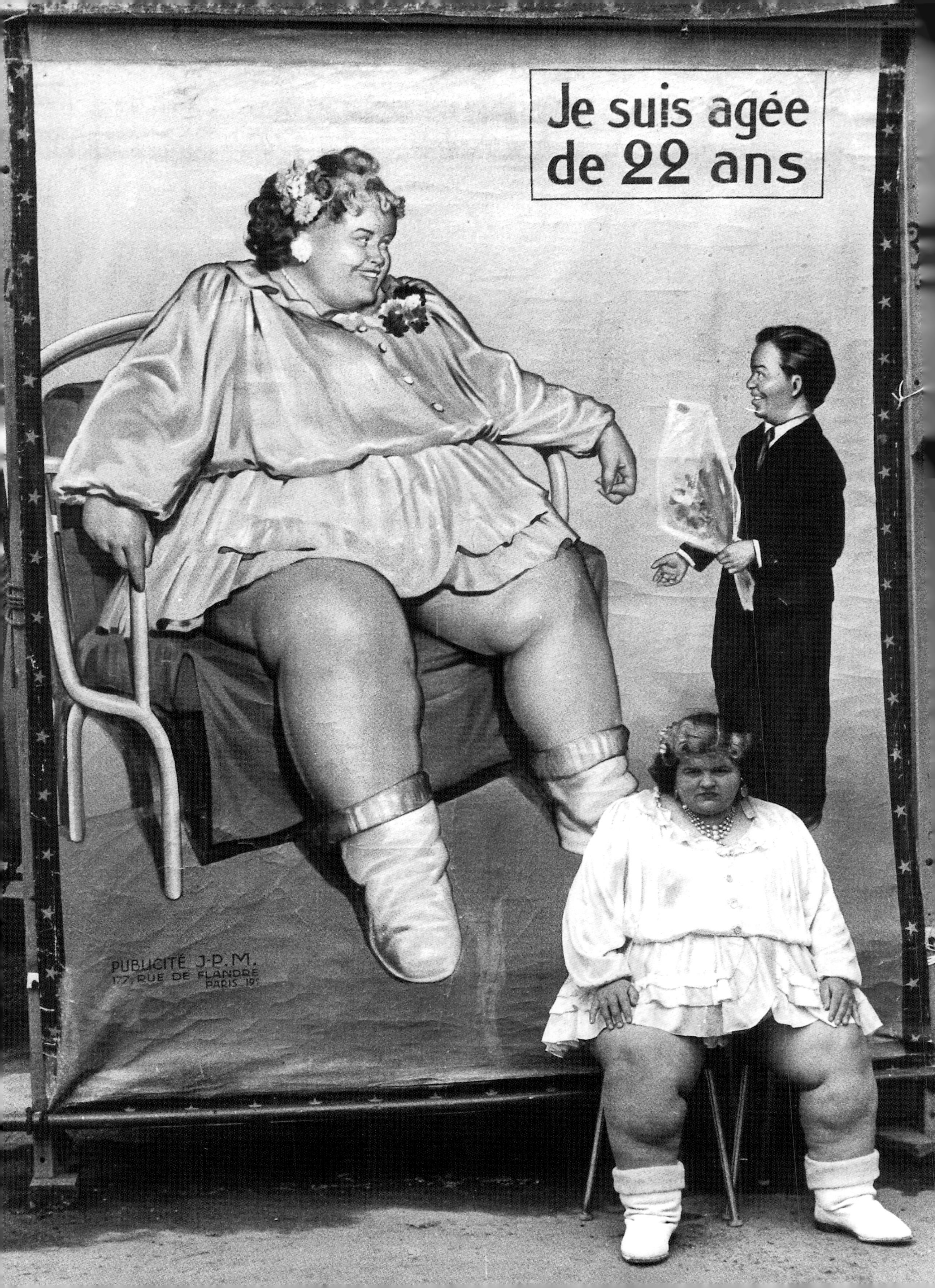
Je suis agée
de 22 ans
PUBLICITÉ J-P.M.
177, RUE DE FLANDRE
PARIS 19

Pyke Koch

Beek, Netherlands, 1901 – Wassenaar, Netherlands, 1991

In 1927 Pieter Frans Christian Koch abandoned his law studies at the University of Utrecht to teach himself painting. His early works, depicting prostitution and poverty in the depressed neighbourhoods of large cities, show the influence of the Neue Sachlichkeit movement and of Magic Realism, which were having a powerful impact in the Netherlands at the time. An avid cinema enthusiast, he drew his initial inspiration from the silent films of the 1920s. Their imprint can be seen not only in the subjects he chose to paint, but also in the recurring image of a world-weary woman[1] modelled on the Danish silent movie star Asta Nielsen, whose portrait he painted in 1929.[2] Like many of the films produced in Germany at the time, including one of his favourites, Ewald Andreas Dupont's *Variety* (1925), Koch's works portray a murky and pitiless world that is the very antithesis of bourgeois society. It is the world evoked in the best-known painting from his youthful period, *The Shooting Gallery* (1931), where his female "type" stands behind the counter of a shooting booth like those at the fairgrounds of his childhood. After several trips to Florence between 1937 and 1939, the influence of the Italian masters of the Quattrocento began to pervade his work, and he did not return to his early themes until 1955. After having been impressed by the skills of a young contortionist nicknamed "Wonderboy," star of the Strassburger Circus, presented at the Koninklijk Theater Oscar Carré in Amsterdam, Koch made a similar figure the subject of two large paintings, *The Contortionist* (1955–1963) and *The Large Contortionist* (cat. no. 133), which were based on shots by the press photographer Aart Klein.

In *The Large Contortionist* Koch has reproduced exactly the spectacular pose of the female acrobat as photographed by Klein: on a round platform placed on a floor strewn with cigarette butts, matches, and scraps of paper, she is shown supporting herself on her hands, her back arched right over and her legs dangling on either side of her shoulders. Wearing a leotard with a little skirt, tights, and acrobat's shoes, she exhibits the lower part of her body to the public. As the Koch specialist Carel Blotkamp has pointed out, the eroticism of the image was more explicit in a preparatory drawing executed the year before: there, the artist placed the figure in front of a backdrop depicting a mountainous landscape that included an erupting volcano – a symbol of sexual power much favoured by the Surrealists.[3] In the final 1957 version, the landscape has been replaced by a dark background against which are silhouetted a painted wood caryatid and the "circus valet" from a small 1952 study, who seems to be observing the audience's reaction to this disconcertingly suggestive performance. The contortionist, whose face resembles that of the woman in *The Shooting Gallery*, has a slight squint, as if she were checking with one eye for a signal from behind the scenes while looking straight at the spectator with the other. Bram Kempers has noted that the sexual allure of the contortionist's figure, her strong, supple, almost androgynous body, is considerably heightened by the extraordinary and immodest position in which she places it.[4]

Between 1970 and 1982 Koch worked at length on one last painting whose subject is from the circus world, *Tightrope Walker III*. Scholars agree that in this work he employed the image of an aging tightrope walker, practicing alone in a decrepit room to the accompaniment of a gramophone record, to conjure his own swan song.

M.R.

1   In a letter to his friend Jan Engelman, Koch wrote: "Here I've obviously painted 'hard-boiled women,' women who know about life." Quoted by Carel Blotkamp in *Pyke Koch* (Paris: Institut Néerlandais, 1982), n.p.

2   Koch executed the portrait using still shots taken from two films in which Asta Nielsen played a leading role: *Die freudlose Gasse* ("The Joyless Street"), 1925, directed by Georg Wilhelm Pabst, and *Dirnentragödie* ("Tragedy of the Street"), 1927, directed by Bruno Rahn.

3   Blotkamp, *Pyke Koch*, n.p.

4   Bram Kempers, "Masquerades and Metaphors: Pyke Koch's Enigmatic Realism," in *Pyke Koch: Schilderijen en Tekeningen / Paintings and Drawings* (Rotterdam: Museum Boymans-van Beuningen, 1995), p. 83.

133
Pyke Koch
The Large Contortionist 1957

134
Albert Birkle
Acrobat Schulz 1924

Albert Birkle

Berlin-Charlottenburg, 1900 – Salzburg, 1986

After leaving the army in 1919, Albert Birkle studied at the
Akademie der Bildenden Künste in Berlin. In 1923 he became
the youngest member of the Berlin Secession movement
led by Lovis Corinth. He worked as an illustrator for Leftist
magazines. During the 1920s his socialist leanings induced
him to create faces whose expressions reflect the psychic
trauma of postwar Germany, where unemployment was ram-
pant. He generally portrayed factory workers and other
members of the working class, including the subject of the
painting *Acrobat Schulz* (cat. no. 134). After working in
Bavaria for a period, he moved to Salzburg in 1933, becoming an Austrian citizen in 1946.

C.N.-R.

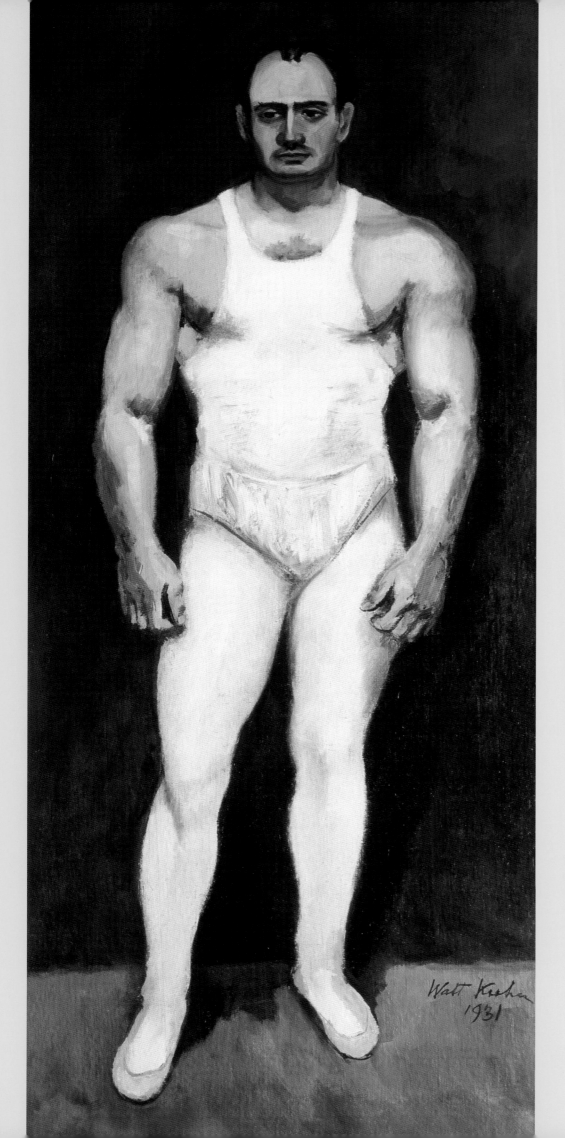

271

135
Walt Kuhn
Top Man 1931

272

Claude Cahun

Nantes, 1894 – Isle of Jersey, 1954

Lucy Schwob, niece of the Symbolist author Marcel Schwob (1867–1905), had a multifaceted career as a photographer, performer, and writer under the pseudonym Claude Cahun. Her art is marked by an obsession with self-representation, cross-dressing, and gender ambivalence that is apparent even in her earliest photographic self-portraits, done around 1914–1915. In a series of photographs from around 1927–1929 she appears in the pose of a weightlifter, with a slight air of the femme fatale, staring defiantly into the camera (cat. no. 136). In others done in 1928–1929 her face is hidden by carnival masks. For an autobiographical essay entitled *Aveux non avenus* (1930), Cahun and her companion Suzanne

Malherbe (also known as Marcel Moore) created ten photomontages using elements from her self-portraits, including a Pierrot head and the weightlifter. In 1932 Cahun joined the Surrealists. In 1937 she photographed enigmatic assemblages of sundry objects for *Le Coeur de Pic*, a collection of poems by Lise Deharme. The fifteenth plate in this book features a skull, a fork, and a clown figurine. That same year she left Paris for the Isle of Jersey, where she was to produce her final self-portraits shortly before her death in 1954.

M.R.

137
Diane Arbus
Tattooed man at a carnival, Md.
1970, printed later

274

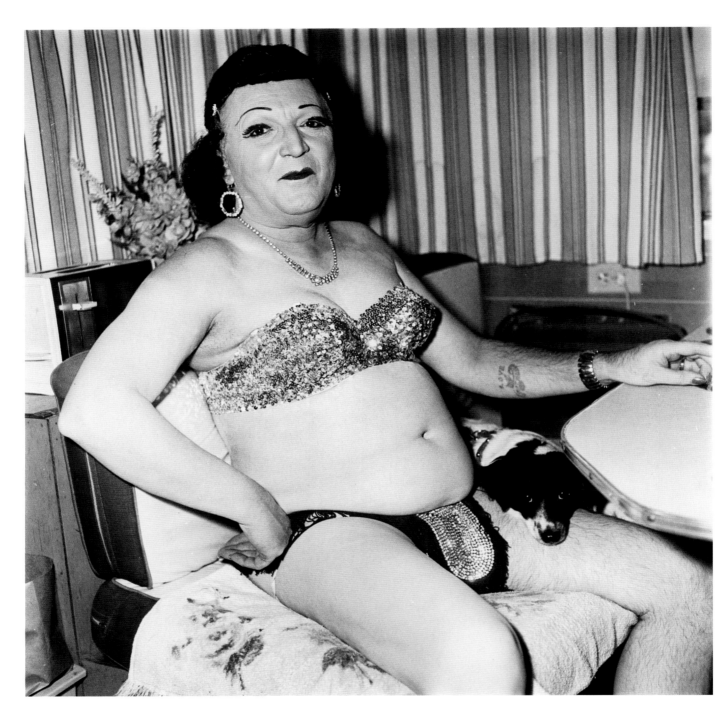

138
Diane Arbus
*Hermaphrodite and a dog in
a carnival trailer, Md.*
1970, printed later

139
Lisette Model
*Albert-Alberta, Hubert's 42nd Street
Flea Circus, New York* c. 1945

140
Izis
Foire du Trône: Sideshow, Crocodile
Woman, Paris 1959

141
Bruce Davidson
The Dwarf 1958

142
Cindy Sherman
Untitled B 1975

Charles Atlas
The Legend of Leigh Bowery 2001

Charles Atlas

Saint Louis, Missouri, born 1949

After making a short film entitled *Blue Studio: Five Segments* (1975–1976) in collaboration with the famed American choreographer and dancer Merce Cunningham, Atlas worked from 1978 to 1983 as filmmaker-in-residence for the Merce Cunningham Dance Company. He became known as the pioneer of a new form closer to video art than documentary, "videodance," in which the combining of different excerpts from a single choreography, often filmed in unusual places, allows him to convey his own perception of the dancers' work. A great admirer of Andy Warhol, he fills his films with references to punk and gay lifestyles, erasing the boundaries between popular culture and the elitist milieu of modern dance. In 1983 he created his first installation, *Times Five, for Merce*, in which extracts of films shot throughout his collaboration with Cunningham, interspersed with images in Super-8 and archival footage, are shown on five video screens. That same year his videodances began featuring unique performances conceived especially for him by such internationally renowned choreographers and dancers as Douglas Dunn, Karole Armitage, Philippe Découflé, John Kelly, and Bill Irwin. A number of Atlas's films were produced for television in Great Britain, France, Spain, and the United States. In 1989 he made a film entitled *Because We Must*, based on a choreography presented at the Sadler's Wells Theatre in London by the company run by Michael Clark, *enfant terrible* of modern dance, with whom Atlas has been collaborating regularly since 1983.

The Australian-born performance artist and costume designer Leigh Bowery, a close friend of Clark's, was among the players in this irreverent, grotesque choreography, which parodies the conventions of modern dance. Bowery, a key figure of London's underground scene, was already known in the milieu for the flamboyant performances he presented alone or with his assistant, Nicola Bateman, at his own clandestine nightclub, Taboo. In these designed-to-shock numbers he would undergo a series of farcical and extravagant metamorphoses that distorted the stereotypes of gay transvestism – wrapping himself in cling film, covering himself with blood and excrement, disguising himself as a retarded showgirl or a hideous clown. But it was when he became the favourite model of Lucian Freud,* in 1990, that he achieved the enduring celebrity he had always sought (cat. no. 144). Five years after Bowery's death from AIDS in 1994, Atlas made a short film entitled *Mrs. Peanut Visits New York* (1999), which shows Bowery strolling through Manhattan's industrial district disguised as a female version of Mr. Peanut, the Planter's Peanut mascot, wearing a floral print dress and transparent-heeled platform shoes. In 2001 Bowery became the subject of a new film by Atlas, *The Legend of Leigh Bowery* (cat. no. 143). This intimate portrayal of the famous provocateur provides insight into the cultural milieu that nourished his prodigious imagination. Atlas's portrayal, which includes many interviews with family members and close friends, extends beyond the myth to reveal the complicated man beneath the mask.

M.R.

144
Lucian Freud
Nude With Leg Up (*Leigh Bowery*)
1992

VIII Celestial Bodies

When Zarathustra arrived at the nearest of the towns … he found in that place many people assembled in the market square: for it had been announced that a tightrope walker would be appearing. And Zarathustra spoke thus to the people:

I teach you the Superman. Man is something that should be overcome. What have you done to overcome him?

…

What is the ape to men? A laughing-stock or a painful embarrassment. And just so shall man be to the Superman: a laughing-stock or a painful embarrassment.

…

Man is a rope, fastened between animal and Superman – a rope over an abyss.

Friedrich Nietzsche

282

145
Francisco Goya
Punctual Folly c. 1816–1824

146
Francisco Goya
A Young Witch Flying on a Rope Swing c. 1824–1828

147
Honoré Daumier
Man on a Rope c. 1858–1860

Edgar Degas
Paris, 1834 – Paris, 1917

After contact with Manet and his young admirers, known from 1874 on as the "Impressionists," Degas abandoned his earlier historical subjects and began depicting modern life. Increasingly, his pictures focused on different forms of entertainment and performance, aimed at both the masses and high society: theatre, music-hall, the dance foyer at the Opéra. The circus, too, provided artists of the period with themes whose evocative power went far beyond that of the traditional, timeworn images of academic art. Degas himself was a regular at the Cirque Fernando, located just at the foot of the Butte Montmartre, not far from his studio. In January 1879 – precisely when Edmond de Goncourt was working on his circus novel, *Les Frères Zemganno* – Degas went several times to see Miss Lala Kaira, known as the "Black Venus" or the "Cannon Woman." One of the most famous acrobats of her time, she put on an act of remarkable strength and daring (minus safety net) that fascinated the artist.[1] He made several preparatory drawings and a pastel portraying the performer being raised to the trapeze hanging only by her teeth. He even had her visit his studio in order to record details for the final canvas, *Miss Lala at the Cirque Fernando* (cat. no. 148).[2] As she is pulled up by the rope, her slightly bent legs and spread arms convey the slow rotation of her body as she rises. We see her from far below, hanging a little off-centre against a markedly three-dimensional space. It is the only painting by Degas that has the circus as its subject.

Until Degas, nineteenth-century images of acrobats in action were limited to sketches by draftsmen working for publishers of engravings or lithographs, made to be framed or sold as part of an album.[3] *Miss Lala* is thus a groundbreaking work. The subject would be explored subsequently by such artists as Seurat,* Toulouse-Lautrec,* Picasso,* Shinn,* and Calder,* and would henceforth be part of the metaphorical repertoire used to support the analogy between the world of the circus and the world of art.

C.N.-R.

1   Henri Loyrette, *Degas* (Paris: Fayard, 1991), p. 382. See also Anne Roquebert, *Degas* (Paris: Cercle d'Art, 1988): "The subject has been identified from the preparatory sketches annotated by Degas and a poster of *Miss Lala, Nicknamed the Cannon Woman*, a mulatto acrobat with the Cirque Fernando who presented an act called *Black Venus* in January 1879" (p. 160).

2   Loyrette, *Degas*, p. 382. The painting was included in the fourth Impressionist exhibition, held from 10 April to 11 May 1879.

3   See Ségolène Le Men, "Le Cirque et le monde de l'art, de Grandville à Courbet," in *Jours de cirque* (Monaco: Grimaldi Forum; Arles: Actes Sud, 2002), pp. 210–226.

148
Edgar Degas
Miss Lala at the Cirque Fernando
1879

149
Georges Seurat
Study for "The Circus" 1890–1891

Georges Seurat

Paris, 1859 – Paris, 1891

Georges Seurat was still an adolescent when he began going to the Cirque Fernando at the corner of Rue des Martyrs and Boulevard Rochechouart in Montmartre, near his parents' home. After his schooling at the École des Beaux-Arts in Paris in 1878–1879, followed by a year of military service in Brest, he took up art in earnest, focusing on contemporary themes. His interest in the Pierrot figure, then much in vogue in literary circles, is evident in two small oil studies of his childhood friend Aman-Jean done in 1883, *The Painter Aman-Jean as Pierrot* and *Pierrot with a White Pipe*. In the summer of 1887 middle-class diversions became one of his favourite subjects. Every evening, after a day's work in the Montmartre studio he had had since 1884, on Boulevard de Clichy, he attended the Cirque Fernando or performances at nearby show bars: Eden Concert, Concert Européen, Gaîté-Rochechouart, Divan Japonais. Many of his drawings from this period feature singers, ballerinas, tumblers, and acrobats, rendered in a simplified, hieratic style.

A painting done around the same time, *Circus Parade* (1887–1888), depicts the Cirque Corvi band at the Foire du Trône (the Foire au Pain d'Épice) on Place de la Nation. And several studies for *The Circus* made in 1890 represent the Cirque Fernando ring, seen in broad view in the compositional study (cat. no. 149). *The Circus*, according to Seurat scholars, is more indicative of a genuine interest in the popular arts than the artist's earlier works. In addition to the fact that it is based on on-site drawings, it also incorporates elements borrowed from Jules Chéret posters, which he collected. The tumbler somersaulting in the background is copied almost exactly from a poster promoting the Persivani and Vandervelde revue (1875) at the Ambassadeurs café. In the foreground, the stance of the clown in the horned wig – similar to the one worn by the famous Geronimo Medrano (see p. 187, fig. 1) – echoes that of one of the clowns in another poster, *L'Horloge, les Frères Léopold* (1877). And the female rider dancing on a white horse in a thrilling display of acrobatics à la Richards[1] shares points in common with yet another, *L'Amant des danseuses* (1888). The ringmaster, who was often the circus owner and here matches contemporary descriptions of Louis Fernando, is cracking his whip to direct the galloping horse, also a traditional circus symbol. Widely favoured by poster designers, the magnificent Pegasus motif appears as well on Picasso's* 1917 stage curtain for *Parade* (cat. 211). Seurat has paid special attention to the audience, using attire and postures to create easily identifiable types and classes. Drawn from all ranks of society, the spectators are arrayed in first-, second-, and third-class seats, matching the layout of the Cirque Fernando. The clown in the foreground, as Richard Thomson has pointed out, serves as a critical observer of the times, drawing attention to these social disparities by raising the curtain that normally precludes access to the ring.[2] A simple denunciation of social inequity, in keeping with Seurat's anarchist leanings? Or narcissistic identification with the clown figure self-exiled to the margins of society, all the better to analyze and parody it?

C.N.-R. and M.R.

---

1   A style of trick riding done on a bareback, unbridled horse developed in 1860 by the American-born performer Davis Richards (he died performing it in Saint Petersburg in 1866). It included numerous acts of bravado, including a somersault. Catherine Zavatta, *Les Mots du cirque* (Paris: Belin, 2001), p. 327.

2   Richard Thomson, *Seurat* (London: Phaidon, 1985), pp. 220–221.

150
Henri de Toulouse-Lautrec
Trained Horse and Monkey 1899

151
Henri de Toulouse-Lautrec
The Flying Trapeze 1899

152
Henri de Toulouse-Lautrec
Pas de Deux 1899

153
Henri de Toulouse-Lautrec
Bareback Rider 1899

154
Henri de Toulouse-Lautrec
Acrobat Rider (*Elle est gentille,
la demoiselle*) 1899

155
Henri de Toulouse-Lautrec
The Curtain Call 1899

156
Henri de Toulouse-Lautrec
Trainer Clown 1899

157
Henri de Toulouse-Lautrec
Clowness 1899

158
Henri de Toulouse-Lautrec
Voltige 1899

159
Henri de Toulouse-Lautrec
Entering the Ring 1899

160
Henri de Toulouse-Lautrec
Tightrope Walker 1899

161
Henri de Toulouse-Lautrec
Work on the Mat 1899

162
Albert Londe
Tumblers c. 1887

299

163
Albert Londe
Tightrope Walker c. 1887

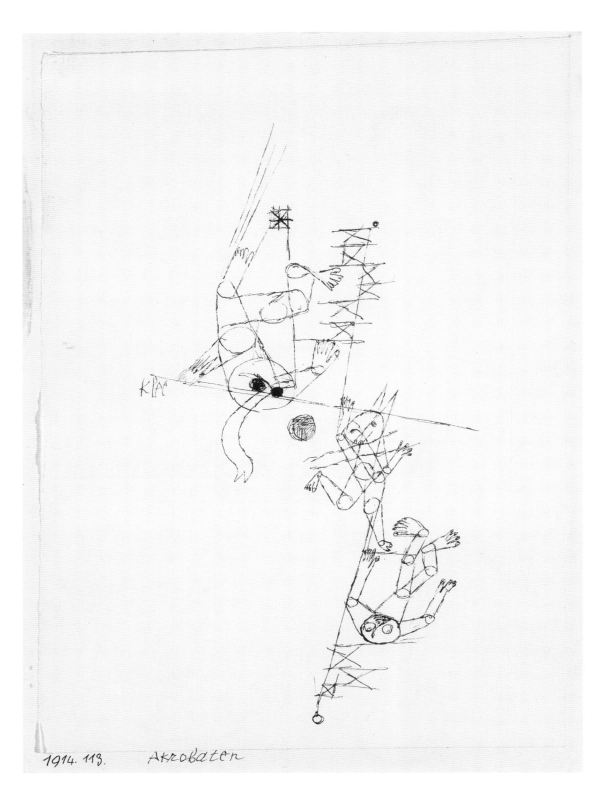

167
Paul Klee
Acrobats 1914

168
Paul Klee
Tightrope Walker 1923

169
Pablo Picasso
Harlequin and Pierrot 1918

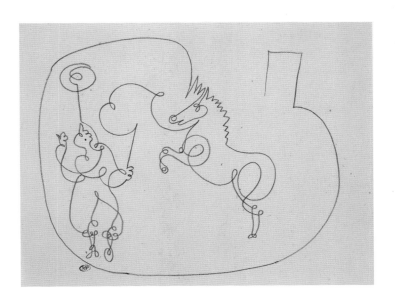

170
Pablo Picasso
Horse and Trainer Juggler 1920

171
Pablo Picasso
Horse and Trainer Juggler 1920

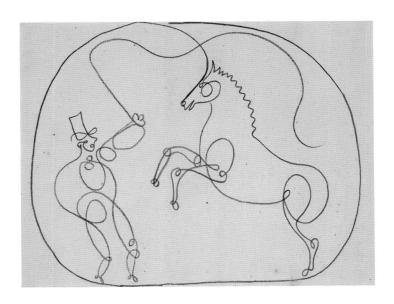

172
Pablo Picasso
Horse and Trainer 1920

173
Pablo Picasso
Horse and Female Trainer 1920

Alexander Calder

Lawnton, Pennsylvania, 1898 – New York, 1976

After graduating in mechanical engineering in 1919, Alexander Calder studied painting with John Sloan* and George Luks* at the Art Students League in New York from 1923 to 1926. In the spring of 1925, equipped with a press pass, he spent days at the Ringling Bros. and Barnum & Bailey Circus making sketches used later that year for a drawing published in the *National Police Gazette*, a sports and entertainment paper. Around the same time, he did two circus paintings in the New York School style, *The Flying Trapeze* (1925) and *Circus* (1926). In 1926 he went to Paris, where frequent visits to the Cirque Medrano inspired him to fashion toy figures made out of wire and assorted materials that became the initial version of the miniature "circus in a suitcase," to which he continued adding until 1932.[1] In the fall of 1926, in his Montparnasse studio at 22 Rue Daguerre, he animated these figures in their first performances, based on the Medrano routines. Before long, the local artistic and literary crowd was flocking to his door.[2] The following year, after the legendary clown Paul Fratellini attended a performance, Calder made him a large-scale model of his rubber-hose-and-wire dachshund, "Miss Tamara," which Albert Fratellini would lead round on a leash in the three-brother act at Cirque Medrano. *Le Cirque Calder* became so famous that the circus reviewer Legrand-Chabrier devoted three articles to it within the space of two years.[3]

The elliptical forms of Calder's wire sculptures evoking acrobatic feats, first made in 1926, reappear in some hundred drawings from 1931 and 1932 (cat. nos. 175–177) that capture the characteristic movements of jugglers and trapeze artists in single, uninterrupted pencil strokes. Done from memory in his Paris studio, these images recall the American circus acts he saw in New York in 1925. Unlike Picasso,* for whom the circus performer allegorically represented the artist, a pariah exiled to the margins of society, Calder had a very positive, Anglo-American notion of the trapeze artist as the uncontested star of a grand form of popular entertainment. He was fascinated with wide-angle views (*The Circus*, cat. no. 175), which allowed him to explore the near and far planes and the spatial tensions generated by the simultaneous presentation of different acts in three rings under the immense big top.

Calder spent the winter of 1927–1928 in New York, where his first one-man show was held at the Weyhe Gallery, on Lexington Avenue. Because the gallery was upstairs, he made a wire sign to attract passers-by, hanging it outside from a single hook to allow the acrobat to swing as if on a trapeze (cat. no. 174). From the 1930s on, he expressed his fascination with the dynamics of bodies in space mainly in abstract mobiles and stabiles, but he continued to look to the circus, and in 1944 exhibited plaster models of trained animals and acrobats (cat. no. 190).

C.N.-R.

1   Once completed, the miniature circus comprised seventy human and animal figures, each about 15 centimetres high. Made of wire, corks, and bits of cloth, they were delightfully funny. See Joy Spergling, "The Popular Sources of Calder's Circus: The Humpty Dumpty Circus, Ringling Brothers and Barnum & Bailey, and the Cirque Medrano," *Journal of American Culture* 17, no. 4 (1994), p. 4.

2   Joan Marter, *Alexander Calder* (Cambridge: Cambridge University Press, 1991), pp. 60–61. For financial reasons, Calder staged the early performances in his studio.

3   Legrand-Chabrier, "Paris-Montparnasse et son cirque," *Patrie*, 6 May 1927; "Un Petit Cirque à domicile," *Candide*, no. 171 (23 June 1927), p. 7; "Alexandre Calder et son cirque automatique," *La Volonté*, 19 May 1929.

175
Alexander Calder
The Circus 1932

176
Alexander Calder
Precision 1932

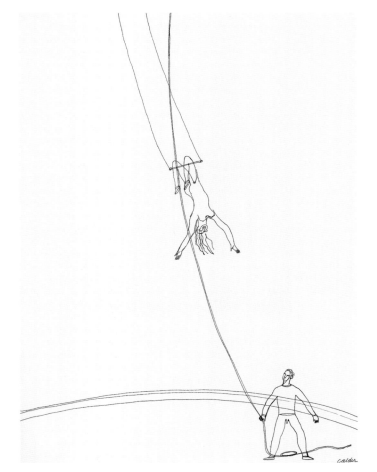

177
Alexander Calder
Woman on Flying Trapeze 1931

178
Le Cirque de Calder, film directed by
Carlos Vilardebó, France, 1961

179
Max Beckmann
The Tightrope Walkers, plate 8 of the portfolio *Der Jahrmarkt* ("The Annual Fair") 1921

180
Otto Dix
Circus Scene 1923

Everett Shinn

Pilesgrove, New Jersey, 1876 – New York, 1953

As a boy, Everett Shinn was enchanted by the circuses that came to Woodstown, New Jersey, where his family had settled in 1887. After training at the Pennsylvania Academy of the Fine Arts in Philadelphia from 1893 to 1895, he moved to New York in 1897, not far from Madison Square Garden, where he often attended the circus. He visited London in May 1900 and made sketches at the Hippodrome theatre on Leicester Square, going on from there to Paris to make the rounds of theatres and show bars in Montparnasse. The theatrical world would continue to provide him with subject matter for many years. In New York in 1901 he exhibited two circus paintings, *In Green Room Circus* and *The Circus*, at Boussod, Valadon & Co. In 1908 he presented *The Hippodrome, London* (1902), and seven other canvases on the show business theme with the group known as The Eight. His predilection for acrobatic exploits resulted in a major work in 1924,

Tightrope Walker (cat. no. 181). From 1917 he worked as art director on a variety of Hollywood films, including the 1929 *Polly of the Circus*, directed by Alfred Santell. During the 1930s and 1940s he painted acrobats and clowns from drawings made at Proctor's Theater in New York, which he had attended since the turn of the century. Not long before his death he made several visits to the Ringling Hotel and the circus's winter quarters in Sarasota, Florida, to make drawings intended as the basis for future paintings.

M.R.

181
Everett Shinn
Tightrope Walker 1924

182
Max Beckmann
Variety Show 1927

183
Marc Chagall
Acrobat 1914

184
Marc Chagall
Acrobat 1930

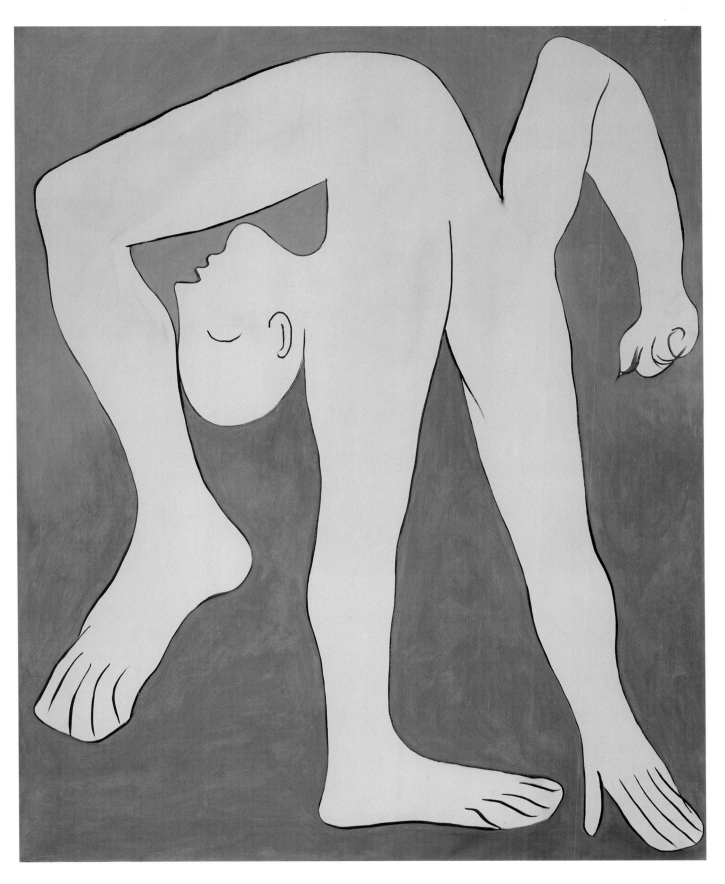

185
Pablo Picasso
The Acrobat 1930

320

Milton Avery

Altmar, New York, 1893 – New York, 1965

During the 1930s Milton Avery occasionally interrupted his landscape and domestic-scene painting to work with circus and music-hall themes. He did his first gouaches on black paper in the summer of 1927, returning to this medium for a later series inspired by the vaudeville performances he regularly attended at the Palace Theater in New York (*Acrobats*, 1931; *Jugglers*, 1932). In the same deliberately naive and spontaneous style, he produced a group of oils that evoke the thrilling feats of circus acts (*Trapeze Artist*, cat. no. 186; *Three Ring Circus*, c. 1939).

M.R.

187
Umbo
Trapeze Artists 1932, printed later

Robert Riggs

Decatur, Illinois, 1896 – Philadelphia, 1970

Robert Riggs's dream at age eleven was to join the travelling carnival troupes that he saw in Decatur and pictured in a hundred or so drawings that reveal his precocious talent. After studies at the Art Students League in New York from 1915 to 1917, he worked as an illustrator for the Philadelphia advertising agency N.W. Ayer and Son. In 1918 he spent time in Paris, where he took courses at the Académie Julian. He produced his first lithographs in 1932, on themes from the popular world of boxing (*Before the Fight*, 1932). When Ringling Brothers came to Philadelphia the following year he made a systematic study of the circus. During the day he sketched and photographed the performers outside the ring,

and in the evening he attended their performances. From this close contact came a series of fifteen meticulously realistic lithographs depicting the top-billed acts of the three-ring show: the clown Felix Adler, the Flying Concellos, the bareback-riding Reiffenach sisters, the high-wire walker Con Colleano, the elephant trainer Larry Davis, and the Wen Hais, Chinese acrobats. In 1934 national acclaim for the technical virtuosity of his lithograph *Center Ring* (cat. no. 188) prompted him to give up painting and devote himself to drawing and printmaking.

M.R.

322

188
Robert Riggs
Center Ring 1933

189
Fernand Léger
The Acrobat and His Partner 1948

191
Max Beckmann
Back Bend (*The Acrobat*) c. 1950

190
Alexander Calder
Acrobats 1944

George Segal

New York, 1924 – Trenton, New Jersey, 2000

George Segal studied art and architecture from 1941 to 1949. He earned his living farming chickens in New Jersey until 1958, at which time he converted his farm into a vast studio. Before long he turned from painting to sculpture, and began fashioning large figures from chicken wire and plaster-soaked burlap. In 1961 he adopted a new technique that consisted of wrapping human models in wet plaster bandages and then assembling the resulting casts of the various body parts with fresh plaster. Frozen in stereotypical poses and surrounded by everyday objects, these often solitary life-size figures play motionless roles in scenes worthy of Beckett's existential theatre.

Segal's passing interest in the circus between 1969 and 1972 resulted in several sculptures that evoke the high-energy routines of tightrope walkers and trapeze artists. In the mid-1970s he began producing works for installation in public spaces. In one of them, *Circus Flyers* (1981), he returned to the acrobat theme, creating two plaster aerialists in dynamic poses that now hang from the atrium ceiling of Butler Square West, a former Minneapolis warehouse. A similar duo is captured in a breathtaking midair catch in the 1988 *Circus Acrobats* (cat. no. 192).

M.R.

192
George Segal
Circus Acrobats 1988
(full view opposite)

193
Lisette Model
Circus, New York 1945

194
Lisette Model
Circus, New York 1945

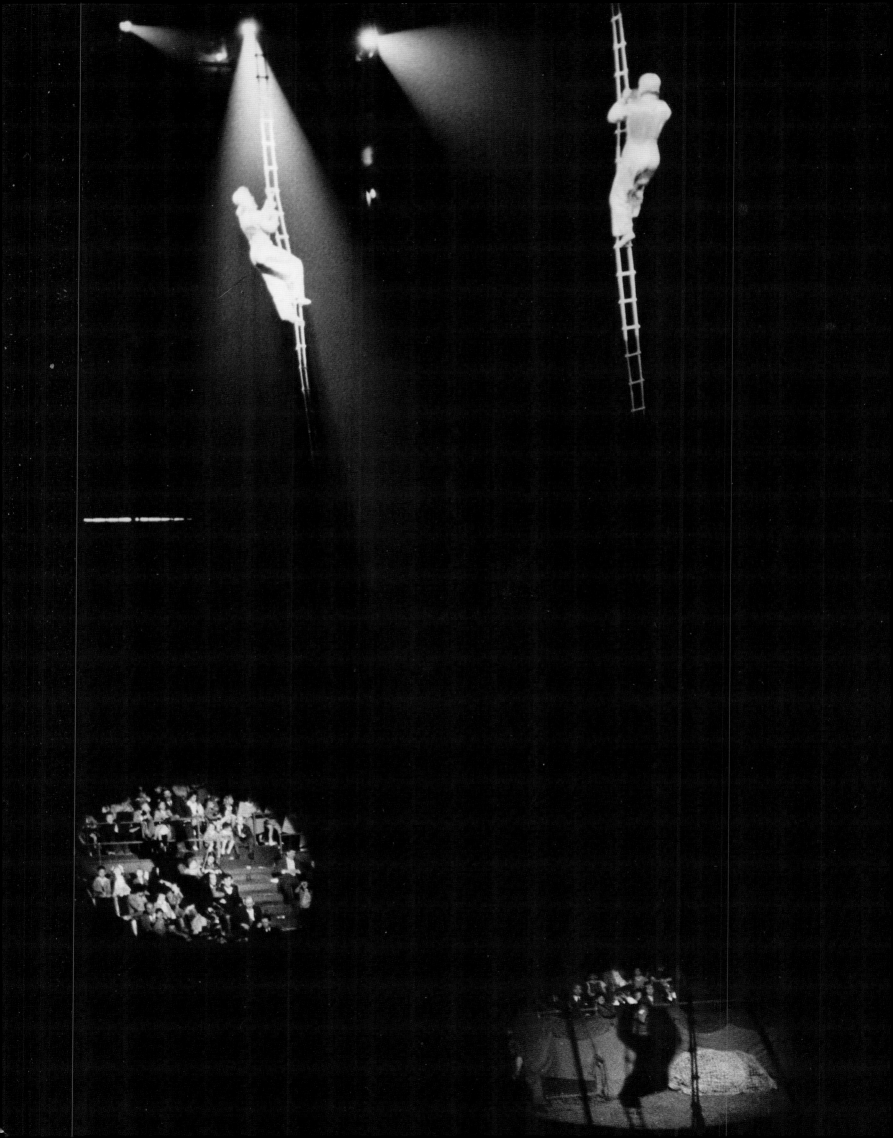

195
Harold Edgerton
Moscow Circus 1963, printed 1985

Harold Edgerton

Fremont, Nebraska, 1903 – Boston, 1990

After studying photography with an uncle between 1915 and 1921, Harold Edgerton earned degrees in electrical engineering (B.Sc., University of Nebraska, 1926; M.Sc. and D.Sc., Massachusetts Institute of Technology, 1927 and 1931). He joined the faculty of the Massachusetts Institute of Technology in 1932, eventually becoming a professor emeritus in 1968. In 1931 he perfected the electronic stroboscope, a device that emits hundreds of flashes per second, enabling photographers to capture motion invisible to the naked eye. In 1938 he revolutionized sports photography by using the strobe technique to deconstruct the movements of gymnasts, divers, and golfers in stop-action images. He also worked on its application in motion pictures. In the 1940s the circus provided him an opportunity to test his high-speed, multiflash system outside the lab. A dozen of his circus photographs appeared in *National Geographic* in 1948. In 1963 Edgerton produced extraordinarily precise shots of the Moscow Circus acrobats in motion (cat. no. 195).

M.R.

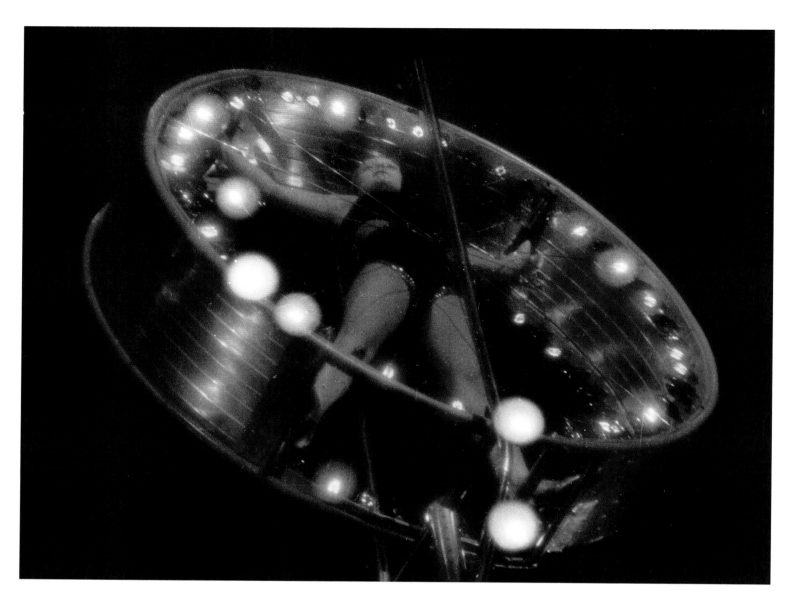

196
Aleksandr Rodchenko
The Rhine Wheel c. 1940,
printed c. 1980–1989

197
Aleksandr Rodchenko
The Pyramid 1937, printed later

Louise Bourgeois

Paris, born 1911

In 1935 Louise Bourgeois abandoned the study of mathematics at the Sorbonne to train as a painter, first at the École des Beaux-Arts and then at several independent academies (Ranson, Julian, Colarossi, and Grande Chaumière). She studied with André Lhote, Othon Friesz, Paul Colin, and Fernand Léger.* She considered Léger to have been her most influential teacher, since it was he who steered her toward sculpture. In 1938 she married the American art historian Robert Goldwater and settled in New York. She trained for two years in Vaclav Vytlacil's painting studio at the Art Students League and spent time with a number of European artists – Giacometti, Duchamp,* Tanguy, Le Corbusier, and Miró – who had sought refuge in the United States during the war. In 1949 she began devoting herself to sculpture. During the 1950s she produced thin, anthropomorphic works in wood that evoke human solitude. These were followed by arrangements of supple, organic forms in plaster and latex that are sometimes suggestive of human body parts. As is evident from her most characteristic sculpture of this period, a large latex phallus called *Fillette* (1968), Bourgeois's art stems from her own personal history and from the most ambiguous of human fantasies. More recently, she has produced monumental works for major international exhibitions, including *Cell (Arch of Hysteria)*, part of a series entitled *Cells*, shown at the Venice Biennale in 1993: in an enclosure of metal doors, a polished bronze sculpture of a male body lies arched in the grip of hysteria, headless and armless, as if dismembered by the nearby circular saw. This distorted figure, which makes its first discreet appearance in the 1991 sculpture *Cell III*, is also featured in a 1992 drawing of a mother and child, *Altered States*, and a year later in another, suspended bronze sculpture, *Arch of Hysteria* (cat. no. 198), where it is arched to the utmost, forming a circle as the hands and feet touch. The exceedingly taut position, as apt to lead to collapse as to flight, implies a surprising blend of strength and fragility that recalls the prowess of circus contortionists and tumblers.

M.R.

198
Louise Bourgeois
Arch of Hysteria 1993

IX Harlequin

The face has been identified as Picasso's. But the figure is also Harlequin. Why is the artist wearing a cocked hat and diamond-patterned suit? What dignity or indignity is he claiming for himself? Could it be that the art of our century goes hand in glove with irony?

Jean Starobinski

Harlequin was originally Hellequin, an animal-faced demon who, deep in the winter forest, led his howling retinue of departed souls. A dweller in the kingdom of death, a messenger from the underworld, he served as ferryman between the realms of the living and the dead. In the Middle Ages he became a good devil, associated with Carnival time and its glimpses of the world beyond. He was a cheerful fellow, uncouth and hairy, but benign. During the eighteenth century, refined by love, he assumed the form in which we know him now, wearing the colourful, diamond-patterned suit that recalls the variegated costume of the jester.

Picasso's Harlequins – like Guillaume Apollinaire's Harlequin "Trismegistus," avatar of the thrice-great Hermes, guide of souls, a mischievous god – have not lost this original connection to the kingdom of death and unreason. They are situated midway between the hell down in the ring, with its creatures of the night, and the circus heaven above, where acrobats and aerialists soar.

J.C.

199
Pablo Picasso
Harlequin 1917

200
Pablo Picasso
The Painter Salvado as Harlequin
1923

201
Pablo Picasso
Paul as Harlequin 1924

202
Pablo Picasso
Portrait of an Adolescent Dressed as Pierrot 1922

204
Pablo Picasso
Study for the Stage Curtain for the Ballet "Parade" 1917

205
Pablo Picasso
Fairground Circus 1922

206
Pablo Picasso
Study for the Stage Curtain for
"Pulcinella": Harlequin in the Ring
with Ballerina and Rider 1920

211
Pablo Picasso
Stage Curtain for the Ballet "Parade"
1917

Chronology

History of the Circus 1500–2000
15th Century

The origin of acrobats, buffoons, and itinerant and theatrical players dates from Greco-Roman antiquity. The Miles Gloriosus of actor-playwright Plautus (d. 180 B.C.) is an ancestor to the Capitano of the sixteenth-century *commedia dell'arte*. The *fabula Atellana*, a form of mime popular in the Roman Campania in the second half of the fourth century, also gave rise to various buffoon characters that have come down through the ages. Later, medieval mystery plays relied on the interplay of characters typifying the human condition, with a religious view to the afterlife. There are no documents describing these early periods because these comic players were so much a part of daily life that no writer felt the need to comment on them. Documents begin to appear in the sixteenth century, along with the formation of the first troupes consisting of professional actors and a leader (*commedia dell'arte* in fact means "comedy of the profession," or "comedy of skill"). Soon, a distinction grew up between the *commedia sostenuta* (with written text and dialogue, a more literary and aristocratic genre, performed on permanent stages in theatres) and the *commedia all'improviso* (with improvisations on a well-known scenario by stock characters, often masked, a more popular genre occupying the temporary stages set up at fairs and in public squares).

The characters of the *commedia* showed their varied regional Italian origins. They often spoke local dialects, which did not matter, since their delivery was based mainly on gestures, props, a mask, acrobatics, pirouettes, leaps, dances, and so forth. Scapin and Beltrame came from Milan, Giandujia from Turin, Coviello from Calabria, Pantalone from Venice, the Dottore from Bologna, Arlecchino and Brighella from Bergamo, and so on.

Through the highly Italianized milieu of the Lyons silk industry and the presence of the Medicis in the French royal family, special bonds were established in the sixteenth century between various regions of France and the Italian *commedia dell'arte* troupes.

1492

France, Paris: March, Louis XI authorized the monks of the Abbey of Saint-Germain-des-Près to establish a fair on the site of the gardens of the king of Navarre to compensate their losses in the wars with England. From then on, the large fairs all functioned along similar lines: the throne granted the religious authorities of an abbey the privilege of organizing a fair and collecting entrance fees. Fairs took place annually, at fixed dates associated with a religious festival. With the advent of the fairs, a new phenomenon occurred: the formation of the first associations, the first companies.

History of the Circus 1500–2000
16th Century

Troupes were often formed around a family of actors. They travelled from town to town throughout Europe with their caravan of wagons. In general, before setting up their stage and performing, they had to obtain permission from the local lord or magistrate, sometimes even the bishop or Parliament, for the Church judged their often crude burlesque farces severely. The troupes performed in public squares for the populace and in theatres or even princely courts for the nobility.

In general, a troupe at this time consisted of the following stock characters: a director, who also acted; two old men, Pantalone and the Dottore (an old pedant); two male lovers (*innamorati*); two female lovers (*prima donna innamorata* and *secunda donna innamorata*); two comic valets (*zannis*), one of them deceitful and cunning, the other oafish, forming a pair of opposites (the most famous eventually being Arlecchino-Brighella); one or two *soubrettes*, Zagna, Fantesca; a Capitano, or a Scaramouche or Scapin; incidental roles: narrator, singer, dancer, acrobat, etc.

In the seventeenth and eighteenth centuries other characters made their appearance on stage: Brighella the schemer, Pulcinella-Polichinelle, Pedrolino-Pierrot, Giglio-Gilles, Isabella, and Columbine.

At this period, Arlecchino was something of an intangible chameleon, a crude faun with a wild imagination and biting wit. His costume was a long jacket laced up the front and trousers with multicoloured strips of cloth sewn on here and there. He wore a black mask and a cap of the period adorned with a rabbit or fox tail. It was, all in all, a rag-picker's getup.

1541

England, Nottingham: First mention of the Goose Fair in the Nottingham town records. This market fair, where tumblers and comedians also performed, had been held on Saint Matthew's Day (21 September) every year since 1284. Beginning in 1752, it took place on 2 October.

1547

Italy: A character named Pedrolino or Piero figured often in scenarios by various authors until 1604, reappearing in 1665. He is an honest, pleasant-looking young valet and a charming suitor of *soubrettes*, so different from the other *zannis*, or valets, that he often took his place alongside them without overlapping them. In fact, the valets often played in pairs, in "couples," so as to create comical situations through the collision of their personalities. Pedrolino was a sensitive and delicate fellow, but he knew how to play jokes and willingly asked forgiveness for others' sins. His white costume with a ruff resembled Pulcinella's but was closer fitting. With his powdered white face, he wore no mask, but he did wear a fairly large hat. During tours in France the Italian Piero soon became Pierrot, wearing much the same costume and showing the same character traits, with perhaps a touch more elegance.

349

1601

France: Founding of the Fedeli, a troupe of comedians, which remained active until 1652.

1603

France, Versailles: Invited to the French court by Marie de Médicis, the Gelosi (including the great actress Isabella Andreini) were a resounding success.

1604

France: Giambattista Andreini, the son of Isabella, took over the direction of the Fedeli, heirs to the Gelosi's tradition.

Lyons: Death of Isabella Andreini, who wrote many poetical pieces, songs, sonnets, madrigals, and scenarios that were published by her husband, Francesco, after the Gelosi disbanded the same year.

1611

Italy: The Confidenti took a new director, Flaminio Scala, and introduced a new character, Scapino, played by Francesco Gabrielli. Scapino was a valet, a jack of all trades. As his name implies (*scappare* means "to escape"), he comes and goes, muddling everything, forgetting everything, a liar, impossible to pin down, an unrepentant lover, a lover for the pleasure of it. He wears a loose-fitting shirt with green and white stripes and trousers, like people of his station. A wide belt slips down over his narrow hips. He wears a mask and a cap with a very long visor and a long feather. Thereafter, this character was part of every troupe; in 1671, in France, Molière put the character Scapin in *Les Fourberies de Scapin*.

1613

France, Paris: Summoned by Marie de Médicis, the Fedeli came to Paris to perform at court and at the Hôtel de Bourgogne. The Italian troupe returned to Paris in 1623 but had less success with its plays; the public did not appreciate the fact that they spoke a mixture of Italian dialects (Venetian, Bergamese, Genoan) with Castillian, French, and German thrown in.

1618

France, Paris: Two itinerant comedians obtained permission to perform at the Saint-Germain fair. One played Arlequin, the other Colombine.

Italy, Naples: 16 April, the first appearance of the stock character Pulcinella, at the carnival of Naples, on the stage of an actual theatre. However, he had existed for a long time in troupes of travelling acrobats. Born "of two different fathers," Maccus and Bocco, this epicurean had a double temperament and a double hump, one on his back and the other on his stomach. Pulcinella can be kind, sensual, crafty, and acrobatic, or he can be clumsy, gross, and slow moving; master or valet, whimsical old bachelor, selfish and cruel. He wears a loose-fitting white shirt with a ruff and large flowing trousers, like the peasants of Acerra (region of Salerno). He wears an immense white skullcap or a big grey hat. Around 1640, in France, his costume in the Mazarin troupe became a jacket with a starched ruff and red and yellow trousers trimmed with green, like the French Polichinelle, cut to fit the two enormous bulges.

The Neapolitan Pulcinella quickly changed elsewhere in Europe according to culture. In France the potbellied, humpbacked Polichinelle who had appeared in the reign of Henry IV was preferred. In England Punchinello, called Punch, was more fiercely ironic and a more aggressive seducer (according to one song, he could satisfy twenty-two women). In Central Europe there already existed a Hanswurst ("John Sausage"), a sort of plump Pulcinella, potbellied and piggish, in Holland a Tonellgey, and in Spain a Don Christoval and a Pulichinela.

1622

Italy: Arlecchino's costume changed somewhat. The rags at random on his jacket and pants became blue, red, and green triangles fastened by a yellow braid. The mask still bore a crafty expression.

1628

Germany, Nuremberg: The Fechthaus presented animal fights, hunting scenes, and burlesque games of comedians and various travelling attractions in a rectangular open-air arena.

1639

France, Paris: Giuseppe Bianchi's troupe was called to Paris by Louis XIII. There they performed several "operas," like *Orfeo*, plays interspersed with songs and dances. The troupe left France in 1648 because of the uprising of the Fronde.

1640

France, Paris: The Saint-Germain fair attained considerable proportions by including on its site the dressing-rooms of the actors, puppeteers, tightrope walkers, and animal exhibitors.

1653

England, London: Opening of Sadler's Wells, which became the favourite theatre for animal exhibits, acrobats, and tightrope walkers. The annals of this variety theatre include the names of famous English circus families, such as Adams, Bell, Bradbury, Bridges, Clarke, Cooke, Keyes, Lee, Newsome, Price, and Woolford.

France, Paris: The Comédiens-Italiens moved into the Théâtre du Petit-Bourbon.

1658

France, Paris: François Datelin dit Brioché, one of the most famous puppeteers of the period, obtained permission to present his show at the Saint-Germain fair. When the fair closed in the spring, he returned to his theatre on Rue Guénégaud.

1660

France, Paris: The Fiorelli-Loccatelli troupe, later called the Ancienne Troupe de la Comédie-Italienne, settled in Paris and moved from the Théâtre du Petit-Bourbon to the Palais-Royal, where it performed alternately with Molière's troupe.

1661

France, Paris: The actor Domenico Biancolelli gave a new form to the costume of Arlequin (Arlecchino was more and more often gallicized to Arlequin, at least in France). The jacket became shorter, the triangles became bicoloured lozenges with blue, red, or green, and a cocked hat replaced the toque. The character changed too: less a tumbler, dancer, and acrobat, less of an ungainly rag picker, he was a more important valet, wittier, sometimes the big lover of the *prima donna*. Louis XIV, who particularly appreciated Biancolelli's performances, once attended a show incognito, on an evening that was less successful than usual. The noble spectator remarked upon this to Arlequin, who answered, "Sire, do not tell the king, or he will throw me out."

1663

France, Paris: Inauguration of the Saint-Laurent fair in its final site, between Rue du Faubourg-Saint-Martin and Rue du Faubourg-Saint-Denis. It was held there at nearly regular intervals thereafter.

1665

France, Paris: 15 February, first appearance in France of the Italian Pedrolino, in Molière's *Dom Juan, ou le Festin de pierre*.

352

1668

France, Paris: First use of French in the comic scenes performed by Domenico Biancolelli.

1673

England, London: After making a name for himself in the role of Scaramouche, Tiberio Fiurelli performed in London. His success was so great that his name quickly became a synonym for clown or buffoon. His mimicry and grimaces had a decisive influence on the style of English actors.

1675

France, Paris: The character of Pantalone developed in the hands of the actor Antonio Riccoboni. He became a good father, a decrepit old man who affected youth, ever the dupe. He wore short trousers, big red socks, a black *zimmara*, and sometimes a large pair of glasses. This red and black outfit is characteristic of Pantalone.

Catarina Biancolelli, Domenico's daughter, debuted in the role of Colombine at the Comédie-Italienne.

1677

England, London: First performance, at Drury Lane, of Ravenscroft's adaptation of *Les Fourberies de Scapin*, entitled *Scaramouche a Philosopher, Harlequin, a Schoolboy, Bravo, Merchant, and Magician*, described as a "comedy in the Italian manner." In this English adaptation of Molière's play the character of Scapin, played by Jo Haines, became a stupid and wicked Harlequin.

1678

France, Paris: The first fairground comedy, *La Force de l'amour et de la magie*, was performed at the Saint-Germain fair by the troupe of the brothers Charles and Pierre Alard. The play's success earned the Alards the privilege of performing before Louis XIV that year. Charmed by the show, the king authorized further performances at the Saint-Germain fair the following year, on the condition that they include no singing or dancing.

1680

France, Paris: 21 October, a royal ordinance combined the actors of the Hôtel de Bourgogne and the Théâtre Guénégaud to form the Comédie-Française. From then on, only the Grands-Comédiens de Sa Majesté had the right to present spoken plays in Paris. This decree did not affect the Comédie-Italienne, where foreign actors performed, or the Opéra, whose productions were of a different kind from "recited plays and comedies." It was aimed most particularly at the Alards' troupe by revoking previous authorizations broadly overstepped by the presentation of actual plays going well beyond the permitted "few speeches accompanied by acrobatics." Throughout its history, the Comédie-Française endeavoured to maintain a monopoly on spoken plays, thus obliging the actors of the great fairs to constantly reinvent new forms of entertainment that enabled them to sidestep the magistrates' surveillance.

1681

France, Paris: In their scenarios, the Comédiens-Italiens began regularly inserting scenes in French, which increased interest for spectators who were unfamiliar with Italian.

c. 1618

France, Paris: Jacques Callot, *Les Trois Pantalons*.

1622

Italy, Florence: In the service of the Medicis, Jacques Callot executed a series of 24 prints entitled *Balli di Sfessania* (*The Asinine Dances* or *Dances of Idiocy*).

1645

Italy, Rome: Jan Miel, *Carnival in the Piazza Colonna Rome* (c. 1645–1650).

1697

France, Paris: After the departure of the Comédiens-Italiens from Paris, the painter Claude Gillot regularly attended the revivals of their shows at the Saint-Germain and Saint-Laurent fairs.

1683

France, Paris: The Comédie-Italienne moved to the Hôtel de Bourgogne.

The character of Colombine "the coquette" was then played by Catarina Biancolelli, daughter of Domenico Biancolelli, the famous Arlequin. As this contemporary quatrain describes her, "Colombine dans ses Amours / trompe ses Amants tous les jours / Comme un singe elle a de l'adresse / et plus qu'un renar de Finesse." ("Colombine all in her loves / Deceives her lovers daily. / She agile as a monkey moves, / She's than a fox more wily.") Similarly, Françoise Biancolelli changed the character of Isabella into a "big flirt who led everyone by the nose."

1684

France, Paris: Giuseppe Giaratone donned the guise of Pierrot in Nolant de Fatouville's play *Arlequin empereur dans la lune*, presented by the Comédiens-Italiens on the stage of the Hôtel de Bourgogne. The play enjoyed such popularity that it was still being performed at the fairgrounds in 1752.

1685

France, Paris: The Comédie-Italienne took the initiative of performing some plays entirely in French.

1687

England, London: First performance, at Drury Lane, of an English adaption of the play *Arlequin empereur dans la lune*. The "spoken pantomime" *Harlequin, Emperor on the Moon* was often revived in England through 1777.

1688

France, Paris: Moritz von der Beck directed a troupe of acrobats at the Saint-Germain fair. His agility on the tightrope immediately won the public's favour.

Death of Domenico Biancolelli. Management of the Comédiens-Italiens assumed by Evaristo Gherardi.

1689

France, Paris: At the Saint-Germain fair, Alexandre Bertrand and his brother Jean rented a space in the closed end of Rue des Quatre-Vents, where they gave their first puppet show. Encouraged by his success, Alexandre Bertrand built a second theatre in the open courtyard of the Saint-Germain fair the following year and called it the Jeu des Victoires. In so doing, he violated the royal ordinance of 21 October 1680 by combining "actors of wood" with real actors who performed plays without interludes of tumbling and dancing. Consequently, on 10 February 1692, Bertrand's theatre was demolished by order of M. de La Reynie, lieutenant general of the police.

1697

France, Paris: The quite vulgar carrying on that was accepted when spoken in Italian was more offensive in French. Informed that the comedians were "making indecent representations and saying various foul things in their comedies," the king warned them in 1696 that if they did not cease immediately, "he would put an end to them and send them all back to Italy." It is easy to detect the influence of Madame de Maintenon, who did not at all like this type of show. *La Fausse Prude* was published in Holland in 1697, a novel directed against Madame de Maintenon. The head of the Italians' troupe had the questionable idea of entitling one of his shows *La finta matrigna* – "The False Stepmother." The king retaliated on 13 May by firing the Comédiens-Italiens and having "their theatre closed permanently." Furthermore, they were banned from coming within 30 leagues (120 kilometres) of Paris.

The expulsion of the Comédiens-Italiens, who had struggled to obtain access to the best stages in Paris, worked to the advantage of the small troupes performing in the theatres at the Saint-Germain and Saint-Laurent fairs. Two troupes moved in almost permanently: that of the Alard brothers and Moritz von der Beck's widow; and that of Bertrand and Dolet. The actors were professionals from large companies, assisted by volunteers and acrobats. They performed the repertory of Arlequin and Scaramouche. Audiences were made up of grand seigneurs eager for such delights, marquises of easy virtue, honest bourgeois, rascals, and adventurers. The Comédie-Française, naturally anxious to protect its privilege of performing stage plays in Paris, lobbied against this competition, often securing the demolition of the fairground theatres, which were rebuilt as if by magic, due to popular pressure and police indulgence. The fair comedians had another way of circumventing royal edicts. They put on *opere* with orchestra, dancing, songs, and pantomimes.

The actor Marc made his debut at the Saint-Germain fair in the role of Gilles, giving birth to the French version of this stock character. The character of Gilles le Niais, created in the mid-seventeenth century by a fairground player, Sieur de la Force, was another incarnation of this naive and foolish valet. Throughout the eighteenth century and into the nineteenth, Gilles was so popular at the fair that he eclipsed Pierrot.

1699

France, Paris: 20 February, police lieutenant d'Argenson reiterated the ban on performing comedies and farces at the fair. Expecting Parliament to intervene, the fair people ignored the decree and continued enlarging their theatres and troupes.

354

1700

France, Paris: The widow of Moritz von der Beck, Jeanne Godefroy, who was known as the Widow Maurice, formed a partnership with Charles Alard to operate a theatrical enterprise until 1706.

1701

England, London: First performance, at Drury Lane, of the pantomime *Italian Night Scene* by a fair troupe of the Alards.

France, Paris: At the Saint-Germain fair, the leaper Crespin played the role of Gilles in the troupe of Alard and Widow Maurice. He was called "Gilles le boîteux" because of a slight limp that did not, however, keep him from rope dancing with grace and agility.

1705

France, Paris: 26 June, Parliament obliged fairground companies to obey the prohibition on presenting comedies. It was a temporary victory for the Comédie-Française, which sought to maintain its exclusive privileges.

1707

France, Paris: Still under the policy of the Comédie-Française, actors at the fairs were prohibited from using dialogue in their plays (which made them similar to the *commedia sostenuta*). To get around this new decision of Parliament, dialogue was written on signboards and shown to the audience, who were delighted with this clever solution.

1709

France, Paris: The fair troupe of Bertrand and Dolet replaced monologues with parodies in Alexandrines, erroneously referred to as "pièces à la muette" (dumbshows). The tone in which the lines were delivered, as well as the accompanying gestures, ironically evoked the acting style of their rivals, the Comédiens-Français.

1712

France, Paris: Back from a tour of the provinces, Jean-Baptiste Hamoche made his debut at the fair in the role of Pierrot. From 1712 to 1718, and from 1721 to 1732, he was a great favourite with the public.

1715

France, Paris: Francisque formed a troupe of comedians at the Saint-Germain fair.

Upon the death of Louis XIV, the Comédiens-Italiens returned to the Palais-Royal, after having been exiled since 1697.

1716

France, Paris: The regent, Philippe d'Orléans, undertook to dispel the doldrums of Paris's theatrical activity. He recalled an Italian troupe under the direction of Luigi Riccoboni, who had surrounded himself with the great names of the period, including the beautiful Silvia, the Parisian elite's darling of the hour, who portrayed roles created by Marivaux. They gave their first performance on the stage at the Palais-Royal on 18 May, before the regent and the Duchess de Berry. A month later, the company performed on the restored stage of the Hôtel de Bourgogne. A phoenix and the motto *Je renais* ("I rise again") were painted above the curtain.

c. 1705

France, Paris: Antoine Watteau, in collaboration with Claude Gillot, *The Departure of the Italian Comedians*, representing their expulsion from Paris under Louis XIV.

c. 1707

France, Paris: Claude Gillot, *The Two Coaches*; *The Tomb of Maître André*.

c. 1708

France, Paris: Antoine Watteau, in collaboration with Claude Gillot, *Harlequin, Emperor on the Moon, a Scene from the Comédie-Italienne*. The subject of the painting is taken from a three-act comedy by Nolant de Fatouville, *Arlequin empereur dans la lune*, first performed by the actors of the Comédie-Italienne on 5 March 1684 and revived in 1707 at the Saint-Laurent fair and in 1717 at the Saint-Germain fair.

c. 1710–1718

France, Paris: Nicolas Lancret, *Scene from the Comédie-Italienne*.

c. 1712

France, Paris: Antoine Watteau, *Pierrot Contented*; *Actors of the Comédie-Française*.

c. 1714

France, Paris: Antoine Watteau, *The Foursome*.

c. 1716–1718

France, Paris: Antoine Watteau, *Love in the Italian Theatre*; *Love in the French Theatre*.

1717

England, London: 2 March, premiere of *The Loves of Mars and Venus: New Dramatic Entertainment of Dancing, after the Manner of the Ancient Pantomimes*, by John Weaver. It was the first show in England to be called a pantomime. Enthusiasm for this type of entertainment was then very high. On 2 April another pantomime by Weaver, *The Shipwreck, or Perseus and Andromeda*, was performed on stage at Drury Lane. The same day, the Lincoln's Inn Fields countered by presenting a similar production, *The Cheats, or the Tavern Bilkers*. On 29 April the pantomime *The Jealous Doctor, or the Intriguing Dame* was on the bill at the same theatre.

1718

England, London: Francisque's fair troupe was the first French company to present in England plays from the repertory of Evaristo Gherardi, interspersed with numbers by acrobats.

France, Paris: 19 January, the Comédiens-Italiens announced to their audience at the Hôtel de Bourgogne that from then on they would perform exclusively in French.

1719

France, Paris: Following a new petition by the Comédie-Française against the theatres at the fairs, the Court decided to eliminate all fair spectacles except tightrope walkers and puppeteers. The regent, who had until then shown them his favour, made a last gesture of sympathy by inviting them to perform the play *Les Funérailles de la foire* at the Palais-Royal. This temporary demise was rapidly followed by a resurrection, for in 1720 Francisque, the leading director of fair theatres, ventured to reopen. To forestall the authorities' wrath, he limited himself to presenting mainly leapers, tightrope walkers, and prestidigitators.

1721

France, Paris: 25 July, the Comédiens-Italiens forsook the Hôtel de Bourgogne for the Saint-Laurent fair, where they performed in a restored theatre they named the Théâtre du Faubourg-Saint-Laurent. Unable to compete with the fair entertainers, they returned in defeat to the Hôtel de Bourgogne in 1723.

1722

France, Chantilly: October, as part of the celebrations for Louis XV's coronation in Rheims, the Duc d'Orléans summoned Francisque's troupe to the Château de Chantilly to present a show of leapers and tumblers disguised as wild animals.

1723

France, Paris: 3 February, Louis XV presided at the inauguration of the Saint-Germain fair.

1724

United States, Philadelphia: The first known travelling troupe appeared before the American public. It included tightrope walkers, sword swallowers, and a clown.

1726

France, Paris: Cardinal de Bissy, owner of the land where the Saint-Germain fair was held, expropriated the fair people and demolished their stalls in order to set up a large hall for rental to merchants, whose business was more profitable. Some comedians of the fair resettled on Rue de Buci, others in the Cul de Sac des Quatre-Vents. It was a first step toward the emancipation of the fair theatres, which were to become the theatres of the Boulevards in the nineteenth century.

Domenico Biancolelli's son Dominique replaced Riccoboni as the head of the Comédiens-Italiens.

1733

France, Paris: The fair actor Jean-Baptiste Hamoche retired. His departure hastened the gradual disappearance of Pierrot from the repertory of the Théâtre de la Foire.

Russia, Saint Petersburg: The troupe of Tommaso Ristori arrived from Warsaw and remained until 1735. Costantini (the famous Arlequin) and Antonio Vulcani (the Pantalone) were also in the capital at the same time. Many collections of Italian scenarios translated into Russian attest to the influence of the *commedia dell'arte* on Russian theatre at this time. The nineteenth-century children's puppet theatres, called "Petrushkas," typically set up at a fair stall, or *balagan*, were a result of the importation of Italian comedy.

1737

Italy, Udine (Venezia): 5 August, birth of Antonio Franconi.

1742

England, Newcastle: 8 January, birth of Philip Astley.

France, Paris: Guillaume Nicolet, founder of a family of fair entertainers, master dancer, and puppeteer, presented his "wooden comedians" at the Saint-Germain and Saint-Laurent fairs.

1745

France, Paris: Following protests by the Comédie-Française, the Opéra-Comique was suppressed. For seven years there were only tightrope walkers and popular dances at the Saint-Germain and Saint-Laurent fairs.

1755

Austria, Vienna: The Frenchman Defraine founded the Hetz Theatre, a sort of open-air amphitheatre famous for its hunts and animal fights. Sumptuous equestrian spectacles with music were also presented.

1758

England, London: Giuseppe Grimaldi, a Genoese promoter of English pantomime, appeared as a dancer and acrobat and was an instant success.

1760

France, Paris: Jean-Baptiste Nicolet, the eldest son of Guillaume Nicolet, opened the Jeu de Nicolet on Boulevard du Temple, where pantomimes and comic operas were performed. A great many tightrope walkers were present.

1761

France, Paris: Invited by the Comédiens-Italiens, Carlo Goldoni came to Paris, where he wrote several scenarios for them.

1762

France, Paris: 16–17 March, a fire destroyed the Saint-Germain fair. It severely affected the theatres of the acrobats and puppets, in particular the Nicolet brothers' two troupes.

1763

France, Paris: Official opening of the Saint-Ovide fair, at first located on Place Vendôme, then transferred to Place Louis XV after a fire. As soon as it was inaugurated, the Nicolets set up their stage there.

1767

England, London: The English horseman-acrobat Price appeared in the yard of the Three Hats, a pub and dance hall run by Mrs. Dobney.

France, Paris: The school rider Jacob Bates presented Paris's first outdoor horse show, in a ring surrounded by stands.

1768

England, London: Philip Astley gave his first equestrian shows in a vacant lot called Halfpenny Hatch. His enterprise was called a riding school, in reference to the lessons he gave to supplement his income.

In July a current event inspired Astley to create an equestrian parody called *Bill Button, or the Tailor's Ride to Brentford*. This comic number ridiculing the clumsiness of a tailor became a classic of the genre and was exported to France under the titles *Rongolet et Passe-Carreau* and *Le Tailleur gascon*.

1769

France, Paris: Audinot, an actor formerly with the Comédie-Italienne, founded the Ambigu-Comique at the Saint-Germain fair. Following his puppet show's tremendous success, he moved his establishment, whose 400 seats were constantly full, to Boulevard du Temple. He soon replaced his puppets with a troupe of children.

1770

England, London: Opening of Astley's Amphitheatre, near Westminster Bridge. It may be considered the first modern circus, as it presented tight-rope walkers, jugglers, acrobats, strong men, and animal trainers from the fair in a 13-metre ring.

1771

United States, Salem, Massachusetts: John Sharp presented the first acrobatic riding act in the United States.

1772

France, outskirts of Paris: 23 April, Jean-Baptiste Nicolet gave a performance in Choisy before Madame du Barry and Louis XV, who granted him the privilege of naming his theatre the Théâtre des Grands-Danseurs du Roi. The honour of being received by the king was also granted that year to the Ambigu-Comique's director, Audinot.

1774

France: Philip Astley's first tour on the Continent.

1775

France, Paris: 23 February, a first five-act version of Beaumarchais's *Barbier de Séville* was presented at the Comédie-Française. This comedy was based on an old *parade*, or sketch, he had composed to entertain the guests of Charles-Guillaume Le Normant, husband of the Marquise de Pompadour, at the Château d'Étioles. The poor reception at the premiere led Beaumarchais to trim the play, and on 26 February he presented a successful four-act revision.

United States, New York: The trick rider Jacob Bates distinguished himself in the equestrian parody *Bill Button, or the Tailor's Ride to Brentford*, made famous by Astley.

1776

France, Rouen: Franconi built a new circus on Rue Duguay-Trouin.

1717

France, Paris: Antoine Watteau, *The Embarkation for Cythera*; *The Pilgrimage to Cythera*.

c. 1718–1719

France, Paris: Antoine Watteau, *Pierrot* (also called *Gilles*).

c. 1718–1720

France, Paris: Antoine Watteau, *Mezzetin*.

c. 1720

England, London: Antoine Watteau, *Italian Comedians*.

1723

France, Paris: Claude Gillot, *The Metamorphoses of Harlequin*.

c. 1724

England, London: Giuseppe Grisoni, *Masquerade on the Stage of the Haymarket Theatre*.

1725

France, Paris: A former singer of the Alard troupe, François Octavien, was made a member of the Académie de Peinture et de Sculpture with the presentation of *The Fair at Bezons*, a painting inspired by the fair that opened every year on the first Sunday of September.

1728–1732

Italy, Rome: Carle van Loo, *Polichinelle*.

c. 1730

France, Paris: Nicolas Lancret, *Actors of the Italian Comedy*.

1733

Italy, Naples: 5 September, premiere at the Teatro San Bartolomeo of Pergolesi's intermezzo opera in two parts, *La serva padrona*, libretto by Gennaro Antonio Federico after Jacopo Angello Nelli's play.

c. 1733–1736

France, Bezons (near Versailles): Jean-Baptiste Pater, *The Fair at Bezons*.

c. 1735

Spain, Madrid: Giambattista Tiepolo, *Punchinellos Cooking*.

1740–1760

Italy, Florence: Giovanni Domenico Ferretti, series of paintings *The Disguises of Harlequin*.

1748

Bohemia, Český Krumlov: Joseph Ledere, frescoes of the Mask Hall, Český Krumlov Castle.

1751

Italy, Venice: Pietro Longhi, *Il rinoceronte*.

Between 1754 and 1765

France, Paris: Hubert Robert, *Triumph of Harlequin*.

1755

France, Paris: Étienne Jeaurat, *Village Fair*.

357

358

1777

France, Paris: A fire destroyed the Saint-Ovide fair. Faced with bankruptcy, the Saint-Laurent fair was now rid of its biggest rival and temporarily regained its popularity. The official opening of the Saint-Laurent fair was celebrated the next year at the Variétés-Amusantes, a new theatre founded by Sieur de l'Écluse.

1779

France, Paris: Again banished, the Comédiens-Italiens were restricted to appearing at fairs and on the stage of the Grands-Danseurs du Roi, the Ambigu-Comique, and the Variétés-Amusantes.

Germany, Hamburg: Francesco Chiarini presented shadow plays at Kneschke's Theater.

1780

France, Versailles: 12 June, the future Charles X demonstrated his acrobatic talents before the king and queen. This major first attests to the French aristocracy's enthusiasm for the fairs' entertainments.

Austria, Vienna: Juan Porté founded a circus whose star performer was the famous Hyam, an English horseman who had worked at the Colisée des Champs-Élysées in Paris in 1774 and at the Hetz Theatre in Vienna the following year.

1782

England, London: November, opening of the Royal Circus and Equestrian Philharmonic Academy of Charles Hughes, a former bareback rider at Astley's Amphitheatre. This first appearance of the word "circus" in modern times was probably suggested by Hughes's associate, Charles Dibdin. This circus's success made it Philip Astley's main rival.

1783

France, Versailles: Upon returning from London, Astley performed for Marie-Antoinette at Versailles.

16 October, Astley's success with the queen enabled him to open his Amphithéâtre Anglais on Rue du Faubourg-du-Temple. It was Paris's first circus. Astley and his son John, whom Marie-Antoinette called "the English Rose," went there every year after their London season. Before becoming Astley's partner and replacing him while he was in England, Antonio Franconi presented trained canaries there, and the English clown Billy Saunders, a comic rider and dog trainer, also performed there to great acclaim. Even though the laws governing theatrical privilege forbade dialogue at the circus, the patter of English comedians like Saunders (famous for his recurrent line, "Volé-vô jouer avé moa?") was tolerated.

1784

France, Paris: After Louis XVI renewed its privileges, the Opéra obtained the right to grant the lease and operation of fair shows to whomever it pleased, in return for a fee.

1785

France, Paris: The Saint-Laurent fair again deserted, its theatres closed one by one. The Variétés-Amusantes moved to Boulevard du Temple.

Another venue that opened on Boulevard du Temple was the Délassements-Comiques, for which Plancher Valcour was director, author, and actor. The hall burned down in 1787 but was rebuilt the next year. After further intervention from the Comédie-Française, the Délassements-Comiques was forbidden to perform anything but pantomimes or to present more than three actors on stage at a time. Furthermore, they had to be separated from the audience by a scrim.

United States, Philadelphia: August, Thomas Pool, billed as the first American acrobat rider, performed in his riding ring before going to New York with a trained horse and a clown. He closed his show with *Bill Button, or the Tailor's Ride to Brentford*, which had been popularized by Astley.

1786

France, Lyons: Franconi went to Lyons, where the English horseman Balp, another of Astley's rivals, had just founded a circus. Franconi in turn built a wooden circus, which he soon replaced with a stone structure.

Paris: Rebuilding of Audinot's Ambigu-Comique, which became one of the largest and most elegant halls in Paris.

1787

England, Liverpool: Astley put on the first entire show under canvas, in what he called the "royal tent."

Sweden, Stockholm: 18 October, Englishman James Price and his troupe of horsemen gave outdoor performances. They then visited other cities in Sweden, among them Göteborg, before travelling to Denmark and Norway.

1789

France, Paris: When the French Revolution broke out, Astley had to close his circus and return to England.

Abolition of the police ordinance requiring troupes of actors and acrobats to gather at the Saint-Germain and Saint-Laurent fairs twice a year, during the first weeks of spring and the last weeks of summer. They settled in fixed establishments nearer the centre of the city: the Palais-Royal, the customary meeting place of leisured socialites, and Boulevard du Temple.

In the face of the success of these little theatres on the Boulevards, the Comédie-Française demanded that the Associés and the Variétés be closed. It agreed to allow Audinot's Ambigu-Comique and Nicolet's Grands-Danseurs du Roi to survive on the condition that the former confine itself to pantomimes and the latter to feats of strength.

Opening of the Cirque du Palais-Royal, which featured curiosities like a mechanical cabriolet drawn by a mechanical stag. It later became mainly a place for balls and concerts.

1790

France, Paris: Inauguration of the Théâtre-Français Comique et Lyrique, on Rue Bondy. In November the play *Nicodème dans la lune, ou la Révolution pacifique* was performed there. Warmly acclaimed by Parisian audiences, it remained on the program until the end of September the following year. This prodigious success raised the Théâtre-Français Comique et Lyrique to the first rank among Paris theatres.

Austria, Vienna: The Liège-born Spanish rider Pierre Mahyeu gave performances in Vienna, which earned him the prestigious title of His Royal and Imperial Majesty's Horseman. Two of Germany's top three circus directors, Briloff and Christophe de Bach, were pupils of Mahyeu.

1791

France, Paris: The decree on the freedom of the theatres, which granted anyone the right to build a public theatre and put on plays of any type, was the coup de grâce for the two large fairs, Saint-Germain and Saint-Laurent.

1792

France, Lyons: In the turmoil of the Revolution, Franconi had to close his Lyons establishment.

Paris: Nicolet renamed his Théâtre des Grands-Danseurs du Roi the Théâtre de la Gaîté.

1793

France, Lyons: During the bombardment of the "Commune Affranchie" Franconi's circus was completely destroyed.

Paris: March, Franconi again took over Astley's, which had been empty since 1789; he remodelled the rotunda and added box seats. On 9 Thermidor Year I (27 July 1793) he reopened "Franconi's Amphitheatre," where he put on shows at odd intervals, often of a patriotic nature, for at this time it was vital to "play to the people."

During the summer Arlequin was the favourite hero of the Boulevard theatres. Every evening, after having watched the cortege of hearses, Parisians went to commiserate with his tribulations. He was at Nicolet's in *Le Mariage turc d'Arlequin* and *Les Précieuses ridicules*; at the Vaudeville in *Arlequin friand*, *Arlequin tailleur*, *Arlequin machiniste*, and *Le Duel d'Arlequin*; at the Variétés in *Arlequin marchand d'almanachs* and *Le Médecin malgré lui*; at the Théâtre Montansier in *Arlequin journaliste* and *Le Lendemain des noces d'Arlequin*; and at the Théâtre-Français Comique et Lyrique in *Arlequin marchand d'esprit*.

United States, Philadelphia: The Scotsman John Bill Ricketts, who claimed to have been a student of Charles Hughes, set up the first true circus in America, Ricketts' Circus.

1795

France, Paris: 25 November, Franconi, who had had to flee Paris because of serious political entanglements, reopened his amphitheatre with the support of his two sons, Laurent and Henri, his son-in-law Bassin, and Bassin's son.

United States, Philadelphia: 19 October, John Bill Ricketts inaugurated the Art Pantheon, one of the first modern permanent circuses.

1796

Bohemia, Kolin: Birth of Jean-Baptiste Gaspard Deburau, nineteenth-century France's successor to the *commedia dell'arte* actors. Baudelaire saw him as the synthesis of the old French and Italian jokesters as he played Pierrot in his very simple costume: a long white jacket, white trousers, fine dancer's shoes, and black skullcap. A master of improvisation and pantomime, he performed for a long time at the little Théâtre des Funambules, on Boulevard du Temple in Gascony.

1797

Canada, Montreal: John Bill Ricketts opened the first circus in Canada.

Visual Arts, Music, and Film 1500–2000
18th Century

1757

France, Paris: Étienne Jeaurat, *Carnival in the Streets of Paris*.

Switzerland, Zürich: Henry Fuseli, *Fool in a Fool's Cap Having His Portrait Painted*.

Italy, Vicenza: Giandomenico Tiepolo, frescoes in the *foresteria*, or guest lodgings, at the Villa Valmarana, including a first version of *Il Mondo Novo*.

1760

France, Paris: Gabriel de Saint-Aubin, *Boulevard Parade*.

1762

France, Paris: Pierre-Antoine De Machy, *Fire at the Saint-Germain Fair on the Night of 16 to 17 March 1762*.

c. 1765

Spain, Madrid: Giandomenico Tiepolo, *Il Mondo Novo*, painting.

c. 1771

Italy, Venice: Pietro Longhi, *L'Elefante*.

1772

Italy, Verona: Marco Marcuola, *An Italian Comedy in Verona*.

c. 1775–1780

France: Jean-Honoré Fragonard, *Les Charlatans*.

1778

Spain, Madrid: January, for the bedroom of the prince of Asturias at the Pardo, Francisco Goya designs a series of seven tapestry cartoons on themes inspired by the annual fair at the Plaza de Cebada.

1783

Austria, Vienna: February, performance of a pantomime by Mozart for a court ball in the Redoutensaal of Hofburg Palace. Mozart played the part of Harlequin.

1791

Spain, Madrid: Francisco Goya executed *The Stilts* and *The Straw Mannikin*, tapestry cartoons for Charles IV's study at the Escorial.

Italy, Zianigo: Giandomenico Tiepolo, *Il Mondo Novo*, large fresco.

1793

Spain, Cádiz: Goya executed some small oils on tin, among them *The Travelling Players* (*Alegoria Menandrea*).

1797–1800

Italy, Zianigo: Giandomenico Tiepolo, *Diversions for Children*, 104 ink and wash drawings of the Neapolitan *commedia dell'arte* character Pulcinella.

1825

England, London: Andrew Ducrow took over the management of Astley's Amphitheatre, and the programs became so famous that they were later held under the patronage of Queen Victoria and Prince Albert. Ducrow owed his success to an equestrian act of his invention, *The Saint Petersburg Courier*. It required the rider to stand with one foot on each of two cantering horses kept far enough apart for other horses to pass between his legs. The rider had to snatch the horses' reins and drive them as a team. Small flags planted in their headstalls indicated the countries a courier would pass through on his way to Saint Petersburg.

France, Paris: Debut of Jean-Baptiste Gaspard Deburau at the Théâtre des Funambules, in the role of Pierrot. With Deburau, Pierrot took on a new dimension. Until then, he had played only a secondary role in pantomime. Portrayed by the great mime, he ceased to be Arlequin's inept whipping boy and became a sly and insolent rascal, cowardly and greedy, capable of all crimes and vices.

Germany: Briloff founded a circus company with which he travelled, especially in North Germany, under the title General Concessionaire of Artistic Riders to His Majesty the King of Prussia.

1826

France, Paris: 16 March, the Franconis' Cirque Olympique was again destroyed by fire. Laurent and Henri became tenants of Louis Dejean, who purchased the lot on Boulevard du Temple where the third Cirque Olympique was inaugurated on 31 March 1827.

Because of their precarious finances, the Franconis withdrew. Henri's adopted son Adolphe, known as "Minette," took their place on 19 June 1827, in partnership with Vilain de Saint-Hilaire and Ferdinand Laloue. The Cirque Olympique now specialized in the production of *gloires militaires*, pantomimes commemorating the exploits of the French army.

Austria, Vienna: The Italian rider Alessandro Guerra left the company of his father-in-law, Christophe de Bach, to found a rival circus with the tightrope walker Ravel. De Bach and his troupe played at the Circus Gymnasticus, while Guerra was in the ring of the Rot Haus.

Denmark, Copenhagen: The French riders and tightrope walkers Baptiste and Louis Foureaux obtained permission to build a wooden circus. They erected a second structure the following year in Stockholm.

United States, New York: Construction of a first permanent circus in New York, directed by General Sandford.

1828

Sweden, Stockholm: The Frenchman Didier Gautier set up a horse ring at Djurgården, a large recreation area.

1829

France, Paris: Henri Martin, the first great French animal trainer, set up his menagerie at the Porte Saint-Denis.

1831

France, Paris: 21 April, the Cirque Olympique put on the play *Les Lions de Mysore*, starring the trainer Henri Martin. In this mimodrama, wild animals were presented at the circus for the first time.

Russia, Saint Petersburg: Christophe de Bach and his troupe performed in Russia.

1834

Germany, Berlin: During the winter seasons of 1834 and 1835 the Briloff company performed in the arena at Brandenburg Gate.

Spain, Madrid: Creation of the Circo Olímpico by M. Avrillon.

1835

France, Paris: Louis Dejean took over the Cirque Olympique. He kept Adolphe Franconi and Ferdinand Laloue on as collaborators.

5 March, in the ring of the Cirque Olympique the public discovered Jean-Baptiste Auriol, a leaper and equilibrist who became one of the leading figures of the French entertainment world. He remained on Dejean's payroll until 1852.

A huge canvas tent was raised by Louis Dejean and Adolphe Franconi at the entrance of Carré Marigny, on the Champs-Élysées. Under the July Monarchy it was the site of a permanent summer fair.

Germany, Berlin: The Briloff company was tremendously successful.

Spain, Madrid: The gymnast and rider Paul Laribeau, related to the Franconi family by marriage, founded the Circo Nuevo.

1836

France, Paris: Clément-Philippe Laurent joined the staff of the Cirque Olympique, leaving the mime Jean-Baptiste Gaspard Deburau alone on the boards of the Théâtre des Funambules. The character of Pierrot now began appearing in roles bearing a degree of importance unprecedented in the history of pantomime.

6 November, death of Antonio Franconi at the age of ninety-nine.

1838

England, London: At Astley's Amphitheatre, Jean Gontard, a clown affiliated with the Franconi Circus, was introduced to English spectators.

France, Paris: The canvas big top on the Champs-Élysées was replaced by a wooden circus building.

25 January, first performance of the play *Les Saltimbanques*, at the Théâtre des Variétés, starring the clown-parodist Jacques-Charles Odry. Its success led to revivals in 1843, 1853, 1854, and 1862, with Frédérick Lemaître in the leading role.

1840

France, Paris: The directors of the Théâtre des Funambules hired Paul Legrand to replace Jean-Baptiste Gaspard Deburau in the role of Pierrot.

1841

England, London: During the night of 7 June a fire completely destroyed Astley's Amphitheatre. The shock was so great that its manager, Andrew Ducrow, had a nervous breakdown. He never recovered and died a year later.

United States, New York: P.T. Barnum bought the American Museum in New York, where thousands of curiosities, phenomena, and wild animals were exhibited and edifying dramas were performed in a large auditorium called the "Lecture Room." The museum burned down in 1868.

1842

France, Paris: *Marrrrchant d'habits*, a pantomime in four tableaus by the establishment's manager, M. Cot d'Ordan, was performed at the Théâtre des Funambules. On 4 September, in the *Revue de Paris*, Théophile Gautier gave a detailed account that laid the foundation of the concept of a romantic Pierrot.

Germany, Berlin: Ernst Jakob Renz took over the old Briloff company. His little troupe included some performers – Wilhelm Carré, Salamonsky, Gotthold Schumann – who in turn became great managers.

Another student of Briloff, Eduard Wollschläger, founded the Prussian Circus.

Austria, Vienna: Following his marriage to Laura de Bach, widow of Christophe de Bach, the French rider Louis Soullier became the manager of the Circus Gymnasticus, which he renamed the Cirque Impérial de Louis Soullier. He stayed in the fixed circus for six months and then toured the rest of the year, going as far as Turkey. Seeing that country inspired him with a new style: from then on he wore only the ceremonial uniform of Turkish colonels, and he named his big top the Caravanserai.

1843

France, Paris: Still under the management of Louis Dejean, a stone building was erected for the Cirque des Champs-Élysées (also called the Cirque d'Été), on the site today occupied by the Théâtre de Marigny. The name was changed to Cirque de l'Impératrice in 1853. In 1870 it returned to the name Cirque des Champs-Élysées, which it kept until it was demolished in 1989. It was in fact a summer circus (*d'été*), for it was open from 1 May to 1 November. It was more a social meeting place than a true circus with a solid reputation: gentlemen would go there to be seen and then leave before the end with a charming lady on their arm.

1845

France, Paris: 3 July, inauguration of the Hippodrome built by Laurent Franconi and his son Victor at the Barrière de l'Étoile, near the Arc de Triomphe.

1846

France, Paris: Death of the mime actor Jean-Baptiste Gaspard Deburau. His son Charles Deburau pursued the same career, though he did not leave as indelible a mark.

Germany, Berlin: 20 December, first performance of Ernst Jakob Renz's Equestrian Circus at the Royal Manege on Sophenstrasse. The buffoon Wilhelm Qualitz made his debut there and almost immediately won popular favour.

Visual Arts, Music, and Film 1500–2000
19th Century

1823–1828

France, Paris: Louis-Léopold Boilly, *Thirty-Five Expressive Heads*, painting.

1824

Spain, Madrid: First appearance of acrobats in the work of Goya, with *The Saltimbanques* (Album F).

France, Bordeaux: Goya attended the circus games at the annual fair, as seen in the chalk drawings of his last album (Album H): *Serpent Four Yards Long in Bordeaux*; *Crocodile in Bordeaux*; *Claudio Ambrosio Surat, known as the Living Skeleton*.

1834

France, Paris: First appearance of the clown in Daumier's work, in *Lower the Curtain, the Farce Is Ended*, a satirical lithograph.

1835

Germany, Leipzig: Robert Schumann, *Carnaval, scènes mignonnes sur quatre notes*, Op. 9; among these twenty-one piano pieces are *Pierrot*, *Arlequin*, and *Pantalon et Colombine*.

1838

France, Paris: Jacques Daguerre invented the daguerreotype.

1839

France, Paris: Honoré Daumier, *The Parade*, published in *Le Charivari*.

1843

France, Paris: First Paris sojourn of Champfleury (Jules Husson), who hastened to see Jean-Baptiste Gaspard Deburau perform at the Théâtre des Funambules.

363

364

1847

England, London: The Hanlon Brothers (Thomas, George, William, Alfred, Edmond, and Frederick) made their debut at the Adelphi Theatre directed by Madame Céleste. They worked under the supervision of a gymnast, Lee, and soon formed the famous Hanlon-Lee troupe.

France, Paris: After the departure of Paul Legrand for London, Charles Deburau made his debut as Pierrot at the Théâtre des Funambules.

Louis Dejean sold the Cirque Olympique, which became the Opéra National under Adolphe Adam, and then went back to being the Cirque Olympique the following year. Dejean kept only the Cirque des Champs-Élysées, until 1873.

Germany, Berlin: Renz renamed his equestrian circus the Olympischer Circus. When the new season opened on 21 January the program included the first grand historical pantomime to play in Germany, *Graf Polowsky*.

Russia, Saint Petersburg: After attending the exercises of Alessandro Guerra, an Italian rider living in Saint Petersburg, Tsar Nicholas I decided to initiate a troupe of young Russians in the arts of the ring. A school was opened. Its director was the Frenchman Paul Cuzent, who had made a reputation in Russia with the Cirque de Paris. This circus school was converted into a riding school until 1927, when the plan for a circus school was revived.

United States, San Francisco: Giuseppe Chiarini, a descendant of the famous Italian dynasty and a student of Franconi, founded his own circus in the New World.

1848

France, Paris: The Cirque des Champs-Élysées (Cirque d'Été), was renamed the Cirque National de Paris by its directors, Louis Dejean and Adolphe Franconi.

England, London: Dejean and Franconi presented their Cirque National de Paris at Drury Lane.

Sweden, Stockholm: After leaving Berlin as a consequence of his standoff with Renz, Alessandro Guerra founded a new circus. He became famous throughout northern Europe.

1850

Germany, Berlin: 22 December, the French circus manager Louis Dejean set out to conquer Berlin with his Cirque National. He met with dazzling success at the circus on Friedrichstrasse.

1852

France, Paris: 11 December, for his first act as emperor, Napoleon III inaugurated the new circus that the architect Hittorff had just built, in eight months, at the corner of Boulevard du Temple and Boulevard des Filles-du-Calvaire. It was called the Cirque Napoléon from then until 1870; after the fall of the Empire it was the Cirque National, and in 1873 it became the Cirque d'Hiver.

Germany, Berlin: It was the German Ernst Jakob Renz's turn to occupy the ring of the circus on Friedrichstrasse. Dejean having left the city on 15 April, Renz became the "absolute king of the circus" in Prussia. He gave performances on Friedrichstrasse until 1876, when the building was expropriated for the construction of a train station.

Austria, Vienna: The Circus Gymnasticus was sold at auction for 6,000 florins and demolished.

1853

England, London: Founding of the Great British Circus of William and George Pinder. In 1854 they raised their modest tent in France. They caused a sensation with their elephants and impressive cavalcade, enhanced with gilded and mirrored carved-wood wagons.

France, Paris: Paul Legrand left the Théâtre des Funambules.

Germany, Berlin: Karl Hinné gave his name to the circus he had founded under the name of his brother-in-law Ducrow, a student of Andrew Ducrow but otherwise unrelated to the famous rider.

Pierre Corty and his son-in-law, the German tightrope walker Dominik Althoff, founded a travelling circus. After their death, the establishment passed to young Pierre Althoff, son of Dominik Althoff and Adèle Corty, who quickly made it prosperous. In the late nineteenth century the Corty-Althoff Circus was one of the best travelling circuses in Central Europe. It ceased operation three years after the death of Pierre Althoff, in 1927.

Austria, Vienna: Ernst Jakob Renz entrusted the building of a circus on Zirkusgasse to the architects May and Schebeck.

Russia, Moscow: The wealthy V. Novosiltzev had the Moscow Circus built on the Petrovka for his wife, Laura Bassin, a well-known rider. In this stationary circus, she and her company presented equestrian acts.

United States, New York: 2 May, opening of the Franconis' Hippodrome, at the corner of Fifth Avenue and 23rd Street.

1854

France, Paris: Demolition of the Hippodrome at Barrière de l'Étoile by the government of Napoleon III. The establishment was transferred with the same dimensions and the same characteristics to Place d'Eylau.

Austria, Vienna: Louis Soullier left for a tour of Russia, China, and Japan. His troupe returned to Austria with some Chinese and Japanese acrobats.

Russia, Saint Petersburg: Opening of the Saint Petersburg Circus, which hosted foreign companies for a number of years.

Serbia, Belgrade: Founding of Wilhelm Carré's circus.

1855

France, Paris: Charles Deburau left the Théâtre des Funambules, which subsequently lapsed into mediocrity.

United States, Chicago: On a tour of the United States, the Hanlon-Lee troupe met the juggler Agoust, who suggested working up an acrobatic pantomime inspired by two of Deburau's scenarios: *Arlequin statue* and *Arlequin squelette*. Upon their return to Paris in 1867, the troupe presented the pantomime *Frater au village* at the Cirque d'Hiver.

1856

France, Rouen: Théodore Rancy founded a circus at the Manège Saint-Sever.

Paris: Founding of the Grand Musée Anatomique Spitzner at the Pavillon de la Ruche.

1857

England, London: First season in England of Seth B. Howes and Joseph Cushing's American circus. It was so successful that the troupe split in two the next year. It toured Europe frequently until 1862.

1858

Spain, Madrid: Thomas Price installed his circus at the site on Calle de Recoletos. His success encouraged him to return every year, and he eventually settled there permanently.

1859

France, Paris: Ferdinand-Constantin Beert, called Fernando, was acclaimed for his riding at the Cirque de l'Impératrice.

12 November, the first flying trapeze artist, Jules Léotard, made his debut at the Cirque Napoléon to general admiration.

Poland, Warsaw: The Hinné Circus was struck by fire. Karl Hinné founded another circus in Frankfurt, then undertook a major tour of Turkey, Greece, and Russia, where he remade his fortune.

Canada, Niagara Falls: The French high-wire acrobat Jean-François Gravelet, called Blondin, crossed Niagara Falls on a tightrope.

1860

France, Paris: Théodore Loyal succeeded Jean-Léonard Houcke as the ringmaster of the Cirque de l'Impératrice. The name "Monsieur Loyal" was his legacy to future ringmasters.

Spain, Barcelona: 20 September, Gaetano Ciniselli and his family inaugurated the Gran Circo Real, near Puerta de Isabel II. He gained the crowds' favour, to the detriment of his rival, Thomas Price, who was trying to establish a branch of his Circo Teatro Price from Madrid in Barcelona.

1862

France, Paris: 20 August, opening of the Nouveau Cirque Olympique, built on Place du Châtelet by the government of Napoléon III to compensate for the destruction of seven theatres on Boulevard du Temple (including the Théâtre des Funambules), required by Haussmann's urban development plan for Paris.

1863

France, Paris: The English clown Chadwick made his debut at the Cirque Napoléon and the Cirque de l'Impératrice, where he became known for his leitmotif "Music!" which he addressed to the band leader after each of his gags.

1864

France, Paris: A law ensuring freedom of performance abolished the theatres' privileges and allowed comedies with dialogue to be performed at the circus. This promoted an increase in the number of circuses and travelling troupes.

1865

Germany, Berlin: Birth of the clown type known as the Auguste. According to some authors, it took place at the Renz Circus, when a rider turned an involuntary act of clumsiness – which had prompted the audience to shout "Auguste!" at him – into a comedy routine.

Netherlands, Amsterdam: Wilhelm Carré built a permanent circus on the Amstelfeld. On 7 May 1868 it officially became the Koninklijk Theater Oscar Carré, named for his son.

1848

France, Paris: First performance, at the Théâtre des Funambules, of Nadar's pantomime *Pierrot ministre*, with Charles Deburau in the role of Pierrot.

1851

Italy, Venice: 11 March, first performance, at the Teatro La Fenice, of Giuseppe Verdi's opera *Rigoletto*.

1853

France, Paris: 29 September, the Théâtre de la Porte-Saint-Martin presented *Les Sept Merveilles du monde: Grande féerie en vingt tableaux et un prologue*, by Adolphe Philippe d'Ennery and Pierre-Eugène Basté (Eugène Grangé). Honoré Daumier designed the costumes for the fourteenth tableau.

1854

France, Paris: Gustave Doré, *Family of Performers*.

Beginning 21 September, in the studio at 11 Boulevard des Capucines, Nadar directed the photographing of Charles Deburau for the "expressive heads" of Pierrot produced by Nadar's brother, Adrien Tournachon.

1855

France, Paris: Three ballet-pantomimes by Jacques Offenbach premiered at the Bouffes-Parisiens: *Arlequin barbier* on 5 July; *Pierrot le clown* on 30 July; *Polichinelle dans le monde* on 19 September.

1856

France, Paris: Gustave Courbet, *Le Bras noir* ("The Black Arm"), a poster design for Fernand Desnoyers's pantomime, presented on 8 February 1856 at the Théâtre des Folies-Nouvelles with Paul Legrand as Pierrot.

The Folies-Nouvelles successfully mounted a second pantomime by Nadar, *Pierrot boursier*.

1857

France, Paris: Gustave Doré dressed as Pierrot for a costume party given by the composer Jacques Offenbach.

Jean-Léon Gérôme, *Duel after a Masked Ball*, completed in 1859.

1858

France, Paris: Thomas Couture, *The Duel after the Masked Ball*.

1860

France, Paris: Jean-Louis-Ernest Meissonier, *Punchinello*.

1861

France, Paris: Charles Baudelaire, "Le Vieux Saltimbanque," prose poem in *Le Spleen de Paris*.

Daumier executed from memory a portrait of Charles Deburau, who had returned from a tour of the provinces.

1862

France, Paris: Édouard Manet, *The Old Musician*.

c. 1863–1865

France, Paris: Honoré Daumier, *Crispin and Scapin*.

c. 1865

France, Paris: Honoré Daumier, *The Sideshow*; *The Strong Man*.

1866

France, Paris: August, the Cirque du Prince Impérial opened on Rue de Malte, but had to close the following year owing to financial difficulties. Its director was Bastien Gillet-Franconi. After a change of management, it took the name Théâtre du Château-d'Eau, from 1869 to 1880, and Opéra Populaire from 1881. In 1903 it changed vocation and became the Alhambra, a famous music-hall.

1867

France, Paris: 31 March, through the appearance of Mademoiselle Cornélie, a former tragic actress at the Comédie-Française, on the stage of the Eldorado, Camille Doucet, Ministre des Théâtres, sanctioned the performance of plays with costumes, dance, and acrobatic interludes at café-concerts. By abolishing the state theatres' privileges, this further decree doubled the number of halls within a few months.

The high-wire acrobat Blondin crossed the Seine above the Exposition Universelle grounds, which further increased his renown.

Marseilles: Charles Deburau was hired by the Alcazar. The future mime Louis Rouffe, who would call himself "l'homme blanc," attended one of his performances and was warmly impressed by his elegance.

1868

England, London: The English rider MacCollum opened the Holborn Amphitheatre, where he presented a show that included the famous acrobat riders Alfred Bradbury and James Robinson, the tumbler George Delavanti, the gymnasts the Hanlon-Lees and the Rizarellis, and the trapeze artist Lulu.

France, Paris: Flécheux set up the Gaîté in a hangar; the first true café-concert on the Butte Montmartre, it became the Gaîté-Rochechouart.

Russia, Saint Petersburg: On the banks of the Fonranka Canal, Karl Hinné built the Ciniselli Circus, which took its name from his brother-in-law Gaetano Ciniselli, who succeeded him as its manager in 1875.

Moscow: Hinné had another circus built on Vozdvichenko Prospect, as a sort of branch of the Saint Petersburg Circus.

1870

France, Paris: During the Prussian siege of Paris the government ordered the closing of entertainment halls. The Cirque de l'Impératrice was converted into a cartridge manufacturing shop.

4 September, following the proclamation of the Third Republic, the Cirque de l'Impératrice again became the Cirque d'Été, and the Cirque Napoléon was named the Cirque National. Louis Dejean retired, and Victor Franconi, Laurent's son, took over the management of both circuses.

1871

England, London: 28 March, Astley's Amphitheatre, put up for auction, was purchased by the Sanger brothers for 11,000 pounds.

Finding Astley's too small for the large-scale pantomimes they wanted to mount, George and John Sanger rented the vast Agricultural Hall for the winter season until 1900. It was London's predecessor to Paris's Hippodrome de l'Alma.

France, Paris: 1 and 2 March, the Prussian army was billeted in the Cirque d'Été.

United States, Bridgeport, Connecticut: P.T. Barnum formed a partnership with William C. Coup and former clown Dan Castello to create P.T. Barnum's Museum, Menagerie, and Circus, a huge travelling show on rails. The large-scale development of rail travel marked the beginning of the golden age of the American circus, which expanded continually until 1910.

1872

France, Paris: July, at the Cirque d'Été, Parisians first saw Geronimo Medrano, the future clown Boum-Boum.

The Hanlon-Lee troupe appeared at the Folies Bergères.

Vierzon: Ferdinand-Constantin Beert (Fernando), a former butcher from Belgium, founded a modest circus with five performers and a half dozen horses.

United States, New York: Winter, construction of a Hippodrome on Madison Square, where P.T. Barnum's Greatest Show on Earth performed for two months before setting out on the road to spend from March to October crossing the continent.

1873

France, Paris: 9 August, inauguration of Ferdinand-Constantin Beert's circus in Montmartre, in a green tent on a vacant lot at the corner of Boulevard de Rochechouart and Rue des Martyrs. The Cirque Fernando soon rivalled the Cirque d'Été, on the Champs-Élysées, and the Cirque d'Hiver, on Rue des Filles-du-Calvaire. It was so successful that Beert had a permanent structure built two years later. This success was largely due to the clown Geronimo Medrano, who ended all his numbers by calling out "Boom! Boom!" to the band (as the English clown Chadwick had shouted "Music!"). Among the famous spectators were Edgar Degas, who drew the trapeze artist Miss Lala, and Toulouse-Lautrec, who sketched the rider Fernando and, later, La Goulue.

The Cirque National, successor to the Cirque Napoléon, became in turn the Cirque d'Hiver, with Victor Franconi as director. Over the years, this building changed vocation various times, but today it is the only surviving permanent circus facility in Paris.

Jean-Baptiste Auriol appeared for the last time at the Variétés in the revue *Le Tour du cadran*.

Austria, Vienna: Death of Wilhelm Carré. His son Oscar set up his circus in Vienna for the World's Fair.

Russia, Penza: The brothers Dmitry, Akim, and Piotr Nikitin, sons of a farmer and balalaika player, founded the first Russian circus with the equipment of Emmanuel Beránek, former owner of a Czech circus. They opened a second establishment the following year in Saratov.

1875

England, London: The Sanger brothers dissolved their partnership; George Sanger became sole proprietor of Astley's Amphitheatre.

France, Paris: 26 June, inauguration of Fernando's stone circus at the corner of Boulevard Rochechouart and Rue des Martyrs.

Russia, Saint Petersburg and Moscow: Gaetano Ciniselli took on the management of the circuses he inherited from his brother-in-law Karl Hinné.

United States, Bridgeport, Connecticut: William C. Coup quit as manager of Barnum's circus.

1876

Germany, Berlin: When his circus on Friedrichstrasse was expropriated, Ernst Jakob Renz had a large circus built on Karlstrasse that became Max Reinhardt's favourite theatre.

Switzerland, Geneva: The Frenchman Théodore Rancy built a wooden circus, which he replaced with a stone building in 1880. He produced equestrian shows interspersed with pantomime.

Spain, Madrid: Thomas Price's Circo Teatro Price was completely destroyed by fire. His son-in-law, William Parish, saw to rebuilding it on Plaza del Rey. The inauguration of the new building, which had room for 3,000 spectators, took place in May 1882.

1877

France, Paris: The ring of the Cirque d'Été was converted into an immense skating rink.

Construction of the Hippodrome de l'Alma. This 8,000-seat establishment of modern design had a movable glass roof that could be opened on fine summer evenings by means of a system of rails.

1878

France, Paris: Revisionist committees met at the Cirque Fernando, where, to make up the deficit, political events were programmed; Boulangist and anti-Boulangist factions clashed outside.

September, Gustave Fratellini, father of the famous clown trio, appeared at the Cirque Fernando.

The Hanlon-Lee troupe attracted notice at the Exposition Universelle and were hired by the Théâtre des Variétés.

James Guyon imported the Auguste clown-type to France, which brought him lasting success in the ring of the Hippodrome de l'Alma. His character quickly became the prototype of all the others. In the new tandem he formed with the clown, the Auguste assumed the role of a blockhead, a compendium of human folly, while the clown abandoned the role of victim, inspired by the *commedia dell'arte* Pierrot, and gradually adopted a new, nobler bearing.

1879

Spain, Barcelona: 21 May, inauguration of the Circo Ecuestre Barcelonès, also called the Circo Alegria, after its owner, Vicente Gil Alegria, Price's former manager. Until 1895, when it was demolished, it staged both theatrical performances and circus shows.

Russia, Moscow: Arrival of the German Albert Salamonsky, who competed with the Italian Gaetano Ciniselli for the monopoly of the circus in Russia. This standoff ended when Ciniselli died in 1881. Salamonsky settled in Moscow, leaving Saint Petersburg to Ciniselli's son, Andrea.

1880

France, Paris: 21 March, Ernest Molier, a wealthy circus aficionado and distinguished horseman, opened a riding ring in a hangar adjoining his home on Rue de Bénouville. Until 1933 the elite of Paris stormed the place once or twice a year to applaud dukes, marquis, counts, and barons performing extemporaneously as riders and trapeze artists.

April, Fernando's troupe left on a Belgian tour, during the course of which his Paris circus became a café-concert on Sundays and holidays.

Russia, Moscow: Albert Salamonsky built a stone circus on Tvetnoy Boulevard. Beginning 20 October, it entertained audiences with artists like Mathias Beketov, Anatoli, and Vladimir Durov, as well as the Sosinis, a family of contortionists.

Visual Arts, Music, and Film 1500–2000
19th Century

c. 1866

France, Paris: Honoré Daumier, *The Departure of the Saltimbanques*; *The Saltimbanques*.

1868

France, Paris: Renoir depicted the clown John Price in *The Clown*.

c. 1872

France, Paris: Last appearance of a clown in Daumier's work, with *Head of a Clown*.

1874

France, Paris: Gustave Doré, *The Performers*.

1876

France, Paris: John Singer Sargent, *Rehearsal of the Pasdeloup Orchestra at the Cirque d'Hiver*.

1878

France, Paris: Félicien Rops, *Woman on a Trapeze*. Also began his suite of *One Hundred Lighthearted Sketches for the Pleasure of Decent People*, completed in 1881.

1879

France, Paris: Degas exhibited *Miss Lala at the Cirque Fernando* at the Fourth Impressionist Exhibition.

Renoir presented the painting *Two Little Circus Girls* at a solo exhibition on the premises of the fashion magazine *La Vie Moderne*.

Jules Chéret created the poster for the Hanlon-Lee pantomime *Do mi sol do*.

1880

France, Paris: Gustave Doré, *The Acrobats*, sculpture.

1881

France, Paris: In the suburbs annexed to Paris in 1860 some of the fairs that had been suppressed by Napoleon III were reinstituted.

1882

France, outskirts of Paris: During the summer Paul Margueritte and his brother Victor converted a workshop in Valvins into a little theatre where they put on pantomimes. Their producer was their uncle, Stéphane Mallarmé.

Paris: Louis Fernando succeeded his father as manager of the Cirque Fernando.

Bordeaux: George Foottit made his debut as a clown at the Cirque Continental.

Italy, Rome: Aristide Togni founded the Victoria Circus (which became the Togni Brothers' Circus somewhat later).

United States, New York. P.T. Barnum's Greatest Show on Earth opened at Madison Square Garden in the spring. The spectators were flabbergasted by the innovation of a show taking place in three rings simultaneously. This circus later became the Barnum & Bailey Circus (1888), then the Ringling Bros. and Barnum & Bailey Circus (1919).

9 April, the circus bought Jumbo the elephant, a colossal creature about 3.5 metres at the shoulder. Jumbo became the menagerie's main attraction.

1883

France, Paris: The rider Fanny Lehmann was the star of the Cirque Fernando. Boum-Boum the clown (Geronimo Medrano) presented Porte-Veine, his trained pig.

United States, Omaha: 17 May, the opening of the Wild West Show, a huge show that travelled by train, instituted by Colonel William Cody, nicknamed "Buffalo Bill," and actor Nate Salisbury. In an outdoor ring surrounded by bleachers, Buffalo Bill's company brought the epic of the Wild West back to life, with horse races, Indians attacking a stagecoach, sharpshooters, and lasso tricks. The tour was so successful that it was repeated three times; the last tour, in 1902, lasted four years.

1884

France, Paris: The pantomime *Les Mirlifiques Aventures d'Aladin et la lampe merveilleuse* brought 200 children into the ring of the Cirque Fernando.

Denmark, Svendborg: 29 June, founding of the "largest equestrian troupe in Scandinavia" by Paul Busch.

United States, Baraboo, Wisconsin: In the spring, in cooperation with Yankee Robinson, the Ringling brothers – Al, Otto, Alf, Charles, and John – founded the Yankee Robinson–Ringling Bros. Circus. They set out on a tour with only three wagons, two horses, and a hand-stitched tent large enough for 600 spectators.

1885

France, Paris: First fairground exhibition of the collection of wax sculptures from the Grand Musée Anatomique Spitzner.

Sweden, Malmö: 16 May, horse trainer Albert Schumann founded the Scandinavian Circus.

1886

France, Paris: Inauguration of the Nouveau Cirque on Rue Saint-Honoré, founded by Joseph Oller (founder also of the Moulin Rouge and the Olympia). With a ring that could be converted into a swimming pool, this circus, the most luxurious in Paris, owed its success to the burlesque aquatic acrobatics it presented, as well as the pantomimes of the clown duo Foottit and Chocolat. Until 1888 the ringmaster was the English clown Chadwick.

Russia, Saint Petersburg: Dmitry, Akim, and Piotr Nikitin became the owners of the Hinné Circus. After the troupe disbanded in 1890, Akim remained alone as the head of the establishment until his death in 1917.

1887

France, Paris: April, first performances of Ferdinand Corvi's little circus at the Foire du Trône, on Place de la Nation.

Mazeppa, a pantomime of Louis Fernando based on the tale by Byron and the poem by Victor Hugo, met with great success at the Cirque Fernando.

First tour in France of Buffalo Bill's Wild West Show.

Germany, Hamburg: Founding, on Heiligengeistfeld, of the Hagenbeck International Circus.

Austria, Vienna: Carl Kludsky succeeded his father as the manager of the little family-run menagerie. The enterprise expanded to include a Hippodrome modelled after Barnum's.

Portugal, Lisbon: 24 December, inauguration of the Real Coliseu, also called the Coliseu da Rua da Palma, under the auspices of a company managed by Antonio Santos and Alexandre Mo Silva. The period's most highly acclaimed performers appeared in the ring, in particular the clowns Tony Grice and Little Walter.

1888

France, Paris: First performance, at the Nouveau Cirque, of Félicien Champsaur's pantomime *Lulu*.

Geronimo Medrano became the Nouveau Cirque's ringmaster.

Creation by Surtac and Alévy (Gabriel Astruc and Armand Lévy) of the first circus revue, *En selle pour la revue*, at the Cirque Fernando. The play parodied a "naturalistic quadrille" mimed by La Goulue, spoofed the Nouveau Cirque with an aquatic ring represented by a tub, and pastiched the Théâtre-Libre d'Antoine with a routine about the "Cirque Libre."

Paul Margueritte, Félix Larcher, and Raoul de Najac founded the Cercle Funambulesque, whose goal was to revive the tradition of the pantomime-tumbler and encourage the writing of plays in the spirit of the *commedia dell'arte*.

Germany, Berlin: Ernst Jakob Renz entirely renovated the Olympischer Circus for 1.5 million marks.

Netherlands, Amsterdam: 2 December, inauguration of a new circus by Albert Carré.

1889

England, London: The Barnum & Bailey Circus's first stay in England.

France, Paris: A performance of *La Noce à Chocolat* at the Nouveau Cirque marked the debut of the celebrated black Auguste known as Chocolat, who was to become Foottit's partner in the first clown duo in circus history.

Raoul Donval, former director of the Alcazar d'Hiver, became the manager of the Nouveau Cirque.

Buffalo Bill made a stop in Paris.

While the Exposition Universelle was running, the Cirque d'Hiver remained open, instead of closing for the summer as usual.

Germany, Berlin: 18 September, Paul Busch built a large circus with a stage and an aquatic ring that could be covered over with coconut matting, near the Boerse train station, not far from the Imperial Palace. He presented equestrian shows, but his preference was pantomimes, on which writers like Hans Heiz Ewers and Alexandre Moskowski collaborated.

Lilienbrau: The seven-year-old Valentin Ludwig Fey, later known by the stage name Karl Valentin, put on the clown's costume for the first time for a show at a hotel.

United States, Baraboo, Wisconsin: After the death of Yankee Robinson two years earlier, the Ringling brothers formed a partnership with Hyatt Frost, the owner and director of the Van Amburgh circus-menagerie. Henceforth their circus took on gigantic proportions.

Visual Arts, Music, and Film 1500–2000
19th Century

1881

France, Paris: Gustave Doré, *Joy (Saute-mouton)*, sculpture.

1882

France, Paris: Félicien Rops, *The Acrobat*.

May, James Tissot was in Paris. He attended the Cirque Molier, where Comte Hubert de la Rochefoucauld performed on the trapeze and Édouard Martell appeared as an English clown.

Belgium, Ostend: James Ensor, *The Music Lesson, after Watteau*.

1883

France, Paris: April, Toulouse-Lautrec spent his evenings at the Ménagerie Pezon, where he drew wild animals.

Georges Seurat, *The Painter Aman-Jean as Pierrot*; *Pierrot with a White Pipe*.

Belgium, Ostend: First appearance of the carnival mask in the work of James Ensor, with the painting *Scandalized Masks*. Also that year, a self-portrait, to which he added a hat in 1888, making it *Ensor with a Flowered Hat*.

1885

France, Paris: James Tissot's *Women of Paris* series exhibited at Galerie Sedelmeyer, with three of the works having a circus theme: *The Amateur Circus*; *Ladies of the Chariots*; *The Acrobat*.

Adolphe Willette, *Parce Domine*, large painting for the Montmartre cabaret the Chat Noir.

Dieppe: During a first stay in Dieppe with Degas, Walter Sickert depicted the ring and spectators at the Pinder big top in *The Circus*, his first painting on the theme.

1886

England, London: Tissot's *Women of Paris* series exhibited at the Arthur Tooth Gallery.

France, Paris: Jules Chéret became the official poster artist of the Nouveau Cirque on Rue Saint-Honoré.

Henri Rousseau, *Pierrot (Carnival Evening)*.

Adolphe Willette, *Pierrot's Widow*.

1887

France, Paris: Albert Londe, *Portraits of Clowns: Hippodrome de l'Alma*; *Clown Acts at the Hippodrome de l'Alma*; *Acrobats*.

Henri de Toulouse-Lautrec: *At the Cirque Fernando: Medrano with a Small Pig* (c. 1887–1888); *At the Circus: Monsieur Loyal* (c. 1887); *At the Cirque Fernando* (c. 1887); *At the Cirque Fernando: Equestrienne* (1887–1888); *Circus Scene* (project for a fan, c. 1887–1888).

Belgium, Ostend: James Ensor, *Carnival on the Beach*.

1888

France, Paris: Albert Londe organized a presentation of photographs of a clown doing a double somersault.

Georges Seurat exhibited *Circus Parade* at the Salon des Indépendants.

Fernand Pelez exhibited *Grimaces and Misery* at the Salon des Artistes Vivants held in the Salon Carré at the Louvre.

To compete with the magazine *Le Chat Noir*, Adolphe Willette and the poet Émile Goudeau founded the satirical illustrated magazine *Le Pierrot*.

Aix-en-Provence: Paul Cézanne, *Mardi Gras*.

Belgium, Brussels: February, Henri de Toulouse-Lautrec exhibited eleven works with Les XX, among them *Rider*, *Circus (Fan)*, and *Drawing of a Clown*.

Ostend: James Ensor, *Christ's Entry into Brussels in 1889*.

1889

France, Paris: Fernand Pelez's *Grimaces and Misery* won a silver medal at the Exposition Universelle.

The Moulin Rouge, opened 5 October by Joseph Oller, had Toulouse-Lautrec's *At the Cirque Fernando: Equestrienne* on permanent display.

Dieppe: Walter Sickert returned to the Cirque Pinder in the summer, during his annual stay in Dieppe.

Belgium, Ostend: First appearance of Pierrot in James Ensor's work, in the painting *Theatre of Masks*. That same year, creation of the paintings *The Amazement of the Mask Wouse* and *Old Woman with Masks*.

369

1890

France, Paris: Audiences flocked to the Nouveau Cirque to see *À la Cravache*, a new revue by Surtac and Alévy. The clown Foottit imitated Sarah Bernhardt as Cleopatra in the play by Victorien Sardou. The great tragic actress attended a performance and laughed heartily.

Germany, Frankfurt: Sarrasani (Hans Stosch) made his debut at the Ciniselli Circus as an animal trainer clown, with three monkeys, three dogs, a donkey, and a pig. His act soon became famous in all the circuses and music-halls of Germany.

Portugal, Lisbon: 14 August, opening of the Coliseu dos Recreios. Better located and with a larger seating capacity than the Real Coliseu, it took over from its predecessor and initiated the golden age of the circus in Portugal.

United States, New York: Madison Square Garden was completely refurbished by the architect Stanford White at a cost of 3 million dollars. At that time, nearly all American circuses had adopted the three-ring format popularized by Barnum.

1891

France, Paris: Yvette Guilbert sang at the Nouveau Cirque in *Garden-Party*, a fantasy by Pierre Delcourt and Victor Meusy.

To compete with the Nouveau Cirque, the Cirque d'Hiver put on an aquatic pantomime.

The pantomime *Néron* was a great success at the Hippodrome de l'Alma.

Germany, Hamburg-Altona: Paul Busch settled into a stationary circus.

United States, Bridgeport, Connecticut: April, death of P.T. Barnum, leaving James A. Bailey alone at the head of the Greatest Show on Earth.

1892

France, Paris: In the ring of the Cirque d'Été audiences saw the Russian clown Durov, one of the most famous small-animal trainers.

Equestrian show at the Nouveau Cirque. Pierantoni and Saltamontès parodied fairground wrestlers. In December the Nouveau Cirque presented a nautical extravaganza of Japanese inspiration entitled *Papa Chrysanthème*. The show revolved around the ceremonial dance that the European wife of a Japanese prince had to perform in order to be accepted by his court. For the occasion, the Nouveau Cirque's aquatic ring was converted into a pond strewn with water-lilies and lotuses; under the electric lights, dancers in diaphanous veils imitated the performances of the celebrated Loie Fuller.

Austria, Vienna: Paul Busch had a circus built by the Drexter brothers on Austellungsstrasse.

1893

England, London: George Sanger had to resign himself to demolishing Astley's Amphitheatre, which was beyond repair. The last performance was given on 4 March before an emotional audience.

France, Paris: The Nouveau Cirque presented a boxing kangaroo act; Surtac and Alévy put on the revue *Paris Clown*; Donval presented *Pierrot soldat*; and Foottit played Pierrot in stage sets by Caran d'Ache.

Demolition of the Hippodrome de l'Alma.

Germany, Berlin: On tour in Germany, Albert Schumann's Scandinavian Circus gave Renz's Olympic Circus solid competition.

1894

France, Paris: Inauguration of the Hippodrome du Champ-de-Mars.

1895

France, Paris: March, the horseback rider Eléna Betty (Foottit's sister) and the clown Gougou Loyal performed triumphantly at the Cirque Fernando.

March, opening of the Chien Noir in the Nouveau Cirque's secondary buildings. It was founded by cabaret singers who had quarrelled with the management of the Chat Noir in Montmartre.

April, Louise Weber, called La Goulue, a quadrille dancer at the Moulin Rouge, Montmartre's idol and a friend of Toulouse-Lautrec, decided to attempt a new career. She set up a booth at the Foire du Trône, where she appeared as an Egyptian belly dancer.

Germany, Berlin: 24 October, inauguration of Paul Busch's Circuspalast, or Circus Busch.

Spain, Barcelona: 29 October, demolition of the Circo Ecuestre Barcelonès. Deprived of permanent installations, the troupe performed in improvised rings, especially the stages of the Bosque, Novedades, Cómico Condal, and Nuevo theatres, until the opening of the Teatro Circo Olympia in 1924.

1896

France, Paris: Triumphant performances, at the Nouveau Cirque, of the rider Blanche Allarty, the most brilliant student of Ernest Molier, whom she married.

Germany, Frankfurt: Albert Schumann founded Frankfurt's stationary circus, which later became a theatre.

1897

France, Paris: Louis Fernando was forced to abandon his circus, which had not been doing well since Medrano left for the Nouveau Cirque in 1888.

December, Medrano bought out the Cirque Fernando and named it Cirque Medrano.

Hippolyte Houcke took over management of the Nouveau Cirque and presented outstanding animal acts, including trained zebras.

The Russian clown Durov appeared at the Cirque d'Hiver with his donkey.

Germany, Berlin: In difficulty since the death of its founder, Ernst Jakob Renz, on 3 April 1892, the Olympic Circus was forced to close.

Switzerland, Geneva: Théodore Rancy's son, Alphonse, razed the old Rancy Circus to build a new one. This circus was later converted into a theatre and, eventually, a movie theatre. It was demolished in 1955.

Denmark, Copenhagen: 28 June, inauguration of the Max Schumann Circus.

United States: Circus director James A. Bailey took the Greatest Show on Earth to Europe for a five-year tour. By this time, the American tent circus had acquired its characteristic format: three rings and two stages or platforms, surrounded by an oval horse track for spectacles and races. Several European circuses took up this model with varying degrees of success: Krone, Sarrasani, and McCaddon.

1898

France, Paris: Closing of the Cirque d'Été following Victor Franconi's death in 1897. Charles Franconi continued to manage the Cirque d'Hiver until 1907 but was obliged to abandon the Cirque d'Été, which was running a deficit, to the demolishers' shovel.

1899

France, Paris: The Fratellini brothers rivalled Foottit and Chocolat at the Nouveau Cirque in the pantomime *La Cascade merveilleuse*. François Fratellini, the trio's future whiteface clown, distinguished himself as a trick rider.

1890

France, Paris: Seurat began his *Circus* in the fall, from studies done at the Cirque Fernando.

Émile Reynaud, *Guillaume Tell*, a Praxinoscope strip based on sketches performed by Foottit and Chocolat.

Belgium, Ostend: James Ensor reworked an academic composition, *Masks Watching a Negro Bargeman* (1878–1879), adding a group of masks.

1891

France, Paris: Georges Seurat, *The Circus* (unfinished).

Belgium, Ostend: James Ensor, *Masquerade*; *The Grotesque Singers*.

1892

France, Paris: Pierre Bonnard's first use of the circus theme, in *The Parade* (or *The Fair*).

28 October, first performance, at the Musée Grévin's Théâtre Fantastique, of Émile Reynaud's "luminous pantomimes," animated magic lantern projections. Reynaud drew, image by image, various sequences lasting a quarter hour, including 500 images for the "cinematic" pantomime *Pauvre Pierrot*.

Belgium, Ostend: James Ensor, *The Strange Masks*; *The Despair of Pierrot* (or *Jealous Pierrot*); *Duel of the Masks*.

Italy, Milan: Ruggero Leoncavallo's *I Pagliacci* premiered at the Teatro dal Verme under the direction of Arturo Toscanini. This *dramma* in a prologue and two acts portrays a clown who must laugh and make others laugh while his lovesick heart is breaking.

Russia: Sergey Rachmaninoff, *Polichinelle*, Op. 3, No. 4, for piano solo.

1893

France, Paris: Pierre Bonnard executed *At the Circus, Haute École* for the album *Petites Scènes familières* by the composer Claude Terrasse, his brother-in-law.

Photographs of a trapeze artist taken by Albert Londe in the ring of the Salpêtrière, inaugurated the same year, made use of the capacities of his new twelve-lens chronophotography camera.

Henri-Gabriel Ibels, *Mademoiselle Olympe*; *At the Circus*.

Georges de Feure, *The Cirque Corvi*.

1894

France, Paris: Pierre Bonnard, *Circus*.

Photograph of Toulouse-Lautrec wearing the clown Foottit's hat.

1895

England, London: Walter Sickert exhibited a circus painting at the Dutch Gallery.

Aubrey Beardsley designed the frontispiece for "Pierrot's Library," a series of books published by John Lane.

France, Paris: 28 December, at the Salon Indien du Grand Café, 14 Boulevard des Capucines, Antoine Lumière demonstrated the cinematograph invented by his sons Auguste and Louis.

Pierre Bonnard painted *Redskins*, after Pawnee Bill's Historic Wild West, then touring Belgium, the Netherlands, and France.

26 January, the magazine *Le Rire* (no. 12, pp. 7–8) published "Théorie de Foottit sur le rapt" by Romain Coolus, with five drawings by Toulouse-Lautrec.

Henri de Toulouse-Lautrec, *The Clowness Cha-U-Kao*; *The Clowness*; *Entrée of Cha-U-Kao*; and panels for La Goulue's booth at the Foire du Trône: *La Goulue Dancing at the Moulin-Rouge* and *La Goulue as an Egyptian Dancer*.

In a supplement to *La Revue Blanche* entitled *Nib*, Toulouse-Lautrec produced a humorous advertisement for Potin chocolate, which featured the clown duo Foottit and Chocolat.

December, Siegfried Bing's first Salon de l'Art Nouveau. The American glassmaker Louis Comfort Tiffany exhibited stained glass after a sketch by Toulouse-Lautrec, *At the Nouveau Cirque: The Clowness with Five Plastrons*.

Spain, Madrid: On summer holiday with his family, Pablo Picasso visited the Prado for the first time, where he made drawings of a dwarf and a buffoon after Velázquez.

1896

England, London: Aubrey Beardsley, *The Death of Pierrot*.

France, Paris: *Elles*, an album of lithographs by Toulouse-Lautrec, included *Seated Clowness*, which depicts Cha-U-Kao, a female clown and dancer at the Nouveau Cirque and the Moulin Rouge.

Rheims: November, Toulouse-Lautrec participated in the Exposition d'Affiches Artistiques, Françaises et Étrangères, Modernes et Rétrospectives at the Cirque de Reims.

United States, New York: 12 April, in the Sunday supplement of the *New York World*, George Luks published a cartoon entitled *The Animals Start a Circus and Make the Men Perform*.

1897

France, Paris: Pierre Bonnard, *Equestrienne*; *At the Circus*; *The Ring*.

Toulouse-Lautrec, *Clowness at the Moulin Rouge*.

November issue of *Le Figaro Illustré* was devoted to the theme "Forains et Saltimbanques."

Belgium, Ostend: James Ensor, *Death and the Masks*.

Spain, Barcelona: Pablo Picasso, *Self-portrait in a Wig*.

Italy, Venice: 6 May, first performance, at the Teatro La Fenice, of Ruggero Leoncavallo's four-act opera *La Bohème*. It is set in the colourful world of circus entertainers.

1898

England, London: 30 April, opening of a Toulouse-Lautrec exhibition at the Goupil Gallery. Among the exhibited works: *A Cavalcade*; *Cha-U-Kao*; *Clown*; *In Clown's Costume*.

France, Paris: František Kupka decorated La Goulue's booth at the Foire du Trône.

1899

France, Paris: 30 December, first performance, at the Théâtre de la Gaîté-Lyrique, of the three-act operetta *Les Saltimbanques*, music by Louis Ganne, libretto by Maurice Ordonneau. The action takes place in Versailles and Normandy: the shy singer Suzanne marries the handsome lieutenant André, with the complicity of three other acrobats, Marion, Paillasse, and Grand Pingouin, the strong man.

Neuilly: Toulouse-Lautrec was interned in the rest home of Dr. Semelaigne, 16 Avenue de Madrid. In the space of eleven weeks he made 40 drawings from memory on the theme of the circus.

Belgium, Ostend: James Ensor, *Ensor with Masks*; *Pierrot with Masks*.

1899–1900

France, Paris: First appearance of the theme of acrobats in the work of Kees Van Dongen, in *Les Débuts de Raoul*.

1900

England, London: 15 January, opening of the Hippodrome in Leicester Square.

France, Paris: Breathtaking equestrian act by the Frediani brothers at the Nouveau Cirque.

Inauguration of the Hippodrome on Place Clichy at the time of the Exposition Universelle.

La Goulue took up a career as an animal trainer, a profession in which Adrien Pezon had initiated her two years earlier. She owned her own menagerie and had a short-lived success with audiences curious to see this former music-hall dancer in the wild animal cage.

Switzerland, Goerlikon (Canton of Thurgau): The Knie family became Swiss citizens.

1901

France, Paris: The Hippodrome on Place Clichy became the Hippo-Palace under the direction of Albert Schumann.

The pantomime *Le Pont Alexandre III* was a huge success at the Nouveau Cirque.

Germany, Annaberg (Saxony): Sarrasani mounted his first circus at the town fair in the fall.

1902

France, Paris: Louis, François, Paul, and Albert Fratellini were hired by the Cirque d'Hiver.

Belgium: Alphonse De Jonghe, founder of Belgium's largest circus, built a semi-permanent wooden structure in which he debuted with the famous athlete Miss Athléa.

Germany, Hamburg: Paul Busch purchased the buildings of the Renz Circus, which had closed in 1897.

1903

France, Paris: American businessman Frank C. Bostock rented the Hippo-Palace for the year. Like Barnum, he presented human and animal phenomena to the Paris public.

Germany, Breslau: Paul Busch purchased the Renz Circus installations in Breslau.

Ukraine, Kiev: Russian aristocrat Piotr Krutikov, who had set up a private circus in his house along the lines of Molier's circus in Paris, built a permanent circus named the Hippo-Palace. It was considered Europe's most modern and commodious circus building.

1904

France, Paris: December, Adrien Wettach, famous as the clown Grock, made his first appearance at the Cirque Medrano with his partner, Marius Galante, called Brick.

Mauricia de Thiers presented "L'Autobolide," a circus act, at the Folies Bergères.

Austria, Vienna: Albert Schumann built a circus for 3,200 spectators on Märzstrasse.

1905

France, Paris: Second Paris stay of Buffalo Bill, who set up his show in the Champ-de-Mars.

Under the management of Mathias Beketov, the Nouveau Cirque of Paris became the Grand Cirque Russe Beketov for the while. It presented a large equestrian troupe and pantomimes with local colour, like *Sibérie*.

Foottit and Chocolat performed in the revue at the Folies Bergères.

Germany, Bremen: 28 May, Carl Krone, Jr., put up a big top 36 metres in diameter at the Freimarkt.

1906

France, Paris: 5 January, inauguration of the Cirque Métropole on Avenue de la Motte-Piquet. The opening show included performances by Valli de Laszewski and his cavalry, the Clarkonians on the flying trapeze, the Josberthos, acrobat athletes, Princess Yvonne de Mayrena and her three elephants, and the rider Baronne de Holstein and her four horses.

Jean Houcke took over management of the Nouveau Cirque and brought back the clown Chocolat.

28 September, Théodore Laugier and the widow of Paul Fanni ended their partnership with the last performance of the Cirque Populaire, which they had operated together. Supported by her eldest son, Théodore, the widow Fanni founded the Cirque Fanni.

United States: Upon the death of James A. Bailey in April, the Ringling brothers took over the management of the Greatest Show on Earth. They simultaneously managed the Ringling Bros. Circus out of Baraboo, Wisconsin, and the Barnum & Bailey Circus out of Bridgeport, Connecticut.

1907

France, Paris: 29 August, the Cirque d'Hiver's gaslights were replaced by electric lamps. While staying on as managing director, Charles Franconi ceded the Cirque d'Hiver to the movie company Pathé.

Tison and Debray took over management of the Nouveau Cirque and brought back Foottit.

Germany, Hamburg-Stellingen: 7 May, Carl Hagenbeck's German circus opened a zoo.

1908

France, Paris: 8 February, the Cirque Métropole closed, reopening two weeks later as the Cirque de Paris.

Madame de Ternann, a rider who rode astride, performed triumphantly at the Nouveau Cirque.

Until 1910 the clown duo Grock and Antonet (Umberto Guillaume) were appearing at the Cirque Medrano. Using the costume and style of Little Walter, Sr. – Antonet's former partner – Grock gradually developed the style for which he became known.

At the Fête de Neuilly, Charles Dullin created the Théâtre de la Foire, which revived the principles of *commedia dell'arte*: a play based on a scenario with *lazzis* and dramatic situations halfway between pantomime and clown acts.

Germany: Carl Krone abandoned the old formula of the menagerie and mounted a three-ring arena inspired by the big American circuses. However, he continued to augment his animal collection, which became a veritable itinerant zoo.

1909

France, Paris: For four months the Cirque de Paris housed the Grand Cirque Rancy. It was followed by the German Hagenbeck Circus. A huge advertising campaign and a show of high quality brought audiences to Avenue de la Motte-Piquet. On the reopening of the Cirque de Paris in September, Hippolyte Houcke, former director of the Hippodrome de l'Alma and the Nouveau Cirque, took the helm.

Albert, Paul, and François Fratellini established their celebrated clown trio. The Fratellinis revitalized clown comedy – until then dominated by the pairing of a whiteface clown and an Auguste – by adding another clown and cleverly reworking the *commedia dell'arte* scenarios.

1900

England, London: During a stay in London, Everett Shinn made sketches of the circus show at the Hippodrome Theatre in Leicester Square. These sketches influenced his paintings over the next few years.

Spain, Barcelona: Pablo Picasso won second prize in the poster competition for the carnival organized by the avant-garde magazine *Pèl i Ploma* with his project entitled *Pierrot Celebrating the New Year* (1899). This design marks the first appearance of Pierrot in his work.

France, Paris: Picasso, *The Blue Dancer*; *Booth at the Fair*.

3 July, inauguration of an exhibition of works by Everett Shinn at Galerie Goupil. Four pastels were included: *The Wrestlers*; *Merry-Go-Round*; *Monkey Cart*; *Luxembourg Garden – Punch and Judy Show*.

František Kupka's drawing *The Fools* won a silver medal at the Exposition Universelle.

Belgium, Ostend: James Ensor, *The Arrest of Pierrot*.

Russia, Saint Petersburg: 10 February, first performance, at the Theatre of the Hermitage, of the ballet *Les Millions d'Arlequin*, score by Riccardo Drigo, choreography by Marius Petipa, the composer conducting.

1901

France, Paris: During a second stay in Paris, Pablo Picasso executed *Harlequin* (*Pierrot*) and *The Two Saltimbanques* (*Harlequin and His Companion*), in which he portrayed himself as Harlequin, who became his alter ego. This was the beginning of the artist's Blue Period (1901–1904).

Spain, Madrid: First appearance of a clown in the work of Picasso, in the painting *Clown with a Monkey*.

Picasso published a drawing of a clown in the 10 March issue of the magazine *Arte Joven*, which he founded with Francisco Asís Soler.

Picasso, *La Nana*.

Italy, Venice: Walter Sickert, *Pierrot and Woman Embracing*, study for *Venetian Stage Scene*.

United States, New York: November, Everett Shinn's paintings *In Green Room Circus* and *The Circus* exhibited at Boussod, Valadon & Co.

1902

France, Paris: First paintings by Georges Rouault on the theme of the circus.

Dieppe: Walter Sickert, *The Fair at Night*.

Spain, Barcelona: Pablo Picasso produced an advertising poster for a health remedy, Agell, depicting a neurasthenic Pierrot.

Austria, Vienna: November, inauguration of an exhibition in the dispatch room of *Die Zeit*, in which František Kupka and Adolphe Willette took part. Kupka presented, among other things, his lithograph *The Fools*.

United States, New York: Everett Shinn, *The Hippodrome, London*.

1903

Ukraine, Kherson: After ending his collaboration with Stanislavski's Moscow Art Theatre, director Vsevolod Meyerhold founded his own theatre company. On the program of their first season was a melodrama by the Austrian playwright Franz von Schönthan; Meyerhold played the role of Landowski, an old clown.

United States, New York: Everett Shinn, *Trapeze*.

1904

France, Paris: 13 April, Pablo Picasso moved into the Bateau-Lavoir, 13 Rue Ravignan. Beginning in December, he went to the Cirque Medrano several evenings a week with Fernande Olivier, Guillaume Apollinaire, Max Jacob, André Salmon, and Paul Fort. He attended the debut of Grock and Brick, and became friends with Ilès, Alex, and Rico. This was the beginning of the artist's Rose Period (1904–1906).

Georges Rouault, *Head of a Tragic Clown*.

Toulouse-Lautrec's panels (1895) for La Goulue's booth at the Foire du Trône exhibited at the Salon d'Automne.

Kees Van Dongen, *Marie Cochon*; *The Parade*; *Saucisse and Pépino*; *Standing Clown*; *A Gymnast*.

1905

France, Paris: After coming home from the circus with Max Jacob, Pablo Picasso created one of his first bronzes, *The Jester*.

Picasso portrayed himself as Harlequin seated at a table at the Lapin Agile, beside Germaine Florentin (née Gargallo) as Columbine and the bistro's proprietor, Frédé, playing the guitar.

25 February to 6 March, Picasso exhibited the first works of his Rose Period at Galerie Serrurier, including eight circus scenes: *Acrobat on a Ball*; *The Acrobat's Family with a Monkey*; *Seated Harlequin*; *Acrobat and Young Harlequin*; *Two Acrobats with a Dog*; *Harlequin's Family*; *Circus Family*; *At the Lapin Agile*.

Pablo Picasso, *La Suite des saltimbanques* (drypoints).

Upon his return from northern Holland, where he spent the summer, Picasso finished his large canvas *Family of Saltimbanques* and decided to leave *Pierrette's Wedding* unfinished.

Kees Van Dongen's regular visits to the Cirque Medrano inspired a series of paintings on the theme of the circus, such as *The Clown Who Believes Himself to Be President of the Republic*, *Equestrienne*, and *Riders at the Cirque Medrano*.

Belgium, Ostend: James Ensor, *Pierrot and Skeletons*.

Russia, Saint Petersburg: Alexandre N. Benois, *Scene from the Commedia dell'arte*.

1906

France, Paris: Staying in Paris in the fall, Walter Sickert was a regular at the café-concerts of Montparnasse and Montmartre, which provided him with material for several paintings, including *Gaîté Rochechouart*, which includes a trapeze artist in the background.

Pablo Picasso, *Two Brothers*.

Félicien Rops, *Saltimbanque*.

Georges Rouault, *Clown with a Bandoneon*; *Clown with a Drum* (c. 1906–1907).

Kees Van Dongen, *The Old Clown*.

Russia, Saint Petersburg: 30 December, first performance, at the Teatr na Ofitserskoi, of Aleksandr Blok's play *Blaganchik*, directed by Meyerhold, who also played the role of Pierrot.

United States, New York: Everett Shinn, *Circus*.

1907

France, Paris: Georges Rouault, *The Parade*.

1908

France, Paris: Georges Rouault, *Clown with Rose*.

Kees Van Dongen, *Equestrienne*; *The White Leotard*.

Germany, Dresden: Ernst Ludwig Kirchner, *Tightrope Walker*.

1910

France, Paris: At the Cirque de Paris, the whiteface clown Foottit and his sons, as well as Chocolat, presented a sensational entrée.

Rico and Alex, master clowns, acrobats, singers, and mimes, made the Cirque Medrano the most popular circus in Paris up until 1914.

Germany, Berlin: The Fratellini trio made its debut at the Circus Busch.

Russia, Saint Petersburg: The Fratellinis presented their act at the Cirque Ciniselli.

1911

France, Paris: At the Nouveau Cirque, Chocolat portrayed La Belle Otéro; Foottit played in *Hamlet* and *La Dame aux Camélias*.

Belgium, Mons: 11 December, the clown, mime, tightrope jumper, and dog trainer Alexandre Palisse inaugurated his circus.

Germany, Berlin: Antonet and Grock's act was poorly received, and the ensuing conflict between them led to their separation in 1913.

1912

France, Paris: June–July, Wilhelm Hagenbeck's travelling circus set up in Paris.

Germany, Dresden: Sarrasani built a circus on the Carolaplatz for 2 million marks. The building was destroyed by bombing on 13 February 1945.

1913

France, Paris: C.B. Cochran presented Hagenbeck's circus-menagerie at the Olympia Theatre.

Russia, Moscow: The Fratellinis performed at the Nikitin Circus.

1914

England, London: Conversion of the Hippodrome in Leicester Square to a variety theatre.

France: Theatres and entertainment halls officially closed for the duration of the war.

Germany, Berlin: 31 March, the Circus Busch closed temporarily. It reopened the following year.

1915

France, Paris: Closed since war was declared in 1914, the Cirque Medrano reopened for the 1915–1916 season. Its director, Rodolphe Bonent, hired Paul, François, and Albert Fratellini and devoted a huge advertising campaign to them.

Spain, Barcelona: The Circo Reina Victoria became the property of the Andreu-Rivel family.

1917

Spain, Madrid: After the death of William Parish, his son Leonardo Parish de Fasso took over the management of the Circo Teatro Price, which he renamed Circo Parish.

United States, Denver, Colorado: Death of Buffalo Bill.

1918

Germany, Nienburg: After acquiring two trained horses and a trained donkey, Julius Gleich and his wife, Caroline Margarete Hänne, founded the Henny Circus. Returning from Holland, where they had stayed during the inflationary period, they were back in Germany in 1923 as the Barnum & Bailey European Circus.

Berlin: 30 March, Albert Schumann's Scandinavian Circus gave its final performance.

1909

France, Paris: Pablo Picasso, *The Harlequin's Family*; *Bust of Harlequin*; *Harlequin Leaning on His Elbow*; *Carnival at the Bistro*.

Germany, Dresden: Ernst Ludwig Kirchner, *Equestrienne*; *Black Stallion, Rider, and Clown*; *Acrobat and Clown*; *Equestrienne at the Circus*; *Tightrope Walker*.

Austria, Vienna: *Der Graf von Luxemburg*, an operetta by Franz Lehár, with the characters Pierrot and Pierrette.

1910

Germany, Berlin: Erich Heckel, *Tightrope Walkers*.

20 May, world premiere, at the Theater das Westens, of *Carnaval*, a one-act pantomime-ballet, danced by the Ballets Russes, music by Robert Schumann (orchestrated by Nikolai Rimsky-Korsakov, Anatoly Liadov, Nikolai Tcherepnin, and Alexander Glazunov), choreography by Michel Fokine, sets and costumes by Léon Bakst.

Spain, Cadaqués: late June, Pablo Picasso, Fernande Olivier, and the Derains were staying in Cadaqués. They struck up friendships with clowns, acrobats, and horsemen whom they met in the cafés and with whom they spent their evenings.

United States, New York: John Sloan painted *Old Clown Making Up* after visiting a professional model, Mr. Wilson, whom he asked to pose in the clown costume he had come to borrow for a costume ball.

1911

France, Paris: Pablo Picasso, *Pierrot*; *Buffalo Bill*.

13 June, world premiere, at the Théâtre du Châtelet, of the ballet *Petrushka*, "Scènes burlesques en quatre tableaux," danced by the Ballets Russes, score by Igor Stravinsky, story by Stravinsky and Alexandre Benois, choreography by Michel Fokine, sets and costumes by Benois.

Germany, Berlin: Emil Nolde, *Pierrot and White Lilies*.

1912

France, Paris: April, during a two-week stay, Paul Klee went to the Cirque Medrano.

Germany, Berlin: 16 October, first performance of Arnold Schoenberg's *Pierrot lunaire*, Op. 21, "thrice seven melodramas" for speaking voice and five instrumentalists, to a cycle of poems by the Belgian author Albert Giraud.

Ernst Ludwig Kirchner, *Japanese Acrobats*.

Munich: Paul Klee's first drawings on the theme of the circus, *Cow and Clown*; *Harlequinade*; *Young Pierrot*.

Stuttgart: First performance, at the Königliches Hoftheater, of the first version of Richard Strauss's one-act opera *Ariadne auf Naxos*, libretto by Hugo von Hofmannsthal, the composer conducting. Abandoned by Theseus on the island of Naxos, Ariadne bemoans her fate until the characters of the Comédie-Italienne step in, determined to cheer her up. The piece ends with Ariadne being carried off by Bacchus in the direction of the Champs-Élysées.

Bonn: August Macke, *Russian Ballet*.

1913

France, Céret: Pablo Picasso, *Head of Harlequin*; *Harlequin*.

Paris: Alexander Archipenko, *Carrousel Pierrot*; *Medrano II*.

Germany, Munich: Ernst Ludwig Kirchner, *Acrobats Somersaulting*; *Circus Scene*.

Berlin: Erich Heckel, *Pierrot Dying*.

1914

France, Paris: Marc Chagall, *Acrobat*.

Monte Carlo: 16 April, world premiere, at the Casino de Monte-Carlo, of *Papillons*, a one-act ballet by Michel Fokine, music by Robert Schumann, sets by Mstislav Dobujinksy, costumes by Léon Bakst. Fokine danced the role of Pierrot.

Germany, Berlin: Ernst Ludwig Kirchner, *Equestrienne*; *The Tent*.

Munich: Paul Klee, *Acrobats*.

United States, New York: Edward Hopper, *Soir Bleu*.

1915

England, London: Back in London after a stay in Brighton during August and September, Walter Sickert painted *Brighton Pierrots*.

France, Paris: The composer Edgar Varèse introduced Jean Cocteau to Pablo Picasso, on Rue Schoelcher.

Self-portrait of Picasso as Harlequin in his Cubist painting *Harlequin*.

Germany, Berlin: Ferruccio Busoni, *Rondo arlecchinesco*, Op. 46, for orchestra.

1916

France, Paris: Cocteau asked Picasso to design the sets and costumes for the ballet *Parade*, score by Erik Satie. The ballet's simple story involves the parade of a troupe of itinerant entertainers on the Boulevards of Paris. To attract customers into their booth, a clown, a little American girl, and a Chinese conjurer perform their acts surrounded by three managers. Picasso made 67 preparatory pencil and gouache sketches for a stage curtain, the set, and costumes. He also contributed directly to the subject by thinking up the characters of the managers, dressed in Cubist constructions.

A stretcher-carrier in Verdun, Fernand Léger, on furlough with Apollinaire, discovered the films of Chaplin.

Germany: Second version of Richard Strauss's opera *Ariadne auf Naxos*. The composer added a long prologue, a musical setting of the longstanding quarrel between the partisans of *opera seria* and *opera buffa*, making fun of the grand tradition of German opera and the popular tradition of the Italian comedy.

Munich: Paul Klee, *Head Jugglers*; *Acrobat and Jugglers*.

1917

Italy, Rome: 17 February, Picasso and Cocteau met up with Diaghilev and Léonide Massine in Rome to work on the ballet *Parade* with the Ballets Russes. While in Italy, the foursome discovered the adventures of Policinella at performances of the *commedia dell'arte* they attended in Naples. Massine instantly wished to dance the role.

France, Paris: 18 May, premiere of *Parade* at the Théâtre du Châtelet. In the midst of the military rout the show caused an outcry of protest, and it was withdrawn from the Ballets Russes's program.

Georges Rouault created the illustrations for *Guerre et Miserere* (1917–1927), which was not published until 1948, under the title *Miserere*. Among this series of prints, *Who Is Not Made Up?* aptly summarizes his conception of the clown as alter ego and emblematic double of the scourged Christ.

Juan Gris, *Harlequin*.

Spain, Barcelona: June, Picasso joined his future wife, the dancer Olga Kokhlova, in Barcelona. He remained there to attend a performance of *Parade* on 10 November. During this stay he made a portrait of choreographer Léonide Massine as Harlequin.

Switzerland, Zürich: After attending a puppet show at the Teatro dei Piccoli in Rome, Ferruccio Busoni composed two short operas, *Arlecchino, oder Die Fenster*, Op. 50 (1916), and *Turandot* (after Carlo Gozzi, 1917), derived from the traditions of the *commedia dell'arte* and eighteenth-century *opera buffa*. The premiere of *Arlecchino* took place on 11 May at the Stadttheater in Zürich, Busoni conducting, sets and costumes by the painter Gino Severini.

Russia, Saint Petersburg: February, first performance, at the Aleksandrinskii Theatre, of Mikhail Lermontov's play *Maskarad*, directed by Meyerhold.

1918

France, Paris: Fernand Léger, *The Cirque Medrano*; *The Circus*; *Circus Acrobats*; *The Acrobats*; *The Clowns*.

Pablo Picasso, *Harlequin with a Violin ("Si tu veux")*; *Harlequin with Mask*; *Harlequin with Guitar*; *Pierrot*.

Jacques Lipchitz, *Harlequin with Accordion*.

Russia, Saint Petersburg: For the first anniversary of the October Revolution, first performance, at the Opera Theatre, of Vladimir Mayakovsky's play *Misteriia-Buff*, directed by Meyerhold. It is a synthesis of *comédie de mystère* and buffoonery.

United States, New York: Gaston Lachaise, *Equestrienne*, bronze.

1919

France, Paris: 10 December, first performance, at the Théâtre Lyrique, of the children's ballet *La Boîte à joujoux*, story by André Hellé, score by Claude Debussy (completed after his death in 1918 by his disciple André Caplet). The story revolves around a quarrel between the wooden soldiers and the polichinelles in a toy box, a sort of city where they live like human beings.

Publication, by H. Floury, of the autobiography of Willette, *Feu Pierrot*.

André Derain, *Harlequin*.

Juan Gris, *Pierrot with Grapes*.

Jacques Lipchitz, *Harlequin with Clarinet*.

1919

France, Paris: Grock performed at the Olympia, and the critics felt they had witnessed the birth of a new genius of clownery.

Germany, Munich: 10 May, inauguration of the Krone Circus. It was destroyed by bombing in 1944.

Switzerland, Bern: The Knies replaced their outdoor variety arena with a circus tent, and the Cirque National Suisse was born. Generations have succeeded one another at the head of the enterprise, which has maintained its independence until today by operating without government subsidies.

Italy, Rome: The Togni Brothers Circus, founded in 1882, became the Togni National Circus.

Russia, Moscow: 26 August, on the recommendation of cultural commissar Lunacharsky, Lenin signed a decree on the "nationalization of theatres and circuses" to remedy circus owners' lack of education and culture. The Salamonsky Circus, on Tsvetnoy Boulevard, thus became the first state circus, and the Nikitin Circus became the second.

United States, Bridgeport, Connecticut, and Baraboo, Wisconsin: The Ringling brothers merged their two circuses into one, the Ringling Bros. and Barnum & Bailey Circus, also known as "The Big One" and "Big Bertha." Four special trains were needed to transport the giant American circus's equipment.

1920

England, London: Bertram Mills, former organizer of horse competitions, founded the Olympia Circus, a permanent circus that gave performances every Christmas season until 1966 (except during the war). They included some of the most famous American circus acts: the Codonas, the Wallendas, the Colleanos, and the Riffenachs.

1921

France, Paris: George Foottit, son of Foottit the clown, and Eugène Grimaldi, son of the Auguste character Chocolat, revived their fathers' comic duo.

1923

France, Paris: May, Gaston Desprez became the owner of the Cirque d'Hiver and restored its original vocation. It reopened on 12 October. Desprez considerably improved the equipment by adding a movable ring and an aquatic ring, then a vast zoo facing Rue de Crussol. Gustave Fratellini's sons Paul, François, and Albert, who came from the Cirque Medrano, presented their clown trio act, which was a huge success.

Austria, Vienna: May, the Zirkus Zentral was launched in a hall built during the First World War on the site of the former "Venice in Vienna" amusement park. In its first year it presented such celebrated performers as Billy Jenkins, Henrik Gautier, and Thérèse Renz, as well as the Knie, Wilhelm Hagenbeck, and Kludsky circus troupes.

Russia, Moscow: Inauguration of the Nijni Novgorod State Circus, which had a monopoly on hiring Western European performers.

1924

France, Paris: 29 June, the Fratellinis' farewell performance at the Medrano.

Spain, Barcelona: 4 December, inauguration of the Teatro Circo Olympia, by the Tivoli company. This building, which could hold up to 6,000 spectators and had a ring that could be converted into a pool, combined all the circus activities in Barcelona.

Madrid: Management of the Circo Parish was assigned to two new partners, Sánchez Reixach and Perezoff, who renamed it Circo Price in honour of its founder. It kept this name until it was demolished in 1970.

1920

France, Paris: Fernand Léger, illustrations for the collection of poems *Die Chaplinade* by Yvan Goll.

February, first performance, at the Comédie des Champs-Élysées, of Jean Cocteau's show *The Nothing Doing Bar*, score by Darius Milhaud, sets by Raoul Dufy. The roles were played by renowned Augustes: François Fratellini as the Red-headed Woman, Paul Fratellini as the Barman, and Albert Fratellini as the Woman in the Low-cut Dress. Cyrillo and Busby, a duo from the Cirque de Paris, portrayed the Negro Boxer and the Policeman respectively; Pinocchio, who was playing at Medrano's, was the Gentleman in evening clothes.

15 May, *Pulcinella*, "ballet with song in one act," was given its first performance at the Opéra by Diaghilev's Ballets Russes, choreography by Léonide Massine, music by Igor Stravinsky, sets and costumes by Picasso, Ernest Ansermet conducting. Massine based the story on an old collection of *commedia dell'arte* scenarios, *I quattro Pulcinella uguali*. Two young women are courted by two suitors, but the women prefer Polichinelle, who has fallen in love with a beautiful peasant girl. There follows a series of mixups that end with the happy marriage of the three couples. Stravinsky adapted and orchestrated the musical numbers from Pergolesi (as well as from works attributed to Pergolesi but actually by Domenica Gallo, Carlo Ignazio Monza, and Unico Wilhelm van Wassenaer). This was the composer's first essay in the neoclassical style following his discovery of traditional Neapolitan theatre.

Juan-les-Pins: During the summer Picasso created *Pierrot and Harlequin*.

Dieppe: Walter Sickert paid a final tribute to Degas, who influenced his early career, in his own version of the famous painting *Miss Lala at the Cirque Fernando* (1879), entitled *The Trapeze*.

Belgium, Brussels: 17 January, first performance, for the Ensor exhibition at Galerie Giroux, of *La Gamme d'amour (Flirt de marionnettes)*, "ballet pantomime, en un acte et deux tableaux," score, libretto, sets, and costumes by James Ensor, under the direction of the composer Léon Delcroix. The scenario is in 26 scenes; the first tableau recounts the frustrated love of Miamia and her suitor Fifrelin in a mask and puppet shop; in the second tableau, the action takes place on a public square, with some fifty colourful characters.

Germany, Frankfurt: 22 February, five days after the end of Carnival, Max Beckmann created the first in a series of preparatory sketches for the painting *Carnival*, where he portrays himself as a masked clown with his dealer, I.B. Neumann, as a Pierrot-Harlequin and his benefactress, Fridel Battenberg, as Columbine.

Munich: Heinrich Maria Davringhausen, *The Acrobat*.

Berlin: Otto Dix, *Suleika, the Tattooed Wonder*.

Spain, Madrid: José Gutiérrez Solana, *The Clowns*.

Russia, Moscow: Chagall created a huge set for the Jewish Theatre, for a show performed by musicians, clowns, and acrobats combining theatre and Hassidic music and dance.

Saint Petersburg: 8 January, inauguration of the Narodnaia Komediia, under the direction of Sergey E. Radlov, a student of Meyerhold. Radlov aspired to renew the classical codes of the theatre based on the popular forms of the circus and the *commedia dell'arte*.

376

1921

England, London: Laura Knight made her first circus drawings at the Olympia Circus of Bertram Mills.

France, Paris: Pablo Picasso, *Three Musicians*, in which the artist portrays himself as Harlequin, alongside Apollinaire as Pierrot with a clarinet and Max Jacob (who had just entered a monastery) as a monk.

17 May, premiere, at the Théâtre de la Gaîté-Lyrique, of *Chout*, "Russian legend in six scenes," danced by the Ballets Russes, score by Sergey Prokofiev, choreography by Mikhail Larionov and Thadée Slavinsky, sets and costumes by Mikhail Larionov.

Germany, Weimar: Opening of the Bauhaus Theatre workshop, under the direction of Lothar Schreyer.

Frankfurt: Max Beckmann, portfolio *Der Jahrmarkt* ("The Annual Fair"); *Self-portrait as Clown*; *Variety Show*.

Berlin: Karl Hofer, *Circus People*.

Italy, Rome: Gino Severini, *Masked Musicians* series (1921–1922).

United States, New York: Edward J. Kelty visited the carnival booths at Coney Island for the first time. Several booth owners ordered photographs from him to promote their attractions: Bobby the Bulldog, the Lobster Boy, the Carlson sisters, the hermaphrodite Jean Eugène, Norma the four-legged woman, and Jolly Irene, America's fattest woman.

Publication of the American painter Marsden Hartley's book *Adventures in the Arts: Informal Chapters on Painters, Vaudeville, and Poets*. One of the chapters, "The Twilight of the Acrobat," is on the circus.

Chicago: 30 December, premiere, at the Chicago Auditorium, of Prokofiev's four-act opera with prologue *The Love for Three Oranges*, libretto by the composer after a *fabia teatrale* of Carlo Gozzi.

1922

France, Paris: Pablo Picasso, *Portrait of an Adolescent Dressed as Pierrot*; *Acrobat*; *Fairground Circus*.

Publication of Henri Church's *Clowns*, illustrations by Georges Rouault.

20 January, premiere, at the Théâtre des Champs-Élysées, of *Skating Rink*, danced by Rolf de Maré's Ballets Suédois, score by Arthur Honegger, sets and costumes by Fernand Léger.

Germany, Düsseldorf: Otto Dix, portfolio *Circus Performers*. Among the ten drypoints in the series, three images are based on acts presented in Germany at the time: *Magic Act* (an act performed by the "spider woman"); *Maud Arizona* (a tattooed woman who performed mainly in port cities); *Lili, Queen of the Air* (the famous trapeze artist Lillian Leitzel of the Ringling Bros. and Barnum & Bailey Circus).

Munich: The clown and cabaret performer Karl Valentin appeared in the Surrealist movie *Mysterien eines Friesersalons* (*The Mysteries of a Hairdresser's Shop*), co-directed by Bertolt Brecht.

George Grosz, *Tightrope Walker*.

Austria, Vienna: First performance of Alexander von Zemlinsky's opera *Der Zwerg* (*The Dwarf*), libretto after Oscar Wilde's *The Birthday of the Infanta* (1888).

Alfred Kubin, *Death of Pierrot*.

Belgium, Deurle: Gustave De Smet, *Parade*.

United States, New York: During the summer Edward J. Kelty followed the circuses touring the East Coast in his studio-van. From 1925 to 1942 he photographed the employees and performers of major and minor American circuses: Ringling Bros. and Barnum & Bailey, Cole Brothers, Hagenbeck-Wallace, Sells-Floto, John Robinson Circus, the circus of Al G. Barnes, Hunt's Circus, Sam B. Dill's Circus, and the Sivan-Drew Motorized Circus.

Gaston Lachaise, *Two Floating Nude Acrobats*, bronze.

1923

England, London: Laura Knight was introduced to Bertram Mills by their mutual friend A.J. Munnings. Mills gave her special permission to paint his troupe during rehearsal and in the wings. Knight became friends with the circus performers, particularly the animal tamer Togare, the dwarf Goliath, and the clown Whimsical Walker.

France, Paris: The Catalan painter Jacinto Salvado posed in a Harlequin costume for Pablo Picasso. That same year Picasso created *Harlequin with a Mirror*, *Harlequin*, and *Saltimbanque Seated with His Arms Crossed*.

Juan Gris, *Pierrot with Guitar*.

Spain, Seville: First concert performance of Manuel de Falla's marionette opera *El retablo de Maese Pedro* (1920), a musical stage adaption of a well-known episode from *Don Quichotte*. In the stable of an inn in La Mancha, puppeteer Master Peter puts on a show about freeing Melisandra, wife of Don Gaiferos, imprisoned in Zaragoza. Don Quixote and Sancho Panza are in the audience.

Germany, Weimar: Oskar Schlemmer replaced Lothar Schreyer as director of the Bauhaus Theatre workshop. That same year he painted *Pierrot and Two Figures*.

Paul Klee, *Captive Clown*; *Tightrope Walker*; *Acrobatic Theatre*.

Frankfurt: Max Beckmann, *The Trapeze*.

Düsseldorf: Otto Dix, *Circus Scene*; *Equestrienne*; *Sketch*; *Five Acrobats on a Trapeze*; *Tightrope Walker*.

Cologne: August Sander, *Showman with Performing Bear in Cologne*.

Italy, Rome: Antonio Donghi, *Carnival*.

1924

France, Monte Carlo: 1 January, performance, at the Théâtre de Monte-Carlo, of the comic opera *La Colombe* (1860), danced by the Ballets Russes to music of Charles Gounod (with two new recitatives by Francis Poulenc), sets and costumes by Juan Gris.

Paris: Publication of Louise Hervieu's *L'Âme du cirque*, with illustrations by Pierre Bonnard and Pablo Picasso.

4 December, performance by the Ballets Suédois of the two-act ballet *Relâche*, with a "cinematographic intermission" in the form of a short film directed by René Clair. The show was a collaboration of Francis Picabia, dancer Jean Börlin, composer Erik Satie, and director René Clair. Some of Picabia's costume designs were inspired by Pierrot's full-cut white tunic.

Juan Gris, *Pierrot and Book*.

André Derain, *Harlequin with Guitar*.

Fernand Léger, *Ballet mécanique*, Dadaist-Cubist film, in collaboration with Man Ray; *Cubist Charlie*.

Juan-les-Pins: Picasso's son Paulo portrayed in costume in *Paul as Harlequin*. That same year Picasso executed *Harlequin Musician*.

Germany, Berlin: Albert Birkle, *Acrobat Schulz*.

Belgium, Antwerp: 27 March, performance, at the Koninklijke Vlaamsche Opera, of the ballet-pantomime *La Gamme d'amour* (*Flirt de marionnettes*) by James Ensor, as *Poppenliefde*, choreography by Sonia Korty, under the direction of Flor Bosmans. There were four more performances in April 1924, and a revival on 7 April 1925.

Deurle: Gustave De Smet, *The Acrobat Admirer*; *The Circus*.

Italy, Rome: Gino Severini, *The Two Punchinellos*; *Pierrot the Musician*.

378

1925

France, Paris: The Codonas, who were from Mexico, presented their flying trapeze act at the Cirque d'Hiver. Only they could execute a death-defying triple somersault. The Paris public was as enthusiastic as it had been over the first appearance of the trapeze artist Léotard at the same circus in 1859.

December, the honour of illuminating the Christmas tree on the Champs-Élysées fell to the Fratellinis.

Austria, Vienna: 1–23 May, the Viennese flocked to Anton Kludsky's Czech circus. Under the gigantic 10,000-seat big top, no fewer than 42 acts were presented in three rings and on two stages.

1926

France, Paris: Demolition of the Nouveau Cirque.

Germany, Berlin: Death of Paul Busch. His daughter, Paula Busch, took over management of the company.

1927

Russia, Moscow: Opening of the State University of Circus and Variety Arts, known as the Moscow Circus School, under the direction of Alexandr Voloshin. The most famous student from the first graduating class was the clown Karandash (Mikhail Nikolaievich Rumiantsev), who gained notoriety with his satires of current Russian politics.

1928

France, Paris: Management of the Cirque Medrano was taken over by Medrano's son Jérôme, who had reached the age of twenty-one. During his term the circus presented high-quality programs and had practically no competition, which made it the best-attended circus in Paris.

Charles Spessardy, Jr., bought out the Cirque Pinder, the French branch of the famous British establishment. During the 1950s he restored its former brilliance by reconstituting a dazzling cavalcade with motorized floats, horses, animals, a dozen elephants, and many extras.

Germany, Berlin: The clown and monologist Karl Valentin appeared on the stage of the cabaret Der Komiker.

1929

France, Paris: 9 September, inauguration of the newly renovated and repainted Cirque Medrano.

United States, Peru, Indiana: John, the last surviving Ringling brother, took control of the American Circus Corporation, a vast syndicate encompassing all but a few independent circuses.

1930

England, London: Bertram Mills organized a first summer circus season under the big top. These summer tours, which continued until 1964, enabled him to hire artists for a longer period than at Christmas and mount his own acts with wild animals and horses.

France, Paris: 15 June, the last performance of the Cirque de Paris, despite the talent of its clowns Antonet and Beby, the most popular ringmasters/emcees. The building was demolished.

Montauban: Gaston Desprez, director of the Cirque d'Hiver, toured France with a tent circus he called the Cirque Fratellini. In addition to the celebrated clowns' entrée, the program highlighted the other members of the family.

United States, New York: Everett Shinn, *The Tightrope Walker*.

Edward J. Kelty photographed the Ringling Bros. and Barnum & Bailey Circus troupe for the first time. One photograph includes all the clowns of the company, another all the freaks and sideshow attractions.

Santa Fe, New Mexico: John Sloan, *Travelling Carnival*.

Hollywood: *He Who Gets Slapped*, film directed by Victor Seastrom (Victor Sjöström), produced by MGM.

Russia: Sergey Prokofiev, *Trapeze*, a ballet.

1925

France, Paris: Pablo Picasso, *Paul as Pierrot*.

Mougins: Francis Picabia, *Mardi Gras* (*The Kiss*); *Mid-Lent* (*Carnival*).

Belgium, Ostend: James Ensor, *The Vile Vivisectors*.

Germany, Frankfurt: Max Beckmann, *Galleria Umberto*; *Pierrette and Clown*; *Double-portrait Carnival*.

Dessau: Paul Klee, *Monsieur Perlenschwein*; *Wintery Mask*; *The Mask with the Little Flag*; *Country Clown*; *Grotesques from the Circus V*.

Krefeld: Heinrich Campendonk, *Pierrot with Sunflower*.

Dresden: First performance of Ferruccio Busoni's three-act opera *Doktor Faust* (completed after his death by his disciple Philipp Jarnach). Busoni's libretto was based on old puppet plays, which Goethe too had used.

Düsseldorf: *Variétés*, film directed by Ewald André Dupont, featuring the Codonas, Lillian Leitzel, and Rastelli, produced by Ufa (Erich Pommer).

Italy, Venice: Gian Francesco Malipiero, *Il finto Arlecchino*, one-act opera with a libretto compiled by the composer from various old literary sources. An ardent supporter of the older music that was gradually being rediscovered at the time, and a devoted bibliophile, Malipiero referred to eighteenth-century thematic and harmonic models in this opera.

Spain: Joan Miró, *The Circus*; *Painting* (*Circus Horse*).

United States, New York: Alexander Calder, *The Flying Trapeze*.

Edward J. Kelty published his first non-illustrated sales catalogue, with a list of all the photographs produced at the circus in the previous seasons.

Hollywood: *Sally of the Sawdust*, film directed by David W. Griffiths, produced by Paramount Pictures.

1926

France, Paris: Georges Rouault executed four lithographs on the theme of the circus for the book *Maîtres et petits maîtres d'aujourd'hui* by Jacques Maritain, published by E. Frapier.

Rouault's first colour etchings for *Cirque* by André Suarès (published in 1936 as *Cirque de l'étoile filante*).

Two paintings by Rouault reproduced in colour on the front and back cover of the December issue of the magazine *Funambules*.

Marc Chagall, *The Three Acrobats*.

3 June, world premiere, at the Théâtre Sarah-Bernhardt, of the ballet *Jack in the Box*, danced by the Ballets Russes, music by Erik Satie (orchestrated by Darius Milhaud), choreography by George Balanchine, sets and costumes by André Derain.

Darius Milhaud, *Le Carnaval d'Aix*, piano concerto.

Le Cannet: Pierre Bonnard, *Circus Vision*, drawing for the book *En suivant la Seine* by Gustave Coquiot.

Germany, Dessau: At the opening of the new building of the Bauhaus, the Hungarian painter Andor Weininger presented a "clownerie," wearing a costume designed by Oskar Schlemmer.

Paul Klee, *Arrival of the Jugglers*.

Cologne: August Sander, between 1926 and 1932: *Girl in a Fairground Caravan*; *Usherettes*; *Circus Artiste*; *Circus Artistes*; *Circus People*; *Fairground Workers*; *Circus Workers*; *Three Generations in Fairground Caravan*.

Berlin: Umbo's first depiction of the circus, in the photomontage *Street Scene*.

United States, New York: January, exhibition of John Quinn's modern art collection at the Art Center. It included Seurat's painting *The Circus*, which Joseph Cornell had the opportunity to see.

Alexander Calder, *Animal Sketching*; *Circus*.

1927

France, Paris: Exhibition *Les Peintres du cirque* at the Cirque d'Hiver. Among the participants, Georges Rouault exhibited four drawings and two poems, and Chagall exhibited two paintings.

Based on drawings done at the Cirque d'Hiver, Marc Chagall executed the 19 gouaches of his *Cirque Vollard*.

Pablo Picasso, *Harlequin*.

Claude Cahun, *I AM IN TRAINING DON'T KISS ME*.

Jacques Lipchitz, *Pierrot Escapes*.

Belgium, Liège: 22 March, performance, at the Théâtre Royal de Liège, of the ballet-pantomime *La Gamme d'amour* (*Flirt de marionnettes*) by James Ensor, choreography by Madame Albers.

Germany, Dessau: Irene Bayer-Hecht photographed Andor Weininger in clown make-up for the Eye-Ear-Nose-Throat Festival at the Bauhaus. T. Lux Feininger photographed the director of the Bauhaus Theatre Workshop, Oskar Schlemmer, as a clown-musician. That same year he also photographed Weininger in his clown-musician costume performing in the pantomime *Treppenwitz*, directed by Schlemmer at the Bauhaus.

Frankfurt: Max Beckmann, *Portrait of N.M. Zeretelli*.

Spain: Joan Miró, *Painting* (*Circus Horse*); *Painting* (*Circus Horse – The Lasso*).

1928

England, London: Laura Knight executed the painting *Charivari* (or *The Grand Parade*), in response to a commission from Major Atherley, a circus devotee.

Germany, Berlin: 31 March, the Beard-Nose-Heart Festival organized at the Bauhaus orchestra.

Frankfurt: Max Beckmann, *Aerial Acrobats*.

Coburg: Gian Francesco Malipiero's one-act opera *Il finto Arlecchino* (1925) was combined with two new short stage works as the centrepiece of a triptych entitled *Il mistero di Venezia*.

Belgium, Deurle: Gustave De Smet, *Equestrienne*.

United States, New York: Alexander Calder gave performances of his miniature *Cirque* in the small room he occupied on Charles Street.

Westport, Connecticut: John Steuart Curry, *State Fair*.

Hadlyme, Connecticut: After visiting the Hadlyme Fair, George Luks began his painting *The Circus Tent*, completed in 1930.

Hollywood: *The Circus*, film directed by and starring Charlie Chaplin, produced by William Hinckley.

1929

England, London: Laura Knight's painting *Charivari* (or *The Grand Parade*) exhibited at the Royal Academy. The work was the basis of a satirical cartoon in *Punch*, where the circus stars were replaced by politicians.

France, Paris: André Kertész photographed Alexander Calder with his *Cirque*.

Belgium, Brussels: On the occasion of a major Ensor retrospective at the Palais des Beaux-Arts, the album *La Gamme d'amour* published by Un coup de dés. It included the scenario, colour drawings of the characters in costumes, and one of the sets, as well as six piano pieces: *Flirt de marionnettes*, *Lento et Andante*, *Gamme d'amour*, *Marche funèbre*, *Enlacements*, and *Pour un orgue de Barbarie*.

Germany, Dessau: Oskar Schlemmer's move to Breslau led to the closing of the Bauhaus Theatre Workshop in the fall.

Paul Klee, *Clown*.

Cologne: 27 April, publication of a group of photographs of Grock by Umbo in the *Kölnische Illustrierte Zeitung*, under the title "Dr. Phil. h.c. Grock. Wie Herr Wettach sich in Grock verwandelt."

Westerwald: August Sander, *Showman with Performing Bear in the Westerwald*.

United States, New York: April, James Steuart Curry presented his painting *Female Acrobat* (*High Diver*) at the exhibition *The Circus in Paint* organized by Juliana Force at the Whitney Studio Galleries.

Edward J. Kelty pioneered the use of flash in photographing the circus games at Madison Square Garden.

Walt Kuhn, *The White Clown*.

Gaston Lachaise, *Acrobat*.

George Luks, *A Clown*.

1930

England, Margate: Laura Knight accompanied the travelling troupe formed that year by Bertram Mills and the "Great Carmo" during its summer tour in the south of England. She made the acquaintance of clown-tumbler Joe Bert and his wife, Ally, with whom she shared a furnished apartment.

London: November, inauguration of the exhibition *Circus Folks* by Laura Knight at the Alpine Art Gallery.

Walter Sickert, *Barnet Fair*.

France, Paris: While finishing the figurines for his miniature *Cirque*, Alexander Calder executed a hundred drawings on the same subject. He performed his *Cirque* for the Abstraction-Création group, which he joined the same year.

Picasso went to the Cirque Medrano with his young son Paulo. The show inspired him to create a series of canvases on the theme of the acrobat.

Marc Chagall, *Acrobat*.

Belgium, Ostend: James Ensor, *The Puzzled Masks*.

Germany, Frankfurt: Max Beckmann, *Carnival, Paris*.

Cologne: August Sander, *Indian with Manager*; *Magician*; *"Test Your Strength" Showman*.

Munich: 16 February, publication of Umbo's photo-reportage "Hier wird Untermann geprobt . . . Das tägliche Brot der akrobatischen Tänzerin" in the *Münchner Illustrierte Presse*.

United States, New York: Milton Avery, *Trapeze Artist*.

Reginald Marsh, *Wonderland Circus, Sideshow, Coney Island*.

1932

France, Paris: The high-wire act of Con Colleano, who had mastered the forward and backward somersault, was the main attraction of the Cirque Medrano.

Jérôme Medrano acquired the Cirque Palisse, a semi-permanent wood, iron, and canvas structure, which enabled him to broaden his sphere of activity beyond touring in rented venues.

5 November, the act titled *Le Cirque sous l'eau*, starring the Auguste character Rhum (Enrico Sprocani) and Georges Loyal, premiered at the Cirque Medrano.

1934

France, Paris: Financial difficulties resulting largely from the failure of *Tarzan* forced the corporation that operated the Cirque d'Hiver to renounce management of the hall. On 17 November it was taken over by the four Bouglione brothers, and the Fratellinis stopped performing there. The Bouglione achieved a certain measure of success, particularly with pantomime operettas, and have continued through successive generations to manage the establishment until today.

The Amar brothers, professional animal trainers, launched their business by acquiring the 15 elephants of Kludsky's Czech circus. Their show was exceptional in its presentation of groups of wild animals.

1935

France, Paris: The Amar brothers took over management of the Empire, a large variety theatre. They built an on-stage ring, and interspersed vocal numbers and vaudeville attractions with regular circus acts.

Germany, Berlin: 23 August, Paula Busch acquired the Strassburger Circus, which enabled her to abandon her stationary circuses and, beginning in 1941, to travel with a big top.

Austria, Linz: 15 May, the rider Carl Rebernigg erected the first four-pole tent in Austria.

United States, New York: Debut of the Works Progress Administration (WPA) circus in the fall, subsidized by the American government. The year-round show gave performances in three rings, in New York and the surrounding area.

1936

France, Paris: Disappearance of the Neuilly fair, owing to the extension of the subway to the Pont de Neuilly.

1937

France, Paris: January, Grock's farewell appearance at the Cirque Medrano.

Germany, Berlin: 11 May, beginning of the demolition of the Circus Busch.

1938

England, London: Death of Bertram Mills. His circus was taken over by his sons Cyrill and Bernard.

1939

France: After war was declared, the Fratellinis went back on the road under the Bouglione banner. Paul, gravely ill, was replaced by Ilès, a former Auguste.

Germany, Kattendorf (near Oebisfelde): After buying the equipment of the Papke brothers' small travelling troupe, Carl Althoff's variety circus set out on its first tour. In 1965 the company became the Californischer National Circus.

United States, Sarasota, Florida: Death of the American circus magnate John Ringling. His nephew, John Ringling North, assumed management of the American Circus Corporation.

380

1931

England, London: 27 May, premiere, at the Lyceum Theatre, of a new production of the ballet *Pulcinella*, story by Léonide Massine, score by Igor Stravinsky after Pergolesi, choreography by Boris Romanov, sets and costumes by Giorgio De Chirico.

France, Mougins: Francis Picabia, *Auguste* (*Bahia*).

United States, New York: Milton Avery, *Acrobats*.

Walt Kuhn, *Top Man*; *The Blue Clown*.

Reginald Marsh, *The Barker*.

Guy Pène du Bois, *Trapeze Performers*.

Westport, Connecticut: John Steuart Curry, *The Medicine Man*.

1932

France, Paris: The collector Marie Cuttoli commissioned two large circus paintings from Georges Rouault, *The Wounded Clown* and *The Little Family*, as tapestry cartoons for the Aubusson manufactory.

Germany, Berlin: 21 February, publication of Umbo's photo-reportage "Der Fotograf 2 Meter über dem Trapez" in the *Berliner Illustrirte Zeitung*.

Umbo, *The Wallendas*; *Trapeze Artists: The Three Codonas*.

United States, New York: April, James Steuart Curry followed the Ringling Circus on a three-month New England tour. This experience resulted in: *The Flying Codonas*; *The Aerialists*; *The Great Wallendas*; *The Reiffenach Sisters*; *Performing Tiger*; *Circus Elephants*; *Baby Ruth*; *The Runway*; *Clyde Beatty*; *Agony of the Clowns*.

Milton Avery, *Jugglers*.

Walt Kuhn, *Tiger Trainer*.

In *Pip and Flip* Reginald Marsh represented a crowd of onlookers gathered at Coney Island, where brightly coloured posters announce the attractions that will be presented by the World Circus Side. One of the posters announces Pip and Flip, the pinhead twins "from Peru" (in reality Elvira and Jenny Snow, born in Georgia).

Hollywood: *Freaks*, film directed by Tod Browning, produced by MGM (Irving Thalberg). Among the freaks are Harry Earles (Hans), Daisy Earles (Frieda), Daisy and Violet Hilton (Siamese Twins), Olga Roderick (Bearded Lady), Peter Robinson (Human Skeleton), Joséphine Joseph (Half-Woman, Half-Man), Johnny Eck (Man with No Legs), Prince Radian (Living Torso), Elvira and Jenny Snow (Pinheads), and Martha Morris and Frances O'Connor (Armless Girls).

Polly of the Circus, film directed by Alfred Santell, produced by MGM.

1933

France, Paris: After attending a show at the Cirque Medrano in early February with Brassaï, Pablo Picasso executed a series of paintings showing an equilibrist "reduced to an ideogram pulsing in the light of the projectors."

Fernand Léger, *Marie the Acrobat*.

Spain, Madrid and Barcelona: New performances of Alexander Calder's *Cirque*.

United States, New York: 3 April, exhibition at Ferargil Galleries of circus paintings executed by James Steuart Curry on his return from the Ringling Circus tour. The Codonas, the Reiffenach sisters, Baby Ruth Pontico, and the "human cannonball" Hugo Zacchini attended the opening.

Milton Avery, *Chariot Race*.

Reginald Marsh, *Smoko, the Human Volcano*.

1934

England, London: Laura Knight decorated the "Circus" line of tableware for the ceramic manufacturer A.J. Wilkinson.

France, Paris: Puppet designs by Fernand Léger for a show, *La Boxe*, presented on 17, 19, and 29 December by his former student Jacques Chesnais's puppet theatre, La Branche de Houx.

United States, New York: Gaston Lachaise, *Acrobat Woman*, bronze.

Westport, Connecticut: John Steuart Curry, *Tragedy* and *Comedy*, mural paintings for the Bedford Junior High School Auditorium.

1935

Russia, Moscow: Aleksandr Rodchenko, paintings: *Equestrienne*; *Romance*; *Circus: Entrée*; photographs: *The Rhine Wheel*; *Circus*.

United States, New York: Joseph Cornell, *Untitled (Harlequin)*, completed in 1938.

Everett Shinn, *The Clown (No Laughs)*.

Gaston Lachaise, *Female Acrobat*.

Chicago: Exhibition of Alexander Calder's *Cirque* at the Renaissance Art Society and Arts Club.

Westport, Connecticut: James Steuart Curry, *Clown and Equestrians*.

1936

France, Paris: Pablo Picasso designed a stage curtain for Romain Rolland's play *Le Quatorze Juillet*, performed from 14 to 23 July at the Alhambra (then the Théâtre du Peuple). Against a background of ruins and rocks, a gigantic man with an eagle's head is depicted carrying in his arms the dead Minotaur dressed as Harlequin.

Mougins: Francis Picabia, *Clown*.

Le Cannet: Pierre Bonnard began *The Circus Horse*, completed in 1946.

Belgium, Ostend: James Ensor, *My Portrait with Masks*.

Germany, Berlin: Max Beckmann, *Artiste*.

Russia, Moscow: *Tsirk*, film directed by Grigori Alexandrov, produced by Mosfilm.

Finland, Helsinki: Jan Sibelius, *Scaramouche*, ballet.

United States, New York: Reginald Marsh, *The Flying Concellos*.

Westport, Connecticut: James Steuart Curry, *At the Circus*.

1937

France, Paris: Marc Chagall represented Lenin as an acrobat in his painting *The Revolution*.

Publication of *Le Coeur de Pic*, poems by Lise Deharme with "photographic tableaus" by Claude Cahun. Among Cahun's illustrations, the fifteenth plate features a skull, a fork, and a clown figurine.

First performance, at the Exposition Universelle, of Darius Milhaud's *Scaramouche*, suite for two pianos.

Mougins: Francis Picabia, *Fratellini the Clown*.

Switzerland, Zürich: 2 June, first performance, at the Stadttheater, of the incomplete two-act version of Alban Berg's opera *Lulu*, libretto by the composer based on two plays by Frank Wedekind.

Bern: Paul Klee, *Travelling Circus*; *Clown in Bed*.

Netherlands, Amsterdam: Max Beckmann, *Birth*.

United States, New York: Publication of James Otis's book *Toby Tyler, or Ten Weeks with a Circus*. The introduction is by Everett Shinn, who reveals his fascination for the figure of the tightrope walker, with whom he identifies.

New Orleans, Louisiana: During Mardi Gras, John Gutmann takes the photographs *In the Background*: *The Pimp*; *Street Musicians*; *White into Black*; *The Game*; *Jitterbug*; *Mardi Gras Crowd on Canal Street*.

1938

England, London: 10 November, first performance, at Sadler's Wells, of the ballet *Harlequin in the Street*, music by François Couperin (orchestrated by Gordon Jacob), choreography by Frederick Ashton, sets by André Derain.

France, Paris: Publication of Georges Rouault's *Cirque de l'étoile filante* by Ambroise Vollard (it had been printed on 5 March 1936).

Netherlands, Amsterdam: Max Beckmann, *Death*.

Spain, Madrid: José Gutiérrez Solana, *Masks*.

Russia, Moscow: Aleksandr Rodchenko portrays himself as a clown in his *Clown with Saxophone*.

United States, New York: Walt Kuhn, *Musical Clown*.

1939

Netherlands, Amsterdam: Max Beckmann, *Acrobats*, triptych.

United States, New York: Milton Avery, *Three Ring Circus*.

Joseph Cornell, *A Dressing Room for Gille*.

San Francisco: John Gutmann, *Bare Back*; *Aerialists*; *Midget Clowns*; *Man Walking by Clown*; *Lady Graffiti*.

1940

France, Paris: 15 November, Medrano reopened under the German management of Paula Busch and her son-in-law partner, Emil Wacker.

20 December, the Cirque d'Hiver reopened as well under the German flag.

1941

France, Paris: 22 March, the Bougliones returned to the management of the Cirque d'Hiver.

11 April, Jérôme Medrano recovered his circus.

Separated from his former partner Porto, Alex the clown teamed up with the Auguste character Achille Zavatta, who was affiliated with the Cirque d'Hiver.

1943

Germany, Hamburg: 24 July, the Busch Circus building was destroyed by bombing.

1945

Germany, Breslau: 5 April, the Busch Circus building was destroyed by bombing.

1946

France, Paris: The Cirque d'Hiver was entirely renovated and again became one of Europe's finest and best-equipped halls.

Germany, Berlin: Paula Busch's Astra Circus gave its first outdoor performance at the Berlin Zoo, where it remained until 12 September 1948.

Franz Althoff presented his first program after the war in a large, three-ring, tent-covered Hippodrome: *The Wonderful World of the Circus*, directed by Erhardt Plath. The production's huge success was sustained during a long tour in Germany, Belgium, the Netherlands, Sweden, North Africa, and Spain.

Hamburg: First performance of the Great Williams Circus Show, founded by the English horseman Harry Williams and Carola Williams, Dominik Althoff and Adèle Corty's eldest daughter. Despite several interruptions, the troupe continued its travels until 27 October 1968.

1947

Spain, Barcelona: 28 February, closing of the Teatro Circo Olympia.

1948

Germany, Bremen: Will Aureden, a former journalist from the *Braunschweiger Allgemeiner Anzeiger*, built a circus in the hangars of the Weser aeronautics company. He called it the Roland Circus, after the emblem of the city of Bremen. The first performance took place on 2 May in Delmenhorst.

1949

France, Paris: On the initiative of Louis Merlin and Jean Coupan, the small Gruss-Jeannet Circus became the Radio-Circus, a mixture of circus, games, and radio advertising. This groundbreaking encounter between the radio and the arts of the ring brought the Grusses fame they upheld for generations.

Germany, Berlin: 1 May, a new circus founded by Paula Busch left on tour. Its last performance took place in Southeast Asia in 1953.

1950

France, Paris: Gravely ill, François Fratellini had to give up the circus. Without resources, Gabriel Geretti, who had been the trio's first Auguste since 1948, threw himself under a subway car.

1940

France, Gordes (Provence): In the spring Chagall returned to the theme of the circus, producing, among other works, the gouache *At the Circus*.

Netherlands, Amsterdam: Max Beckmann, *The Wagon*; *Acrobat on the Trapeze*.

Russia, Moscow: In collaboration with the photojournalist Georgy Petrusov, Aleksandr Rodchenko photographed acrobats, clowns, and the trainer Vladimir Durov at the Moscow Circus for an issue of *SSSR na Stroike* devoted entirely to the circus. Because of the war, the issue was never published.

United States, New York: 10–26 December, the exhibition *Joseph Cornell: Exhibition of Objects, Daguerreotypes, Miniature Glass Bells, Soap Bubble Sets, Shadow Boxes, Homage to the Romantique Ballet* was presented at the Julien Levy Gallery. Designed by Cornell, the exhibition poster reproduced Watteau's celebrated *Pierrot* (also called *Gilles*).

Everett Shinn, *Trapeze Artists* (*Proctor's Theater*); *Over the Audience*.

Reginald Marsh, *Continuous Performance*.

San Francisco: John Gutmann met and photographed Fernand Léger.

John Gutmann, *The Beautiful Clown*; *Alice from Dallas, World's Fattest Girl*.

1941

Netherlands, Amsterdam: Max Beckmann, *Actors*, triptych.

1942

Netherlands, Amsterdam: Max Beckmann, *Carnival*, triptych.

United States, New York: Last circus photographs by Edward J. Kelty.

On the initiative of John Ringling North, Ringling Bros. and Barnum & Bailey Circus presented *Circus Polka*, a ballet danced by 50 elephants, choreography by George Balanchine, score by Igor Stravinsky. The premiere took place in the spring at Madison Square Garden.

Walt Kuhn, *Clown with Ball*.

1943

France, Paris: The artist's book *Divertissement* by Georges Rouault, published by Tériade.

Belgium, Brussels: Paul Delvaux, *Musée Spitzner*.

Russia, Moscow: Aleksandr Rodchenko, *Circus Mask*, gouache.

United States, New York: Alexander Calder gave a performance of his *Cirque* for Fernand Léger and his friends in the studio of the American photographer Herbert Matter. Matter took some pictures of the event.

18 April, the magazine *PM* published Weegee's photographs *Resourceful Girl Manages to Watch Man on the Flying Trapeze and Feed Hot Dog to Escort at Same Time* and *Boy at the Circus*. On 28 June Weegee photographed Victoria Zacchini propelled from the mouth of a cannon. That same year he also photographed the clown Jimmy Armstrong. On 9 July the magazine published the photograph *Weegee as Clown Covers Circus from the Inside*.

1944

France, Paris: Publication of *Correspondances*, text and illustrations by Pierre Bonnard. In a letter of 1886 to his brother Charles, which is reproduced in the book, Bonnard reports his regular visits to the Cirque Medrano.

United States, New York: Weegee's *Naked City*, published by Essential Books. Chapter 7, entitled "The Escapists," has eight circus photographs, including *Tired Man at the Circus* (c. 1942) and *The Cannon Act* (1943).

Walt Kuhn, *Acrobat in Red*.

1945

France, Paris: Henri Sauguet, *Les Forains*, ballet, story by Boris Kochno, choreography by Roland Petit, sets by Christian Bérard. The work is dedicated to Erik Satie.

Les Enfants du paradis, film directed by Marcel Carné, produced by Pathé Cinéma, with the actor and theatre director Jean-Louis Barrault in a moving portrayal of the Pierrot character Baptiste (a reference to the celebrated mime Jean-Baptiste Gaspard Deburau).

United States, New York: Fernand Léger, *Big Julie*.

Lisette Model, *Circus, Living Skeleton*; *Albert-Alberta, Hubert's 42nd Street Flea Circus, New York*; *Female Impersonators*; *Circus, New York*.

Weegee photographed the famous American clown Emmett Kelly at Madison Square Garden. He also produced *Danger: Do Not Walk on Ceiling* (*Hanging Clown Effigy*).

1946

Germany, Hemmenhofen: After being imprisoned by the French in Alsace during the war, Otto Dix returned to Hemmenhofen (near the Swiss border) just in time for Carnival. This event inspired the painting *Masks in Ruins*.

United States, New York: A collage by Joseph Cornell reproducing Seurat's painting *The Circus* published on the cover of the June issue of *Dance Index*.

1947

France, Paris: The artist's book *Jazz*, text and illustrations by Henri Matisse, published by Tériade.

Italy, Rome: Giorgio De Chirico, *Self-portrait in Seicento Costume*.

United States, New York: Walt Kuhn, *Bobby Barry*.

Los Angeles: Exhibition of a dozen paintings of clowns by Everett Shinn at the James Vigeveno Gallery.

1948

France, Paris: Fernand Léger, *The Acrobat and His Partner*.

Italy, Rome: Giorgio De Chirico, *Self-portrait in Black Costume*; *Self-portrait in Armour*.

United States: Alexander Calder takes part, with Marcel Duchamp, Max Ernst, and Fernand Léger, in Hans Richter's film *Dreams That Money Can Buy*, produced by Art of This Century. One of the film's sequences features Calder's miniature *Cirque*.

1949

France, Paris: Fernand Léger, *Homage to Louis David: Les Loisirs*.

Francis Picabia, *Acrobat*.

Joseph Kosma, *L'Écuyère*, ballet.

Vallauris: August, Robert Capa photographed Pablo Picasso wearing a clown mask.

Marseilles: Izis photographed acts by a fair troupe at the Vieux-Port.

United States, New York: Everett Shinn, *Ringling Brothers Circus, Winter Quarters, Sarasota, Florida*.

1950

France, Paris: The artist's book *Cirque*, text and illustrations by Fernand Léger, published by Tériade.

France and Germany: *Au revoir, Monsieur Grock*, film directed by Pierre Billon, produced by Le Trident.

United States, New York: Max Beckmann, *The Acrobat* (bronze); *Carnival Mask, Green, Violet, and Pink* (*Columbine*).

383

1951

Germany, Hamburg: 24 March, first performance, on the Heiligengeistfeld, of the Grock Circus. This circus was spawned by the collaboration of the famous Swiss clown and the German Kurt Collien, former impresario of the Plötz-Althoff Circus, which he inherited when it closed. Under a red and white four-pole big top with a revolving stage (which precluded the presentation of animals), the show offered cabaret numbers in the first half and a recital by Grock and his partner, Alfred Schatz, in the second half.

Switzerland, Lausanne: Anton Bühlmann's widow and children put up a 36-metre tent with ten rows of bleachers, a new ring fence, box seats, and a bandstand. From the start of the 1952 season, full houses cheered the new Pilatus Circus, named after the mountain that borders the Lake of Lucerne. However, difficulties during the 1957–1958 winter season got the better of the fledgling enterprise, which went bankrupt in 1959.

1953

Germany, Hamburg: The Carl Hagenbeck Circus ceased operation, and the Hagenbecks now devoted themselves exclusively to their zoo, to which they added a dolphin tank.

1954

France, Paris: Death of Alexandre Bouglione. The management of the Cirque d'Hiver passed to his younger brother Joseph.

United States, Baraboo, Wisconsin: Founding of the Circus World Museum, containing the world's largest collection of circus carts and wagons from Europe and America.

1955

France, Paris: Albert Fratellini took to the ring for the last time, at the Palais des Sports, in a threesome with Maïss and Polo Rivel.

1956

France, Paris: Achille Zavatta starred in *Zavatarzan* at the Cirque Medrano, where he was acclaimed not only as a clown but also as a comic rider and lion tamer.

Jérôme Medrano brought the Budapest Circus to Paris.

The Gruss-Jeannet corporation broke off its association with radio.

The Moscow City Circus came to Paris for the first time and set up in the Palais des Sports. Popov the clown performed to critical and public acclaim.

Germany, Mannheim: 31 March, a new Sarrasani Circus was officially inaugurated by the company's former director of operations, Fritz Mey, and Sarrasani's only daughter, Hedwige.

Spain, Barcelona: Impresario Juan Martínez Carcelle and former clown Arturo Castilla organized the first World Circus Festival, at the Palacio de Deportes.

United States, Pittsburgh, Pennsylvania: 16 July, John Ringling North abandoned the big top formula and adapted his show to the arenas and stadiums of big American cities.

1957

France, Paris: Medrano hosted one of the great West German circuses, the Carola Williams Circus.

Germany, Hamburg: 30 June, the last performance of the former Grock Circus, which had become the Collien Circus in 1955.

1958

France, Paris: François Fratellini's sons Kiko, Paupaul, and Baba presented a new Fratellini clown trio at the Cirque Medrano.

1959

France, Paris: The Grusses founded the Grand Cirque de France, with the support of Radio-Luxembourg. The main attraction of their program was the pantomime *Ben-Hur*, which was highly successful in France and the neighbouring countries for over three years. Their radio contract lasted until 1966.

1961

Germany, Lauterbach: 5 June, closing of the Paula Busch Circus.

1962

Germany, Munich: 23 December, inauguration of the new Krone building, where three different programs were presented each winter.

1963

France, Paris: 7 January, last performance of the Cirque Medrano. A few days later, under the management of the Bougliones, it became Cirque de Montmartre, a branch of the Cirque d'Hiver.

Ringling Bros. and Barnum & Bailey Circus's first visit to Paris since the beginning of the century. Paris audiences were not taken with the standard American three-ring format, and the tour ended earlier than planned.

1964

France, Paris: Following the death of Paul (Paupaul) Fratellini, Henri (Kiko) took on his role as Auguste and passed the role of clown to his son Gino.

1951

France, Paris: Izis photographed acrobats near the Porte de Vanves.

1952

England, London: Izis, *Chained Woman; August Holiday Fair*.

France, Paris: Izis photographed the Cirque Fanni, which had set up its big top on Boulevard Pasteur, as well as a fair troupe installed on Place de la Bastille.

The Hungarian-born French composer Joseph Kosma composed his first pantomimes for the mime Marcel Marceau. That same year he composed the ballet *Pierrot de Montmartre*.

Cimiez (outside Nice), Hôtel Régina: Henri Matisse, *Acrobat*.

Germany, Hemmenhofen: Otto Dix, *Masks in the Street*.

United States, Hollywood: *The Greatest Show on Earth*, film directed by Cecil B. de Mille, produced by Paramount, shot in part at the Ringling Bros. and Barnum & Bailey Circus.

1953

France, Gif-sur-Yvette (Seine-et-Oise): Fernand Léger, *The Great Parade on a Red Background*.

Saché (Touraine): *Le Cirque de Calder*, documentary film directed by Carlos Vilardebó. The artist gave a complete performance of his *Cirque*, with musical assistance from his wife, Louisa.

Sweden, Stockholm: *Sawdust and Tinsel*, film directed by Ingmar Bergman, produced by Sandrews Productions.

1954

France, Paris: At the Foire du Trône on Place de la Nation, Izis photographed performing dogs. That same year he met Marc Chagall.

Lyons: Izis photographed the clowns at the International Circus Festival.

Cannes and Toulon: Izis photographed the clown Grock.

Gif-sur-Yvette (Seine-et-Oise): Fernand Léger, *The Great Parade*, definitive state.

Vence: Marc Chagall, *Acrobat and Mauve Sky*.

Germany, Hemmenhofen: Otto Dix, *Alemannic Masks*.

Italy, Rome: *La Strada*, film directed by Federico Fellini, produced by Ponti–De Laurentis, with Giulietta Masina as the clown Gelsomina.

United States, Hollywood: *Ring of Fear*, film directed by James Edward Grant, produced by Warner Bros, shot in part at the Clyde Beatty Circus.

Three Ring Circus, film directed by Joseph Pevney, produced by Paramount, shot in part at the Clyde Beatty Circus, starring Jerry Lewis.

1955

Germany and France, Munich and Paris: *Lola Montès*, film directed by Max Ophüls, produced by Florida Films, Gamma Film, and Oska-Film.

Netherlands, Amsterdam: Pyke Koch, *The Contortionist*, completed in 1963.

1956

France, Paris: At the Foire du Trône, Izis photographed the animal tamer Jim Rose, as well as the sideshows and the attractions of the Ménagerie Lambert. He also made a portrait of Albert Fratellini in his dressing-room at the Cirque Medrano and a photograph of the Cirque Fanni.

Vence: Marc Chagall, *Clown with Violin*.

United States, New York: Lisette Model, *Ringling Brothers Circus, New York*.

Hollywood: *Trapeze*, film directed by Carol Reed, produced by United Artists and Hecht-Hill-Lancaster Productions, shot in part at the Cirque d'Hiver, Paris.

1957

England, London: Laura Knight, *Old Time Clowns*.

France, Paris: At the Foire du Trône, Izis photographed Charlot Van Krienes and his trained dogs as well as Mademoiselle Noël and her goat Reinette. He photographed the Grand Cirque at the Palais des Sports.

Bordeaux: Izis photographed the Bordeaux fair.

Netherlands, Amsterdam: Pyke Koch, *The Large Contortionist*.

United States, New York: George Grosz, *Grosz as Clown and Showgirl*.

1958

France, Paris: Izis photographed the animal tamer Philip Guss and Capellini's chimpanzees at the Cirque Medrano. He also photographed the clowns Emilio Zavatta, Rolphe Zavatta, Léonor, Ludo, and Roberto, stars of the Cirque Napoléon Rancy.

United States, Palisades, New Jersey: Bruce Davidson, *The Dwarf*, series of photographs.

1959

France, Paris: At the Foire du Trône, Izis photographed the clown-acrobat William Leméni. He also watched a fire-eater perform on Boulevard Rochechouart in Montmartre.

Lagny (Seine-et-Marne): Izis, *Foire du Trône: Sideshow, Crocodile Woman, Paris*.

Germany, Frankfurt: Marc Chagall, *Commedia dell'arte*, wall decoration for the Frankfurt Theatre, and new circus works.

United States, Sarasota and Hollywood: *The Big Circus*, film directed by Joseph M. Newman, produced by Allied Artists.

1960

France, Cavaillon: Izis, *Cirque Amar*.

Villejuif: Izis, *Showman with Performing Bear*.

1961

France, Paris: Izis, *Foire du Trône: Sideshow, Leopard Woman*.

United States, New York: Diane Arbus, *Jack Dracula, the Marked Man, NYC 1961; Siamese twins in a carnival tent, NJ 1961*. Arbus also photographed Lentini the "Three-legged Wonder."

1962

England, London: Publication of the biography of the clown Joe Bert, *A Proper Circus Omie*, written by Laura Knight and illustrated with her circus drawings.

France, Paris: Izis photographed the English clown Austin Fosset at the Cirque d'Hiver.

Mougins: Pablo Picasso returned to the theme of the circus with *The Clown*.

1963

United States, New York: Diane Arbus, *Russian midget friends in a living room on 100th Street, NYC 1963*.

Weegee used optical distortions in photographing a clown.

1964

United States, New York: Sixteen of the circus drawings that Alexander Calder executed in 1931–1932 were reproduced in facsimile in the magazine *Art in America* as "Calder's Circus."

Hollywood: *Circus World*, film directed by Henry Hathaway, produced by Paramount Pictures, shot in part under the big top of Franz Althoff, with John Wayne as the circus owner. Harry and Marianne Althoff doubled for John Smith and Claudia Cardinale.

1965

France, Paris: Jean Clairjois presented the Gonka horsemen from Moscow, a superb cavalcade combining rhythm and bravery with humour.

Germany, Berlin and Bremen: Merger of the Paula Busch Circus and Roland Circus as the Busch-Berlin and Roland-Bremen Circus. It was sold to Heinz Geier in 1970.

1967

England, London: 21 January, last performance of the Bertram Mills Circus at the Olympia.

United States, Florida: 11 November, John Ringling North sold the Ringling Bros. and Barnum & Bailey Circus to a group headed by Irvin Feld, an American recording industry kingpin. The agreement was signed in a ceremony at the Colosseum in Rome.

1968

Germany, Bremerhaven: 2 November, the *Atlantic Sage* set sail carrying the Williams Circus to the United States, with 17 elephants, 25 horses, 9 tigers, 50 pigeons, and 11 parakeets on board. Under the direction of Carola Williams's son-in-law, the famous animal tamer Gunther Gebel-Williams, the troupe took part in a tour lasting several years organized by the Ringling Bros. and Barnum & Bailey Circus. Gebel-Williams made his first American appearance on 6 January 1969.

United States, Venice, Florida: Irvin Feld founded Ringling Bros. and Barnum & Bailey Clown College to preserve the tradition of the art of the clown.

1969

France, Rungis: The Cirque Jean Richard set out on a tour of France. It featured Alexis Gruss's horses, Gilbert Houcke's tigers, the trapeze artist Gérard Edon, and the Auguste character Achille Zavatta.

United States, Florida: The Ringling Bros. and Barnum & Bailey Circus split into two units, the Blue Unit and the Red Unit, which toured the major American cities. The program changed every other year.

1970

England, London: Brian Austen and Gerry Cottle launched the Cottle and Austen London Festival Circus.

France, Paris: The Grusses split up. André and his sons attempted to keep the Grand Cirque de France in operation without radio advertising support. Alexis and his family joined the team of Jean Richard.

Spain, Madrid: Demolition of the Circo Price.

1971

France, Paris: 8 January, last performance of the Cirque de Montmartre (formerly the Cirque Medrano).

Germany, Berlin: Heinz Geier acceded to the directorship of the Busch-Roland Circus, becoming its sole proprietor in 1975.

United States, Florida: The Ringling Bros. and Barnum & Bailey Circus was bought by the Mattel Corporation, toy manufacturers. Irvin Feld and his son Kenneth stayed on as general managers.

1972

France, Sucy-en-Brie: Jean Richard acquired the Cirque Pinder, which took the name Pinder–Jean Richard. He operated it until 1983.

Russia, Moscow: Inauguration of the New Moscow Circus (later named the Bolshoi Circus). This modern building had four movable rings (a regular ring, an aquatic ring, an ice ring, and a trick ring for conjurers) that could be replaced in a matter of minutes at the command of the stage director.

Outskirts of Moscow: Opening of the Moscow Studio (Moscow Academy) on the initiative of Rosgotsirk, the central organization of Russian circuses. The institution's mandate was to define and produce acts of exceptional quality for presentation at the circuses in major Russian cities and on foreign tours.

1973

France, Paris: 9 October, the closing of the Amar brothers' circus following a crushing bankruptcy. Its equipment was sold to Firmin Bouglione, Jr.

Demolition of the Cirque de Montmartre (formerly the Cirque Medrano).

1974

France, Paris: Annie Fratellini and her husband, Pierre Étaix, who formed a "lady Auguste" and clown duo, founded the École Nationale du Cirque.

Jean Richard erected the Nouvel Hippodrome de Paris, a tent with over 5,000 seats, at the Porte de Pantin.

Alexis Gruss, Jr., and the comedian Silva Monfort founded the Cirque du Nouveau Carré in the former Gaîté-Lyrique building. This "old-fashioned circus" aspired to renew the circus show tradition by giving priority to its two basic elements: equestrian vaulting and acrobatics.

Principality of Monaco: December, the first Festival International du Cirque de Monte-Carlo was inaugurated by Prince Rainier III of Monaco. The awarding of "Gold Clowns" and "Silver Clowns" to the most outstanding acts helped contribute to the revival of the circus.

Austria, Stockerau (near Vienna): 13 April, first performance of the Austrian National Circus, founded by Elfi Althoff-Jacobi with state approval.

1975

England, London: Camera crews were at Gerry Cottle's circus tent to make a television series.

1976

France, Paris: 3 April, with the support of the Rechs, a family of acrobats, Firmin Bouglione, Jr., mounted a travelling circus to which he gave the prestigious name Amar. The circus toured throughout France until September 1981.

Germany, Bonn: 18 May, first performance of the Roncalli Circus, founded by two young Austrians, stage director André Heller and graphic designer Bernhard Paul. In 1977 Paul became the sole director. Every year from April to late November, the circus toured to four or five regional German and Austrian capitals. Besides his job as manager, Paul played the Auguste character Zippo in the ring. His partners were the clowns Fumagalli (Darix Huesca) and Francesco, a famous whiteface clown from the Cairoli family.

1977

Denmark, Copenhagen: 28 April, inauguration of the new Max Schumann Circus.

Visual Arts, Music, and Film 1500–2000
20th Century

1965

France, Paris: *Le Cirque d'Izis*, with a preface by Jacques Prévert and four original compositions by Marc Chagall, published by A. Sauret. Besides circus photographs taken by Izis between 1949 and 1962, the book includes excerpts of previous texts, illustrations, and press clippings collected by the photographer over many years.

Yoyo, film directed by Pierre Étaix, produced by Paul Claudion, shot in part under the big top of the Pinder Circus.

United States, New York: Weegee used mirror effects in photographing an acrobatic duo.

4 February, first performance, at the New York State Theater, of the ballet *Harlequinade*, choreographed by George Balanchine to Riccardo Drigo's score for the ballet *Les Millions d'Arlequin*.

Edward Hopper, *Two Comedians*.

1967

France, Paris: The book *Cirque*, text and illustrations by Marc Chagall, published by Tériade.

1967–1968

United States, Mill Valley, California: Bruce Nauman, *Art Make-Up*, video.

1968

Germany, Göttingen: *Die Artisten in der Zirkuskuppel: Ratlos* (*Artists at the Top of the Big Top: Disoriented*), film directed by Alexander Kluge, produced by Kairos-Film.

United States, Mill Valley, California: Bruce Nauman, *First Hologram Series: Making Faces (A–K)*.

1969

United States, New Jersey: George Segal, *The Girl on the Flying Trapeze*; *The Tightrope Walker*.

1970

France, Mougins: Pablo Picasso, etchings of *Suite 156*.

Italy and Germany, Rome and Munich: *The Clowns*, film directed by Federico Fellini, produced by Bavaria Film and Compagnia Leone Cinematografica, with Charlie Rivels, Alex, Nino, Bario, Jean Houcke, Victoria Chaplin, Pierre Étaix, Tristan Rémy, Annie Fratellini, and Victor Fratellini.

United States, Maryland: Diane Arbus photographed members of a fair troupe, including a female albino sword-swallower, a girl in circus costume, a tattooed man, and a hermaphrodite.

1971

France, Mougins: Pablo Picasso, series of head drawings of Harlequin and Pierrot.

United States, New Jersey: George Segal, *Man on the Flying Trapeze*; *Trapeze*.

1972

United States, New York: The Whitney Museum of American Art acquired Alexander Calder's miniature *Cirque*. The book *Calder's Circus* was published by Jean Lipman for the work's inaugural exhibition. The event was also underscored by a parallel exhibition of drawings and paintings on the same theme at Perls Galleries.

New Jersey: George Segal, *Girl on Swing*.

France, Paris: Christian Boltanski sent out invitations in which he proposed to "perform, surrounded by all his props, authentic relics, and his famous talking doll, in sets representing the real places where the decisive scenes of his childhood took place, his celebrated childhood memories."

Parade, film directed by Jacques Tati, produced by Gray Films, shot in part at the Scott Circus (Sweden).

La Rochelle: During the summer Christian Boltanski performed as a clown for an audience of children.

Germany, Munich: Inauguration of the exhibition *Affiches, Accessoires, Décors: Documents photographiques* by Christian Boltanski at the Westfälischer Kunstverein, inspired by Munich's Karl Valentin Museum, devoted to the popular German comedian of the 1920s and 1930s.

Christian Boltanski, *Quelques Interprétations par Christian Boltanski* and *Les Morts pour rire*, artist's books.

1975

France, Vence: Marc Chagall, *The Large Grey Circus*.

United States, Buffalo, New York: Cindy Sherman photographed herself as an Auguste in *Untitled, A–E*.

1976

United States, Hollywood: *Buffalo Bill and the Indians, or Sitting Bull's History Lesson*, film directed by Robert Altman, produced by De Laurentis–Talent Associated Ltd.

1978

France, Paris: Achille Zavatta put together a travelling circus with the cooperation of the Rech family, who provided several acts. This circus made many tours until 1992, when it ceased operation.

1980

France, Paris: The Cirque Bidon, founded by Pierrot Bidon, became Archaos.

United States, New York: The Big Apple Circus, the first contemporary American circus to return to the European one-ring format, set up at Lincoln Center for the winter season. Its manager, Paul Binder, succeeded in winning over New Yorkers to the congenial charm of an intimate circus.

1982

France, Paris: The Cirque du Nouveau Carré became the Cirque National Alexis Gruss.

United States, Florida: 17 March, Irvin Feld and his son Kenneth, co-directors of the Ringling Bros. and Barnum & Bailey Circus, bought the business back from the Mattel Corporation.

Canada, Baie-Saint-Paul, Quebec: Stilt walker and fire breather Guy Laliberté organized a summer festival called the Fête Foraine with the Club des Talons Hauts, a band of street entertainers.

1984

France, Franche-Comté: The Cirque Plume, founded by Bernard Kudlak, undertook its first tour.

The rider Bartabas founded Zingaro, a troupe specializing in equestrian arts.

United States, Florida: Following the sudden death of Irvin Feld, his son Kenneth took over management of the Ringling Bros. and Barnum & Bailey Circus.

Canada, Baie-Saint-Paul, Quebec: During the celebration of the 450th anniversary of Jacques Cartier's first voyage to Canada the Fête Foraine became the Cirque du Soleil, Quebec's first circus to achieve international renown. From the outset, the Cirque du Soleil was noted for its theatrical style and high-calibre acrobatic acts.

1985

Belgium, Brussels: Firmin Bouglione and his son Alexandre, a tiger and elephant trainer, founded the Cirque Alexandre Bouglione, which toured Belgium in 1985 and 1986.

Germany: The leading German television station broadcast a series of six shows chronicling the Roncalli Circus's first ten years.

Switzerland, Wohlen: Two former school teachers, Hildegarde and Guido Muntwyler, founded the Cirque Monti and travelled with it through the villages of German-speaking Switzerland.

1986

France, Châlons-en-Champagne: 13 January, Jack Lang, Minister of Culture, inaugurated the Centre National Supérieur de Formation aux Arts du Cirque (CNAC), the first state circus school in Western Europe.

1987

France, Paris: The Cirque Plume conquered Parisian audiences with its *Spectacle de cirque et merveilles*.

United States: First American tour of the Cirque du Soleil, with the show *Le Cirque réinventé*, which was acclaimed in Los Angeles, San Diego, Santa Monica, San Francisco, New York, and Washington, D.C.

1989

France, Paris: The Bouglione brothers decided to lease their name to big tops of varying size: Variétés Bouglione (Mordon family), Gerda Bouglione (Dassonneville), Linda Bouglione (Bino Beautour), Spectacle Bouglione (Klising-Dumas family), Grégory Bouglione (Lamberty family), Esther Bouglione (Victor Rech).

Aubervilliers: In a new permanent hall, Zingaro presented *Cabaret équestre III*, *Opéra équestre*, and *Chimère*, three shows inspired by the circus, gypsy cabaret, and opera.

United States, Florida: Animal tamer Gunther Gebel-Williams's farewell tour with the Ringling Bros. and Barnum & Bailey Circus. He was replaced by his son, Mark Oliver Gebel. In 1994 Gunther Gebel-Williams made a brief comeback with a Ringling Bros. and Barnum & Bailey tour of ten American cities. Excerpts of the tour were broadcast in a CBS special, *The Return of Gunther Gebel-Williams*.

1990

Italy, Rome: After redesigning a tent according to plans by their grandfather Darix Togni, the Togni brothers launched the show *Florilegio*.

Russia, Moscow: Teresa Durova, granddaughter of the Russian clown Durov, organized the first Moscow Clown Festival.

1991

France: The Archaos Circus presented a huge travelling show, *Métal Clown*, in the "cathedral," a big top specially designed to accommodate stage sets updating the classic pantomimes. Breaking with the traditional 13-metre ring, this modern tent covered an 80-by-15-metre blacktop street with stands set up along either side.

Blois: Désiré Rech raised a tent and gave it the Amar name.

Russia, Moscow: Reconstruction of the Moscow City Circus on the site of the former Salamonsky Circus. Its manager was Yuri Nikulin, one of Russia's most popular movie and circus stars.

United States: David Larible began appearing as the star clown of the Ringling Bros. and Barnum & Bailey Circus.

1992

Germany, Berlin: Bernhard Paul, André Heller, and Peter Schwenkov founded the Wintergarten Variety Theatre.

Switzerland: In cooperation with the Cirque National Suisse Knie, the Cirque du Soleil gave shows in more than 60 Swiss towns.

Canada, Montreal: The Cirque du Soleil's show *Saltimbanco* set out on a 19-month North American tour.

1993

France, Blois: Désiré Rech and partner William Brand engaged a troupe of Russian performers who had never appeared in France. It was the most remarkable French show of the year.

Germany, Cologne: Inauguration of the Roncalli Circus's new tent, designed to resemble Milan's La Scala.

United States, Los Angeles: Encouraged by the success of its show *Nouvelle expérience*, which had been touring the United States since 1990, the Cirque du Soleil set up in a new specially outfitted hall in the Treasure Island Hotel for its new production, *Mystère*.

388

1978

United States, California: Jonathan Borofsky, *Man on a Tightrope at 2,354,128 and 2,531,117*, mural drawing.

1979

France, Paris: 24 February, first performance, at the Opéra, of the entire three-act version of Alban Berg's opera *Lulu* (Act III completed by Friedrich Cerha), Pierre Boulez conducting, stage direction by Patrice Chéreau.

Vence: Marc Chagall, *The Great Parade*, completed in 1980.

1980

United States, Minneapolis: George Segal, *The Circus Flyers*.

Los Angeles: David Hockney, *Harlequin*.

1981

Germany, Derneburg: Georg Baselitz, *Clown*.

West Berlin: Marcus Lüpertz, *Pierrot lunaire*.

United States, New York: First performance, at the Metropolitan Opera House, of a new production of the ballet *Parade*, score by Erik Satie, story by Jean Cocteau, sets by David Hockney.

1981–1983

England, London: Lucian Freud, *Large Interior, W11 (after Watteau)*.

1982

United States, New York: Robert Longo, *Pressure*, completed in 1983.

1983

United States, New York: Exhibition of Jonathan Borofsky's kinetic sculpture *The Dancing Clown at 2,845,325* at the Paula Cooper Gallery.

1984

Switzerland, Zürich: Exhibition of Christian Boltanski's *Comic Vignettes* (1974) at the Kunsthaus.

1985

United States, Pasadena, California: Bruce Nauman executed two neon signs inspired by burlesque theatre: *Mean Clown Welcome* and *Punch and Judy: Kick in the Groin, Slap in the Face*.

1987

United States, New York: Exhibition of Bruce Nauman's video installation *Clown Torture* at the Leo Castelli Gallery.

1988

United States, Hollywood: *Killer Klowns from Outer Space*, film directed by Stephen Chiodo, produced by Chiodo Brothers and TransWorld Entertainment.

1989

United States, Venice, California: Installation of Jonathan Borofsky's kinetic sculpture *Ballerina Clown* on the facade of a building at a busy intersection where street entertainers often performed.

1990

England, London: Lucian Freud, *Leigh Bowery (Seated)*.

Switzerland, Basel: Exhibition of Bruce Nauman's video installation *Shadow Puppets and Instructed Mime*.

United States, New York: Rhona Bitner produced a first series of Cibachrome prints, entitled *Circus*.

1992

England, London: Lucian Freud, *Naked Man, Back View*.

1993

England, London: Lucian Freud, *Painter Working, Reflection*; *Leigh in Taffeta Skirt*.

Italy, Venice: Presentation of Louise Bourgeois's sculpture *Cell (Arch of Hysteria)* in the American pavilion at the Venice Biennale.

United States, New York: Louise Bourgeois, *Arch of Hysteria*.

389

1994

France, Piolenc (Provence): Alexis Gruss founded a circus museum and school in the Château de Piolenc.

Austria, Vienna: After leaving the family circus in 1993, tiger and elephant trainer Louis Knie took over the Austrian National Circus from Elfi Althoff-Jacobi, wife of a cousin of the German Althoff dynasty.

Canada, Montreal: The Cirque du Soleil celebrated its tenth anniversary with *Alegria*, which toured North America for the next two years.

1995

France, Marseilles: The Archaos Circus launched a new show, *Game Over*, an "electronico-totalitarian high mass" that incorporated television into the circus for the first time.

Lyons: Alexis Gruss organized the Biennale du Cirque.

1996

Canada, Montreal: After a home stand, the Cirque du Soleil's new production, *Quidam*, began a three-year North American tour.

1997

France, Massy: To distinguish itself from other circuses using the Amar company name, Désiré Rech named his enterprise Les Kino's Présentent Amar.

United States, Sarasota, Florida: Closing of Ringling Bros. and Barnum & Bailey Clown College.

Canada, Montreal: February, inauguration of the Cirque du Soleil's "Studio," their international headquarters and production centre.

1998

United States, Las Vegas: October, the Cirque du Soleil's aquatic show *Ô* began playing permanently at the Bellagio.

Orlando, Florida: December, inauguration of another stationary Cirque du Soleil show, *La Nouba*, at Disney World Resort.

1999

France, Paris: The Bougliones' Cirque d'Hiver returned to its circus vocation. The 1999–2000 season hosted the show *Salto*.

Lannion: The Archaos Circus presented *In Vitro* in the arena of the Carré Magique.

United States, Biloxi, Missouri: The Cirque du Soleil's show *Alegria* became a permanent fixture at the Beau Rivage.

Canada, Montreal: Inauguration of a new Cirque du Soleil production, *Dralion*.

1994

England, London: Lucian Freud, *Leigh under the Skylight*.

France, Nantes: Pierrick Sorin, *La Bataille des tartes*, video installation.

1995

United States, New York: Cindy Sherman, *Untitled #319*, photograph from the series *Horror Pictures*.

Los Angeles: Paul McCarthy, *Painter*, installation and video performance.

1996

France, Nantes: Pierrick Sorin, *Un Spectacle de qualité*, video installation that incorporates trick mirrors in such a way that the viewer sees his own head emerging from the bubbles in a real bathtub, in front of which the artist, whose filmed image appears superimposed over a table, performs some silly routines.

1998

Brazil, São Paulo: Presentation of Pierrick Sorin's installation *It's Really Nice* at the XXIV Bienal de São Paulo. Each of the work's 32 video screens shows a close-up of a composite digital portrait made up of parts of different people's faces. These strange faces, which look like reflections in a fun-house mirror, make swallowing noises while rolling their bulging eyes, some of them whispering "It's really nice . . . I like the work very much."

1999

France, Nantes: Pierrick Sorin, *Sorino le magicien*.

2001

United States, New York: Rhona Bitner begins her *Clown* series.

Bibliography

The Circus: General Studies and Specialized Articles

Adams, Bluford. *E Pluribus Barnum: The Great Showman and the Making of U.S. Popular Culture*. Minneapolis: University of Minneapolis Press, 1997.

Adams, Rachel. *Sideshow U.S.A.: Freaks and the American Cultural Imagination*. Chicago: University of Chicago Press, 2001.

Adrian, [Paul]. *Histoire illustrée des cirques parisiens d'hier et d'aujourd'hui*. Bourg-la-Reine: Paul Adrian, 1957.

———. *Le Cirque commence à cheval*. Bourg-la-Reine: P. Adrian, 1968.

———. *Ce Rire qui vient du cirque*. Bourg-la-Reine: Paul Adrian, 1969.

———. *En Piste, les acrobates*. Bourg-la-Reine: Paul Adrian, 1973.

———. *Cirque parade*. Paris: Solar, 1974.

———. *À Vous les jongleurs*. Paris: Paul Adrian, 1977.

———. *Cirque au cinéma, cinéma au cirque*. Paris: P. Adrian, 1984.

———. *Ils donnent des ailes au cirque*. Paris: Paul Adrian, 1988.

———. *Le Sens de l'équilibre*. Paris: Paul Adrian, 1993.

Albert, Maurice. *Les Théâtres de la foire (1660–1789)*. 1900. Geneva: Slatkine, 1969.

Albrecht, Ernest. *A Ringling by Any Other Name: The Story of John Ringling North and His Circus*. Metuchen, N.J.: Scarecrow Press, 1989.

———. *The New American Circus*. Gainesville: University Press of Florida, 1995.

Amiard-Chevrel, Claudine, ed. *Du Cirque au théâtre*. Lausanne: L'Âge d'Homme, 1983.

Arnauld, Céline. "Le Cirque, art nouveau." *L'Esprit Nouveau: Revue Internationale d'Esthétique* 1 (15 October 1920), pp. 97–98.

Baisez, Mathilde. "Étude du clown dans une perspective sociale." Master's thesis, Université du Québec à Montréal, 1986.

Ballantine, Bill. *Wild Tigers and Tame Fleas*. New York: Rinehart, 1958.

———. *Horses and Their Bosses*. Philadelphia: Lippincott, 1964.

———. *Clown Alley*. Boston: Little, Brown and Company, 1982.

Barnum, Phineas Taylor. *Struggles and Triumphs*. 1869. New York: Arno, 1970.

Barrier, Robert, and Philippe Barrier. *Cent Cirques français sur le voyage*. Crépy-en-Valois: Robert Barrier, 1994.

Basch, Sophie. *Romans de cirque*. Paris: Bouquins, 2002.

Beaulieu, Henri. *Les Théâtres du boulevard du Crime*. 1905. Geneva: Slatkine, 1977.

Berton, Claude. *Les Spectacles à travers les âges*. Paris: Éditions du Cygne, 1931–1932.

Blackstone, Sarah J. *Buckskins, Bullets, and Business: A History of Buffalo Bill's Wild West*. Westport, Conn.: Greenwood, 1986.

Bogdan, Robert. *Freak Show: Presenting Human Oddities for Amusement and Profit*. Chicago: University of Chicago Press, 1988.

———. "Le Commerce des monstres." *Actes de la Recherche en Sciences Sociales* 104 (1994), pp. 34–46.

Bost, Pierre. *Le Cirque et le music-hall*. Paris: Au Sans Pareil, 1951.

Bouissac, Paul. "Pour une sémiotique du cirque." *Semiotica* 3 (1971), pp. 93–120.

———. *Circus and Culture: A Semiotic Approach*. Bloomington: Indiana University Press, 1976.

———. "Circus Performances as Texts: A Matter of Poetic Competence." *Poetics* 5 (1976), pp. 101–118.

———. "La Pyramide et la roue: Jeux formels et effets de sens dans les spectacles de cirque." *Anthropologica* 27, no. 1–2 (1985), pp. 101–121.

———. "Introduction: The Circus – A Semiotic Spectroscopy." *Semiotica* 85 (1991), pp. 189–199.

———. "From Calculus to Language: The Case of Circus Equine Displays." *Semiotica* 85 (1991), pp. 291–317.

Braithwaite, David. *Fairground Architecture: The World of Amusement Parks, Carnivals, and Fairs*. New York: Praeger, 1968.

Brown, T. Allston. *Amphitheatres and Circuses: A History from the Earliest Date to 1861, with Sketches of Some of the Principal Performers*. Edited by William L. Slout. San Bernardino: Borgo, 1994.

Campardon, Émile. *Les Comédiens du roi de la troupe italienne pendant les deux derniers siècles*. 2 vols. 1882. Geneva: Slatkine, 1970.

Care, Jean-Marc, and Carmen Mata Barreiro. *Le Cirque: Une Simulation globale*. Paris: B.E.L.C., 1984.

Carlyon, David. *Dan Rice: The Most Famous Man You've Never Heard Of*. New York: Public Affairs, 2001.

Carmeli, Yoram S. "Played by Their Own Play: Fission and Fusion in British Circuses." *The Sociological Review* 35 (1987), pp. 744–774.

———. "Performing the 'Real' and 'Impossible' in the British Travelling Circus." *Semiotica* 80 (1990), pp. 193–220.

———. "Performance and Family in the World of British Circus." *Semiotica* 85 (1991), pp. 257–289.

———. "The Invention of Circus and Bourgeois Hegemony: A Glance at British Circus Books." *Journal of Popular Culture* 29 (Summer 1995), pp. 213–221.

Carter, Robert A. *Buffalo Bill Cody: The Man behind the Legend*. New York: John Wiley & Sons, 2000.

Chamber, Ross. "*Frôler ceux qui rôdent*: Le Paradoxe du saltimbanque." *Revue des Sciences Humaines* 44, no. 167 (July–September 1977), pp. 347–363.

Champfleury. *Souvenirs des funambules*. 1859. Geneva: Slatkine, 1971.

Chindahl, George Leonard. *A History of the Circus in America*. Caldwell, Idaho: Caxton Printers, 1959.

Christen, Kimberly A. *Clowns and Tricksters: An Encyclopedia of Tradition and Culture*. Denver: ABC-CLIO, 1998.

Clarke, John Smith. *Circus Parade*. London: B.T. Batsford, 1936.

Clayton, J. Douglas. *Pierrot in Petrograd: The Commedia dell'arte / Balagan in Twentieth-Century Russian Theatre and Drama*. Montreal and Kingston: McGill-Queen's University Press, 1993.

Clubb, Louise George. *Italian Drama in Shakespeare's Time*. New Haven and London: Yale University Press, 1989.

Cooper, Diana Starr. *Night after Night*. Washington, D.C.: Island Press, 1994.

Coup, William Cameron. *Sawdust and Spangles: Stories & Secrets of the Circus*. Chicago: Herbert S. Stone and Company, 1901.

Croft-Cooke, Rupert. *The Circus Has No Home*. London: Falcon, 1950.

Croft-Cooke, Rupert, and Peter Cotes. *Circus: A World History*. London: Elek, 1976.

Csergo, Julia. "Extension et mutation du loisir citadin: Paris XIXe–début XXe siècle." In *L'Avènement des loisirs, 1850–1960*, ed. Alain Corbin, pp. 121–168. Paris: Aubier, 1995.

Csida, Joseph, and June Bundy. *American Entertainment: A Unique History of Popular Show Business*. New York: Watson-Guptill, 1978.

Culhane, John. *The American Circus: An Illustrated History*. New York: Henry Holt, 1990.

Dahlinger, Fred, Jr. *Trains of the Circus, 1872–1956*. Hudson, 2000.

Dahlinger, Fred, Jr., and Stuart Thayer. *Badger State Showmen: A History of Wisconsin's Circus Heritage*. Exhibition catalogue. Madison: Grote, 1998.

Dalsème, A.-J. *Le Cirque à pied et à cheval*. Paris: Librairie Illustrée, 1888.

Davis, Jamet M. *The Circus Age: Culture and Society under the American Big Top*. Chapel Hill: University of North Carolina Press, 2002.

Denis, Dominique. *Le Livre du clown*. Strasbourg: Éditions du Spectacle, 1985.

——. *Dictionnaire illustré des mots usuels et locutions en trois volumes du cirque*. 3 vols. Paris: Association Arts des 2 Mondes, 1997–2001.

Depping, Guillaume. *Les Merveilles de la force et de l'adresse: Agilité, souplesse, dextérité, les exercices de corps chez les anciens et les modernes*. Paris: Hachette, 1886.

De Selva, Martia. *Petite Histoire du cirque en Belgique et ailleurs*. Brussels: EVO, 2000.

Despot, Adriane Lea. *Three Clowns: Pierrot, Charlie and "Jean Genet."* Ann Arbor: UMI Research Press, 1983.

Dick, Kay. *Pierrot*. London: Hutchinson, 1960.

Disher, Maurice Willson. *Clowns and Pantomimes*. 1925. New York: B. Blom, 1968.

——. *Fairs, Circuses and Music Halls*. London: Collins, 1942.

Douglas, Mary. "My Circus Fieldwork." *Semiotica* 85 (1991), pp. 201–204.

Drake, Sylvie, et al. *Cirque du Soleil*. New York: Rizzoli, 1994.

Duchartre, Pierre-Louis. *La Commedia dell'arte et ses enfants*. Paris: Éditions d'Art et Industrie, 1955.

Dumur, Guy, ed. *Histoire des spectacles*. Paris: Gallimard, 1965.

Dupavillon, Christian. *Architectures du cirque: Des origines à nos jours*. Paris: Moniteur, 1982.

Durant, John, and Alice Durant. *A Pictorial History of the American Circus*. New York: Barnes, 1957.

Eckley, Wilton. *The American Circus*. Boston: Twayne, 1984.

Feiler, Bruce. *Under the Big Top*. New York: Scribner's, 1995.

Fenner, Mildred Sandison, and Wolcott Fenner, ed. *The Circus: Lure and Legend*. Englewood Cliffs: Prentice-Hall, 1970.

Fox, Charles Philip. *The Circus in America*. Waukesha: Country Beautiful, 1969.

Fox, Charles Philip, ed. *Old-Time Circus Cuts: A Pictorial Archive of 202 Illustrations*. New York: Dover, 1979.

Fox, Charles Philip, and Tom Parkinson. *The Circus Moves by Rail*. Newton: Carstens, 1993.

Frichet, Henry. *Le Cirque et les Forains*. Tours: Mame, 1898.

Frost, Thomas. *Circus Life and Circus Celebrities*. London: Tinsley Bros., 1875.

Gallop, Alan. *Buffalo Bill's British Wild West*. Stroud: Sutton, 2001.

Gebel-Williams, Gunther. *Untamed: The Autobiography of the Circus's Greatest Animal Trainer*. New York: William Morrow, 1991.

Giret, Noëlle, ed. *Des Clowns: Cahiers d'une exposition*. Exhibition catalogue. Paris: Bibliothèque Nationale, 2001.

Gladiateur II (Édouard Cavailhon). *Le Cirque Fernando*. Paris: Paul Libéral et Cie, 1875.

Gomez de la Serna, Ramon. *Le Cirque: Première Chronique officielle du cirque avec une illustration et un portrait de l'auteur*. Paris: S. Kra, 1927.

Green, Martin, and John Swan. *The Triumph of Pierrot: The Commedia dell'arte and the Modern Imagination*. New York: Macmillan, 1986.

Greenwood, Isaac John. *The Circus: Its Origin and Growth Prior to 1835*. New York: B. Franklin, 1970.

Gregor, Jan T., and Tim Cridland. *Circus of the Scars: The True Inside Odyssey of a Modern Circus Sideshow*. Seattle: Brennan Dalsgard, 1998.

Grock. *Grock, ich lebe gern!* Munich: Knorr & Hirth, 1930.

——. *Sans blague, ma carrière de clown*. Paris: Flammarion, 1948.

Haenlein, Carl Albrecht, and Wolfgang Till, ed. *Menschen, Tiere, Sensationen: Zirkusplakate 1880–1930*. Exhibition catalogue. Hannover: Kestner Gesellschaft, 1978.

Hagen, Ursula. *Masken und Narren: Traditionen der Fastnacht*. Exhibition catalogue. Cologne: Kölnisches Stadtmuseum, 1972.

Hammarstrom, David Lewis. *Big Top Boss: John Ringling North and the Circus*. Urbana: University of Illinois Press, 1992.

Handelman, Don. "Symbolic Types, the Body, and Circus." *Semiotica* 85 (1991), pp. 205–225.

Harding, Les. *Elephant's Story: Jumbo and P.T. Barnum under the Big Top*. Jefferson, N.C.: McFarland, 2000.

Hatch, Alden, and Henry Ringling North. *The Circus Kings: Our Ringling Family Story*. Garden City: Doubleday, 1960.

Hergibo, Marie-Laure, and Jean Villiers. *Quand passent les clowns*. Exhibition catalogue. Paris: Syros-Alternatives, 1990.

Hippisley Coxe, Antony. *A Seat at the Circus*. Rev. ed. Hamden, Conn: Archon Books, 1980.

Hodak, Caroline. "Le Cirque en France et en Angleterre." Ph.D. diss., EHESS, Paris, 1993.

Hoh, LaVahn G., and William H. Rough. *Step Right Up! The Adventure of Circus in America*. White Hall, Va.: Betterway, 1990.

Hotier, Hugues. *Vocabulaire du cirque et du music-hall*. Paris: Maloine, 1981.

——. *Signes du cirque: Approche sémiologique*. Brussels: Tréteaux, 1984.

——. "La Transgression au cirque." *Kodikas/Code* 7, no. 1–2 (1984), pp. 9–16.

——. *Cirque, culture, communication*. Bordeaux: Presses Universitaires de Bordeaux, 1995.

Isherwood, Robert M. *Farce and Fantasy: Popular Entertainment in Eighteenth-Century Paris*. New York: Oxford University Press, 1986.

Jay, Ricky. *Jay's Journal of Anomalies*. New York: Farrar Strauss and Giroux, 2001.

Jean-Leo. *Histoire illustrée du cirque à Bruxelles: Saltimbanques et gens du voyage depuis le dix-septième siècle*. Brussels: Archives Générales du Royaume, 1998.

Jenkins, Ronald Scott. *Acrobats of the Soul: Comedy and Virtuosity in Contemporary American Theatre*. New York: Theatre Communications Group, 1988.

Jones, Louisa E. *Sad Clowns and Pale Pierrots: Literature and the Popular Comic Arts in 19th-Century France*. Lexington: French Forum, 1984.

Jours de cirque. Exhibition catalogue. Monaco: Grimaldi Forum; Arles: Actes Sud, 2002.

Kasson, Joy S. *Buffalo Bill's Wild West: Celebrity, Memory and Popular History*. New York: Hill and Wang, 2000.

Kober, A.H. *Circus Nights and Circus Days*. New York: W. Morrow & Company, 1931.

Koch, Gerd, and Florian Vassen, ed. *Lach- und Clownstheater: Die Vielfalt des Komischen in Musik, Literatur, Film, und Schauspiel*. Frankfurt am Main: Brandes & Apsel, 1991.

Kunhardt, Philip B., Jr., Philippe B. Kunhardt III, and Peter W. Kunhardt. *P.T. Barnum: America's Greatest Showman*. New York: Knopf, 1995.

Lea, K.M. *Italian Popular Comedy: A Study in the Commedia dell'arte, 1560–1620, with Special Reference to the English Stage*. 2 vols. New York: Russell & Russell Inc., 1962.

Lehmann, A.G. "Pierrot and Fin de Siècle." In *Romantic Mythologies*, ed. Ian Fletcher, pp. 209–223. London: Routledge & Kegan Paul, 1967.

393

Le Roux, Hugues. *Les Jeux du cirque et la vie foraine* (*Les Banquistes*). Paris: Plon et Nourrit, 1889.

Leroy, Dominique. *Histoire des arts du spectacle en France: Aspects économiques, politiques et esthétiques de la Renaissance à la Première Guerre mondiale*. Paris: L'Harmattan, 1990.

Levy, Pierre Robert. *Les Clowns et la tradition clownesque*. Sorvillier: Éditions de la Gardine, 1991.

——. *Les Fratellini: Trois Clowns légendaires*. Arles: Actes Sud, 1997.

Little, Kenneth W. "The Rhetoric of Romance and the Simulation of Tradition in Circus Clown Performance." *Semiotica* 85 (1991), pp. 227–255.

Lorant, Terry, and Jon Carroll. *The Pickle Family Circus*. San Francisco: Chronicle Books, 1986.

Loxton, Howard. *The Golden Age of the Circus*. London: Regency House, 1997.

Manning-Sanders, Ruth. *The English Circus*. London: Laurie, 1952.

Manser, Rodney N. *Circus: The Development and Significance of the Circus, Past, Present and Future*. Blackburn: Richford, 1987.

Markschiess-van Trix, Julius, and Bernhard Nowak. *Circus People and Posters*. Leipzig: Edition Leipzig, 1977.

Martin, Edward. *Mud Show: American Tent Circus Life*. Albuquerque: University of New Mexico Press, 1988.

Matlaw, Myron, ed. *Conference on the History of American Popular Entertainment*. Westport, Conn.: Greenwood, 1979.

May, Earl Chapin. *The Circus from Rome to Ringling*. New York: Duffield and Green, 1932.

McConnell, John H. *A Ring, A Horse, and a Clown: An Eight Generation History of the Hannefords*. Detroit: Astley and Ricketts, 1992.

McKechnie, Samuel. *Popular Entertainments through the Ages*. 1931. New York: Blom, 1969.

McKennon, Joe. *A Pictorial History of the American Carnival*. Sarasota: Carnival, 1972.

——. *Logistics of the American Circus Written by a Man Who Was There*. Sarasota: Carnival, 1977.

Medrano, Jérôme. *Une Vie de cirque*. Paris: Arthaud, 1983.

Mehl, Dieter. *The Elizabethan Dumb Show: The History of a Dramatic Convention*. London: Methuen, 1965.

Michel-Andino, Andreas. *Unterhaltung und Image: Artistische Unterhaltungskunst in sozialwissenschaftlicher Perspektive*. Frankfurt am Main: Haag & Herchen, 1993.

Mishler, Doug A. "It Was Everything Else We Knew Wasn't: The Circus and American Culture." In *The Cultures of Celebrations*, ed. Ray B. Browne and Michael T. Marsden. Bowling Green: Bowling Green State University Popular Press, 1994.

Moreau de Tours, Paul. *Fous et bouffons: Étude physiologique, psychologique et historique*. Paris: J.B. Baillière et fils, 1885.

Mourey, Gabriel. *Fêtes foraines de Paris*. 1906. Paris: André Delpeuch, 1927.

Murray, Marian. *Circus: From Rome to Ringling*. Westport, Conn.: Greenwood, 1973.

Ogden, Tom. *Two Hundred Years of the American Circus: From Aba-Daba to the Zoppe-Zavatta Troupe*. New York: Facts on File, 1993.

O'Nan, Stewart. *The Circus Fire: A True Story*. New York: Doubleday, 2000.

Palacio, Jean de. *Pierrot fin-de-siècle ou les Métamorphoses d'un masque*. Paris: Séguier, 1990.

Pandolfi, Vito. *La Commedia dell'arte: Storia e testo*. 6 vols. Florence: Edizioni Sanzoni Antiquariato, 1957–1961. Florence: Le Lettere, 1988.

Péricaud, Louis. *Le Théâtre des Funambules, ses mimes, ses acteurs et ses pantomimes, depuis sa fondation jusqu'à sa démolition*. Paris: L. Sapin, 1897.

Py, Christiane, and Cécile Ferenczi. *La Fête foraine d'autrefois: Les Années 1900*. Lyons: La Manufacture, 1987.

Reddin, Paul. *Wild West Shows*. Urbana: University of Illinois Press, 1999.

Rémy, Tristan. *Les Clowns*. Paris: Grasset, 1945.

——. *Le Cirque de Moscou*. Paris: Cercle d'Art, 1956.

——. *Entrées clownesques*. Paris: L'Arche, 1962.

——. *Le Cirque: Iconographie*. Paris: Bibliothèque Nationale, 1969.

——. "Le Cirque Fernando, 25 ans de cirque (1873–1897)." *Le Cirque dans l'Univers*, supplement to no. 115 (1979), pp. 1–72.

Renevey, Monica J., ed. *Le Grand Livre du cirque*. 2 vols. Paris and Lausanne: Bibliothèque des Arts, 1977.

Rennert, Jack. *100 Years of Circus Posters*. London: Michael Dempsey, 1975.

Richards, Kenneth, and Laura Richards. *The Commedia dell'arte: A Documentary History*. Oxford: Blackwell, 1989.

Romain, Hippolyte. *Histoire des bouffons, des augustes et des clowns*. Paris: Joëlle Losfeld, 1997.

Rose, Jim, and Melissa Rossi. *Freak Like Me: Inside the Jim Rose Circus Sideshow*. New York: Dell, 1995.

Russell, Don. *The Wild West: A History of the Wild West Shows*. Exhibition catalogue. Fort Worth: Amon Carter Museum of Western Art, 1970.

Russo, Mary. *The Female Grotesque: Risk, Excess and Modernity*. New York: Routledge, 1994.

Sand, Maurice. *Masques et bouffons*. 2 vols. Paris: M. Levy, 1860.

Sarrazin, Bernard. "Prémices de la dérision moderne: Le Polichinelle de Jean Paul et le clown anglais de Baudelaire." *Romantisme*, no. 74 (1991), pp. 37–47.

Saxon, Arthur Hartley. *Enter Foot and Horse: A History of Hippodrama in England and France*. New Haven: Yale University Press, 1968.

——. *The Life and Art of Andrew Ducrow and the Romantic Age of the English Circus*. Hamden, Conn.: Archon Books, 1978.

——. *P.T. Barnum: The Legend and the Man*. New York: Columbia University Press, 1989.

——. *Circus Language: A Glossary of Circus Terms*. Fairfield, Conn.: Jumbo's Press, 2000.

Schechter, Joel. *The Pickle Clowns: New American Circus Comedy*. Carbondale: Southern Illinois University Press, 2001.

Semprini, Andrea. "*Old Regnas* et le droit chemin: Analyse sémiotique et opérateurs topologiques." *Semiotica* 85 (1991), pp. 319–333.

Senelick, Laurence. *The Age and Stage of George L. Fox, 1825–1877*. Iowa City: University of Iowa Press, 1999.

Serge. *Le Monde du cirque*. Paris: Librairie des Champs-Élysées, 1939.

——. *Histoire du cirque*. Paris: Gründ, 1947.

Simonet, Alain. *Programmes des cirques en France de 1860 à 1910*. Paris: Arts des 2 Mondes, 2000.

Slout, William L. *Theatre in a Tent: The Development of a Provincial Entertainment*. Bowling Green: Bowling Green University Popular Press, 1972.

——. *Clowns and Cannons: The American Circus during the Civil War*. San Bernardino: Borgo, 1997.

——. *Olympians of the Sawdust Circle: A Biographical Dictionary of the Nineteenth-Century American Circus*. San Bernardino: Borgo, 1997.

Smelstor, Marjorie. "'Damn Everything but the Circus': Popular Art in the Twenties and *him*.'" *Modern Drama* 17, no. 1 (March 1974), pp. 43–55.

Smith, Eleanor. *British Circus Life*. London: George G. Harrap & Co., 1948.

Soulé, Michel. "Oedipe au cirque devant le numéro de l'Auguste et du Clown blanc." *Revue Française de Psychanalyse* 44 (January–February 1980), pp. 99–125.

Speaight, George. *A History of the Circus*. London: Tantivy; San Diego: A.S. Barnes, 1980.

Stoddart, Helen. *Pierrots on the Stage of Desire: Nineteenth-Century French Literary Artists and the Comic Pantomime*. Princeton: Princeton University Press, 1985.

——. *Rings of Desire: Circus History and Representation*. Manchester: Manchester University Press, 2000.

Storey, Robert F. *Pierrot: A Critical History of a Mask*. Princeton: Princeton University Press, 1978.

Strehly, Georges. *L'Acrobatie et les acrobates*. 1903. Paris: S. Zlatin, 1977.

Swortzell, Lowell. *Here Come the Clowns*. New York: Viking, 1978.

Taylor, Robert Lewis. *Center Ring: The People of the Circus*. Garden City: Doubleday, 1956.

Thayer, Stuart. *Annals of the American Circus, 1793–1829*. Manchester: Rymack Printing Co., 1976.

——. *Annals of the American Circus, 1830–1847*. Seattle: Peanut Butter Publishing, 1986.

——. *Annals of the American Circus, 1848–1860*. Seattle: Dauven & Thayer, 1992.

——. *Traveling Showmen: The American Circus Before the Civil War*. Morristown: Astley and Ricketts, 1997.

Thayer, Stuart, and William L. Slout. *Grand Entrée: The Birth of the Greatest Show on Earth, 1870–1875*. San Bernadino: Borgo, 1998.

Thétard, Henry. *Coulisses et secrets du cirque*. Paris: Plon, 1934.

——. *La Merveilleuse Histoire du cirque*. Paris: Prisma, 1947. Revised edition, including *Le Cirque depuis la guerre* by L.-R. Dauven. Paris: Julliard, 1978.

Thomas, Frank J. *Circus Wagon*. Los Angeles: Tenfingers, 1972.

Thomson, Rosemarie Garland, ed. *Freakery: Cultural Spectacles of the Extraordinary Body*. New York: New York University Press, 1996.

Tyrwhitt-Drake, Garrard. *The English Circus and Fair Ground*. London: Methuen, 1947.

Ulanov, Ann Belford, and Barry Ulanov. *The Witch and the Clown: Two Archetypes of Human Sexuality*. Wilmette: Chiron, 1987.

Vanderveen, Bart Harmannus, ed. *Fairground and Circus Transport*. London and New York: F. Warne, 1973.

Van Papen, Robert J. "Pierrot Postcard Collection." *Idea* 43, no. 248 (January 1995), pp. 94–97.

Vigouroux-Frey, Nicole, ed. *Le Clown: Rire et/ou dérision*. Rennes: Presses Universitaires de Rennes, 1999.

Wallis, Michael. *The Real Wild West: The 101 Ranch and the Creation of the American West*. New York: St. Martin's, 1999.

Ward, Richard, and Geoff Weedon. *Fairground Art: The Art Forms of Travelling Fairs, Carousels and Carnival Midways*. New York: Abbeville, 1981.

Weeks, David C. *Ringling: The Florida Years, 1911–1936*. Gainesville: University Press of Florida, 1993.

Weill, Alain, ed. *Le Cirque français*. Exhibition catalogue. Paris: Musée de l'Affiche, n.d.

Welsford, Enid. *The Fool: His Social and Literary History*. London: Faber and Faber, 1935.

Wilkins, Charles. *The Circus at the Edge of the Earth: Travels with the Great Wallenda Circus*. Toronto: McClelland & Stewart, 1998.

Wilmeth, Don B. *The Language of American Popular Entertainment: A Glossary of Argot, Slang, and Terminology*. Westport, Conn.: Greenwood, 1981.

——. *Variety Entertainment and Outdoor Amusements: A Reference Guide*. Westport, Conn.: Greenwood, 1982.

Wilson, R.L. *Buffalo Bill's Wild West: An American Legend*. New York: Random House, 1998.

Zavatta, Catherine. *Les Mots du cirque*. Paris: Belin, 2001.

Zucker, Wolfgang M. "The Image of the Clown." *Journal of Aesthetics* 12 (March 1954), pp. 310–317.

The Circus and the Visual Arts

Ahlander, Leslie Judd. *The Circus in Art*. Exhibition catalogue. Sarasota: John and Mable Ringling Museum of Art, 1977.

Baugé, Isabelle. "Pantomime, littérature et arts visuels, une crise de la représentation." Ph.D. diss., Paris III, 1995.

Berger, Roland, and Dietmar Winkler. *Künstler, Clowns und Akrobaten: Der Zirkus in der Bildenden Kunst*. Exhibition catalogue. Stuttgart: Kohlhammer, 1983.

Borowitz, Helen Osterman. "Painted Smiles: Sad Clowns in French Art and Literature." *Bulletin of the Cleveland Museum of Art* 71, no. 1 (1984), pp. 23–35.

Boustany, Bernadette. *En Piste! Le cirque en image des soeurs Vesque*. Paris: Découvertes Gallimard, 1992.

Brown, Marilyn. *Gypsies and Other Bohemians: The Myth of the Artist in Nineteenth-Century France*. Ann Arbor: UMI Research Press, 1985.

Cate, Philip Dennis. "The Cult of the Circus." In *The Pleasures of Paris: Daumier to Picasso*, ed. Barbara Stern Shapiro. Boston: Museum of Fine Arts / D.R. Godine, 1991.

Ciret, Yan, ed. "Le Cirque au-delà du cercle." *Art Press*, no. 20, special issue (September 1999).

De Marco, Gabriella. "La maschere della Commedia dell'arte nella pittura francese negli anni del Cubismo." *Ricerche di storia dell'arte* 37 (1989), pp. 40–54.

Depietro, Anne Cohen. *Under the Big Top: The Circus in Art*. Exhibition catalogue. Huntington: Hecksher Museum of Art, 1991.

Dery, Mark. "Jokers Wild." *World Art*, no. 3 (1995), pp. 66–73.

Dufrene, Thierry. *Acrobate, mime parfait: L'Artiste en figure libre*. Exhibition catalogue. Paris: Paris Musées, 1997.

Fahrendes Volk: Spielleute, Schausteller, Artisten. Exhibition catalogue. Recklinghausen: Städtische Kunsthalle, 1981.

Forell, Janina. *Pierrot und Harlekin: Die Quellen der Inspiration und die Bedeutung dieses Themas für die französische Malerei des 19. und beginnenden 20. Jahrhunderts*. Munich, 1985.

Friedrichs, Y. "Fahrendes Volk." *Weltkunst* 51, no. 11 (1 June 1981), pp. 1649–1651.

Goodrich, Lloyd. *The Circus in Paint*. Exhibition catalogue. New York: Whitney Studio Galleries, 1928.

Greco, Franco Carmelo, ed. *Pulcinella maschera del mondo*. Exhibition catalogue. Naples: Electa, 1990.

Gustafson, Donna, et al. *Images from the World Between: The Circus in 20th Century American Art*. Exhibition catalogue. Cambridge, Mass.: MIT Press; New York: American Federation of Arts, 2001.

Harlequin und Akrobat: Die Welt der Artisten im rheinischen Expressionismus. Exhibition catalogue. Bonn: Verein August Macke Haus, 1997.

Haskell, Francis. "The Sad Clown: Some Notes on a 19th Century Myth." In *French 19th Century Painting and Literature*, ed. Ulrich Finke, pp. 2–16. Manchester: Manchester University Press, 1972.

Henkes, Robert. *Themes in American Painting: A Reference Work to Common Styles and Genres*. Jefferson, N.C.: McFarland, 1993.

Jamieson, David, ed. *Clowns of the 20th Century! Photographs of 100 Years of Circus Clowns*. Exhibition catalogue. Buntingford: Circus Friends Association and Aardvark Publishing, 2000.

Januszczak, Waldema. "La Grande Parade." *Studio International* 198, no. 1009 (1985), pp. 36–39.

Jensen, Dean. *Center Ring: The Artist, Two Centuries of Circus Art*. Exhibition catalogue. Milwaukee: Milwaukee Art Museum, 1981.

Julig, Suzanne L., and Lane Talbot Sparkman. *Center Stage: Entertainment in American and European Art*. Exhibition catalogue. New York: Hirschl and Adler Galleries, 1995.

Kellein, Thomas. *Pierrot: Melancholie und Maske*. Exhibition catalogue. Munich: Haus der Kunst; New York: Prestel, 1995.

La Grande Parade: Hoogtepunten van de schilderkunst na 1940. Exhibition catalogue. Amsterdam: Stedelijk Museum, 1984.

Laude, Jean. "Le Monde du cirque et ses jeux dans la peinture." *Revue d'Esthétique* 6 (1953), pp. 411–433.

Lawner, Lynne. *Harlequin and the Moon: Commedia dell'arte and the Visual Arts*. New York: Harry N. Abrams, 1998.

Le Men, Ségolène. "French Circus Posters." *Print Quarterly* 8, no. 4 (1991), pp. 363–387.

Malhotra, Ruth. *Manege frei! Artisten und Circusplakate von Adolph Fiedländer*. Dortmund: Harenberg, 1979.

McMullan, Richard Dale, and Kneeland McNulty. *Circus in Art*. Exhibition catalogue. Boston: Boston Public Library, 1985.

Merkert, Jörn, ed. *Zirkus, Circus, Cirque*. Exhibition catalogue. Berlin: Nationalgalerie, 1978.

Minguet-Battlori, Joan M. "El payaso en la pintura contemporanea: tres momentos en la representacion de un personaje." *Cuadernos de arte e iconografia: Actes de los II Coloquios de iconografia* 4, no. 8 (1991), pp. 204–211.

Newman, T. "French Painting and the Circus." *Antique Dealer and Collector's Guide*, November 1976, pp. 80–83.

Ritter, Naomi. *Art as Spectacle: Images of the Entertainer since Romanticism*. Columbia: University of Missouri Press, 1989.

Schardt, H. *Schausteller, Gaukler und Artisten: Schaubuden-Graphik der Vormarzeit*. 2 vols. Essen: Fredebeul & Koenen, 1980.

Schneider, M. "Gilles und Pierrot, Gaukler und Harlekin." *Kunst und das Schöne Heim* 94, no. 6 (June 1982), pp. 380–386, 434–435.

Silver, Kenneth E. *Esprit de corps: The Art of the Parisian Avant-Garde and the First World War, 1914–1925*. Princeton: Princeton University Press, 1989.

Starobinski, Jean. "Notes sur le bouffon romantique." *Cahiers du Sud* 61, no. 387–388 (1966), pp. 270–275.

———. *Portrait de l'artiste en saltimbanque*. Geneva: Skira, 1970. Geneva: Skira; Paris: Flammarion, 1983.

Sterling, Charles. "Early Paintings of the Commedia dell'arte in France." *Metropolitan Museum of Art Bulletin*, Summer 1943, pp. 11–32.

Toole-Stott, Raymond. *Circus and Allied Arts: A World Bibliography*. 4 vols. Derby: Harpur, 1958–1971.

———. *Circus and Allied Arts: A World Bibliography*, vol. 5. Liverpool: Circus Friends Association, 1992.

Verhagen, Marcus. "Re-figurations of Carnival: The Comic Performer in Fin-de-Siècle Parisian Art." Ph.D. diss., University of California, Berkeley, 1994.

Wagner, Geoffrey. "Art and the Circus." *Apollo* 82, no. 42 (August 1965), pp. 134–136.

Walch, Josef. "Maske, Maskierung, Maskerade." *Kunst + Unterricht*, no. 161 (April 1992), pp. 20, 23–30.

Wallon, Emmanuel, ed. *Le Cirque au risque de l'art*. Arles: Actes Sud, 2002.

Diane Arbus

Adams, Rachel. "Strange Company: Women, Freaks and Others in Twentieth-Century America." Ph.D. diss., University of California, Santa Barbara, 1997.

Alexander, M. Darsie. "Diane Arbus: A Theatre of Ambiguity." *History of Photography* 19, no. 2 (Summer 1995), pp. 120–123.

Arbus, Doon, and Yolanda Cuomo, ed. *Diane Arbus*. New York: Aperture, 1995.

Arbus, Doon, and Marvin Israel, ed. *Diane Arbus: Magazine Work*. Millerton: Aperture, 1984.

Badger, Gerry. "Notes from the Margin of Spoiled Identity: The Art of Diane Arbus." In *Photo Texts*, by Gerry Badger and Peter Turner, pp. 162–173. London: Travelling Light, 1988.

Bertelli, Pino. *Della fotografia trasgressiva dall'estetica dei "freaks" all'etica della ribellione*. Piombino: TraccEdizioni, 1992.

Bosworth, Patricia. *Diane Arbus: A Biography*. New York: Avon, 1984.

Budick, Ariella G. "Subject to Scrutiny: Diane Arbus's American Grotesque." Ph.D. diss., New York University, 1996.

"Diane Arbus." *Picture*, special issue, 1980.

Diane Arbus: Revelations. Exhibition catalogue. New York: Random House, 2003.

Green, Roy. "Circus Work in Camera." *Photographic Journal* 137 (May 1997), pp. 162–164.

Hulick, Diana Emery. "Diane Arbus' Expressive Methods." *History of Photography* 19, no. 2 (Summer 1995), pp. 107–116.

Jeffrey, Ian. "Diane Arbus and the American Freaks." *Studio International Journal of Art* 187 (March 1974), pp. 133–134.

———. "Diane Arbus and the American Grotesque." *Photographic Journal* 114 (May 1974), pp. 224–229.

McPherson, Heather. "Diane Arbus's Grotesque 'Human Comedy.'" *History of Photography* 19, no. 2 (Summer 1995), pp. 117–120.

Roegiers, Patrick. *Diane Arbus, ou Le rêve du naufrage*. Paris: Chêne, 1985.

Charles Atlas

Yokobosky, Matthew. "The Real Charles Atlas: An Interview." *Performing Arts Journal* 19, no. 3 (September 1997), pp. 21–33.

Milton Avery

Haskell, Barbara. *Milton Avery*. Exhibition catalogue. New York: Whitney Museum of American Art / Harper and Row, 1982.

Hobbs, Robert Carlton. *Milton Avery*. New York: Hudson Hills, 1990.

Kramer, Hilton. *Milton Avery: Paintings 1930–1960*. New York: T. Yoseloff, 1962.

Milton Avery: Paintings and Watercolours. Exhibition catalogue. London: Waddington Galleries, 1996.

Owens, Carlotta J. *Milton Avery: Early and Late*. Exhibition catalogue. Annandale-on-Hudson: Edith C. Blum Art Institute, 1981.

Price, Marla. "The Paintings of Milton Avery." Ph.D. diss., University of Virginia, 1982.

Irene Bayer-Hecht

Eskildsen, Ute, and Jan-Christopher Horak. *Film und Foto der zwanziger Jahre: Eine Betrachtung der Internationalen Werkbundausstellung Film und Foto 1929*. Exhibition catalogue. Stuttgart: Württembergischer Kunstverein, 1979.

Fiedler, Jeannine, ed. *Photography at the Bauhaus*. Cambridge, Mass.: MIT Press, 1990.

Glüher, Gerhard, and Suzanne Pastor. *Photographie und Bauhaus*. Hannover: Kestner Gesellschaft, 1986.

Herzogenrath, Wulf. *Bauhausfotografie*. Exhibition catalogue. Stuttgart: Institut für Auslandsbeziehungen, 1983.

Prakapas, Eugene, et al. *Bauhaus Photography*. Cambridge, Mass.: MIT Press, 1985.

Rosenblum, Naomi. *A History of Women Photographers*. 2nd ed. New York: Abbeville, 2000.

Max Beckmann

Anderson, Eleanor. "Max Beckmann's Carnival Triptych." *Art Journal* 24, no. 3 (Spring 1965), pp. 218–225.

Beckmann, Max. *Écrits*. Edited by Barbara Stehlé-Akhtar, translated from the German by Philippe Dagen. Paris: École Nationale Supérieure des Beaux-Arts, 2002.

Bezzola, Tobia, and Cornelia Homburg, ed. *Max Beckmann and Paris: Matisse, Braque, Léger, Rouault*. Exhibition catalogue. Cologne: Taschen, 1998.

Busch, Günter, Gerhard Gerkens, and Jürgen Schultze. *Max Beckmann, seine Themen, seine Zeit: Zum 100. Geburtstag des Künstlers*. Exhibition catalogue. Bremen: Kunsthalle Bremen, 1984.

Danzker, Jo-Anne Birnie, and Amelie Ziersch, ed. *Max Beckmann, Welt-Theater: Das Graphische Werk 1901 bis 1946*. Exhibition catalogue. Stuttgart: Hatje, 1993.

Döring, Thomas, and Christian Lenz. *Max Beckmann: Selbstbildnisse – Zeichnung und Druckgraphik*. Heidelberg: Edition Braus, 2000.

Elger, Dietmar. *Circus Beckmann: Werke aus dem Sprengel-Museum Hannover, der Sammlung Ahlers und Internationalen Sammlungen*. Exhibition catalogue. Hannover: Sprengel-Museum, 1998.

Gallwitz, Klaus, ed. *Max Beckmann: Gemälde, 1905–1950*. Exhibition catalogue. Stuttgart: Hatje, 1990.

Grunewald, Dietrich. "Zum Beispiel: Max Beckmann 'Pierrette und Clown.'" *Kunst und Unterricht*, no. 189 (January 1995), pp. 14–15.

Heusinger von Waldegg, Joachim. *Kunst + Dokumentation: Max Beckmann Pierrette und Clown, 1925*. Exhibition catalogue. Mannheim: Städtische Kunsthalle, 1980.

Jatho, Heinz. *Max Beckmann: Schauspieler-Triptychon: Eine Kunst-Monographie*. Frankfurt am Main: Insel-Taschenbuch, 1989.

Kessler, Charles S. *Max Beckmann's Triptychs*. Cambridge, Mass.: Harvard University Press, 1970.

Lackner, Stephen. *Max Beckmann: Die neun Triptychen*. Berlin: Safari-Verlag, 1965.

Max Beckmann: Works on Paper – Sculptures. Exhibition catalogue. Chicago: Worthington Gallery, 1985.

O'Brien Twohig, Sarah. *Beckmann: Carnival*. London: Tate Gallery, 1984.

Ottinger, Didier. *Beckmann*. Exhibition catalogue. Paris: Centre Pompidou, 2002.

Ottinger, Didier, ed. *Max Beckmann: Gravures, 1911–1946*. Exhibition catalogue. Paris: Réunion des Musées Nationaux; Sables d'Olonne: Abbaye Sainte-Croix, 1994.

Schultz-Hoffmann, Carla, and Judith C. Weiss, ed. *Max Beckmann Retrospective*. Exhibition catalogue. Munich: Prestel-Verlag; New York: W.W. Norton & Co., 1984.

Schulze, Ingrid. "Zirkus, Karussell und Schaubude: Im Beitrag zu Max Beckmanns Graphikmappe Der Jahrmarkt." *Bildende Kunst* 8 (1990), pp. 60–63.

———. "Zirkus, Karussell und Schaubude: Max Beckmanns Graphikmappe Der Jahrmarkt von 1921 im lichte literarischer und bildkünstlerischer Uberlieferungen." *Weimarer Beiträge* 37, no. 2 (1991), pp. 196–212.

Selz, Peter. *Max Beckmann*. Exhibition catalogue. New York: Museum of Modern Art, 1964.

———. *Max Beckmann: The Self-Portraits*. Exhibition catalogue. New York: Gagosian Gallery / Rizzoli, 1992.

———. "Max Beckmann: The Self-Portraits." In *Beyond the Mainstream: Essays on Modern and Contemporary Art*, pp. 91–106. Cambridge: Cambridge University Press, 1997.

Spieler, Reinhard. "Pictorial Worlds, World Views: Max Beckmann's Triptychs." In *Max Beckmann in Exile*, pp. 57–80. Exhibition catalogue. New York: Solomon R. Guggenheim Museum / Harry N. Abrams, 1996.

Joseph Beuys

Adriani, Götz, Winfried Konnertz, and Karin Thomas. *Joseph Beuys, Life and Works*. Woodbury: Barron's Educational Series, 1979.

Borer, Alain, and Lothar Schirmer. *The Essential Joseph Beuys*. Cambridge, Mass.: MIT Press, 1997.

De Domizio Durini, Lucrezia. *Joseph Beuys: The Image of Humanity*. Exhibition catalogue. Milan: Silvana, 2001.

Getlinger photographiert Beuys, 1950–1963. Cologne: DuMont, 1990.

Hergott, Fabrice, and Marion Hohlfeldt. *Joseph Beuys*. Exhibition catalogue. Paris: Centre Pompidou, 1994.

Stachelhaus, Heiner. *Joseph Beuys*. Düsseldorf: Claassen, 1988.

Thistlewood, David, ed. *Joseph Beuys: Diverging Critiques*. Liverpool: Tate Gallery Liverpool / Liverpool University Press, 1995.

Tisdall, Caroline. *Joseph Beuys*. Exhibition catalogue. New York: Solomon R. Guggenheim Museum, 1979.

———. *Joseph Beuys: We Go This Way*. London: Violette, 1998.

Zweite, Armin. *Joseph Beuys: Natur, Materie, Form*. Exhibition catalogue. Düsseldorf: Kunstsammlung Nordrhein Westfalen; Munich: Schirmer/ Mosel, 1991.

Zweite, Armin, ed. *Beuys zu Ehren: Drawings, Sculptures, Objects, Vitrines, and the Environment 'Show Your Wound' / by Joseph Beuys; Paintings, Sculptures, Drawings, Watercolours, Environments and Video Installations by 70 Artists*. Exhibition catalogue. Munich: Städtische Galerie im Lenbachhaus, 1986.

Albert Birkle

Schaffer, Nikolaus. *Albert Birkle*. Exhibition catalogue. Salzburg: Museum Carolino Augusteum, 2001.

Rhona Bitner

Rhona Bitner. Exhibition catalogue. New York: CRG Gallery, 2001.

Rhona Bitner: Circus. Exhibition catalogue. Salamanca: Universidad de Salamanca, 1998.

Rhona Bitner: Circus. Exhibition catalogue. Mendrisio: Massimo Martino Gallery, 2001.

Olivier Blanckart

Corréard, Stéphane. "Blanckart scotche les icônes." *Beaux-Arts Magazine*, no. 214 (March 2002), pp. 58–63.

Labelle-Rojoux, Arnaud. "Der Parodistische Geist." *Neue Bildende Kunst*, no. 5 (October–November 1996), pp. 36–41.

Labelle-Rojoux, Arnaud, and Olivier Blanckart. "Un Rêve de fiasco." *Art Press*, no. 20, special issue (September 1999), pp. 143–144.

Quintane, Nathalie, Hervé Legros, and Olivier Blanckart. *Blanckart*. Bordeaux: Confluences, 2000.

Louis-Léopold Boilly

Delafond, Marianne. *Louis Boilly 1761–1845*. Exhibition catalogue. Paris: Musée Marmottan, 1984.

Hallam, John Stephen. "The Two Manners of Louis-Léopold Boilly and French Genre Painting in Transition." *The Art Bulletin* 63, no. 4 (December 1981), pp. 618–633.

———. *The Genre Works of Louis-Léopold Boilly*. Ann Arbor: UMI Research Press, 1984.

Siegfried, Susan. *The Art of Louis-Léopold Boilly: Modern Life in Napoleonic France*. New Haven and London: Yale University Press, 1995.

Siegfried, Susan, et al. *Boilly, 1761–1845: Un Grand Peintre français de la Révolution à la Restauration*. Exhibition catalogue. Lille: Musée des Beaux-Arts, 1988.

Christian Boltanski

Blistène, Bernard, et al. *Boltanski*. Exhibition catalogue. Paris: Centre Pompidou, 1984.

Eccher, Danilo, ed. *Christian Boltanski*. Exhibition catalogue. Milan: Charta, 1997.

Ehlers, Fiona. "Unter dem Zirkusdach wird die Kunst zum sinnlichen Erlebnis." *ART – Das Kunstmagazin*, no. 8 (August 1999), pp. 60–65.

Gumpert, Lynn. *Christian Boltanski*. Paris: Flammarion, 1994.

Honnef, Klaus. "Un Magicien moderne: Réflexions à propos de l'oeuvre de Christian Boltanski." *Artstudio*, no. 5 (1987), pp. 107–116.

Honnef, Klaus. Introduction to *Recueil de saynètes comiques interprétées par Christian Boltanski / Sammlung lustiger Einakter dargestellt von Christian Boltanski / Collection of Comical One-act Plays Performed by Christian Boltanski*. Exhibition catalogue. Munich: Westfälischer Kunstverein; Stuttgart: Württembergischer Kunstverein, 1974.

Lascault, Gilbert. "Deux Expositions de Boltanski: Portraits de l'artiste en huissier et en clown." *Chroniques de l'Art Vivant*, no. 52 (October 1974), pp. 32–34.

———. "Huit Critiques grotesques pour un travail de Christian Boltanski." In *Vers une esthétique sans entraves*, ed. Mikel Dufrenne. Paris: Éditions 10/18, 1975.

Semin, Didier, Tamar Garb, and Donald Kuspit. *Christian Boltanski*. London: Phaidon, 1997.

Van Drathen, Doris. "Der Clown als schlechter Prediger: Interview mit Christian Boltanski." *Kunstforum International*, no. 113 (May–June 1991), pp. 314–331.

Pierre Bonnard

Bozo, Dominique, ed. *Bonnard*. Exhibition catalogue. Paris: Centre Pompidou, 1984.

Clair, Jean. *Bonnard*. Paris: H. Scrépel / Weber, 1975.

———. *Pierre Bonnard*. Exhibition catalogue. Milan: Palazzo Reale / Mazotta, 1988.

Cogeval, Guy. *Bonnard*. Paris: Hazan, 1993.

Fermigier, André. *Pierre Bonnard*. London: Thames & Hudson, 1987.

Giambruni, Helen Emery. "Early Bonnard." Ph.D. diss., University of California, Berkeley, 1983.

Hyman, Timothy. *Bonnard*. London: Thames & Hudson, 1998.

Le Leyzour, Philippe, et al. *Hommage à Bonnard*. Exhibition catalogue. Bordeaux: Galerie des Beaux-Arts, 1986.

Newman, Sasha, ed. *Bonnard: The Late Paintings*. Exhibition catalogue. Washington, D.C.: Phillips Collection; Dallas: Dallas Museum of Art, 1984.

Pierre Bonnard. Exhibition catalogue. Paris: Fondation Dina Vierny–Musée Maillol / Réunion des Musées Nationaux, 2000.

Pierre Bonnard 1867–1947. Exhibition catalogue. Lausanne: Fondation de l'Hermitage, 1991.

Prat, Jean-Louis, ed. *Bonnard*. Exhibition catalogue. Martigny: Fondation Pierre Gianadda, 1999.

Terrasse, Antoine. *Bonnard*. Paris: Gallimard, 1988.

Turner, Elizabeth Hutton. *Pierre Bonnard: Early and Late*. Exhibition catalogue. London: Philip Wilson; Washington, D.C.: Phillips Collection, 2002.

Watkins, Nicholas. *Bonnard*. London: Phaidon, 1994.

Whitfield, Sarah, and John Elderfield. *Bonnard*. Exhibition catalogue. London: Tate Gallery, 1998.

Jonathan Borofsky

Jarrell, Joseph. "The Disquieting Mind of Jonathan Borofsky." *Sculpture* 9, no. 5 (September–October 1990), pp. 48–52.

Kittelmann, Udo. *Jonathan Borofsky: Dem Publikum gewidmet / Dedicated to the Audience*. Stuttgart: Edition Cantz, 1993.

Mahoney, Robert. "Pygmalion à Disneyland: L'Histoire de l'art et l'histoire de la mécanique chez Jonathan Borofsky." *Artstudio*, no. 22 (Fall 1991), pp. 116–127.

Marks, Ben. "Jonathan Borofsky's *Ballerina Clown*." *Artspace* 14, no. 3 (March–April 1990), p. 23.

Rosenthal, Mark, and Richard Marshall. *Jonathan Borofsky*. Exhibition catalogue. Philadelphia: Philadelphia Museum of Art, 1984.

Scott, D.E. *Horizons: Jonathan Borofsky*. Exhibition catalogue. Kansas City: Nelson-Atkins Museum of Art, 1988.

Louise Bourgeois

Bernadac, Marie-Laure. *Louise Bourgeois*. Paris: Flammarion, 1995.

Bernadac, Marie-Laure, and Marie-Odile Peynet. *Louise Bourgeois: Pensées-plumes*. Exhibition catalogue. Paris: Centre Pompidou, 1995.

Clair, Jean. *Cinq Notes sur l'oeuvre de Louise Bourgeois*. Paris: L'Échoppe, 1999.

Crone, Rainer, and Petrus Graf Schaesberg. *Louise Bourgeois: The Secret of the Cells*. New York: Prestel, 1998.

Gardner, Paul. *Louise Bourgeois*. New York: Universe Publishing, 1994.

Gorovoy, Jerry. *Louise Bourgeois and the Nature of Abstraction*. New York: Bellport, 1986.

Kotik, Charlotta, Terrie Sultan, and Christian Leigh. *Louise Bourgeois: The Locus of Memory – Works 1982–1993*. New York: Harry N. Abrams, 1994.

Kuspit, Donald. *Bourgeois*. New York: E. Avedon Editions, 1988.

Louise Bourgeois: Recent Works. London: Serpentine Gallery, 1997.

Storr, Robert. *Louise Bourgeois Drawings*. New York: Robert Miller; Paris: Daniel Lelong, 1988.

Tilkin, Danielle, Jerry Gorovoy, et al. *Louise Bourgeois: Memory and Architecture*. Exhibition catalogue. Madrid: Museo Nacional Centro de Arte Reina Sofia / Aldeasa, 1999.

Weiermair, Peter, and Cornelia Walter. *Louise Bourgeois*. Exhibition catalogue. Frankfurt am Main: Frankfurter Kunstverein, 1989.

Wye, Deborah, and Carol Smith. *The Prints of Louise Bourgeois*. Exhibition catalogue. New York: Museum of Modern Art / Harry N. Abrams, 1994.

Claude Cahun

Cottingham, Laura. *Cherchez Claude Cahun*. Lyons: Carobella ex-natura, 2002.

Leperlier, François. *Claude Cahun: L'Écart et la métamorphose*. Paris: Jean-Michel Place, 1992.

Leperlier, François, ed. *Claude Cahun: Photographe*. Exhibition catalogue. Paris: Paris Musées / Jean-Michel Place, 1995.

Leperlier, François. Introduction to *Claude Cahun*. Paris: Nathan, 1999.

Monahan, Laurie. "Radical Transformations: Claude Cahun and the Masquerade of Womanliness." In *Inside the Visible: An Elliptical Traverse of Twentieth Century Art in, of, and from the Feminine*, ed. Catherine De Zegher, pp. 125–133. Cambridge, Mass.: MIT Press, 1996.

Alexander Calder

Alexander Calder: A Retrospective Exhibition. Exhibition catalogue. New York: Solomon R. Guggenheim Museum, 1964.

Alexander Calder: Circus Drawings, Wire Sculptures, and Toys. Exhibition catalogue. Houston: Museum of Fine Arts, 1964.

Alexander Calder: Recent Mobiles and Circus Gouaches. Exhibition catalogue. New York: Peris Galleries, 1975.

Alexander Calder 1898–1976. Exhibition catalogue. Paris: Paris Musées, 1996.

Arnason, Harvard H., ed. *An Autobiography with Pictures*. New York: Pantheon Books, 1966.

Calder, Alexander. "Voici une petite histoire de mon cirque." In *Permanence du Cirque*, pp. 37–42. Paris: Revue Neuf, 1952.

Calder fait son cirque. Exhibition catalogue. Paris: Musée d'Art Moderne de la Ville de Paris: 1996.

Elsen, Albert. *Alexander Calder: A Retrospective Exhibition, Works from 1925 to 1974*. Exhibition catalogue. Chicago: Museum of Contemporary Art, 1974.

Gray, Cleve. "Calder's Circus." *Art in America* 52, no. 5 (October 1964), p. 2248.

Jouffroy, Alain. "Calder's Circus or the Demystification." In *Homage to Alexander Calder*, special issue of *XXᵉ Siècle Review*, pp. 37–42. New York: Tudor, 1972.

Legrand-Chabrier. "Paris-Montparnasse et son cirque." *Patrie*, 6 May 1927.

———. "Un Petit Cirque à domicile." *Candide*, no. 171 (23 June 1927), p. 7.

———. "Alexandre Calder et son cirque automatique." *La Volonté*, 19 May 1929.

Lipman, Jean. *Calder's Universe*. Exhibition catalogue. New York: Whitney Museum of American Art / Viking, 1976.

Lipman, Jean, and Nancy Foote. *Calder's Circus*. Exhibition catalogue. New York: E.P. Dutton & Co., 1972.

Marchesseau, Daniel. *Calder intime*. Paris: Solange Thierry, 1989.

Marter, Joan. *Alexander Calder*. Cambridge: Cambridge University Press, 1991.

Prather, Marla, ed. *Alexander Calder, 1898–1976*. Exhibition catalogue. Washington, D.C.: National Gallery of Art; New Haven and London: Yale University Press, 1998.

Roarr: Calder's Circus. Exhibition catalogue. New York: Whitney Museum of American Art, 1991.

Spergling, Joy. "Calder in Paris: The Circus and Surrealism." *Archives of American Art Journal* 28, no. 2 (1988), pp. 16–29.

———. "The Popular Sources of Calder's Circus: The Humpty Dumpty Circus, Ringling Brothers and Barnum & Bailey, and the Cirque Medrano." *Journal of American Culture* 17, no. 4 (1994), pp. 1–14.

Sweeney, James Johnson. *Alexander Calder*. Exhibition catalogue. New York: Museum of Modern Art, 1943.

Robert Capa

Capa, Robert. "Picasso (1950)." In *Robert Capa, 1913–1954*, ed. Cornell Capa and Bhupendra Karia. New York: Grossman, 1974.

Capa, Robert. *Slightly Out of Focus*. New York: Holt, 1947. Rev. ed. New York: Modern Library, 2001.

Kershaw, Alex. *Blood and Champagne: The Life and Times of Robert Capa*. London: Macmillan, 2002.

Lacouture, Jean. Introduction to *Robert Capa*. Exhibition catalogue. Paris: Centre National de la Photographie; New York: Pantheon Books, 1989.

Righini, M. "La piu leggendaria e pazza agenzia del mondo: Quelle prime donne isteriche del 'circo' magnum." *BolaffiArte*, special issue, 1977, pp. 30–35.

Robert Capa: Photographs. Exhibition catalogue. San Diego: Museum of Photographic Arts, 1998.

Robert Capa: Retrospectiva 1932–1954. Exhibition catalogue. Barcelona: Fundación Caja de Pensiones, 1989.

Whelan, Richard. *Robert Capa: A Biography*. New York: Alfred A. Knopf, 1985.

———. *Robert Capa: The Definitive Collection*. London: Phaidon, 2001.

Marc Chagall

Chagall: Bilder, Traume, Theater, 1908–1920. Exhibition catalogue. Vienna: Jüdisches Museum / C. Brandstätter, 1994.

Chagall connu et inconnu. Exhibition catalogue. Paris: Réunion des Musées Nationaux, 2003.

Chagall et le théâtre. Exhibition catalogue. Toulouse: Musée des Augustins, 1967.

Chagall: Gouaches and Wash Drawings for the Book "Circus." Exhibition catalogue. Lucerne: Galerie Rosengart, 1972.

Chiappini, Rudy, ed. *Marc Chagall*. Exhibition catalogue. Milan: Skira, 2001.

Compton, Susan P. *Chagall*. Philadelphia: Philadelphia Museum of Art, 1985.

———. *Marc Chagall: My Life, My Dreams – Berlin and Paris, 1922–1940*. Munich: Prestel, 1990.

Le Cirque: Estampes, livres illustrés, monotypes, dessins. Geneva: Galerie Gérald Cramer, 1972.

Marc Chagall. Exhibition catalogue. Paris: Réunion des Musées Nationaux, 1969.

Marc Chagall and the Jewish Theater. Exhibition catalogue. New York: Solomon R. Guggenheim Museum, 1992.

Marc Chagall: Oeuvres sur papier. Exhibition catalogue. Paris: Centre Pompidou, 1984.

Marc Chagall: Le Cirque – Paintings 1969–1980. Exhibition catalogue. New York: The Gallery, 1981.

Marc Chagall: Peintures récentes, 1967–1977. Paris: Musée du Louvre / Centre Pompidou, 1977.

Marc Chagall: 25 livres illustrés. Exhibition catalogue. Geneva: Galerie P. Cramer, 1982.

McMullen, Roy. *The World of Marc Chagall*. Garden City: Doubleday, 1968.

Meyer, Franz. *Marc Chagall: Leben und Werk*. Cologne: M. DuMont Schauberg, 1961.

Pertocoli, Domenico. *Marc Chagall: Il teatro dei sogni*. Milan: Mazzotta, 1999.

Rabinow, Rebecca A. "The Legacy of La Rue Férou: 'Livres d'Artiste' Created for Tériade by Rouault, Bonnard, Matisse, Léger, Le Corbusier, Chagall, Giacometti and Miro." Ph.D. diss., New York University, 1995.

Sorlier, Charles. *Les Céramiques et les sculptures de Chagall*. Monaco: A. Sauret, 1972.

———. *Marc Chagall et Ambroise Vollard*. Paris: Galerie Matignon, 1981.

Jean-Baptiste-Siméon Chardin

Conisbee, Philip. *Chardin*. Oxford: Phaidon, 1986.

Cros, Philippe. *Chardin*. Paris: Adam Biro, 1999.

Janson, Horst Woldemar. *Apes and Ape Lore in the Middle Ages and the Renaissance*. London: Warburg Institute / University of London, 1952.

Rosenberg, Pierre. *Chardin, 1699–1779*. Exhibition catalogue. Cleveland: Cleveland Museum of Art, 1979.

Rosenberg, Pierre, and Renaud Temperini. *Chardin*. Paris: Flammarion; Munich and New York: Prestel, 1999.

Rosenberg, Pierre, ed. *Chardin*. Exhibition catalogue. New Haven and London: Yale University Press, 2000.

Snoep-Reitsma, Ella. "Chardin and the Bourgeois Ideals of His Time." *Nederlands Kunsthistorisch Jaarboek*, no. 24 (1973), pp. 147–243. Also in *Verschuivende betekenissen*. The Hague: Deventer, 1975.

Gustave Courbet

Banville, Théodore de. "Échos de Paris." *Le Figaro*, 10 February 1856.

Courbet und Deutschland. Exhibition catalogue. Hamburg: Hamburger Kunsthalle, 1978.

Dessins, destins: Gustave Courbet, 1819–1877. Exhibition catalogue. Ornans: Musée Maison Natale Gustave Courbet, 1982.

Duret, Théodore. "Courbet graveur et illustrateur." *Gazette des Beaux-Arts* 39 (1908), pp. 421–432.

———. *Courbet*. Paris: Bernheim-Jeune et Cie, 1918.

Faunce, Sarah, and Linda Nochlin. *Courbet Reconsidered*. Exhibition catalogue. Brooklyn: Brooklyn Museum; New Haven and London: Yale University Press, 1988.

Gustave Courbet, 1819–1877. Exhibition catalogue. Paris: Réunion des Musées Nationaux, 1977.

Herding, Klaus. *Courbet: To Venture Independence*. New Haven and London: Yale University Press, 1991.

Nochlin, Linda. *Gustave Courbet: A Study of Style and Society*. New York: Garland, 1976.

Rubin, James Henry. *Courbet*. London: Phaidon, 1997.

John Steuart Curry

Dennis, James M. *Renegade Journalism: The Modern Independence of Grant Wood, Thomas Hart Benton and John Steuart Curry*. Madison: University of Wisconsin Press, 1998.

Jaffe, Irma B. "Religious Content in the Painting of John Steuart Curry." *Winterthur Portfolio* 22, no. 1 (Spring 1987), pp. 23–45.

John Steuart Curry. Exhibition catalogue. Lawrence: University of Kansas Museum of Art, 1970.

John Steuart Curry, 1897–1946: An Exhibition of Paintings and Drawings by the Noted Kansas Artist. Exhibition catalogue. Lawrence, 1957.

Junker, Patricia. "John Steuart Curry: Inventing the Middle West." *American Art Review* 10, no. 3 (May–June 1998), pp. 128–135.

Junker, Patricia, et al. *John Steuart Curry: Inventing the Middle West*. Exhibition catalogue. New York: Hudson Hills, 1998.

Kendall, M. Sue. *Rethinking Regionalism: John Steuart Curry and the Kansas Mural Controversy*. Washington, D.C.: Smithsonian Institution, 1986.

Schmeckebier, Laurence E. *John Steuart Curry's Pageant of America*. New York: American Artists Group, 1943.

Honoré Daumier

Blanton, Catherine W. "Unpublished Daumier Panel in the Fogg Art Museum: Scapin and Geronte." *The Burlington Magazine* 108, no. 763 (October 1966), pp. 511–518.

Borowitz, Helen Osterman. "Three Guitars: Reflections of Italian Comedy in Watteau, Daumier, and Picasso." *The Bulletin of the Cleveland Museum of Art* 71 (April 1984), pp. 116–129.

Bransten, E.H. "The Significance of the Clown in Paintings by Daumier, Picasso and Rouault." *Pacific Art Review* 3 (1944), pp. 21–39.

Cherpin, Jean. *Daumier et le théâtre*. Paris: Éditions de l'Arche, 1958.

Fohr, Robert. *Daumier: Sculpteur et peintre*. Paris: Adam Biro, 1999.

Fohr, Robert, ed. *Honoré Daumier, Georges Rouault*. Exhibition catalogue. Rome: Accademia di Francia a Roma; Milan: Electa, 1983.

Füglister, Robert L. "Der Gaukler und Akrobat als Alter Ego des Künstlers: Das Saltimbanque-Motiv bei Baudelaire, Banville und Daumier." *Neue Zürcher Zeitung* 15, no. 10 (1967).

Harper, Paula Hays. *Daumier's Clowns: Les Saltimbanques et les Parades, New Biographical and Political Functions for a Nineteenth-Century Myth*. New York: Garland, 1981.

Ives, Colta, Margret Stuffmann, and Martin Sonnabend. *Daumier Drawings*. Exhibition catalogue. New York: Metropolitan Museum of Art / Harry N. Abrams, 1992.

Laughton, Bruce. *Honoré Daumier*. New Haven and London: Yale University Press, 1996.

Lévêque, Jean-Jacques. *Honoré Daumier*. Paris: ACR, 1999.

Loyrette, Henri, Michael Pantazzi, et al. *Daumier, 1808–1879*. Exhibition catalogue. Ottawa: National Gallery of Canada, 1999.

Maison, K.E. "An Unrecorded Daumier Drawing." *Master Drawings* 9, no. 3 (1971), p. 264.

Rothe, Hans, ed. *Daumier und das Theater: 64 Tiefdruckreproduktionen nach Originallithographien, mit einer Einleitung und Bildtexten*. Leipzig, P. List, 1925.

Wechsler, Judith. *Daumier: Le Cabinet des dessins*. Paris: Flammarion, 1999.

Zugazagoitia, Julián, ed. *Daumier: Scènes de vie et vies de scène*. Exhibition catalogue. Milan: Electa, 1998.

Bruce Davidson

Bruce Davidson. Exhibition catalogue. Paris: Centre National de la Photographie, 1984.

Geldzahler, Henri. Introduction to *Bruce Davidson: Photographies*. Paris: Chêne, 1978.

Heinrich Maria Davringhausen

Eimert, Dorothea. *Heinrich Maria Davringhausen, 1894–1970: Monographie und Werkverzeichnis*. Cologne: Wienand, 1995.

Giorgio De Chirico

Baldacci, Paolo, and Wieland Schmied, ed. *Die andere Moderne: De Chirico, Savinio*. Exhibition catalogue. Ostfildern-Ruit: Hatje Cantz, 2001.

Bossaglia, Rossana, ed. *I De Chirico e i Savinio del Teatro alla Scala*. Milan: Edizione Amici della Scala, 1988.

Bucci, Moreno, and Chiara Bartoletti, ed. *Giorgio De Chirico e il teatro in Italia*. Exhibition catalogue. Florence: Cabinetto Disegni e Stampe degli Uffizi / Ente Aut. Teatro Communale, 1989.

De Chirico nel centenario della nascita. Exhibition catalogue. Venice: Museo Correr, 1988.

Fagiolo dell'Arco, Maurizio, et al. *De Chirico*. Paris: Chêne et Hachette, 1979.

Fagiolo dell'Arco, Maurizio, et al. *Giorgio De Chirico: Romantico e barocco – Gli anni quaranta e cinquanta*. Exhibition catalogue. Italy: Farsettiarte, 2001.

Fagiolo dell'Arco, Maurizio, and Ida Gianelli, ed. *Sipario / Staged Art: Balla, De Chirico, Savinio, Picasso, Paolini, Cucchi*. Exhibition catalogue. Milan: Charta, 1997.

Giorgio De Chirico, pictor optimus: Pittura, disegno, teatro. Exhibition catalogue. Rome: Carte Segrete, 1992.

Jewell, Keala Jane. *The Art of Enigma: The De Chirico Brothers and the Politics of Modernism*. Philadelphia: Pennsylvania State University Press, 2004.

Late De Chirico 1940–1975. Exhibition catalogue. Bristol: Galleria Arnolfini, 1985.

Lista, Giovanni. *De Chirico et l'avant-garde*. Paris: L'Âge d'Homme, 1983.

——. *De Chirico*. Paris: Hazan, 1991.

Marziali, Luca. "A proposito di De Chirico: Quella pittura che ha del Dio e dell'acrobata." *Critica d'arte* 59, no. 8 (October–December 1996), pp. 39–44.

Pillon, Giorgio. *De Chirico e il fascino di Rubens*. Rome: Seracangeli, 1991.

Roos, Gerd. *Giorgio De Chirico e Alberto Savinio: Ricordi e documenti*. Bologna: Bora, 1999.

Rubin, William, ed. *De Chirico*. New York: Museum of Modern Art, 1982.

Rubin, William, Wieland Schmied, and Jean Clair. *Giorgio De Chirico*. Exhibition catalogue. Paris: Centre Pompidou, 1983.

Sakraischik, Claudio Bruni, ed. *Giorgio De Chirico: Post-Metaphysical and Baroque Paintings, 1920–1970*. Exhibition catalogue. New York: Robert Miller Gallery, n.d.

Edgar Degas

Degas: Images of Women. Exhibition catalogue. London: Tate Gallery, 1989.

Loyrette, Henri. *Degas*. Paris: Fayard, 1991.

Pencenat, Corinne. "Miss Lala au cirque Fernando." *Beaux-Arts Magazine*, no. 55 (March 1988), p. 59.

Reff, Theodore. *Degas: The Artist's Mind*. London: Thames & Hudson; New York: Metropolitan Museum of Art, 1976. Cambridge, Mass.: Harvard University Press, 1987.

Roquebert, Anne. *Degas*. Paris: Cercle d'Art, 1988.

Thomson, Richard. *The Private Degas*. Exhibition catalogue. Manchester: Whitworth Art Gallery, 1987.

Fortunato Depero

Belli, Gabriella. *Fortunato Depero, futuriste: De Rome à Paris, 1915–1925*. Exhibition catalogue. Paris: Paris Musées, 1996.

Belli, Gabriella, ed. *Depero: Teatro magico*. Exhibition catalogue. Milan: Electa, 1989.

——, ed. *La casa del mago: Le arti applicate nell'opera di Fortunato Depero, 1920–1942*. Exhibition catalogue. Milan: Charta, 1992.

——, ed. *Depero après Depero*. Exhibition catalogue. Milan: Charta, 1993.

——, ed. *Depero: Dal Futurismo alla Casa d'Arte*. Exhibition catalogue. Milan: Electa, 1994.

Cremoncini, Roberta. *Fortunato Depero: Carnival of Colour*. Exhibition catalogue. Salford (Quays): Lowry, 2000.

Depero: Capri, il teatro. Exhibition catalogue. Naples: Electa, 1988.

Fagiolo dell'Arco, Maurizio, ed. *Depero*. Exhibition catalogue. Milan: Electa, 1988.

Passamani, Bruno, ed. *Depero e la scena, da "Colori" alla scena mobile, 1916–1930*. Turin: Martano, 1970.

——, ed. *Fortunato Depero*. Exhibition catalogue. Rovereto: Musei Civici, Galleria Museo Depero, 1981.

Scudiero, Maurizio. *Casa d'arte futurista Depero*. Rovereto: Il Castello, 1992.

——. *Il segno di Depero*. Exhibition catalogue. Rovereto: Il Castello, 1992.

——. *Depero: Stoffe futuriste*. Calliano: Manfrini-UCT, 1995.

——. *Fortunato Depero: Attraverso il futurismo – Opere 1913–1958*. Exhibition catalogue. Florence: Galleria Poggiali & Forconi, 1998.

Otto Dix

Barton, Brigid S. *Otto Dix and Die Neue Sachlichkeit, 1918–1925*. Ann Arbor: UMI Research Press, 1981.

Granof, Corinne D. "Otto Dix: Circus Imagery as Metaphor." Master's thesis, University of Wisconsin, 1986.

Hofchen, Heinz, Suse Pfäffle, and Adolf Smitmans. *Otto Dix, zum 100. Geburtstag: Zeichnungen, Pastelle, Aquarelle, Kartons, Druckgraphik, Glasfenster, aus eigenen Berstanden*. Exhibition catalogue. Albstadt: Galerie Albstadt, 1991.

Karcher, Eva. *Otto Dix*. New York: Crown, 1987.

Karsh, Florian, ed. *Otto Dix: Das Graphische Werk*. Hannover: Fackelträger-Verlag Schmidt-Küster, 1970.

Löffler, Fritz. *Otto Dix: Life and Work*. New York: Holmes and Meier, 1982.

McGreevy, Linda F. *The Life and Work of Otto Dix: German Critical Realist*. Ann Arbor: UMI Research Press, 1981.

Otto Dix: Eros and Death. Exhibition catalogue. New York: Lafayette Parke Gallery, 1987.

Otto Dix, 1891–1969. Exhibition catalogue. London: Tate Gallery, 1992.

Prat, Jean-Louis, ed. *Otto Dix: Metropolis*. Exhibition catalogue. Saint-Paul-de-Vence: Fondation Maeght, 1998.

Rüdiger, Ulrike. *Otto Dix: Gemälde, Zeichnungen, Druckgraphik*. Exhibition catalogue. Gera: Kunstsammlung Gera; Munich: Klinkhart & Biermann, 1997.

Kees Van Dongen

Diehl, Gaston. *Van Dongen*. Paris: Flammarion, 1968.

Hopmans, Anita. *Van Dongen retrouvé, l'oeuvre sur papier, 1895–1912*. Exhibition catalogue. Paris: Réunion des Musées Nationaux, 1997.

——. *The Van Dongen Nobody Knows: Early and Fauvist Drawings 1895–1912*. Exhibition catalogue. Rotterdam: Museum Boymans-van Beuningen, 1996.

Kees Van Dongen. Exhibition catalogue. Rotterdam: Museum Boymans-van Beuningen, 1989.

Marchesseau, Daniel, ed. *Van Dongen*. Exhibition catalogue. Martigny: Fondation Pierre Gianadda, 2001.

Van Dongen, le peintre: 1877–1968. Exhibition catalogue. Paris: Paris Musées, 1990.

Gustave Doré

Geyer, Marie-Jeanne, and Nadine Lehni. *Gustave Doré: Une Nouvelle Collection*. Exhibition catalogue. Strasbourg: Musée de la Ville de Strasbourg, 1993.

Gustave Doré, 1832–1883. Exhibition catalogue. Strasbourg: Musée d'Art Moderne, 1983.

401

Kaenel, Philippe. *Gustave Doré: Réaliste et visionnaire*. Exhibition catalogue. Geneva: Éditions du Tricorne; Bevaix: Galerie Arts Anciens, P.-Y. Gabus, 1985.

———. *Le Métier d'illustrateur, 1830–1880: Rodolphe Töpffer, J.-J. Grandville, Gustave Doré*. Paris: Messene, 1996.

Renonciat, Annie. *La Vie et l'oeuvre de Gustave Doré*. Paris: ACR / Bibliothèque des Arts, 1983.

Marcel Duchamp

Ades, Dawn. "Duchamp's Masquerades." In *The Portrait in Photography*, ed. Graham Clarke, pp. 94–114. London: Reaktion Books, 1992.

Clair, Jean. *Duchamp et la photographie: Essai d'analyse d'un primat technique sur le développement d'une oeuvre*. Paris: Chêne, 1977.

———. *Marcel Duchamp*. 4 vols. Paris: Centre Pompidou, 1977.

———. *Sur Marcel Duchamp et la fin de l'art*. Paris: Gallimard, 2000.

Damisch, Hubert. "La Défense Duchamp." In *Marcel Duchamp: Tradition de la rupture ou rupture de la tradition?* ed. Jean Clair, pp. 65–115. Paris: Union Générale d'Éditions, 1979.

D'Harnoncourt, Anne, and Kynaston McShine, ed. *Marcel Duchamp*. Exhibition catalogue. Philadelphia: Philadelphia Museum of Art, 1973.

Ehlers, Fiona. "Unter dem Zirkusdach wird die Kunst zum sinnlichen Erlebnis." *ART – Das Kunstmagazin*, no. 8 (August 1999), pp. 60–65.

Joselit, David. "Marcel Duchamp's Monte Carlo Bond Machine." *October* 59 (Winter 1992), pp. 7–26.

———. *Infinite Regress: Marcel Duchamp, 1910–1941*. Cambridge, Mass.: MIT Press, 1998.

Judovitz, Dalia. *Unpacking Duchamp: Art in Transit*. Berkeley: University of California Press, 1995.

Kuenzli, Rudolf, and Francis M. Naumann, ed. *Marcel Duchamp: Artist of the Century*. Cambridge, Mass.: MIT Press, 1989.

Naumann, Francis M. *Marcel Duchamp: The Art of Making Art in the Age of the Mechanical Reproduction*. Gand: Ludion; New York: Harry N. Abrams, 1999.

Joseph Ducreux

Armingeat, Jacqueline. "Ducreux et la grimace." *Gazette des Beaux-Arts*, May 1960, pp. 357–359.

Dorbec, Prosper. "Joseph Ducreux (1735–1802)." *Gazette des Beaux-Arts* 36 (1906), pp. 199–216.

Lyon, Georgette. *Joseph Ducreux (1735–1802), premier peintre de Marie-Antoinette: Sa Vie, son oeuvre*. Paris: La Nef de Paris, 1958.

Harold Edgerton

Edgerton, Harold, and James R. Killian, Jr. *Moments of Vision: The Stroboscopic Revolution in Photography*. Cambridge, Mass.: MIT Press, 1979.

Jussim, Estelle. *Stopping Time: The Photographs of Harold Edgerton*. New York: Harry N. Abrams, 1987.

James Ensor

Berman, Patricia G. *James Ensor: Christ's Entry into Brussels in 1889*. Los Angeles: J. Paul Getty Museum, 2002.

Brown, Carol, ed. *James Ensor, 1860–1949: Theater of Masks*. Exhibition catalogue. London: Barbican Art Gallery, 1997.

Delahousse, Anne. *Les Masques singuliers de James Ensor*. Brussels: Musées Royaux des Beaux-Arts de Belgique, 1999.

De Maeyer, Marcel. "Derrière le Masque: L'Introduction du masque, du travesti et du squelette comme motifs dans l'oeuvre de James Ensor." *L'Art Belge* (special Ensor issue), December 1965, pp. 17–30.

Draguet, Michel. *James Ensor ou la fantasmagorie*. Paris: Gallimard, 1999.

James Ensor, Visionär der Moderne: Gemälde, Zeichnungen und das druckgraphische Werk aus der Sammlung Gerard Loobuyck. Exhibition catalogue. Albstadt: Galerie Albstadt, 1999.

Lesko, Diane. *James Ensor: The Creative Years*. Princeton: Princeton University Press, 1985.

Morrisey, Leslie Dixon. "James Ensor's Self-Portraits." *Arts Magazine* 54 (1979), pp. 90–95.

Ollinger-Zinque, Gisèle. *Ensor par lui-même*. Brussels: Laconti, 1976.

Ollinger-Zinque, Gisèle, ed. *Ensor*. Exhibition catalogue. Tournai: La Renaissance du livre, 1999.

Triaca-Fabrizi, Fabrizia. "Una verita tragica: Le maschere di Ensor." *Grafica d'arte* 8, no. 32 (October–December 1997), pp. 12–15.

Tricot, Xavier. "Métaphores et métamorphoses de James Ensor." *Artstudio*, no. 18 (1990), pp. 46–59.

———. *Ensoriana*. Antwerp: Pandora, 1994.

Waldegg, Joachim Heusinger von. *James Ensor: Legende vom Ich*. Cologne: DuMont, 1999.

T. Lux Feininger

Büche, Wolfgang, ed. *T. Lux Feininger: Von Dessau nach Amerika – Der Weg eines Bauhäuslers*. Exhibition catalogue. Halle: Staatliche Galerie Moritzburg, 1998.

Fiedler, Jeannine, ed. *Photography at the Bauhaus*. Cambridge, Mass.: MIT Press, 1990.

Prakapas, Eugene. *T. Lux Feininger: Photographs of the Twenties and Thirties*. Exhibition catalogue. New York: Prakapas Gallery, 1980.

Rödiger-Diruf, Erika, Ursula Merkel, and Sylvia Bieber. *Feininger, eine Künstlerfamilie*. Exhibition catalogue. Ostfildern-Ruit: Hatje Cantz, 2001.

Scimé, Giuliana, ed. *Bauhaus e razionalismo nelle fotografie di Lux Feininger, Franco Grignani, Xanti Schawinsky, Luigi Veronesi*. Exhibition catalogue. Milan: Mazotta, 1993.

Lucian Freud

Benjamin, Andrew. "Betraying Faces: Lucian Freud's Self-Portraits." In *Art, Mimesis and the Avant-Garde: Aspects of a Philosophy of Difference*, pp. 61–74. London: Routledge, 1991.

Bernard, Bruce, and Derek Birdsall, ed. *Lucian Freud*. London: Jonathan Cape, 1996.

Feaver, William, and Frank Auerbach. *Lucian Freud*. Exhibition catalogue. London: Tate Gallery, 2002.

Gowing, Lawrence. *Lucian Freud*. London: Thames & Hudson, 1982.

Lampert, Catherine. *Lucian Freud: Recent Work*. New York: Rizzoli, 1993.

Lauter, Rolf, ed. *Lucian Freud: Naked Portraits – Werke der 40er bis 90er Jahre / Works from the 1940s to the 1990s*. Exhibition catalogue. Frankfurt am Main: Museum für Moderne Kunst; Ostfildern-Ruit: Hatje Cantz, 2001.

Lucian Freud: Recent Works 1997–2000. New York: Acquavella Contemporary Art, 2000.

Mellor, David Alan. *Interpreting Lucian Freud*. London: Tate Gallery, 2002.

Richardson, John. "Lucian Freud and His Models." In *Sacred Monsters, Sacred Masters: Beaton, Capote, Dalí, Picasso, Freud, Warhol, and More*, pp. 322–341. London: Jonathan Cape, 2001.

Henry Fuseli

Antal, Frederick. *Fuseli Studies*. London: Routledge & Paul, 1956.

Hofmann, Werner, ed. *Johann Heinrich Füssli, 1741–1825*. Exhibition catalogue. Hamburg: Hamburger Kunsthalle; Munich: Prestel, 1974.

Johann Heinrich Füssli, 1741–1825. Exhibition catalogue. Paris: Association Française d'Action Artistique, 1975.

Johann Heinrich Füssli, 1741–1825: Gemälde und Zeichnungen. Exhibition catalogue. Zürich: Kunsthaus, 1969.

Klemm, Christian. *Johann Heinrich Füssli: Zeichnungen*. Exhibition catalogue. Zürich: Kunsthaus, 1986.

Schiff, Gert. *Johann Heinrich Füssli, 1741–1825*. 2 vols. Zürich: Verlag Berichthaus, 1973.

Vitali, Lamberto, ed. *Johann Heinrich Füssli: Disegni e Dipinti*. Exhibition catalogue. Milan: Electa, 1977.

Weinglass, David H. *Henry Fuseli and the Engraver's Art*. Exhibition catalogue. Kansas City: University of Missouri / Kansas City Library, 1982.

Francisco Goya

Arnaiz, José Manuel. *Francisco de Goya: Cartones y tapices*. Madrid: Espasa Calpe, 1987.

Baticle, Jeannine. *Goya*. Paris: Fayard, 1992.

Chan, Victor. "Goya's Tapestry Cartoon of the Straw Manikin: A Life of Games and a Game of Life." *Arts Magazine* 60, no. 2 (1985), pp. 50–58.

Crombie, Theodore. "Goya and the Stage." *Apollo* 98, no. 137 (July 1973), pp. 22–27.

Gassier, Pierre. *Les Dessins de Goya: Les Albums*. 2 vols. Fribourg: Office du Livre, 1973.

——. *Goya: Témoin de son temps*. Fribourg: Office du Livre, 1983.

Gassier, Pierre, and Juliet Wilson. *Vie et oeuvre de Francisco Goya*. Fribourg: Office du Livre, 1970.

Held, Jutta. *Die Genrebilder der Madrider Teppichmanufaktur und die Anfänge Goyas*. Berlin: Mann-Verlag, 1971.

——. "Between Bourgeois Enlightenment and Popular Culture: Goya's Festivals, Old Women, Monsters and Blind Men." *History Workshop Journal* 23 (1987), pp. 39–58.

——. "Los cartones para tapices." In *Goya: Obras maestras del Museo del Prado*. Madrid: Museo del Prado, 2001.

Held, Jutta, ed. *Goya, Neue Forschungen: Das internationale Symposium in 1991 Osnabrück*. Berlin: Mann-Verlag, 1994.

Herrero, Concha, José Luis Sancho, and Juan Martinez Cuesta. *Tapices y cartones de Goya*. Exhibition catalogue. Madrid: Palacio Real; Barcelona: Lunwerg Editores, 1996.

Kornmeier, Barbara. *Goya und die populäre Bilderwelt*. Frankfurt am Main: Vervuert, 1999.

Lorenzo de Márquez, Teresa. "Carnival Traditions in Goya's Iconic Language." In *Goya and the Spirit of Enlightenment*, ed. Alfonso E. Pérez Sánchez and Eleanor A. Sayre, pp. xxxv–xciv. Boston: Museum of Fine Arts, 1989.

Luna, Juan J. *Goya: 250 aniversario*. Exhibition catalogue. Madrid: Museo del Prado, 1996.

Malbert, Roger. *Goya: The Disparates*. Exhibition catalogue. London: Hayward Gallery / South Bank Centre, 1997.

Permanencia de la memoria: Cartones para tapiz y dibujos de Goya. Exhibition catalogue. Saragossa: Museo de Zaragoza, 1997.

Stoichita, Victor I., and Anna Maria Coderch. *Goya: The Last Carnival*. London: Reaktion Books, 1999.

Tomlinson, Janis A. *Francisco Goya: The Tapestry Cartoons and Early Career at the Court of Madrid*. Cambridge: Cambridge University Press, 1989.

——. *Francisco Goya y Lucientes 1746–1828*. London: Phaidon, 1994.

——. "Nouveau Regard sur les cartons de tapisserie." In *Goya: Un Regard libre*, ed. Arnaud Brejon de Lavergnée, pp. 60–66. Paris: Réunion des Musées Nationaux, 1999.

——. *Goya: Images of Women*. Exhibition catalogue. Washington, D.C.: National Gallery of Art; New Haven and London: Yale University Press, 2002.

Wilson-Bareau, Juliet, and Tom Lubbock. *Goya: Drawings from His Private Albums*. Exhibition catalogue. London: Hayward Gallery / Lund Humphries, 2001.

Wilson-Bareau, Juliet, and Manuela B. Mena Marqués, ed. *Goya: Truth and Fantasy – The Small Paintings*. Exhibition catalogue. New Haven and London: Yale University Press, 1994.

Philip Guston

Ashton, Dore. *Yes, but ...: A Critical Study of Philip Guston*. New York: Viking, 1976.

Auping, Michael, ed. *Philip Guston Retrospective*. Fort Worth: Modern Art Museum of Fort Worth; London: Thames & Hudson, 2003.

Balken, Debra Bricker. *Philip Guston's Poor Richard*. Chicago: University of Chicago Press, 2001.

Corbett, William. *Philip Guston's Late Work: A Memoir*. Cambridge, Mass.: Zoland Books, 1994.

Dabrowski, Magdalena. *The Drawings of Philip Guston*. Exhibition catalogue. New York: Museum of Modern Art, 1988.

Feld, Ross. *Guston in Time: Remembering Philip Guston*. New York: Counterpoint, 2003.

Ottinger, Didier. *La Trahison de Philip Guston*. Paris: Échoppe, 2000.

Ottinger, Didier, ed. *Philip Guston: Peintures 1947–1979*. Exhibition catalogue. Paris: Centre Pompidou, 2000.

Schreier, Christoph, ed. *Philip Guston: Gemälde 1947–1979*. Exhibition catalogue. Bonn: Kunstmuseum; Ostfildern-Ruit: Hatje Cantz, 1999.

Storr, Robert. *Philip Guston*. New York: Abbeville, 1986.

Weber, Joanna, and Harry Cooper. *Philip Guston: A New Alphabet, the Late Transition*. Exhibition catalogue. New Haven: Yale University Art Gallery, 2000.

John Gutmann

Humphrey, John. *As I Saw It: Photographs by John Gutmann*. Exhibition catalogue. San Francisco: San Francisco Museum of Modern Art, 1976.

John Gutmann, 1934–1939. Exhibition catalogue. Valencia: Generalitat Valenciana, 1985.

John Gutmann: A Selection of Unpublished Images. Exhibition catalogue. San Francisco: Zuzzyva, 1987.

John Gutmann: 99 Photografias, America 1934–1954. Exhibition catalogue. Barcelona: Fundacio Caixas de Pensions, 1989.

John Gutmann: Beyond the Document. Exhibition catalogue. San Francisco: San Francisco Museum of Modern Art, 1989.

Phillips, Sandra, et al. *The Photography of John Gutmann: Culture Shock*. Exhibition catalogue. Stanford: Iris and B. Gerald Cantor Center for Visual Arts at Stanford University; London: Merrell Holberton, 2000.

Sutnik, Maia-Mari, and Michael Mitchell. *Gutmann*. Exhibition catalogue. Toronto: Art Gallery of Ontario, 1985.

Thomas, Lew, ed. *The Restless Decade: John Gutmann's Photographs of the Thirties*. New York: Harry N. Abrams, 1984.

403

Edward Hopper

Bonnefoy, Françoise. *Edward Hopper*. Exhibition catalogue. Marseilles: Musée Cantini; Paris: Adam Biro, 1989.

Edward Hopper. Exhibition catalogue. Brussels: Société des Expositions du Palais des Beaux-Arts, 1992.

Goodrich, Lloyd. *Edward Hopper*. New York: Harry N. Abrams, 1971.

———. *Edward Hopper: An Intimate Biography*. New York: Knopf, 1995.

Levin, Gail. *Edward Hopper: The Art and the Artist*. Exhibition catalogue. New York: W.W. Norton & Co., 1980.

Izis

Clébert, Jean-Paul. Introduction to *Izis*. Paris: Centre National de la Photographie / Paris Audiovisuel, 1994.

Prévert, Jacques. *Le Cirque d'Izis (avec quatre compositions originales de Marc Chagall)*. Monte Carlo: A. Sauret, 1965.

Rétrospective Izis. Exhibition catalogue. Paris: Caisse Nationale des Monuments Historiques et des Sites / Paris Musées, 1988.

Edward J. Kelty

Barth, Mile, and Alan Siegel. *Step Right This Way: The Photographs of Edward J. Kelty*. New York: Barnes & Noble / Michael Friedman Publishing Group, 2002.

Paul Klee

Allmen, Pierre von, and Félix Klee. *Paul Klee, marionnettes, sculptures, reliefs, masques, théâtre*. Exhibition catalogue. Neuchâtel: Galerie Suisse de Paris, 1979.

Franciscono, Marcel. *Paul Klee: His Work and Thought*. Chicago: University of Chicago Press, 1991.

Kersten, Wolfgang. *Paul Klee Übermut: Allegorie der künstlerischen Existenz*. Frankfurt am Main: Fischer, 1990.

Kort, Pamela, ed. *Paul Klee: In der Maske des Mythos*. Exhibition catalogue. Cologne: DuMont, 1999.

Matuschka, Georg Graf von. *Annäherungen an Paul Klee, 20 Bildinterpretationen*. Nuremberg: Kunstpädagogisches Zentrum im Germanischen Nationalmuseum, 1987.

McCullagh, Janice. "The Tightrope Walker: An Expressionist Image." *The Art Bulletin* 66, no. 4 (December 1984), pp. 633–644.

Plant, Margaret. *Paul Klee: Figures and Faces*. London: Thames & Hudson, 1978.

Rosenthal, Mark. "Paul Klee's 'Tightrope Walker': An Exercise in Balance." *Arts Magazine* 53, no. 1 (1978), pp. 106–111.

Wedekind, Gregor. *Paul Klee: Inventionen*. Berlin: Reimer, 1996.

Zweite, Armin. *Paul Klee: Zauber Theater*. Munich: Piper, 1979.

Dame Laura Knight

Dunbar, Janet. *Dame Laura Knight*. London: Collins, 1975.

Fox, Caroline. *Dame Laura Knight*. Oxford: Phaidon, 1988.

Grimes, Theresa. *Five Women Painters*. Oxford: Lennard, 1989.

Salaman, Malcolm C. *Modern Masters of Etching: Laura Knight, D.B.E., A.R.A.* London: The Studio, 1932.

Pyke Koch

Blotkamp, Carel. *Pyke Koch*. Amsterdam: De Arbeiderspers, 1972.

Blotkamp, Carel, and Annelys Meijer. *Pyke Koch*. Exhibition catalogue. Paris: Institut Néerlandais, 1982.

Blotkamp, Carel, et al. *Pyke Koch: Schilderijen en Tekeningen / Paintings and Drawings*. Exhibition catalogue. Rotterdam: Museum Boymans-van Beuningen, 1995.

Eitner, Lorenz. *Paintings of Pyke Koch*. Exhibition catalogue. Minneapolis: Walker Art Center, 1960.

Pyke Koch: Réalisme magique aux Pays-Bas. Exhibition catalogue. Lausanne: Musée des Beaux-Arts, 1995.

Walt Kuhn

Adams, Philip Rhys. *Walt Kuhn, Painter: His Life and Work*. Columbus: Ohio State University Press, 1978.

Frost, Rosamund. "Kuhn under the Big Top." *Art News* 40 (December 1941), p. 13.

———. "Walt Kuhn Clowns in a Great Tradition." *Art News* 42 (May 1943), p. 11.

Getlein, Frank. Introduction to *Walt Kuhn*. Exhibition catalogue. New York: Kennedy Galleries, 1967.

Perlman, Bernard B. *Walt Kuhn 1877–1949*. Exhibition catalogue. New York: Midtown Galleries, 1989.

Spies, Kathleen Mary. "Burlesque Queens and Circus Divas: Images of the Female Grotesque in the Art of Reginald Marsh and Walt Kuhn, 1915–1945." Ph.D. diss., Indiana University, 1999.

Walt Kuhn (1877–1949). Exhibition catalogue. Portland: Barridoff Galleries, 1984.

František Kupka

Rowell, Margit. *František Kupka 1871–1957: A Retrospective*. Exhibition catalogue. New York: Solomon R. Guggenheim Foundation, 1975.

Salé, Marie-Pierre, Markéta Theinhardt, and Pierre Brüllé, ed. *Vers des temps nouveaux: Kupka, oeuvres graphiques, 1894–1912*. Exhibition catalogue. Paris: Réunion des Musées Nationaux, 2002.

Arnaud Labelle-Rojoux

Jouannais, Jean-Yves. "Arnaud Labelle-Rojoux: L'Ésotérisme troupier." *Art Press*, no. 231 (January 1998), pp. 37–41.

Labelle-Rojoux, Arnaud, and Olivier Blanckart. "Un Rêve de fiasco." *Art Press*, no. 20, special issue (September 1999), pp. 143–144.

Gaston Lachaise

Gaston Lachaise 1882–1935: Sculptures and Drawings. Exhibition catalogue. Los Angeles: Los Angeles County Museum of Art, 1974.

Gaston Lachaise: Sculpture and Drawings. Exhibition catalogue. Rochester: Memorial Art Gallery of the University of Rochester, 1979.

Kramer, Hilton, et al. *The Sculptures of Gaston Lachaise*. New York: Eakins, 1967.

Nordland, Gerald. *Gaston Lachaise: The Man and His Work*. New York: George Braziller, 1974.

Rétrospective Gaston Lachaise (1882–1935). Exhibition catalogue. Paris: Gallimard, 2003.

Sims, Patterson. *Gaston Lachaise: A Concentration of Works from the Permanent Collection of the Whitney Museum of American Art*. Exhibition catalogue. New York: Whitney Museum of American Art, 1980.

Fernand Léger

Bauquier, Georges. *Fernand Léger: Vivre dans le vrai*. Paris: Adrien Maeght, 1987.

Peter de Francia. *Peter de Francia on Léger's "The Great Parade."* London: Cassell and Co., 1969.

——. *Fernand Léger*. New Haven and London: Yale University Press, 1983.

Fell, H.G. "Pictures of Circus Life at the Léger Galleries." *Connoisseur* 99 (January 1937), p. 45.

Fernand Léger: Recent Paintings & Le Cirque. New York: Buchholz Gallery, 1950.

Fernand Léger, oeuvres récentes 1953–1954. Exhibition catalogue. Paris: Maison de la Pensée Française, 1954.

Fernand Léger. Exhibition catalogue. Paris: Réunion des Musées Nationaux, 1971.

Füglister, Robert L. *Fernand Léger: "Akrobaten im Zirkus."* Exhibition catalogue. Basel: Öffentliche Kunstsammlung Basel, 1964–1966.

Lanchner, Carolyn, ed. *Fernand Léger*. Exhibition catalogue. New York: Museum of Modern Art / Harry N. Abrams, 1998.

Léger, Fernand. "Le Cirque" (1949). In *Fonctions de la peinture*, pp. 263–276. Paris: Gallimard, 1997.

Monod-Fontaine, Isabelle, and Claude Laugier, ed. *Fernand Léger*. Exhibition catalogue. Paris: Centre Pompidou, 1997.

Rabinow, Rebecca A. "The Legacy of La Rue Férou: 'Livres d'Artiste' Created for Tériade by Rouault, Bonnard, Matisse, Léger, Le Corbusier, Chagall, Giacometti and Miro." Ph.D. diss., New York University, 1995.

——. "*Cirque*: A Fernand Léger and Henry Miller Story." *The Print Collector's Newsletter* 26, no. 6 (January–February 1996), pp. 209–212.

Serota, Nicolas, ed. *Fernand Léger: The Later Years*. Exhibition catalogue. London: Whitechapel Art Gallery; Munich: Prestel, 1987.

Leon Levinstein

Shamis, Bob. *The Moment of Exposure*. Exhibition catalogue. Ottawa: National Gallery of Canada, 1995.

Stourdzé, Sam, Helen Gee, and A.D. Coleman. *Leon Levinstein: Obsession*. Exhibition catalogue. Paris: L. Scheer, 2000.

Jean-Étienne Liotard

Bull, Duncan, with the assistance of Tomas Macsotay Bunt. *Jean-Étienne Liotard (1702-1789)*. Amsterdam: Rijksmuseum; Zwolle: Uitgeverij Waanders, 2002.

Herdt, Anne de. *Dessins de Liotard, suivi du catalogue de l'oeuvre dessiné*. Exhibition catalogue. Geneva: Musée d'Art et d'Histoire; Paris: Réunion des Musées Nationaux, 1992.

Holleczek, Andreas. *Jean-Étienne Liotard: Erkenntnisvermögen und Künstlerischer Anspruch*. Frankfurt am Main / New York: P. Lang, 2001.

Jean-Étienne Liotard, 1702-1789: Dans les Collections du Musée d'Art et d'Histoire de Genève. Exhibition catalogue. Geneva: Musée d'Art et d'Histoire; Paris: Somogy, 2002.

Loche, Renée. *Jean-Étienne Liotard, 1702-1789*. Exhibition catalogue. Zürich: Kunsthaus; Geneva: Musée d'Art et d'Histoire, 1978.

Reichler, Claude. "Liotard avec variations: Les Autoportraits de Jean-Étienne Liotard." *Genava* 26 (1978), pp. 221–228.

Traz, Georges de. *La Vie, les voyages et les oeuvres de Jean-Étienne Liotard*. Lausanne: Bibliothèque des Arts, 1956.

Trivias, Numa S. "Les Portraits de J.-É. Liotard par lui-même." *Revue de l'Art Ancien et Moderne* 70, no. 374 (November 1936), pp. 153–162.

Albert Londe

Albert Londe. Exhibition catalogue. Paris: Mission du Patrimoine Photographique, 1999.

Albert Londe: La Photographie moderne. Exhibition catalogue. Paris: Cripto, 1986.

Bernard, Denis, and André Gunthert. *L'Instant rêvé: Albert Londe*. Nîmes: J. Chambon; Laval: Trois, 1993.

Gunthert, André. "La Conquête de l'instantané: Archéologie de l'imaginaire photographique en France (1841–1895)." Ph.D. diss., École des Hautes Études en Sciences Sociales, Paris, 1999.

Gunthert, André. Introduction to *Albert Londe*. Paris: Nathan, 1999.

Gunthert, André, and Yan Ciret. "La Piste de la Salpêtrière, Albert Londe." *Art Press*, no. 20, special issue (September 1999), pp. 164–165.

George Luks

City Life Illustrated, 1890–1940: Sloan, Glackens, Luks, Shinn, Their Friends and Followers. Exhibition catalogue. Wilmington: Delaware Art Museum, 1980.

George Luks. Exhibition catalogue. New York: Bernard Danenberg Galleries, 1967.

George Luks, 1866–1933: An Exhibition of Paintings and Drawings Dating from 1889 to 1931. Exhibition catalogue. Utica: Munson-William-Proctor Institute, Museum of Art, 1973.

George Luks: Expressionist Master of Color – The Watercolors Rediscovered. Exhibition catalogue. Canton, Ohio: Canton Museum of Art, 1994.

Kasanof, Nina. "The Illustrations of Everett Shinn and George Luks." Ph.D. diss., University of Illinois, Urbana-Champaign, 1992.

O'Toole, Judith H., ed. *George Luks: An American Artist*. Exhibition catalogue. Wilkes-Barre: Sordoni Art Gallery, 1987.

Paul McCarthy

Cameron, Dan, et al. *Paul McCarthy*. Exhibition catalogue. Los Angeles: Museum of Contemporary Art; Ostfildern-Ruit: Hatje Cantz, 2000.

Meyer-Hermann, Eva, ed. *Paul McCarthy: Dimensions of the Mind*. Cologne: Oktagon, 2001.

Monk, Philip, et al. *Mike Kelley and Paul McCarthy: Collaborative Works*. Exhibition catalogue. Toronto: Power Plant Contemporary Art Gallery, 2000.

Paul McCarthy. Exhibition catalogue. Liverpool: Tate Gallery Liverpool, 2001.

Paul McCarthy – Mike Kelley: Videos 1970–1998. Exhibition catalogue. Munich: Kunstbunker Tumulka, 1999.

Paul McCarthy: Pinocchio. Exhibition catalogue. Paris: Réunion des Musées Nationaux, 2002.

Rugoff, Ralph, Kristine Stiles, and Giacinto Di Pietrantonio. *Paul McCarthy*. New York: Phaidon, 1996.

Schwerfel, Heinz Peter. "Der Clown spiegelt meine Verfassung wider." *Art* 12 (December 1997), pp. 54–57.

Wurtinger, Werner. *Paul McCarthy – Mike Kelley: Sod and Sodie Sock*. Exhibition catalogue. Vienna: Vereinigung Bildender Kunstler, 1999.

Reginald Marsh

Aspects of New York: A Summer Exhibition and Sale of Works by Reginald Marsh. Exhibition catalogue. New York: Bernard Danenberg Galleries, 1969.

Cohen, Marilyn. *Reginald Marsh's New York*. Exhibition catalogue. New York: Whitney Museum of American Art / Dover, 1983.

——. "Reginald Marsh: An Interpretation of His Art." Ph.D. diss., New York University, 1987.

405

East Side – West Side: All Around the Town: A Retrospective Exhibition of Paintings, Watercolors and Drawings by Reginald Marsh. Exhibition catalogue. Tucson: University of Arizona Museum of Art, 1969.

Garver, Thomas H. *Reginald Marsh: A Retrospective Exhibition*. Exhibition catalogue. Newport Beach: Newport Harbor Art Museum, 1972.

Goodrich, Lloyd. "Reginald Marsh, Painter of New York in Its Wildest Profusion." *American Artist* 19 (September 1955), pp. 18–23, 61–63.

———. *Reginald Marsh*. New York: Harry N. Abrams, 1972.

Kerr, Walter. "The Theatre World Drawings of Reginald Marsh." *Bulletin, William Benton Museum of Art* 1, no. 2 (1973), pp. 4–10.

Miller, Michele Lynne. "The Charms of Exposed Flesh: Reginald Marsh and the Burlesque Theater." Ph.D. diss., University of Pennsylvania, 1997.

Photographs of New York by Reginald Marsh. Washington, D.C.: Middendorf Gallery, 1977.

Spies, Kathleen. "Burlesque Queens and Circus Divas: Images of the Female Grotesque in the Art of Reginald Marsh and Walt Kuhn, 1915–1945." Ph.D. diss., Indiana University, 1999.

Franz Xaver Messerschmidt

Behr, Hans-Georg, Herbert Grohmann, and Bernd-Olaf Hagedorn. *Charakterköpfe – Der Fall F.X. Messerschmidt: Wie verrückt darf Kunst sein?* Basel, 1983.

Bükling, M. "Wien: Der Bildhauer F.X. Messerschmidt – Ein exemplarisches Künstleroeuvre der Umbruchzeit." In *Mehr Licht: Europa um 1770 – Die bildende Kunst der Aufklärung*, p. 101ff. Exhibition catalogue. Munich: Klinkhardt & Biermann, 1999.

Glandien, Otto. *Franz Xaver Messerschmidt (1736–1783): Ausdrucksstudien und Charakterköpfe*. Cologne: Forschungsstelle des Instituts für Geschichte der Medizin der Universität zu Köln, 1981.

Keleti, M. *František Xaver Messerschmidt*. Exhibition catalogue. Bratislava: Slovenka Narodna Galéria, 1983.

Keleti, M., and L. Thevenon, ed. *La Galerie nationale slovaque de Bratislava expose à Nice F.X. Messerschmidt "Têtes de caractères."* Nice: Musée d'Art et d'Histoire, Palais Massena, 1993.

Krapf, Michael, ed. *Franz Xaver Messerschmidt, 1736–1783*. Exhibition catalogue. Ostfilder-Ruit: Hatje Cantz, 2003.

Pölzl-Malikova, Maria. *Franz Xaver Messerschmidt*. Vienna and Munich, 1982.

Skreiner, W. "F.X. Messerschmidt – Charakterköpfe: Einige Gedanken zu ihrer Interpretationsmöglichkeit." In *Körpersprache / Bodylanguage*, ed. H.G. Haberl. Exhibition catalogue. Graz, 1973.

Lisette Model

Abbott, Berenice. *Lisette Model: An Aperture Monograph*. New York: Aperture, 1979.

Abbott, Berenice. Introduction to *Lisette Model Portfolio*. Exhibition catalogue. Washington, D.C.: Lunn Gallery / Graphics International, 1976.

Cohen, Alan, and David Vestal. *Lisette Model: Retrospectiva, 1937–1970*. Exhibition catalogue. Madrid, 1987.

Faber, Monika, et al. *Lisette Model: Fotografien, 1934–1960*. Exhibition catalogue. Vienna: Kunsthalle Wien, 2000.

"Lisette Model." *Camera*, no. 12, special issue (December 1977).

Lisette Model: A Retrospective. Exhibition catalogue. New Orleans: New Orleans Museum of Art, 1981.

Stourdzé, Sam, ed. *Lisette Model*. Paris: Baudoin-Lebon / L. Scheer, 2002.

Sussman, Elisabeth. *Lisette Model*. London and New York: Phaidon, 2001.

Thomas, Ann. *Lisette Model*. Ottawa: National Gallery of Canada, 1990.

Thomas, Ann, and Reinhold Misselbeck. *Lisette Model*. Exhibition catalogue. Cologne: Museum Ludwig, 1990.

Nadar (Félix Tournachon) and Adrien Tournachon

Baldwin, Gordon, and Judith Keller. *Nadar-Warhol, Paris-New York: Photography and Fame*. Exhibition catalogue. Los Angeles: J. Paul Getty Museum, 1999.

Gosling, Nigel. *Nadar*. London: Secker & Warburg, 1976.

Greaves, Roger. *Nadar ou le paradoxe vital*. Paris: Flammarion, 1980.

Hambourg, Maria Morris. "Nadar (Félix Tournachon) and Adrien Tournachon: Pierrot Laughing (Charles Deburau)." *Metropolitan Museum of Art Bulletin* 56, no. 2 (Fall 1998), p. 45.

Hambourg, Maria Morris, Françoise Heilbrun, Philippe Néagu, et al. *Nadar*. New York: Metropolitan Museum of Art / Harry N. Abrams, 1995.

Hamon, Philippe. "Pierrot photographe." *Romantisme*, no. 105 (1999), pp. 35–43.

Jammes, André. "Duchenne de Boulogne: La Grimace provoquée et Nadar." *Gazette des Beaux-Arts*, no. 92 (December 1978), pp. 215–220.

———. *Nadar*. Paris: Centre National de la Photographie, 1983.

Rubin, James Henry. *Nadar*. London and New York: Phaidon, 2001.

Bruce Nauman

Adriani, Götz, ed. *Bruce Nauman*. Exhibition catalogue. Ostfildern-Ruit: Hatje Cantz, 1999.

Assche, Christine van, ed. *Bruce Nauman: Image–texte, 1966–1996*. Exhibition catalogue. Paris: Centre Pompidou, 1997.

Bismarck, Beatrice von. *Bruce Nauman, der wahre Kunstler*. Ostfildern-Ruit: Hatje Cantz, 1998.

Brundage, Susan, ed. *Bruce Nauman, 25 Years*. New York: Rizzoli / St. Martin's, 1994.

Chapuis, Yvane. "To Be Clown: Figures de clown dans l'oeuvre de Bruce Nauman." *Art Press*, no. 20, special issue (September 1999), pp. 152–153.

Chiong, Kathryn. "Nauman's Beckett Walk." *October*, no. 86 (Fall 1998), pp. 63–81.

Criqui, Jean-Pierre. "Pour un Nauman." *Les Cahiers du Musée National d'Art Moderne* 62 (Winter 1997), pp. 4–25.

Eble, Bruno. *Le Miroir sans reflet: Considérations autour de l'oeuvre de Bruce Nauman*. Paris: L'Harmattan, 2001.

Folie, Sabine, and Michael Gasmeier. *Samuel Beckett, Bruce Nauman*. Exhibition catalogue. Vienna: Kunsthalle, 2000.

Kraynak, Janet. *Pay Attention Please: Bruce Nauman's Words, Writings and Interviews*. Cambridge, Mass.: MIT Press, 2003.

Livingston, Jane, and Marcia Tucker. *Bruce Nauman: Works from 1965–1972*. Exhibition catalogue. Los Angeles: Los Angeles County Museum of Art, 1972.

Morgan, Robert C., ed. *Bruce Nauman*. Baltimore: Johns Hopkins University Press, 2002.

Oxenaar, Rudolf, and Katharina Schmidt, ed. *Bruce Nauman, 1972–1981*. Exhibition catalogue. Otterlo: Rijksmuseum Kröller-Müller; Baden-Baden: Staatliche Kunsthalle, 1981.

Richardson, Brenda. *Bruce Nauman: Neons*. Exhibition catalogue. Baltimore: Baltimore Museum of Art, 1982.

Rondeau, James E. "*Clown Torture*, 1987." *Museum Studies* 25, no. 1 (1999), pp. 62–63.

Schaffner, Ingrid, and Jill Snyder. *Bruce Nauman, 1985–1996: Drawings, Prints, and Related Works*. Exhibition catalogue. Ridgefield: Aldrich Museum of Contemporary Art, 1996.

Simon, Joan, ed. *Bruce Nauman: Exhibition Catalogue and Catalogue Raisonné*. Exhibition catalogue. Minneapolis: Walker Art Center, 1994.

Van Bruggen, Coosje. *Bruce Nauman*. New York: Rizzoli, 1988.

Zutter, Jörg, ed. *Bruce Nauman, sculptures et installations, 1985–1990*. Exhibition catalogue. Brussels: Ludion, 1991.

Fernand Pelez

Burollet, Thérèse. *Présence et vie d'une peinture oubliée*. Exhibition catalogue. Paris: Bibliothèque Trocadéro / Association Parisienne d'Action Culturelle, n.d.

Rosenblum, Robert. "Fernand Pelez, or the Other Side of the Post-Impressionist Coin." In *Art, the Ape of Nature: Studies in Honor of H.W. Janson*, ed. Moshe Barasch and Lucy Freeman Sandler. New York: Harry N. Abrams; Englewood Cliffs: Prentice-Hall, 1981.

Thalaso, Adolphe. "Le Mois artistique, exposition rétrospective de Fernand Pelez." *L'Art et les Artistes*, no. 106 (January 1914), pp. 195–196.

Francis Picabia

Borràs, Maria Lluïsa. *Picabia*. Paris: Albin-Michel, 1985.

Camfield, William A. *Francis Picabia*. Exhibition catalogue. New York: Solomon R. Guggenheim Foundation, 1970.

———. *Picabia: His Art, Life and Times*. Princeton: Princeton University Press, 1979.

Felix, Zdenek, ed. *Francis Picabia: The Late Works 1933–1953*. Exhibition catalogue. Hamburg: Deichtorhallen; Rotterdam: Museum Boyjmans-van Beuningen, 1998.

Martin, Jean-Hubert, and Hélène Seckel. *Francis Picabia*. Exhibition catalogue. Paris: Centre Pompidou, 1976.

Ottinger, Didier. "*Dresseur d'animaux* (1923) de Francis Picabia." *Les Cahiers du Musée National d'Art Moderne*, no. 72 (Summer 2000), pp. 80–91.

Pagé, Suzanne, and Gérard Audinet, ed. *Francis Picabia: Singulier idéal*. Exhibition catalogue. Paris: Musée d'Art Moderne de la Ville de Paris / Paris Musées, 2003.

Picabia 1879–1953. Exhibition catalogue. Edinburgh: Scottish National Gallery of Modern Art; Frankfurt am Main: Galerie Neuendorf, 1988.

Pablo Picasso

Ameline, Jean-Paul. *Parade pour "Parade."* Exhibition catalogue. Paris: Centre Pompidou, 1986.

Axsom, Richard Hayden. *"Parade": Cubism as Theater*. New York: Garland Outstanding Dissertations in the Fine Arts, 1979.

Blanckenhagen, Peter H. von. "Rilke und 'La Famille des saltimbanques' von Picasso." *Das Kunstwerk* 5, no. 4 (1951), pp. 43–54.

Blunt, Anthony, and Phoebe Pool. *Picasso, the Formative Years: A Study of His Sources*. New York: Studio Books, 1962.

Borowitz, Helen Osterman. "Three Guitars: Reflections of Italian Comedy in Watteau, Daumier, and Picasso." *The Bulletin of the Cleveland Museum of Art* 71 (April 1984), pp. 116–129.

Bransten, E.H. "The Significance of the Clown in Paintings by Daumier, Picasso and Rouault." *Pacific Art Review* 3 (1944), pp. 21–39.

Cardwell, Richard A. "Picasso's Harlequin: Icon of the Art of Lying." *Leeds Papers on Symbol and Image in Iberian Arts*, 1994, pp. 249–281.

Carmean, E.A., Jr. *Picasso: The Saltimbanques*. Exhibition catalogue. Washington, D.C.: National Gallery of Art, 1980.

Cassou, Jean. "Le Rideau de *Parade* de Picasso au Musée d'Art Moderne." *Revue des Arts, Musées de France* (Paris), January–February 1957, pp. 15–18.

Clair, Jean. "Picasso à Venise." *Connaissance des Arts*, no. 548 (March 1998), pp. 98–103.

Clair, Jean, ed. *Picasso: The Italian Journey, 1914–1924*. Exhibition catalogue. New York: Rizzoli; Milan: RCS Libri S.P.A., 1998.

Cooper, Douglas. *Picasso: Theatre*. London: Weidenfeld & Nicolson, 1968.

Cortenova, Giorgio. "Analisi di *Parade*." In *Picasso in Italia*, pp. 80–88. Verona: Galleria d'Arte Moderna e Contemporanea; Milan: Mazotta, 1990.

Danilowitz, Brenda Mary Ann. "The Iconography of Picasso's Ballet Design: 1917–1924." Ph.D. diss., University of the Witwatersrand, Johannesburg, 1985.

De Bold, Conrad. "Parade and Le Spectacle Intérieur: The Role of Jean Cocteau in an Avant-Garde Ballet." Ph.D. diss., Emory University, 1982.

Eberiel, Rosemary. "Clowns: Apollinaire's Writings on Picasso." *Res*, no. 14 (Fall 1987), pp. 143–159.

Emadian, Mitra. "The Easel and the Stage: An Historical Study of Picasso as a Theatrical Designer." Ph.D. diss., University of Southern California, 1981.

Fagiolo dell'Arco, Maurizio, and Ida Gianelli, ed. *Sipario / Staged Art: Balla, De Chirico, Savinio, Picasso, Paolini, Cucchi*. Exhibition catalogue. Milan: Charta, 1997.

Glaesemer, Jürgen, ed. *Der junge Picasso: Frühwerk und blaue Periode*. Exhibition catalogue. Bern: Kunstmuseum Bern, 1984.

Harbec, Jacinthe. "Parade: Les Influences cubistes sur la composition musicale d'Érik Satie." Ph.D. diss., McGill University, 1987.

Henning, Edward B. "Picasso: Harlequin with Violin (*Si tu veux*)." *The Bulletin of the Cleveland Museum of Art* 63 (January 1976), pp. 2–11.

Johnson, R. "Picasso's Parisian Family and the Saltimbanques." *Arts Magazine* 51 (January 1977), pp. 90–95.

Kattner, Elizabeth Marie. "The Artistic Collaboration Resulting in the Creation of the Ballet 'Parade.'" Master's thesis, University of Nevada, 1997.

Keller, Cordula von. *Ballet Dancers and Harlequins in Picasso's "Neoclassical" Period (1915–1925)*. London: Courtauld Institute, 1986.

Kozloff, Max. "Cubism and the Human Comedy." *Art News* 71 (September 1972), pp. 35–41.

Lascault, Gilbert. "Notes sur les bateleurs." *L'Arc*, no. 82 (1981), pp. 7–13.

Léal, Brigitte. "In viaggio per Parade." In *Picasso in Italia*, pp. 89–96. Verona: Galleria d'Arte Moderna e Contemporanea; Milan: Mazotta, 1990.

———. "Pulcinella." In *Picasso in Italia*, pp. 137–141. Verona: Galleria d'Arte Moderna e Contemporanea; Milan: Mazotta, 1990.

———. *Carnets: Catalogue des dessins, Musée Picasso*. Paris: Réunion des Musées Nationaux, 1996.

———. "Arlequins et saltimbanques." *L'Oeil*, no. 502 (December 1998–January 1999), pp. 48–55.

Léal, Brigitte, et al. *Picasso, jeunesse et génèse: Dessins 1893–1905*. Exhibition catalogue. Paris: Musée Picasso; Nantes: Musée des Beaux-Arts, 1991.

Martin, Marianne. "The Ballet *Parade*: A Dialogue Between Cubism and Futurism." *Art Quarterly*, no. 2 (Spring 1978), pp. 101–104.

McCully, Marilyn. "Magic and Illusion in the Saltimbanques of Picasso and Apollinaire." *Art History* 3, no. 4 (December 1980), pp. 425–434.

McCully, Marilyn, ed. *Picasso: The Early Years, 1892–1906*. Exhibition catalogue. Washington, D.C.: National Gallery of Art, 1997.

McQuillan, Melissa A. "Painters and the Ballet, 1917–1926: An Aspect of the Relationship Between Art and Theatre." Ph.D. diss., New York University, 1979.

Menaker Rothschild, Rebecca M. "From Street to the Elite: Popular Sources in Picasso's Designs for 'Parade.'" Ph.D. diss., New York University, 1989.

———. *Picasso's "Parade" from Street to Stage*. New York: The Drawing Center; London: Sotheby's Publications, 1991.

Messinger, Lisa M. "Pablo Picasso: Harlequin." *Metropolitan Museum of Art Bulletin* 55, no. 2 (Fall 1997), pp. 68–69.

Milhau, Denis, Robert Mesuret, and Douglas Cooper. *Picasso et le théâtre*. Exhibition catalogue. Toulouse: Musée des Augustins, 1965.

Mosch, Ulrich. "De quelques relations entre musique et art pictural dans les ballets classicisants *Pulcinella* et *La Giara*." In *Canto d'amore: Modernité et classicisme dans la musique et les beaux-arts entre 1914 et 1935*, pp. 222–240. Paris: Flammarion, 1996.

Muller, Hans Joachim. "Pablo Picasso: Arlequin au loup." In *Nafea: La Collection Rudolf Staechelin*. Basel: Wiese, 1990.

Ocaña, Maria Teresa, ed. *Picasso y el teatro: Parade, Pulcinella, Cuadro Flamenco, Mercure*. Exhibition catalogue. Barcelona: Museu Picasso / Ambit Serveis Editorials, 1996.

Ocaña, Maria Teresa, and Hans Christoph von Tavel. *Picasso 1905–1906: Période rose, Gósol*. Exhibition catalogue. Barcelona: Museo Picasso; Milan: Electa, 1992.

Olivier, Fernande. *Picasso et ses amis*. 1933. Paris: Stock, 1973.

Palau I Fabre, Josep. *Picasso: The Early Years, 1881–1907*. Barcelona: Ediciones Poligrafa, 1985.

Perneczky, Géza. "Picasso after Picasso." *Annales de la Galerie Nationale Hongroise*, 1980–1988, pp. 59–65.

Picasso 1923: Arlequin con espejo y la flauta de Pan. Exhibition catalogue. Madrid: Fundación Colección Thyssen-Bornemisza, 1995.

Picasso and the Circus. Videocassette. Washington, D.C.: National Gallery of Art, 1981.

Picasso et le théâtre: Les Décors d'Oedipe-Roi. Exhibition catalogue. Antibes: Musée Picasso; Paris: Réunion des Musées Nationaux, 1999.

Pool, Phoebe. "Picasso's Neo-Classicism: First Period, 1905–6." *Apollo* 81, no. 36 (February 1965), pp. 122–127.

Ratcliff, Carter. "Picasso's Harlequin: Remarks on the Modern Harlequin." *Arts Magazine* 51, no. 5 (January 1977), pp. 124–126.

Read, Peter. *Picasso et Apollinaire: Les Métamorphoses de la mémoire*. Paris: Jean-Michel Place, 1995.

Reff, Theodore. "Harlequins, Saltimbanques, Clowns, and Fools in Picasso's Art." *Artforum* 10 (October 1971), pp. 30–43.

———. "Picasso and the Circus." In *Essays in Archeology and the Humanities: In Memoriam Otto J. Brendel*, ed. Larissa Bonfante and Helga von Heintze, pp. 237–248. Mayence: Philipp von Zabern, 1976.

———. "Picasso's Three Musicians: Maskers, Artists and Friends." *Art in America* 68, no. 10 (December 1980), pp. 125–142.

———. "À propos d'Arlequin et de Pierrot dans l'oeuvre de Picasso après 1917." In *Canto d'amore: Modernité et classicisme dans la musique et les beaux-arts entre 1914 et 1935*, pp. 140–141. Paris: Flammarion, 1996.

Rewald, Sabine. "Pablo Picasso: *Harlequin*." *Metropolitan Museum of Art Bulletin* 55, no. 2 (Fall 1997), p. 76.

Richardson, John. *A Life of Picasso, Volume I: 1881–1906*, New York: Random House, 1991.

Ritter, Naomi. "The *Saltimbanque* as Savior: Rilke, Picasso and Apollinaire." In *Art as Spectacle: Images of the Entertainer since Romanticism*, pp. 151–176. Columbia: University of Missouri Press, 1989.

Rosenblum, Robert. *The Sculpture of Picasso*. Exhibition catalogue. New York: Pace Gallery, 1982.

Russell, John. "In Detail: Picasso's Three Musicians." *Portfolio*, June–July 1979, pp. 12–16, 18.

Schultze, Franz, and Bruce Wolmer. "Splendid Harlequinade of Pablo Picasso." *Art News* 79, no. 7 (September 1980), pp. 79–83.

Seckel, Hélène. *Max Jacob et Picasso*. Exhibition catalogue. Paris: Réunion des Musées Nationaux, 1994.

Spector, Naomi. "Notes on Picasso's Designs for *Parade*." In *Picasso: 200 Masterworks from 1898 to 1972*, ed. Bernice B. Rose and Bernard Ruiz Picasso, pp. 133–139. London: Bulfinch; Boston: Little, Brown and Company, 2002.

Spies, Werner. "*Parade*: La Démonstration antinomique – Picasso aux prises avec les 'Scene popolari di Napoli' d'Achile Vianelli." In *Il se rendit en Italie: Études offertes à André Chastel*, pp. 679–687. Rome: Edizioni dell'Elefante; Paris: Flammarion, 1987.

Starobinski, Jean. "Passeurs et trépassés." In *Canto d'amore: Modernité et classicisme dans la musique et les beaux-arts entre 1914 et 1935*, pp. 130–133. Paris: Flammarion, 1996.

Walther, Ingo F., ed. *Picasso 1881–1973, Part I: The Works 1890–1936*. Cologne and London: Taschen, 1997.

Weiss, Jeffrey. "Le Spectacle Intérieur: *Parade*, Popular Cubism, and the Law of Systematic Confusion." In *The Popular Culture of Modern Art: Picasso, Duchamp, and Avant-Gardism*, pp. 167–253. New Haven and London: Yale University Press, 1994.

———. "Picasso, Collage and the Music-Hall." In *The Popular Culture of Modern Art: Picasso, Duchamp, and Avant-Gardism*, pp. 82–115. New Haven and London: Yale University Press, 1994.

Herbert Ploberger

Herbert Ploberger, 1902–1977. Exhibition catalogue. Linz: Nordico–Museum der Stadt Linz, 1977.

Lipp, Franz. "Herbert Ploberger." *Kunstjahrbuch der Stadt Linz*. Linz: Nordico–Museum der Stadt Linz, 1979.

Thaler, Herfried, and Katharina Weinberger. *Herbert Ploberger*. Exhibition catalogue. Linz: Nordico–Museum der Stadt Linz, 2002.

Weinberger, Katharina. *Herbert Ploberger: Das Graphische und Malerische Werk 1918-1945*. Exhibition catalogue. Innsbruck: Dipl.-Arb., 2001.

Robert Riggs

"Artist Robert Riggs Wins Prizes: His Favorite Lithographic Subject Is the Circus." *Life*, 13 September 1937, pp. 46–48.

Bassham, Ben L. *The Lithographs of Robert Riggs, with a Catalogue Raisonné*. Philadelphia: Art Alliance; London: Associated University Presses, 1986.

Aleksandr Rodchenko

Dabrowski, Magdalena, Leah Dickerman, and Peter Galassi. *Aleksandr Rodchenko*. Exhibition catalogue. New York: Museum of Modern Art / Harry N. Abrams, 1998.

Foray, Jean-Michel, ed. *Alexandre Rodtchenko*. Exhibition catalogue. Paris: ADAGP / Réunion des Musées Nationaux, 2000.

Gassner, Hubertus. *Rodcenko Fotografien*. Munich: Schirmer/Mosel, 1982.

Karginov, German. *Rodtchenko*. Paris: Chêne, 1975.

Khan-Magomedov, Selim O. *Rodchenko: The Complete Work*. Cambridge, Mass.: MIT Press, 1986.

Lavrentjev, Alexander. *Rodchenko Photography*. New York: Rizzoli, 1982.

———. *Alexandre Rodtchenko: Photographies 1924-1954*. Paris: Gründ, 1996.

Lavrentjev, Alexander, Varvara Fedorovna Stepanova, and Alexander Rodchenko. *Alexander Rodchenko: Possibilities of Photography*. Exhibition catalogue. Cologne: Galerie Gmurzynska, 1982.

Nakov, Andréi B. *Rodtchenko photographe*. Exhibition catalogue. Paris: Musée d'Art Moderne de la Ville de Paris, 1977.

Weiss, Evelyn, ed. *Rodtschenko Fotografien 1920–1938*. Exhibition catalogue. Cologne: Museum Ludwig / Wienand, 1978.

Ugo Rondinone

Bovier, Lionel. "Ugo Rondinone … Doesn't Live Here Anymore!" *Flash Art* 30, no. 193 (March–April 1997), pp. 106–107.

Heyday: Ugo Rondinone. Exhibition catalogue. Zürich: Memory / Cage, 1996.

Janus, Elizabeth. "Openings: Ugo Rondinone." *Artforum* 37, no. 3 (November 1998), pp. 102–103.

Mack, Gerhard. "Ugo Rondinone: Warten auf Godot." *ART – Das Kunstmagazin*, no. 10 (October 1999), pp. 56–61.

Troncy, Eric. "Ugo Rondinone: Where Do We Go, Ugo? – Clown and Out with Ugo Rondinone." *Art Press*, no. 227 (September 1997), pp. 32–37.

"Ugo Rondinone." *Parkett*, no. 52 (1998), pp. 104–145.

Félicien Rops

Bonnier, Bernadette, ed. *Félicien Rops: Rops suis, aultre ne veulx estre*. Exhibition catalogue. Brussels: Complexe, 1998.

Bonnier, Bernadette, and Véronique Leblanc. *Félicien Rops: Vie et oeuvre*. Bruges: Stichting Kunstboek, 1997.

Bonnier, Bernadette, and Michel Draguet. *Rops: Cent légers croquis sans prétention pour réjouir les honnêtes gens*. Exhibition catalogue. Namur: Province de Namur, Service de la Culture, 1998.

Bory, Jean-François, ed. *Félicien Rops 1833–1898: Aquarelles, dessins, gravures*. Exhibition catalogue. Paris: Centre Culturel de la Communauté Française de Belgique, 1980.

De Croës, Catherine, ed. *Félicien Rops 1833–1898*. Exhibition catalogue. Paris: Musée des Arts Décoratifs / Flammarion; Brussels: Lebeer Hossmann, 1985.

Delevoy, Robert, et al. *Félicien Rops*. Paris: Bibliothèque des Arts; Brussels: Lebeer Hossmann, 1985.

Draguet, Michel. *Rops: Le Cabinet des dessins*. Exhibition catalogue. Paris: Flammarion / Musée-Galerie de la Seita, 1998.

Georges Rouault

Bransten, E.H. "The Significance of the Clown in Paintings by Daumier, Picasso and Rouault." *Pacific Art Review* 3 (1944), pp. 21–39.

Chapon, François. *Le Livre des livres de Rouault*. Paris: A. Sauret, 1992.

Chiappini, Rudy, ed. *Georges Rouault*. Exhibition catalogue. Milan: Skira, 1997.

Courthion, Pierre. *Georges Rouault*. With a catalogue compiled in collaboration with Isabelle Rouault. Paris: Flammarion, 1962.

Dorival, Bernard. *Georges Rouault*. Exhibition catalogue. Munich: Haus Der Kunst; Manchester: City Art Gallery, 1974.

Fohr, Robert, ed. *Honoré Daumier, Georges Rouault*. Exhibition catalogue. Rome: Accademia di Francia a Roma; Milan: Electa, 1983.

Hergott, Fabrice, and Sarah Whitfield. *Georges Rouault: The Early Years, 1903–1920*. Exhibition catalogue. London: Royal Academy, 1993.

Hoog, Michel. *Georges Rouault: Exposition du centenaire*. Exhibition catalogue. Paris: Réunion des Musées Nationaux, 1971.

Pontiggia, Elena, ed. *Rouault: Il circo, la guerra, la speranza – Opere grafiche dalle collezioni milanesi*. Exhibition catalogue. Milan: Medusa, 2001.

Rouault, Isabelle, and Kurt Scholz. *Georges Rouault, Zirkus Sternschnuppe: 17 Farbradierungen und 8 Holzschnitte mit einer Einführung von Wolf Stadler*. Fribourg: Herder, 1984.

August Sander

August Sander: Photographs from the J. Paul Getty Museum. Exhibition catalogue. Los Angeles: J. Paul Getty Museum, 2000.

Green, Roy. "Circus Work in Camera." *Photographic Journal* 137, no. 4 (May 1997), pp. 162–164.

Hartz, John von. *August Sander*. Millerton: Aperture, 1977.

Heiting, Manfred, ed. *August Sander, 1876–1964*. Cologne and New York: Taschen, 1999.

Lange, Susan. *August Sander*. Paris: Centre National de la Photographie, 1995.

Lange, Susan, Gabriele Conrath-Scholl, and Gerd Sander. *August Sander: Menschen des 20. Jahrhunderts*. 7 vols. Munich: Schirmer/Mosel, 2002.

Newhall, Beaumont, and Robert Kramer. *August Sander: Photographs of an Epoch, 1904–1959*. Millerton: Aperture, 1980.

Sander, Gerd, ed. *August Sander: "In Photography There Are No Unexplained Shadows!"* Exhibition catalogue. London: National Portrait Gallery, 1996.

Sander, Gunther. *August Sander: Photographer Extraordinary*. London: Thames & Hudson, 1973.

Sander, Gunther, ed. *August Sander: Citizens of the Twentieth Century: Portrait Photographs, 1892–1952*. Cambridge, Mass.: MIT Press, 1986.

Arnold Schoenberg

Bass, Ruth. "The Same as Making Music: The Painting of Arnold Schoenberg." *Art News* 84 (3 March 1985), pp. 94–96.

Castor, Markus, et al. *Zu Arnold Schönberg als Maler*. Klagenfurt: Ritter-Verlag, 1991.

Da Costa Meyer, Esther, and Fred Wasserman. *Schoenberg, Kandinsky, and the Blue Rider*. Exhibition catalogue. New York: Jewish Museum, 2003.

Eisler, Georg. "Schönberg peintre." *Les Cahiers du Musée National d'Art Moderne*, no. 3 (1980), pp. 37–45.

Kallir, Jane. "Arnold Schoenberg et Richart Gerstl." In *Vienne 1880–1938: L'Apocalypse joyeuse*, pp. 454–469. Exhibition catalogue. Paris: Centre Pompidou, 1986.

Leibowitz, René. *Schoenberg*. Paris: Le Seuil, 1969.

Pagé, Suzanne, ed. *Arnold Schoenberg: Regards*. Exhibition catalogue. Paris: Paris Musées, 1995.

George Segal

Friedman, Martin, and Graham W.J. Beal. *George Segal: Sculptures*. Exhibition catalogue. Minneapolis: Walker Art Center, 1978.

Hunter, Sam. *George Segal*. New York: Rizzoli, 1989.

Hunter, Sam, and Don Hawthorne. *George Segal*. New York: Rizzoli, 1984.

Livingstone, Marco. *George Segal Retrospective: Sculptures, Paintings, Drawings*. Exhibition catalogue. Montreal: Montreal Museum of Fine Arts, 1997.

Marck, Jan van der. *George Segal*. New York: Harry N. Abrams, 1979.

Mercurio, Gianni, ed. *George Segal: The Artist Studio*. Exhibition catalogue. Rome: De Luca, 2002.

Pillsbury, Edmund P. *George Segal and the Nobility of Everyday Life: A Memorial Exhibition*. Exhibition catalogue. Dallas: Pillsbury Peters Fine Arts; Santa Fe: Gerald Peters Gallery, 2001.

Teuber, Dirk. *George Segal: Wege zur Körperüberformung*. Frankfurt am Main and New York: P. Lang, 1987.

Tuchman, Phyllis. *George Segal*. New York: Abbeville, 1983.

Seitz, William C. *Segal*. New York: Harry N. Abrams, 1972.

Georges Seurat

Balas, Edith. "A Contribution Towards the Understanding of Seurat's Late Works." *Gazette des Beaux-Arts* 136, no. 1581 (October 2000), pp. 155–158.

Cachin, Françoise, and Robert L. Herbert, ed. *Seurat*. Exhibition catalogue. Paris: Réunion des Musées Nationaux, 1991.

Darragon, Éric. "Pégase à Fernando: À propos de *Cirque* et du réalisme de Seurat en 1891." *Revue de l'Art*, no. 86 (1989), pp. 44–57.

LeMen, Ségolène. *Seurat & Chéret. Le peintre, le cirque et l'affiche*. Paris: CNRS Editions, 1994.

Thomson, Richard. *Seurat*. London: Phaidon, 1985.

Cindy Sherman

Cindy Sherman. Exhibition catalogue. Shiga: Museum of Modern Art, 1996.

Cruz, Amanda, Elizabeth Smith, and Amelia Jones. *Cindy Sherman: Retrospective*. Exhibition catalogue. London: Thames & Hudson, 1997.

Felix, Zdenek, and Martin Schwander, ed. *Cindy Sherman, Photoarbeiten 1975–1995*. Exhibition catalogue. Munich: Schirmer/Mosel, 1995.

Krauss, Rosalind, and Norman Bryson. *Cindy Sherman, 1975–1993*. New York: Rizzoli, 1993.

Schampers, Karel, and Talitha Schoon. *Cindy Sherman*. Exhibition catalogue. Rotterdam: Museum Boymans-van Beuningen, 1996.

Schjeldahl, Pierre. Introduction to *Cindy Sherman*. New York: Pantheon Books, 1984.

Everett Shinn

De Shazo, Edith. *Everett Shinn, 1876–1953: A Figure in His Time*. New York: Clarkson N. Potter, 1974.

Ferber, Linda S. "Stagestruck: The Theater Subjects of Everett Shinn." *Marsyas: Studies in the History of Art* 37 (1990), pp. 50–67.

Rand, Barbara. "The Art of Everett Shinn." Ph.D. diss., University of California, Santa Barbara, 1992.

Weintraub, Laural. "Fine Art and Popular Entertainment: The Emerging Dialogue Between 'High' and 'Low' in American Art of the Early Twentieth Century." Ph.D. diss., City University of New York, 1996.

Wong, Janay. *Everett Shinn: The Spectacle of Life*. Exhibition catalogue. New York: Berry-Hill Galleries, 2000.

———. "The Early Work of Everett Shinn (1897–1911): Art at the Crossroads of a New Century." Ph.D. diss., City University of New York, 2002.

Yount, Sylvia. "Consuming Drama: Everett Shinn and the Spectacular City." *American Art*, Fall 1992, pp. 82–109.

Walter Sickert

Baron, Wendy. *Sickert*. London: Phaidon, 1973.

Baron, Wendy, and Richard Shone, ed. *Sickert: Paintings*. Exhibition catalogue. London: Royal Academy of Arts; New Haven and London: Yale University Press, 1992.

Corbett, David Peters. "Seeing into Modernity: Walter Sickert's Music-Hall Scenes, c. 1887–1907." In *English Art 1860–1914: Modern Artists and Modernity*, pp. 150–167, 248–253. Manchester: Manchester University Press, 2000.

———. *Walter Sickert*. Princeton: Princeton University Press, 2001.

Emmons, Robert. *The Life and Opinions of Walter Richard Sickert*. London: Faber and Faber, 1941.

Shone, Richard. *Walter Sickert*. London: Phaidon, 1988.

Sickert: Pages Torn from the Book of Life. Exhibition catalogue. London: Fine Arts Society, 2002.

Sutton, Denys. *Walter Sickert: A Biography*. London: Joseph, 1976.

John Sloan

Brooks, Van Wyck. *John Sloan: A Painter's Life*. New York: E.P. Dutton & Co., 1955.

Elzea, Rowland. *John Sloan: Spectator of Life*. Exhibition catalogue. Wilmington: Delaware Art Museum, 1988.

Goodrich, Lloyd. *John Sloan*. Exhibition catalogue. New York: Whitney Museum of American Art / Macmillan, 1952.

Kraft, James. *John Sloan in Santa Fe*. Exhibition catalogue. Washington, D.C.: Smithsonian Institution, 1981.

Loughery, John. *John Sloan: Painter and Rebel*. New York: H. Holt, 1995.

St. John, Bruce. *John Sloan*. New York: Praeger, 1971.

St. John, Bruce, ed. *John Sloan's New York Scene, from the Diaries, Notes, and Correspondence, 1906–1913*. New York: Harper and Row, 1965.

Scott, David W. *John Sloan*. New York: Watson-Guptill, 1975.

Scott, David W., and E. John Bullard. *John Sloan, 1871–1951*. Exhibition catalogue. Washington, D.C.: National Gallery of Art, 1971.

Udall, Sharyn R. "Carousels in the Clouds: Circus Themes in New Mexico Art." *El Palacio* 95, no. 1 (Fall–Winter 1989), pp. 51–56.

Weintraub, Laural. "Fine Art and Popular Entertainment: The Emerging Dialogue Between 'High' and 'Low' in American Art of the Early Twentieth Century." Ph.D. diss., City University of New York, 1996.

José Gutiérrez Solana

Ascoaga, Enrique. *Gutiérres Solana, el desenmascarador*. La Corogne: Publicaciós do Museo Carlos Maside / Ediciós do Castro, 1972.

Barrio Garay, José Luis. *José Gutiérrez Solana: Paintings and Writings*. Lewisburg: Bucknell University Press; London: Associated University Presses, 1978.

Campoy, Antonio Manuel. *Solana*. Madrid: Epesa, 1971.

Gómez de la Serna, Ramón. *José Gutiérrez Solana*. Barcelona: Ediciones Picazo, 1972.

Tunissen, Marie-Anne, Francisco Umbral, and Luis Alonso Fernandez. *Sorolla / Solana*. Exhibition catalogue. Liège: Salle Saint-Georges, 1985.

Pierrick Sorin

Davila, Thierry. *Pierrick Sorin*. Exhibition catalogue. Antibes: Musée Picasso, 1997.

Fibische, Bernard. *Pierrick Sorin: Video-installationen*. Exhibition catalogue. Zürich: Kunsthaus, 1996.

Fraser, Marie. *Le Ludique*. Exhibition catalogue. Quebec City: Musée du Québec, 2001.

Giquel, Pierre. *Pierrick Sorin*. Paris: Hazan, 2000.

Million, Élisabeth. *Pierrick Sorin: Petite Nostalgie du burlesque*. Paris: Au Figuré, 1993.

Morice, Jacques. *Pierrick Sorin: Films, vidéos et installations*. Exhibition catalogue. Bordeaux: CAPC / Musée d'Art Contemporain, 1995.

Pierrick Sorin: Artiste solitaire, stupide et trop agité. Exhibition catalogue. Tokyo; Shiseido Gallery, 1996.

410

Giambattista Tiepolo

Brugerolles, Emmanuelle, and David Guillet. *Les Dessins vénitiens des collections de l'École des Beaux-Arts*. Exhibition catalogue. Paris: École Nationale Supérieure des Beaux-Arts, 1990.

Giambattista Tiepolo, 1696–1770. Exhibition catalogue. Paris: Paris Musées, 1998.

Levey, Michael. *Giambattista Tiepolo, His Life and Art*. New Haven and London: Yale University Press, 1986.

Knox, George. "The Punchinello Drawings of Giambattista Tiepolo." In *Interpretazioni Veneziane: Studi di storia dell'arte in onore di Michelangelo Muraro*, ed. David Rosand. Venice: Arsenale, 1984.

Giandomenico Tiepolo

Byam Shaw, James. *The Drawings of Domenico Tiepolo*. Boston: Boston Book and Art Shop, 1962.

Francis, H.S. "Six Drawings from the Life of Pulcinella by the Younger Tiepolo." *Bulletin of the Cleveland Museum of Art* 26, no. 4 (April 1939), pp. 46–49.

Gealt, Adelheid M. *Domenico Tiepolo: The Punchinello Drawings*. New York: George Braziller, 1986.

Gealt, Adelheid M., and Marcia E. Vetrocq. *Domenico Tiepolo's Punchinello Drawings*. Exhibition catalogue. Bloomington: Indiana University Press, 1979.

Gealt, Adelheid M., and George Knox, ed. *Giandomenico Tiepolo: Maestria e gioco – Disegni dal mondo*. Milan: Electa, 1996.

Gealt, Adelheid M., et al. *Domenico Tiepolo: Master Draftsman*. Exhibition catalogue. Bloomington: Indiana University Press, 1996.

Hannegan, Barry, and Edward F. Weeks. *The Tiepolos: Painters to Princes and Prelates*. Exhibition catalogue. Birmingham: Birmingham Museum of Art; Springfield: Museum of Fine Arts, 1978.

Knox, George. "Domenico Tiepolo's Punchinello Drawings: Satire or Labor of Love?" In *Satire in the 18th Century*, ed. John Browning, pp. 124–146. New York: Garland, 1983.

Loire, Stéphane. *Settecento: Le Siècle de Tiepolo*. Exhibition catalogue. Paris: Réunion des Musées Nationaux, 2000.

Mariuz, Adriano. "Giandomenico Tiepolo e la Civiltà Veneta di Villa." In *Atti del Congresso Internazionale di Studi sul Tiepolo*, pp. 16–18. Udine: Electra, 1970.

———. *Giandomenico Tiepolo*. Venice: Alfieri, 1971.

———. "I disegni di Pulcinella di Giandomenico Tiepolo." *Arte Veneta* 42 (1986), pp. 265–272.

Mathews, Harry. *Giandomenico Tiepolo*. Paris: Flohic, 1993.

Newberry, John S., Jr. "Punchinello Drawings Representing Punchinello Carried in a Triumphal Procession." *Bulletin of the Detroit Institute of Arts* 35, no. 4 (1955–1956), pp. 92–94.

Pedrocco, Filippo. *Disegni di Giandomenico Tiepolo*. Milan: Berenice, 1990.

Pignatti, Terisio. *Tiepolo Disegni*. Florence: La Nuova Italia, 1974.

Succi, Dario, ed. *I Tiepolo: Virtuosismo e ironia – Catalogo della mostra*. Exhibition catalogue. Turin: Umberto Allemandi, 1988.

Wolk-Simon, Linda. "Domenico Tiepolo's Late Drawings." *Metropolitan Museum of Art Bulletin* 54 (Winter 1996–1997), pp. 45–67.

James Tissot

Ash, Russell. *James Tissot*. New York: Harry N. Abrams, 1992.

Brooke, David S. "James Tissot's Amateur Circus." *Boston Museum Bulletin* 67, no. 347 (1969), pp. 4–17.

Brooke, David S., Michael Wentworth, and Henri Zerner. *James Jacques Joseph Tissot, 1836–1902: A Retrospective Exhibition*. Exhibition catalogue. Providence: Museum of Art / Rhode Island School of Design, 1968.

James Tissot, 1836–1902. Exhibition catalogue. Besançon: Musée des Beaux-Arts, 1985.

Lochnan, Katharine, ed. *Seductive Surfaces: The Art of Tissot*. New Haven: Yale University Press, 1999.

Marshall, Nancy Rose, and Malcolm Warner. *James Tissot: Victorian Life, Modern Love*. Exhibition catalogue. New Haven: Yale University Press, 1999.

Misfeldt, Williard. "James Jacques Joseph Tissot: A Bio-Critical Study." Ph.D. diss., Washington University, 1971.

———. "James Tissot and Alphonse Daudet: Friends and Collaborators." *Apollo* 123 (February 1986), pp. 110–115.

———. *J.J. Tissot: Prints from the Gotlieb Collection*. Exhibition catalogue. Alexandria, Va.: Art Service Collection, 1991.

Wentworth, Michael Justin. *James Tissot*. Oxford: Clarendon, 1984.

Wood, Christopher. *Tissot: The Life and Work of Jacques Joseph Tissot, 1836–1902*. Boston: Little, Brown and Company, 1986.

Henri de Toulouse-Lautrec

Abélès, Luce. *Toulouse-Lautrec: La Baraque de la Goulue*. Exhibition catalogue. Paris: Musée d'Art et d'Essai, 1984.

Casey, Dorothy N. "Equestrienne, by H. de Toulouse-Lautrec." *Bulletin of the Rhode Island School of Design* 93 (July 1935), pp. 38–39.

Castelman, Riva, and Wolfgang Wittrock. *Henri de Toulouse-Lautrec: Images of the 1890s*. Exhibition catalogue. New York: Museum of Modern Art, 1985.

Coquiot, Gustave. "Les Dessins sur le thème du cirque." In *Toulouse-Lautrec: Un Peintre, une vie, une oeuvre*, ed. Gale Murray, pp. 299–300. Paris: Belfond, 1991.

Frèches, Claire, Anne Roquebert, and Françoise Cachin, ed. *Toulouse-Lautrec*. Exhibition catalogue. Paris: Réunion des Musées Nationaux, 1991.

Frey, Julia Bloch. *Toulouse-Lautrec: A Life*. New York: Viking, 1994.

Greig, James. "Toulouse-Lautrec and the Circus." *The Studio* 7, no. 107 (May 1934), pp. 255–259.

Heller, Reinhold. *Toulouse-Lautrec: The Soul of Montmartre*. Munich and New York: Prestel, 1997.

Julien, Edouard. *Toulouse-Lautrec at the Circus*. London: Methuen, 1957.

Murray, Gale, ed. *Toulouse-Lautrec: A Retrospective*. Exhibition catalogue. New York: Hugh Lauter Levin Associates, 1992.

O'Connor, Patrick. *Nightlife of Paris: The Art of Toulouse-Lautrec*. New York: Universe, 1991.

Post, Hermann. "Lautrecs Zeichnungen 'Au Cirque.'" *Die Kunst* 65 (March 1932), pp. 162–165.

Randall, Richard H., Jr. "A Drawing by Toulouse-Lautrec." *Walters Art Gallery Bulletin* 28, no. 6 (March 1976), pp. 3–4.

Sagne, Jean. *Toulouse-Lautrec au cirque*. Paris: Flammarion / Arthaud, 1991.

Seitz, William C. *Au Cirque*. New York: Harry N. Abrams, 1967.

The Circus by Toulouse-Lautrec. Exhibition catalogue. New York: Knoedler Gallery, 1931.

Toulouse-Lautrec: Woman as Myth. Exhibition catalogue. Turin: Umberto Allemandi, 2001.

Verhaegen, Marcus. "Whipstrokes." *Representations*, no. 58 (Spring 1997), pp. 115–140.

Umbo

Fiedler, Jeannine, ed. *Photography at the Bauhaus*. Cambridge, Mass.: MIT Press, 1990.

Molderings, Herbert. *Umbo: Otto Umbehr, 1902–1980*. Düsseldorf: Richter, 1995.

Molderings, Herbert. Introduction to *Umbo*. Paris: Centre National de la Photographie, 1996.

Umbo: Vom Bauhaus zum Bildjournalismus. Exhibition catalogue. Düsseldorf: Kunstverein / Kestner-Gesellschaft, 1996.

Robert Walker

Walker, Robert. *New York Inside Out*. Don Mills, Ont.: Skyline, 1984.

Walker, Robert, Max Kozloff, and Jan Andriesse. *Color Is Power: Robert Walker Fotograaf / Photographer*. Amsterdam: Ludion; London: Thames & Hudson, 2002.

Antoine Watteau

Adhémar, Hélène, and René Huyghe. *Watteau, sa vie – son oeuvre*. Paris: Tisné, 1950.

Boerlin-Brodbeck, Yvonne. "Antoine Watteau und das Theater." Ph.D. diss., Bibliothek der Öffentlichen Kunstsammlung, Basel, 1973.

Borowitz, Helen Osterman. "Three Guitars: Reflections of Italian Comedy in Watteau, Daumier, Picasso." *The Bulletin of the Cleveland Museum of Art* 71 (April 1984), pp. 116–129.

Boucher, François. "À propos d'une récente acquisition du Louvre: Gillot et Watteau." *Gazette des Beaux-Arts* 8 (September–October 1923), pp. 165–178.

Brookner, Anita. *Watteau*. London: Hamlyn, 1967.

Chan, Victor. "Watteau's *Les Comédiens Italiens* Once More." *Canadian Art Review* 5 (1978–1979), pp. 107–112.

Cornec, Gilles. *Gilles, ou Le Spectateur français*. Paris: Gallimard, 1999.

Eidelberg, Martin "Watteau and Gillot: A Point of Contact." *The Burlington Magazine* 115, no. 841 (April 1973), pp. 232–239.

———. "Watteau and Gillot: An Additional Point of Contact." *The Burlington Magazine* 116, no. 858 (September 1974), pp. 538–539.

Fourcaud, Louis de. "Antoine Watteau: Scènes et figures théâtrales." *Revue de l'Art Ancien et Moderne* 15 (1904), pp. 135–150, 193–213.

Grasselli, Margaret Morgan, and Pierre Rosenberg. *Watteau 1684–1721*. Exhibition catalogue. Washington, D.C.: National Gallery of Art, 1984.

Harbison, Robert. "Looking at Art: Harlequin and Columbine." *Art News* 89 (January 1990), pp. 101–102.

Jones, Louisa E. *Pierrot-Watteau: A Nineteenth Century Myth*. Tübingen: G. Narr, 1984.

Mirimonde, A.P. de. "Les Sujets musicaux chez Antoine Watteau." *Gazette des Beaux-Arts* 63, no. 5 (1961), pp. 248–288.

Moureau, François. *Présence d'Arlequin sous Louis XIV: De Gherardi à Watteau*. Paris: Klincksieck, 1992.

Moureau, François, and Margaret Morgan Grasselli. *Antoine Watteau (1684–1721): Le Peintre, son temps et sa légende*. Paris: Champion-Slatkine, 1987.

Panofsky, Dora. "Gilles or Pierrot? Iconographic Notes on Watteau." *Gazette des Beaux-Arts* 39 (January 1952), pp. 319–340.

Plax, Julie Anne. *Watteau and the Cultural Politics of Eighteenth-Century France*. Cambridge: Cambridge University Press, 2000.

Posner, Donald. "Another Look at Watteau's Gilles." *Apollo* 117, no. 252 (February 1983), pp. 97–99.

———. *Antoine Watteau*. London and Ithaca: Cornell University Press, 1984.

Quinn, Michael L. "Watteau's Commedia and the Theatricality of French Painting." *Theatre Symposium: A Journal of the Southeastern Theatre Conference*, no. 1 (1993), pp. 77–93.

Roland-Michel, Marianne, and Daniel Rabreau. *Les Arts du théâtre, de Watteau à Fragonard*. Exhibition catalogue. Bordeaux: Galerie des Beaux-Arts, 1980.

Rosenberg, Pierre. *Vies anciennes de Watteau*. Paris: Hermann, 1984.

Tomlinson, Robert. *La Fête galante: Watteau et Marivaux*. Geneva: Droz, 1981.

Wintermute, Alan, ed. *Watteau and His World: French Drawing from 1700 to 1750*. Exhibition catalogue. New York: American Federation of Arts; London: Merrell Holberton, 1999.

Weegee (Arthur Fellig)

Bar-Am, Micha, ed. *Arthur (Usher) Fellig alias "Weegee the Famous": Gifts of Michael S. Sachs*. Exhibition catalogue. Tel Aviv: Tel Aviv Museum of Art, 1990.

Barry, Les. "Weegee Covers the Circus." *Popular Photography* 42, no. 4 (April 1958), pp. 126–127.

Barth, Miles, ed. *Weegee's World*. Exhibition catalogue. Boston: Little, Brown and Company; New York: International Center of Photography, 1997.

Stettner, Louis, ed. *Weegee*. New York: Knopf, 1977.

Weegee. *Naked City*. New York: Essential Books, 1945.

Weegee and Roy Ald. *Weegee's Creative Camera*. Exhibition catalogue. New York: Hannover House, 1959.

Weegee. New York: Aperture, 1978.

Weegee: Photographies 1935–1960. Paris: Denoël, 1982.

Weegee's New York: 335 Photographs 1935–1960. Munich: Schirmer, 1982.

Weegee and the Human Comedy. Exhibition catalogue. San Francisco: San Francisco Museum of Modern Art, 1984.

Zuckriegl, Margit, ed. *Weegee's Story: From the Berinson Collection*. Exhibition catalogue. Salzburg: Rupertinum, 1999.

List of Works

1
Antoine Watteau
Italian Comedians
probably 1720
Oil on canvas, 63.3 x 76.2 cm
National Gallery of Art, Washington, D.C.

2
James Ensor
The Puzzled Masks
1930
Oil on canvas, 50.5 x 61.5 cm
Öffentliche Kunstsammlung Basel
Not exhibited

3
Jean-Baptiste-Siméon Chardin
The Monkey as Painter
c. 1739–1740
Oil on canvas, 73 x 59 cm
Musée du Louvre, Paris

4
Henry Fuseli
Fool in a Fool's Cap Having His Portrait Painted
1757–1759
Pen and ink and wash, 30 x 20.9 cm
Kunsthaus Zürich, Graphische Sammlung

5
Giambattista Tiepolo
Punchinellos Cooking
c. 1735
Pen and brown ink and brown wash over black chalk, 22.8 x 38 cm
École Nationale Supérieure des Beaux-Arts, Paris
Exhibited in Paris only

6
Giandomenico Tiepolo
Il Mondo Novo
c. 1765
Oil on canvas, 32 x 56 cm
Musée des Arts Décoratifs, Paris

7
Giandomenico Tiepolo
An Encounter during a Country Walk
c. 1791
Pen and brown ink and brown wash over black chalk on laid paper, 28.8 x 41.7 cm
National Gallery of Canada, Ottawa, Gift of Mrs. Samuel Bronfman, O.B.E., Westmount, Quebec, 1973, in honour of her late husband, Mr. Samuel Bronfman, C.C., LL.D.

8
Giandomenico Tiepolo
Punchinello Visits a Circus
c. 1797–1804
Pen and brown ink and brown wash over black chalk on laid paper (watermark), 35.4 x 47.3 cm
National Gallery of Canada, Ottawa, Gift of Mrs. Samuel Bronfman, O.B.E., Westmount, Quebec, 1973, in honour of her late husband, Mr. Samuel Bronfman, C.C., LL.D.

9
Giandomenico Tiepolo
The Lion's Cage
c. 1791
Pen and brown ink and grey wash over graphite on laid paper, laid down on mounting board, 29.6 x 41.1 cm
National Gallery of Canada, Ottawa, Gift of Mrs. Samuel Bronfman, O.B.E., Westmount, Quebec, 1973, in honour of her late husband, Mr. Samuel Bronfman, C.C., LL.D.

10
Francisco Goya
The Straw Mannikin
1791–1792
Oil on canvas, 267 x 160 cm
Museo Nacional del Prado, Madrid

11
Franz Xaver Messerschmidt
An Arch Rascal
after 1770
Tin-lead alloy, 38.5 cm high
Österreichische Galerie Belvedere, Vienna

12
Franz Xaver Messerschmidt
A Dismal and Sinister Man
after 1770
Tin-lead alloy, 43.5 cm high
Österreichische Galerie Belvedere, Vienna

13
Franz Xaver Messerschmidt
An Old Cheerful Smiler
after 1770
Limewood with wax coating, 36 cm high
Österreichische Galerie Belvedere, Vienna

14
Jean-Étienne Liotard
Liotard Laughing
c. 1770
Oil on canvas, 84 x 74 cm
Musée d'Art et d'Histoire, Geneva

15
Joseph Ducreux
Portrait of the Artist with the Features of a Mocker
c. 1793
Oil on canvas, 91 x 72 cm
Musée du Louvre, Paris

16
Louis-Léopold Boilly
Thirty-Five Expressive Heads
c. 1825
Oil on board, 19 x 25 cm
Musée des Beaux-Arts, Tourcoing

17
Honoré Daumier
The Sideshow
c. 1865
Pen and ink, watercolour, black and red chalk, grey wash, Conté crayon, and gouache on laid paper, 27 x 36.8 cm
Musée d'Orsay, Paris
Exhibited in Paris only

18
James Tissot
Ladies of the Chariots
1883–1885
Oil on canvas, 146 x 100.6 cm
Museum of Art, Rhode Island School of Design, Providence, Gift of Walter Lowry

19
Fernand Pelez
Grimaces and Misery (Circus Performers)
1888
Oil on canvas, in 5 sections, 222 x 627 cm
Musée du Petit Palais, Paris

20
Frantisek Kupka
The Fools
1899
Lithograph, 49 x 71 cm
Collection of Bernard Houri

21
Pierre Bonnard
The Parade (or The Fair)
1892
Oil on canvas, 30 x 22 cm
Private collection, courtesy Galerie Bellier, Paris

22
Georges Rouault
Circus (The Parade)
1905
Watercolour, 41.5 x 51.5 cm
Musée d'Art Moderne de la Ville de Paris
Exhibited in Ottawa only

23
Georges Rouault
The Wrestler (Parade)
1905
Watercolour, India ink, and oil on paper, 22 x 12 cm
Musée d'Art Moderne de la Ville de Paris
Exhibited in Paris only

24
Georges Rouault
The Parade
1907
Watercolour and pastel on paper over cardboard, 65 x 96.5 cm
Öffentliche Kunstsammlung Basel

25
Walter Sickert
Brighton Pierrots
1915
Oil on canvas, 63.5 x 76.2 cm
Tate Britain, London, Purchased with assistance from the National Art Collections Fund and the Friends of the Tate Gallery, 1996

26
Fortunato Depero
My Plastic Ballets
1918
Oil on canvas, 180 x 189 cm
Private collection

27
Max Beckmann
The Tall Man, plate 4 of the portfolio *Der Jahrmarkt* ("The Annual Fair")
1921
Drypoint on handmade paper, 52.7 x 38.1 cm (sheet), 30.6 x 20.8 cm (plate)
Los Angeles County Museum of Art, Los Angeles, The Robert Gore Rifkind Center for German Expressionist Studies

28
Dame Laura Knight
Charivari (or The Grand Parade)
1928
Oil on canvas, 102 x 127 cm
Newport City Council Museum and Heritage Service, Newport, Wales

29
Reginald Marsh
Pip and Flip
1932
Tempera on paper mounted on canvas, 122.6 x 122.6 cm
Terra Foundation for the Arts, Daniel J. Terra Collection
Exhibited in Ottawa only

30
Fernand Léger
The Great Parade on a Red Background
1953
Oil on canvas, 114 x 154 cm
Musée National Fernand Léger, Biot, Gift of Nadia Léger and Georges Bauquier, 1969

31
Fernand Léger
The Parade, first state
1950
Oil on canvas, 72.7 x 91.4 cm
Courtesy the Calder Foundation, New York
Exhibited in Ottawa only

32
Nadar and Adrien Tournachon
Pierrot Imploring
1854–1855
Salted paper print, 28.9 x 20.8 cm
Musée d'Orsay, Paris, Gift of Marie-Thérèse and André Jammes, 1991

33
Nadar and Adrien Tournachon
Pierrot Surprised
1854–1855
Salted paper print, 29 x 21.1 cm
Musée d'Orsay, Paris, Gift of Marie-Thérèse and André Jammes, 1986

34
Nadar and Adrien Tournachon
Pierrot the Photographer
1854–1855
Salted paper print, 27.3 x 20.1 cm
Musée Carnavalet, Paris

35
Nadar and Adrien Tournachon
Pierrot
1854–1855
Modern gelatin silver print, 29.8 x 21.7 cm
Musée Carnavalet, Paris

36
Les Enfants du paradis, film directed by **Marcel Carné**, France, 1945

37
Unidentified photographer
(American, mid-19th century)
William G. Worrell of Welch's National Circus and Theater
1855
Daguerreotype, 14 x 10.9 cm
Collection of W. Bruce Lundberg

38
Unidentified photographer
(American, mid-19th century)
Portrait of an Acrobat, Valentine Denzer
c. 1855
Daguerreotype, 10.7 x 8.3 cm
George Eastman House, International Museum of Photography and Film, Rochester, New York, Gift of Howard Denzer

39
Gustave Courbet
The Black Arm
1856
Charcoal and black chalk on wove paper, 47.3 x 51.8 cm
National Gallery of Canada, Ottawa

40
Honoré Daumier
Crispin and Scapin
c. 1863–1865
Oil on canvas, 60.5 x 82 cm
Musée d'Orsay, Paris, Gift of the Friends of the Louvre with the support of the children of Henri Rouart, 1912

41
James Ensor
The Strange Masks
1892
Oil on canvas, 100 x 80 cm
Koninklijke Musea voor Schone Kunsten van België, Brussels

42
Gustave Doré
Pierrot Grimacing
Watercolour, 64.2 x 50.5 cm
Musée d'Art Moderne et Contemporain, Strasbourg

43
Albert Londe
Portraits of Clowns
1887
Albumen silver prints, 14 x 9.9 cm (left), 14.1 x 10 cm (right)
Collections de la Société Française de Photographie, Paris

44
Georges Rouault
Clown with a Drum
c. 1906–1907
Watercolour and oil on paper mounted on canvas, 72 x 57 cm
Musée National d'Art Moderne, Centre Pompidou, Paris, Gift of Madame Rouault and her children, 1959
Exhibited in Ottawa only

45
Georges Rouault
Head of a Tragic Clown
1904
Watercolour, pastel, and gouache on paper, 37 x 26.5 cm
Kunsthaus Zürich

46
Georges Rouault
Parade (detail), *Acrobat*
c. 1907–1910
Watercolour, pastel, and oil on paper mounted on canvas, 63 x 45 cm
Musée National d'Art Moderne, Centre Pompidou, Paris
Exhibited in Paris only

47
Kees Van Dongen
The Clown Who Believes Himself to Be President of the Republic
c. 1905–1907
Oil on canvas, 100 x 81 cm
Landau Fine Art, Montreal
Exhibited in Ottawa only

48
Pablo Picasso
Head of a Jester
1905
Bronze, 48.2 x 39.1 x 23 cm
Hirshhorn Museum and Sculpture Garden, Smithsonian Institution, Washington, D.C., Gift of Joseph H. Hirshhorn, 1966

49
Vasily Shukhayev and Aleksandr Yakovlev
Self-portraits (*Harlequin and Pierrot*)
1914
Oil on canvas, 210 x 142 cm
The State Russian Museum, Saint Petersburg
Not exhibited

50
Pablo Picasso
Pierrot
1918
Oil on canvas, 92.7 x 73 cm
The Museum of Modern Art, New York, Sam A. Lewisohn Bequest, 1952

51
José Gutiérrez Solana
The Clowns
1920
Oil on canvas, 98 x 124 cm
Museo Nacional Centro de Arte Reina Sofia, Madrid

52
Paul Klee
Wintery Mask
1925
Watercolour on wove paper, laid down on cardboard, 53.5 x 34.6 cm
National Gallery of Canada, Ottawa

53
Umbo
Grock 18
1929
Gelatin silver print, 29.6 x 21.4 cm
Courtesy Gallery Kicken, Berlin

54
Umbo
Grock
1929
Gelatin silver print, 23.8 x 17.8 cm
Courtesy Gallery Kicken, Berlin

55
George Luks
A Clown
1929
Oil on canvas, 61.3 x 50.8 cm
Museum of Fine Arts, Boston, Bequest of John T. Spaulding, 1948

56
Walt Kuhn
The Blue Clown
1931
Oil on canvas, 76.2 x 63.5 cm
Whitney Museum of American Art, New York

57
Weegee (Arthur Fellig)
The Clown Jimmy Armstrong
1943
Gelatin silver print, 25.4 x 20.6 cm
Galerie Berinson, Berlin

58
Izis
Grock, Toulon
1954
Gelatin silver print, 43 x 33.5 cm
Madame Izis

59
Izis
Grock, Toulon
1954
Gelatin silver print, 43 x 33.5 cm
Madame Izis

60
Izis
Grock, Toulon
1954
Gelatin silver print, 43 x 33.5 cm
Madame Izis

415

61
He Who Gets Slapped, film directed
by **Victor Seastrom** (Victor Sjöström),
United States, 1924

62
Leon Levinstein
Circus
c. 1965
Gelatin silver print, 35.8 x 34.5 cm
Courtesy Howard Greenberg Gallery,
New York

63
Pierrick Sorin
La Bataille des tartes
1994
Video installation in 3 parts
Fondation Cartier pour l'Art Contem-
porain, Paris

64
Paul McCarthy
Painter
1995
DVD, 50 min.
National Gallery of Canada, Ottawa

65
James Ensor
Ensor with a Flowered Hat
1883–1888
Oil on canvas, 76.5 x 61.5 cm
Museum voor Schone Kunsten,
Ostend

66
Pablo Picasso
Self-portrait in a Wig
1897
Oil on canvas, 55.8 x 46 cm
Museu Picasso, Barcelona

67
Henri de Toulouse-Lautrec
Cover for "Jouets de Paris"
1901
Lithograph, 21.6 x 11.1 cm
San Diego Museum of Art, Gift of
the Baldwin M. Baldwin Foundation

68
Unidentified photographer
*Henri de Toulouse-Lautrec with
Jane Avril's Fur Boa*
c. 1892
Gelatin silver copy print
Musée Toulouse-Lautrec, Albi

69
Unidentified photographer
*Henri de Toulouse-Lautrec with
Foottit's Hat*
c. 1894
Gelatin silver copy print
Musée Toulouse-Lautrec, Albi

70
Arnold Schoenberg
Vision
1910
Oil on canvas, 32 x 20 cm
Library of Congress, Washington, D.C.
Exhibited in Ottawa only

71
Arnold Schoenberg
Hatred
c. 1912
Oil on canvas, 43 x 30.5 cm
Private collection, courtesy Galerie
St. Etienne, New York

72
Irene Bayer-Hecht
*Andor Weininger at the Eye-Ear-
Nose-Throat Festival at the Bauhaus,
Dessau*
1927
Gelatin silver print, 11.5 x 8 cm
National Gallery of Canada, Ottawa

73
T. Lux Feininger
Oskar Schlemmer as Musical Clown
c. 1927
Gelatin silver print, 16.8 x 12.5 cm
Courtesy the Oskar Schlemmer
Theatre Estate

74
T. Lux Feininger
*Oskar Schlemmer as Musical Clown
with Mechanical Cello*
c. 1927
Gelatin silver prints, 7.8 x 10.9 cm
(top), 7.6 x 11 cm (middle),
8.3 x 11.2 cm (bottom)
Courtesy the Oskar Schlemmer
Theatre Estate

75
Herbert Ploberger
Scherben bringen Glück (*Broken
Crockery Brings Good Luck*)
c. 1925
Oil on canvas, 39 x 49 cm
Private collection

76
Pierre Bonnard
The Boxer (*Self-portrait*)
1931
Oil on canvas, 54 x 74 cm
Musée d'Orsay, Paris. Private collec-
tion, Gift (with life interest retained)
to the French State, 2000

77
Francis Picabia
Fratellini the Clown
1936
Oil on canvas, 92 x 73 cm
Private collection

78
Aleksandr Rodchenko
The Clown Vitaly Lasarenko
1940, printed later
Gelatin silver print, 28.6 x 19.2 cm
National Gallery of Canada, Ottawa,
Gift of Varvara Rodchenko and
Aleksandr Lavrentiev, Moscow, 2003

79
Marcel Duchamp
Monte Carlo Bond
1924–1938
Offset lithograph in red, black, green,
and yellow ink on wove paper,
31.4 x 20.3 cm (image, irregular)
National Gallery of Canada, Ottawa

80
Robert Capa
*Pablo Picasso, Vallauris, France,
1949*
1949, printed c. 1992
Gelatin silver print, 35 x 32.8 cm
Collection of Cornell Capa, courtesy
the International Center of Photography, New York

81
Marc Chagall
Untitled
1967
Lithograph on wove paper,
42.5 x 32.5 cm
Collection of Félix Quinet

82
Giorgio De Chirico
Self-portrait in Seicento Costume
1947
Oil on canvas, 82.5 x 59 cm
Galleria Nazionale d'Arte Moderna,
Rome

83
Joseph Beuys
La rivoluzione siamo Noi (*We Are
the Revolution*)
1972
Silkscreen on polyester with handwritten text in black felt pen, blue
ink stamp, 191 x 100 cm
National Gallery of Canada, Ottawa

84
Lucian Freud
Painter Working, Reflection
1993
Oil on canvas, 101.6 x 81.7 cm
Private collection

85
Philip Guston
Painter's Head
1975
Oil on canvas, 185 x 205 cm
The Estate of Philip Guston, cour-
tesy McKee Gallery, New York

86
**Olivier Blanckart and Arnaud
Labelle-Rojoux**
Clowns
1997
DVD, 10 min., 22 sec.
Courtesy Galerie Loevenbruck, Paris

87
Christian Boltanski
The Joker
1974
Mixed media on paper mounted on
canvas, 100 x 75 cm
Private collection

88
Christian Boltanski
Comic Vignettes: The Reward
1974
4 photographs, heightened with
wax crayon, 4 texts in white pastel,
103 x 74 cm (each photograph),
15.5 x 31.5 cm (each text)
Fondation Cartier pour l'Art Contemporain, Paris
Exhibited in Paris only

89
Cindy Sherman
Untitled #411
2003
Dye coupler print, 114.9 x 79 cm,
with frame
Courtesy the artist and Metro
Pictures, New York

90
Honoré Daumier
The Wrestler
c. 1852–1853
Oil on panel, 42 x 28.5 cm
Ordrupgaard, Copenhagen

91
Honoré Daumier
Performers Resting (*Strong Man
and Pierrot in the Wings*)
c. 1865–1870
Pencil, pen and ink, and watercolour
on paper, 32 x 25 cm
Collection of Michael and Judy
Steinhardt, New York

92
Gustave Doré
The Performers
1874
Oil on canvas, 240 x 207 cm, with
frame
Musée d'Art Roger-Quilliot,
Clermont-Ferrand

93
Félicien Rops
The Intermission of Minerve
c. 1878
Pastel, pencil, and watercolour,
22.5 x 15.5 cm
Ministère de la Culture de la
Communauté Française Wallonie-
Bruxelles, on loan to the Musée
Félicien Rops, Namur

94
Félicien Rops
*Venus and Cupid: Love Blowing
His Nose*
c. 1878
Pastel and gouache over black
chalk, 21.8 x 14.8 cm
Ministère de la Culture de la
Communauté Française Wallonie-
Bruxelles, on loan to the Musée
Félicien Rops, Namur

95
Pablo Picasso
The Acrobat's Family with a Monkey
1905
Gouache, watercolour, pastel, and
ink on cardboard, 104 x 75 cm
Göteborgs Konstmuseum, Göteborg
Exhibited in Ottawa only

96
John Sloan
Old Clown Making Up
1910
Oil on canvas, 81.6 x 66 cm
The Phillips Collection, Washington,
D.C.

97
Edward Hopper
Soir Bleu
1914
Oil on canvas, 91.4 x 182.9 cm
Whitney Museum of American Art,
New York, Josephine N. Hopper
Bequest
Exhibited in Paris only

98
August Sander
Circus Artistes
1926–1932, printed 1975
Gelatin silver print, 18.9 x 24.7 cm
Collection of Gerd Sander

99
August Sander
Circus Workers
1926–1932, printed 1974
Gelatin silver print, 26 x 19 cm
Collection of Gerd Sander

100
August Sander
Circus Artiste
1926–1932, printed 1980
Gelatin silver print, 28.1 x 20.4 cm
Collection of Gerd Sander

101
Max Beckmann
The Circus Wagon
1940
Oil on canvas, 86.3 x 118.5 cm
Städtische Galerie im Städelschen
Kunstinstitut, Frankfurt am Main
Exhibited in Paris only

102
Aleksandr Rodchenko
In the Interval
1940, printed later
Gelatin silver print, 39.4 x 26.2 cm
Collection of Gerd Sander

103
Leon Levinstein
Circus
c. 1965
Gelatin silver print, 43.2 x 32 cm
Courtesy Howard Greenberg
Gallery, New York

104
Bruce Davidson
Circus Dwarf, Palisades, N.J.
1958, printed 2003
Gelatin silver print, 47.5 x 32 cm
Courtesy Bruce Davidson/Magnum
Photos

105
Robert Walker
Backstage – Cirque du Soleil
1990, printed 2002
Giclée print, 104.8 x 69.8 cm
Courtesy the artist

106
Henri de Toulouse-Lautrec
The Clowness Cha-U-Kao
1895
Oil on cardboard, 64 x 49 cm
Musée d'Orsay, Paris, Bequest of
Count Isaac de Camondo, 1911

107
Henri de Toulouse-Lautrec
*Seated Clowness – Mademoiselle
Cha-U-Kao* (from *Elles*)
1896
Lithograph, 52 x 40 cm
San Diego Museum of Art, Gift of
the Baldwin M. Baldwin Foundation

108
Heinrich Maria Davringhausen
The Acrobat
c. 1920
Oil on canvas, 220 x 150 cm
Private collection, Hamburg

109
Fernand Léger
Cubist Charlie
1924
Wood assemblage, 74 x 34 cm
Musée National d'Art Moderne,
Centre Pompidou, Paris

110
Gaston Lachaise
Female Acrobat, also called
Abstract Figure
c. 1935
Bronze, 50.2 cm high
Courtesy Salander-O'Reilly Galleries,
New York

111
Lisette Model
Circus, New York
1945
Gelatin silver print, 35.3 x 25.4 cm
National Gallery of Canada, Ottawa,
Gift of the Estate of Lisette Model,
1990, by direction of Joseph G. Blum,
New York, through the American
Friends of Canada

112
Weegee (Arthur Fellig)
Weegee as Clown
1943
Gelatin silver print, 34.2 x 26.5 cm
Collection of Gerd Sander

113
Weegee (Arthur Fellig)
The Human Cannonball
1943
Gelatin silver print, 34.1 x 27.1 cm
Galerie Berinson, Berlin

114
Diane Arbus
*Albino sword swallower at a
carnival, Md.*
1970, printed 1973
Gelatin silver print, 36.6 x 37 cm
National Gallery of Canada, Ottawa

115
Jonathan Borofsky
The Dancing Clown at 2,845,325
1982–1983
Mixed media, 373 x 203 x 447 cm
The Edward R. Broida Collection

116
Bruce Nauman
Clown Torture (*Dark and Stormy
Night with Laughter*)
1987
2 video monitors, 2 DVD players,
2 DVDs
Collection of Barbara Balkin Cottle
and Robert Cottle

117
Rhona Bitner
from the series: Clown
2001
Azo dye (Ilfochrome) print mounted
on aluminum, 194 x 107 cm
The artist and CRG Gallery, New York

118
Ugo Rondinone
*If There Were Anywhere but Desert:
Tuesday*
2002
Fibreglass, paint, clothing,
51 x 183 x 137 cm
Courtesy Fundación Almine y
Bernard Ruiz-Picasso para el Arte

119
Edward J. Kelty
Congress of Freaks
1929
Gelatin silver print, 22.9 x 38.1 cm
Collection of Alan Siegel, New York

120
Unidentified photographer
(American, mid-19th century)
Tom Thumb
c. 1847–1848
Daguerreotype, heightened with
gold-coloured paint and incised
lines, 9.6 x 6.5 cm
National Gallery of Canada, Ottawa,
Gift of Peter Zegers, Ottawa, 1983

121
Irena Rabinowicz-Rüther
François (*Dwarf from the Sarrasani
Circus*)
1925
Oil on canvas, 114 x 92.2 cm
Städtische Sammlungen Freital

122
John Gutmann
Midget Clowns
1939
Gelatin silver print, 24.7 x 18.4 cm
Hallmark Photographic Collection,
Hallmark Cards, Inc., Kansas City,
Missouri

123
Freaks, film directed by **Tod
Browning**, United States, 1932

124
Pablo Picasso
La Nana
1901
Oil on cardboard, 104.5 x 61 cm
Museu Picasso, Barcelona
Not exhibited

417

125
Otto Dix
Disdainers of Death – Two Artistes
1922
Watercolour and pencil, 58.5 x 48 cm
Otto Dix Foundation, Vaduz

126
Otto Dix
Female Animal Tamer
1922
Drypoint, 39.9 x 29.7 cm
Otto Dix Foundation, Vaduz

127
Otto Dix
Female Animal Tamer
1922
Watercolour, 64.5 x 47.5 cm
The Marvin and Janet Fishman
Collection, Milwaukee

128
Félicien Rops
Saltimbanque
Pencil heightened with watercolour
and gouache on paper, 22 x 15 cm
Musée d'Ixelles, Brussels

129
Max Beckmann
The Snake Woman, plate 10 of
the portfolio *Der Jahrmarkt*
("The Annual Fair")
1921
Drypoint on handmade paper,
52.4 x 36.8 cm (sheet), 29.1 x 25.6 cm
(plate)
Los Angeles County Museum of Art,
Los Angeles, The Robert Gore Rifkind
Center for German Expressionist
Studies

130
Max Beckmann
The Negro, plate 6 of the portfolio
Der Jahrmarkt ("The Annual Fair")
1921
Drypoint on handmade paper,
52.9 x 38.3 cm (sheet), 28.9 x 26 cm
(plate)
Los Angeles County Museum of Art,
Los Angeles, The Robert Gore Rifkind
Center for German Expressionist
Studies

131
John Steuart Curry
Baby Ruth
1932
Oil on canvas, 65.4 x 50.8 cm
Brigham Young University Museum
of Art, Provo, Utah, Gift of Mr. and
Mrs. William H. Child

132
Izis
Foire du Trône
1960
Gelatin silver print, 43 x 33.5 cm
Madame Izis

133
Pyke Koch
The Large Contortionist
1957
Oil and tempera on canvas,
168.5 x 120 cm
Stedelijk Museum, Amsterdam

134
Albert Birkle
Acrobat Schulz
1924
Oil on canvas, 70 x 50 cm
Galerie Heinze, Salzburg

135
Walt Kuhn
Top Man
1931
Oil on canvas, 182.9 x 81.3 cm
Huntington Library, Art Collections,
and Botanical Gardens, San Marion,
California, Gift of the Virginia Steele
Scott Foundation
Exhibited in Ottawa only

136
Claude Cahun
*Untitled (I AM IN TRAINING DON'T
KISS ME)*
1927–1929
Gelatin silver print, 13.9 x 8.8 cm
San Francisco Museum of Modern
Art, Gift of Robert Shapazian

137
Diane Arbus
Tattooed man at a carnival, Md.
1970, printed later
Gelatin silver print, 36.5 x 36 cm
The Museum of Contemporary Art,
Los Angeles, The Ralph M. Parsons
Photography Collection

138
Diane Arbus
*Hermaphrodite and a dog in a carni-
val trailer, Md.*
1970, printed later
Gelatin silver print, 36.5 x 36.5 cm
The Museum of Fine Arts, Houston,
The Collection of Gay Block

139
Lisette Model
*Albert-Alberta, Hubert's 42nd Street
Flea Circus, New York*
c. 1945
Gelatin silver print, 49.1 x 39 cm
National Gallery of Canada, Ottawa,
Gift of the Estate of Lisette Model,
1990, by direction of Joseph G. Blum,
New York, through the American
Friends of Canada

140
Izis
*Foire du Trône: Sideshow, Crocodile
Woman, Paris*
1959
Gelatin silver print, 27 x 19.4 cm
Collection of Gerd Sander

141
Bruce Davidson
The Dwarf
1958
Gelatin silver print, 47.6 x 32.1 cm
Courtesy Bruce Davidson/Magnum
Photos

142
Cindy Sherman
Untitled B
1975
Gelatin silver print, 50.8 x 40.6 cm
Museum of Contemporary Art,
Chicago, Gift of Lannan Foundation

143
Charles Atlas
The Legend of Leigh Bowery
2001
Colour film, 60 min.
Courtesy Electronic Arts Intermix,
New York

144
Lucian Freud
Nude With Leg Up (Leigh Bowery)
1992
Oil on canvas, 183 x 228.5 cm
Hirshhorn Museum and Sculpture
Garden, Smithsonian Institution,
Washington, D.C., Joseph H.
Hirshhorn Purchase Fund, 1993

145
Francisco Goya
Punctual Folly
c. 1816–1824
Etching and aquatint with drypoint
on laid japan paper, 28.1 x 38 cm
(sheet), 24.5 x 35 cm (plate)
National Gallery of Canada, Ottawa

146
Francisco Goya
*A Young Witch Flying on a Rope
Swing*
c. 1824–1828
Black chalk and lithographic crayon
on greenish-white laid paper
(watermark), 19.1 x 15.5 cm
National Gallery of Canada, Ottawa

147
Honoré Daumier
Man on a Rope
c. 1858–1860
Oil on canvas, 110.7 x 72.5 cm
National Gallery of Canada, Ottawa,
Gift of H.S. Southam, Ottawa, 1950

148
Edgar Degas
Miss Lala at the Cirque Fernando
1879
Oil on canvas, 117 x 77 cm
The National Gallery, London

149
Georges Seurat
Study for "The Circus"
1890–1891
Oil on canvas, 55.5 x 46.5 cm
Musée d'Orsay, Paris, Gift of Madame
Jacques Doucet in accordance with
her husband's will, 1937
Exhibited in Paris only

150
Henri de Toulouse-Lautrec
Trained Horse and Monkey
1899
Facsimile lithograph, from the
artist's drawing of 1899, published
posthumously in the limited-edition
portfolio *Au Cirque* (Paris: Manzi,
Joyant et Cie, 1905), 26.8 x 18.4 cm
Bibliothèque Nationale de France,
Paris
Exhibited in Paris only

151
Henri de Toulouse-Lautrec
The Flying Trapeze
1899
Facsimile lithograph, from the
artist's drawing of 1899, published
posthumously in the limited-edition
portfolio *Au Cirque* (Paris: Manzi,
Joyant et Cie, 1905), 28.6 x 18.1 cm
Bibliothèque Nationale de France,
Paris
Exhibited in Paris only

152
Henri de Toulouse-Lautrec
Pas de Deux
1899
Facsimile lithograph, from the
artist's drawing of 1899, published
posthumously in the limited-edition
portfolio *Au Cirque* (Paris: Manzi,
Joyant et Cie, 1905), 26.4 x 18.3 cm
Bibliothèque Nationale de France,
Paris
Exhibited in Paris only

153
Henri de Toulouse-Lautrec
Bareback Rider
1899
Facsimile lithograph, from the
artist's drawing of 1899, published
posthumously in the limited-edition
portfolio *Au Cirque* (Paris: Manzi,
Joyant et Cie, 1905), 25.9 x 17.8 cm
Bibliothèque Nationale de France,
Paris
Exhibited in Paris only

154
Henri de Toulouse-Lautrec
Acrobat Rider (*Elle est gentille,
la demoiselle*)
1899
Facsimile lithograph, from the
artist's drawing of 1899, published
posthumously in the limited-edition
portfolio *Au Cirque* (Paris: Manzi,
Joyant et Cie, 1905), 27.6 x 21 cm
Bibliothèque Nationale de France,
Paris
Exhibited in Paris only

155
Henri de Toulouse-Lautrec
The Curtain Call
1899
Facsimile lithograph, from the
artist's drawing of 1899, published
posthumously in the limited-edition
portfolio *Au Cirque* (Paris: Manzi,
Joyant et Cie, 1905), 26 x 18.4 cm
Bibliothèque Nationale de France,
Paris
Exhibited in Paris only

156
Henri de Toulouse-Lautrec
Trainer Clown
1899
Facsimile lithograph, from the
artist's drawing of 1899, published
posthumously in the limited-edition
portfolio *Au Cirque* (Paris: Manzi,
Joyant et Cie, 1905), 16.4 x 27.6 cm
The New York Public Library
Exhibited in Ottawa only

157
Henri de Toulouse-Lautrec
Clowness
1899
Facsimile lithograph, from the
artist's drawing of 1899, published
posthumously in the limited-edition
portfolio *Au Cirque* (Paris: Manzi,
Joyant et Cie, 1905), 27.5 x 21 cm
The New York Public Library
Exhibited in Ottawa only

158
Henri de Toulouse-Lautrec
Voltige
1899
Facsimile lithograph, from the
artist's drawing of 1899, published
posthumously in the limited-edition
portfolio *Au Cirque* (Paris: Manzi,
Joyant et Cie, 1905), 18.7 x 26.5 cm
The New York Public Library
Exhibited in Ottawa only

159
Henri de Toulouse-Lautrec
Entering the Ring
1899
Facsimile lithograph, from the
artist's drawing of 1899, published
posthumously in the limited-edition
portfolio *Au Cirque* (Paris: Manzi,
Joyant et Cie, 1905), 27.9 x 17.8 cm
The New York Public Library
Exhibited in Ottawa only

160
Henri de Toulouse-Lautrec
Tightrope Walker
1899
Facsimile lithograph, from the
artist's drawing of 1899, published
posthumously in the limited-edition
portfolio *Au Cirque* (Paris: Manzi,
Joyant et Cie, 1905), 27.6 x 18.7 cm
The New York Public Library
Exhibited in Ottawa only

161
Henri de Toulouse-Lautrec
Work on the Mat
1899
Facsimile lithograph, from the
artist's drawing of 1899, published
posthumously in the limited-edition
portfolio *Au Cirque* (Paris: Manzi,
Joyant et Cie, 1905), 27.6 x 18.9 cm
The New York Public Library
Exhibited in Ottawa only

162
Albert Londe
Tumblers
c. 1887
Albumen silver print, 11.1 x 17.2 cm
Collections de la Société Française
de Photographie, Paris

163
Albert Londe
Tightrope Walker
c. 1887
Albumen silver print, 22.3 x 28.3 cm
Collections de la Société Française
de Photographie, Paris

164
Pablo Picasso
Saltimbanques
1905
Drypoint on Arches paper,
28.8 x 32.6 cm
Musée Picasso, Paris

165
Pablo Picasso
At the Circus (from *La Suite des
saltimbanques*)
1905
Drypoint on Van Gelder paper,
21.9 x 13.9 cm
Fine Arts Museums of San Francisco,
Achenbach Foundation for Graphic
Arts, Museum Purchase, M.H.
deYoung Memorial Museum, 1931

166
Pablo Picasso
Salomé (from *La Suite des
saltimbanques*)
1905
Drypoint on Van Gelder paper,
40.1 x 34.9 cm
Fine Arts Museums of San Francisco,
Achenbach Foundation for Graphic
Arts, Museum Purchase, M.H.
deYoung Memorial Museum, 1931

167
Paul Klee
Acrobats
1914
Pen and ink mounted on cardboard,
20.9 x 15.1 cm
Solomon R. Guggenheim Museum,
New York, Gift, Katherine Kuh, 1982

168
Paul Klee
Tightrope Walker
1923
Lithograph, 52.1 x 38.1 cm
Solomon R. Guggenheim Museum,
New York

169
Pablo Picasso
Harlequin and Pierrot
1918
Ink on paper, 13.4 x 10.3 cm
Musée Picasso, Paris

170
Pablo Picasso
Horse and Trainer Juggler
1920
Pencil, 21.5 x 27.3 cm
Musée Picasso, Paris

171
Pablo Picasso
Horse and Trainer Juggler
1920
Pencil, 21.2 x 27.2 cm
Musée Picasso, Paris

172
Pablo Picasso
Horse and Trainer
1920
Pencil, 21.5 x 27.1 cm
Musée Picasso, Paris

173
Pablo Picasso
Horse and Female Trainer
1920
Pencil, 21 x 27 cm
Musée Picasso, Paris

174
Alexander Calder
Wire Sculpture by Calder
1928
Wire, 122.6 x 65.7 x 12.4 cm
Whitney Museum of American Art,
New York, Purchased with funds
from Howard and Jean Lipman

175
Alexander Calder
The Circus
1932
Pen and black ink on wove paper,
51.4 x 74.3 cm
National Gallery of Art, Washington,
D.C., Gift of Mr. and Mrs. Klaus G.
Perls, 1996

176
Alexander Calder
Precision
1932
Pen and India ink, 48.3 x 35.9 cm
Philadelphia Museum of Art,
Purchased with the Thomas Skelton
Harrison Fund, 1941

177
Alexander Calder
Woman on Flying Trapeze
1931
Pen and black ink, 76.8 x 56.8 cm
Museum of Fine Arts, Boston,
Abraham Shuman Collection

178
Le Cirque de Calder, film directed
by **Carlos Vilardebó**, France, 1961
Courtesy the Roland Collection of
Films on Art

419

179
Max Beckmann
The Tightrope Walkers, plate 8
of the portfolio *Der Jahrmarkt*
("The Annual Fair")
1921
Drypoint on handmade paper,
52.7 x 38.1 cm (sheet), 25.7 x 25.6 cm
(plate)
Los Angeles County Museum of Art,
Los Angeles, The Robert Gore Rifkind
Center for German Expressionist
Studies

180
Otto Dix
Circus Scene
1923
Watercolour over pencil and collage,
49.5 x 35.5 cm
Otto Dix Foundation, Vaduz

181
Everett Shinn
Tightrope Walker
1924
Oil on canvas, 59.7 x 45.7 cm
The Dayton Art Institute, Dayton,
Ohio, Museum purchase with funds
provided by the James F. Dicke
Family and the E. Jeanette Myers
Fund

182
Max Beckmann
Variety Show
1927
Oil on canvas, 50.5 x 71.1 cm
Collection of Richard L. Feigen,
New York

183
Marc Chagall
Acrobat
1914
Oil on brown paper mounted on
canvas, 42.5 x 33 cm
Albright-Knox Art Gallery, Buffalo,
New York, Room of Contemporary
Art Fund, 1941
Exhibited in Ottawa only

184
Marc Chagall
Acrobat
1930
Oil on canvas, 117 x 73.5 cm
Musée National d'Art Moderne,
Centre Pompidou, Paris, on loan
to the Musée National Message
Biblique Marc Chagall, Nice

185
Pablo Picasso
The Acrobat
1930
Oil on canvas, 165.5 x 130 cm
Musée Picasso, Paris

186
Milton Avery
Trapeze Artist
1930
Oil on canvas, 91.4 x 61 cm
Milton Avery Trust

187
Umbo
Trapeze Artists
1932, printed later
Gelatin silver print, 24 x 18 cm
Herbert and Barbara Molderings
Archive, Paris and Cologne

188
Robert Riggs
Center Ring
1933
Lithograph, 37 x 49.5 cm
The New York Public Library

189
Fernand Léger
The Acrobat and His Partner
1948
Oil on canvas, 130.2 x 162.6 cm
Tate Britain, London, Purchased
1980

190
Alexander Calder
Acrobats
1944
Bronze, 51.4 cm high
Fondation Marguerite et Aimé
Maeght, Saint-Paul

191
Max Beckmann
Back Bend (*The Acrobat*)
c. 1950
Bronze, 21.6 x 30 x 9 cm
Collection of Jeffrey Steiner,
New York

192
George Segal
Circus Acrobats
1988
2 suspended plaster figures,
183 x 366 x 51 cm
Courtesy the George and Helen Segal
Foundation and Carroll Janis Inc.

193
Lisette Model
Circus, New York
1945
Gelatin silver print, 34.6 x 27 cm
National Gallery of Canada, Ottawa,
Gift of the Estate of Lisette Model,
1990, by direction of Joseph G. Blum,
New York, through the American
Friends of Canada

194
Lisette Model
Circus, New York
1945
Gelatin silver print, 34.6 x 27 cm
National Gallery of Canada, Ottawa,
Gift of the Estate of Lisette Model,
1990, by direction of Joseph G. Blum,
New York, through the American
Friends of Canada

195
Harold Edgerton
Moscow Circus
1963, printed 1985
Dye transfer print, 36.2 x 45.6 cm
National Gallery of Canada, Ottawa,
Gift of the Harold and Esther
Edgerton Family Foundation, Santa
Fe, New Mexico, 1997

196
Aleksandr Rodchenko
The Rhine Wheel
c. 1940, printed c. 1980–1989
Gelatin silver print, 23.2 x 30.3 cm
National Gallery of Canada, Ottawa,
Gift of George R. Carmody, Ottawa,
1998

197
Aleksandr Rodchenko
The Pyramid
1937, printed later
Gelatin silver print, 19.3 x 28.5 cm
National Gallery of Canada, Ottawa,
Gift of Varvara Rodchenko and
Aleksandr Lavrentiev, Moscow, 2003

198
Louise Bourgeois
Arch of Hysteria
1993
Bronze, polished patina,
83.8 x 101.6 x 58.4 cm
Louise Bourgeois Studio

199
Pablo Picasso
Harlequin
1917
Oil on canvas, 116 x 90 cm
Museu Picasso, Barcelona

200
Pablo Picasso
The Painter Salvado as Harlequin
1923
Oil on canvas, 130 x 97 cm
Musée National d'Art Moderne,
Centre Pompidou, Paris, Bequest of
Baroness Eva Gourgaud, 1965

201
Pablo Picasso
Paul as Harlequin
1924
Oil on canvas, 130 x 97.5 cm
Musée Picasso, Paris

202
Pablo Picasso
*Portrait of an Adolescent Dressed
as Pierrot*
1922
Gouache and watercolour,
11.8 x 10.5 cm
Musée Picasso, Paris

203 (not illustrated)
Georges Rouault
Pierrot in Black Socks
1932
Oil on paper mounted on canvas,
101 x 69 cm
Musée National d'Art Moderne, Centre
Pompidou, Paris, Gift of Madame
Rouault and her children, 1963
Exhibited in Paris only

204
Pablo Picasso
*Study for the Stage Curtain for the
Ballet "Parade"*
1917
Watercolour and pencil,
27.3 x 39.5 cm
Musée Picasso, Paris

205
Pablo Picasso
Fairground Circus
1922
Gouache, 11 x 14.5 cm
Musée Picasso, Paris

206
Pablo Picasso
*Study for the Stage Curtain for
"Pulcinella": Harlequin in the Ring
with Ballerina and Rider*
1920
Oil on paper, 16 x 25 cm
Musée Picasso, Paris

207 (not illustrated)
Pablo Picasso
Clown and Acrobats
1905
Gouache, India ink, and wash on
bluish grey paper, 23.5 x 15.6 cm
Musée Picasso, Paris

208
Pablo Picasso
*Design for the Costume of an
Acrobat*
1917
Watercolour and pencil, 28 x 20.5 cm
Musée Picasso, Paris

209
Pablo Picasso
*Design for the Costume of a Female
Acrobat*
1917
Watercolour and pencil,
27.5 x 20.7 cm
Musée Picasso, Paris

210
Pablo Picasso
Study for "The Death of Harlequin"
1905–1906
Pen and black ink and watercolour
on laid paper, 10.5 x 16.8 cm
National Gallery of Art, Washington,
D.C., Collection of Mr. and Mrs. Paul
Mellon, 1996

211
Pablo Picasso
*Stage Curtain for the Ballet
"Parade"*
1917
Distemper on canvas, 10.5 x 16.4 m
Musée National d'Art Moderne,
Centre Pompidou, Paris
Exhibited in Ottawa only

Index of Artists

This index covers artists who are represented in the exhibition or whose works are otherwise illustrated in the catalogue. References are to page numbers (those in bold pointing to reproductions), followed by catalogue numbers. Details on the works in the exhibition, in order of catalogue number, can be found in the "List of Works" immediately above.